For Love or for Money

For Love or for Money
Balzac's Rhetorical Realism

Armine Kotin Mortimer

 THE OHIO STATE UNIVERSITY PRESS | COLUMBUS

Copyright © 2011 by The Ohio State University.
All rights reserved.

Library of Congress Cataloging-in-Publication Data
Mortimer, Armine Kotin, 1943–
  For love or for money : Balzac's rhetorical realism / Armine Kotin Mortimer.
    p. cm.
  Includes bibliographical references and index.
  ISBN 978-0-8142-1169-4 (cloth : alk. paper)—ISBN 978-0-8142-9268-6 (cd)
  1. Balzac, Honoré de, 1799–1850. Comédie humaine. 2. Realism in literature. 3. Love in literature. 4. Money in literature. I. Title.
  PQ2159.C72M57 2011
  843'.7—dc23
                               2011019881
Paper (ISBN: 978-0-8142-5667-1)
Cover design by James Baumann
Text design by Juliet Williams
Type set in Adobe Sabon

Contents

List of Illustrations	vii
Acknowledgments	ix

Chapter 1	Introduction: The Prime Movers	1

I Rhetorical Forms of Realism

Chapter 2	Mimetic Figures of Semiosis	15
Chapter 3	From Heteronomy to Unity: *Les Chouans*	32
Chapter 4	Tenebrous Affairs and Necessary Explications	47
Chapter 5	Self-Narration and the Fakery of Imitation	63
Chapter 6	The Double Representation of the History of César Birotteau	80
Chapter 7	*La Maison Nucingen*, a Financial Narrative	94

II Semiotic Images of Realism

Chapter 8	Myth and Mendacity: *Pierrette* and Beatrice Cenci	109
Chapter 9	The Corset of *La vieille fille*	128
Chapter 10	Genealogy and the Unmarried in *La Rabouilleuse*	139
Chapter 11	*Ursule Mirouët*: Genealogy and Inheritance	152
Chapter 12	*Un prince de la bohème* and *Pierre Grassou*, or How Love Makes Money	167
Chapter 13	Voyages of Reflection, Reflections on Voyages	175

III Mimetic Structures of Realism

Chapter 14	Balzac and Poe: Realizing Magnetism	195
Chapter 15	Chemistry and Composition: *La recherche de l'Absolu*	208
Chapter 16	The Capital of Money and the Science of Magnetism: *Melmoth réconcilié*	221
Chapter 17	Love, Music, and Opium: Medical Semiotics of *Massimilla Doni*	230
Chapter 18	The Language of Sex	242
Chapter 19	Composed Past and Historical Present	259
Chapter 20	Problems of Closure	270
Chapter 21	Conclusion: Balzac's Invention of Realism	292
Bibliography		307
Index		317

Illustrations

Figure 8.1	*Pierrette* genealogy	111
Figure 8.2	Presumed portrait of B. Cenci	125
Figure 10.1	Handwritten *La Rabouilleuse* genealogy	142
Figure 10.2	Computer-generated genealogy	143
Figure 11.1	*Ursule Mirouët* genealogy	156
Figure 14.1	Waltz by Reissiger	197

Acknowledgments

I would like to thank three research assistants who were doctoral students at the University of Illinois at Urbana-Champaign. Juliette Dade helped with translations and became proficient at rendering Balzac (and sometimes Mortimer) into English. In addition, she tracked down references and typed up my illegible handwritten notes from pre-computer days. Ingrid Ilinca contributed speedy and thorough background research on several topics. Leila Ennaïli brought her intelligence and fine mind to a reading of the manuscript and provided judicious criticisms. All three gave generously of their considerable intellectual gifts, and I am grateful to them for their contributions.

It does not fail to amaze me how valuable teaching Balzac has been, and I have much to acknowledge from the students in all the classes where I have taught Balzac. In particular, let me mention Jordan Stump, who has since translated Balzac's *L'envers de l'histoire contemporaine* and whose understanding of the opus grew deep and broad; and James Madden, whose excellent reading skills and ability to retain the myriad details of *La Comédie humaine* outshone anyone's, and to whom the whole class would turn when a point needed remembering and verifying.

Colleagues of the Nineteenth Century French Studies Association heard me deliver papers mostly on Balzac at the annual conferences and gave me the benefit of their reactions. I am grateful for their listening and to the leadership of this organization and the hosts of the annual meetings for affording me this opportunity to try out my ideas and to pursue them from year to year, I hope without becoming too predictable.

I also thank the members of the Groupe international de recherches balzaciennes who invited me to present a paper on voyages in Balzac in 2001 in the suitably Balzacian location of Tours, in particular Paule Pétitier, who hosted the conference, and the GIRB's chief animator, Nicole Mozet. Similarly, I thank the England-based Society of Dix-Neuviémistes who heard my papers on *La recherche de l'Absolu* and on *Melmoth réconcilié* in 2002 and 2003.

Illinois colleagues Larry Schehr and Andrea Goulet provided helpful comments and always fine, stimulating dialogue. I also thank a good reader and a hearty supporter for many years, Allan Pasco, one of the distinguished American Balzacians, for his valuable and encouraging criticism.

Finally, I cannot omit recognizing the person who started me on this journey through *La Comédie humaine,* Peter Brooks, whose graduate seminar on Balzac at Yale in 1971 opened the vein I have continued to mine for my entire professional career.

The University of Illinois at Urbana-Champaign has supported my research in the form of travel funding and research assistants. The editors of the journals and the collective volumes in which earlier versions of parts of some chapters were published have allowed me to reuse those materials in this book, and I thank them. And I am grateful to the two anonymous readers of the manuscript for The Ohio State University Press, whose reports provided insightful feedback and helped me improve the manuscript.

A word about translations:
I have translated French quotations for the convenience of the non-Francophone reader, with the hope that the presence of both French and English will not distract either sort of reader. I thank Juliette Dade for her collaboration in the task of translating.

The following articles contained earlier versions of certain parts of this book:

"*La Maison Nucingen,* ou le récit financier." *Romanic Review* 69 (1978): 60–71.
"Problems of Closure in Balzac's Stories." *French Forum* 10 (1985): 20–39.

"Mimetic Figures of Semiosis in Balzac." In *Repression and Expression: Social Codes and Literary Visions in Nineteenth-Century France*, ed. Carrol Coates, 47–54. New York: Lang, 1996.

"Le corset de *La Vieille Fille* de Balzac." In *L'œuvre d'identité: Essais sur le romantisme de Nodier à Baudelaire*, ed. Didier Maleuvre and Catherine Nesci, 39–48. *Paragraphes* 13. Université de Montréal, 1996.

"Balzac: Tenebrous Affairs and Necessary Explications." In *The Play of Terror in Nineteenth-Century France*, ed. John T. Booker and Allan H. Pasco, 241–55. Newark: University of Delaware Press, 1997.

"Balzac's *Ursule Mirouët*: Genealogy and Inheritance." *The Modern Language Review* 92 (1997): 851–63.

"Myth and Mendacity: Balzac's *Pierrette* and Beatrice Cenci." *Dalhousie French Studies* 51 (Summer 2000): 12–25.

"Balzac and Poe: Realizing Magnetism." *Dalhousie French Studies* 63 (Summer 2003): 22–30.

"Voyages de réflexion, réflexions de voyages." In *Balzac voyageur: Parcours, déplacements, mutations,* ed. Nicole Mozet and Paule Petitier, 119–36. Tours: Université François Rabelais, 2004.

Introduction
The Prime Movers

> Toutes les femmes, tous les hommes créés par Balzac peuvent répéter le mot de Mme de Beauséant: "J'ai voulu vivre."
>
> [All the women, all the men created by Balzac could repeat Mme de Beauséant's mot: "I wanted to live."]
>
> —Gadenne

Eugène and Delphine

Consider the effect of money on Eugène de Rastignac when he is still a poor student in *Le père Goriot*:

> A l'instant où l'argent se glisse dans la poche d'un étudiant, il se dresse en lui-même une colonne fantastique sur laquelle il s'appuie. Il marche mieux qu'auparavant, il se sent un point d'appui pour son levier, il a le regard plein, direct, il a les mouvements agiles; la veille, humble et timide, il aurait reçu des coups; le lendemain il en donnerait à un premier ministre. Il se passe en lui des phénomènes inouïs: il veut tout et peut tout, il désire à tort et à travers, il est gai, généreux, expansif. Enfin, l'oiseau naguère sans ailes a retrouvé son envergure. . . . Paris lui appartient tout entier. (3: 131)[1]

---

1. All references to *La Comédie humaine*, including editorial material, are to the Pléiade edition listed at the head of the bibliography, except where noted.

[The instant money finds its way into a student's pocket, there arises inside him a fantastic column on which he leans. He walks better than before, he feels a fulcrum for his lever, his gaze is full and direct, his movements are agile; humble and timid the night before, he would have accepted blows; the next day he would strike a prime minister. Unheard-of phenomena occur within him. He wishes for everything and can do everything, he desires wildly, he is cheerful, generous, and expansive. In all, the once wingless bird has recovered his wingspan. . . . All Paris belongs to him.]

This apparently minor moment in the student's life gives a rhetorical image of the power of money to make things happen. It is typical of Balzac's rhetoric that the small event—money finding its way into the pocket—connects to the momentous by means of rhetorical embellishment. A metaphorical column rises up, the first result of the agency of money; the pocket change metamorphoses into a major support, such as one might find not only in the pompous façade of a monumental building, but also, suggestively, as the base upholding the statue of a famous person; money is that support instantly raising the indebted student to ranks of power. In a society where demeanor and style indicate social position, the physical changes—walking better, a full, direct gaze, agile movements—are the literal expressions of an expansion that develops from sentence to sentence and places the poor student among the elite to which he aspires. By the device of hypothesis, expressed by the verbs in the conditional tense, Balzac offers an image of his character so outranking a prime minister that he would hypothetically give blows. Finally, the image of the wingless bird regaining his wingspan and his grandeur along with his power of flight adds by another metaphor to the soaring effect of money, and the all-embracing vision of Paris that ensues multiplies the perspective and crowns the rhetorical inflation.

These devices of rhetoric raise the agency of money to the highest level of importance. In the language of this passage, at least two connections internal to *La Comédie humaine* expand the minor moment further. The non-metaphorical description "il veut tout et peut tout, il désire à tort et à travers" connects Eugène de Rastignac to Raphaël de Valentin in *La peau de chagrin*. Encompassing the reference to "vouloir" and "pouvoir," these words about Rastignac restate the foundation of Balzac's philosophy of energy and desire found throughout *La Comédie humaine*. "*Vouloir* nous brûle et *Pouvoir* nous détruit" [*Will* burns us up and *Power* destroys us] (10: 85), according to the antiquarian as he presents Raphaël with the magic skin, and these two actions of the "great mysteries of human life" are also the two causes of death. The final phrase, "Paris lui appartient tout entier," anticipates the famous challenge Rastignac addresses to the city from the heights of the Père Lachaise cemetery at the end of the novel, "À nous deux maintenant" [It's between you and me now], marking the final point of his evolution in this novel and the entry into the other increasingly powerful manifestations of this much reappearing character. Money is the dangerous talisman that would procure Rastignac's every desire, as the magic skin is for Valentin, and the possession of Paris, so vigorously sought after in the novel's closure, is presented in this passage as something achieved thanks to a few coins, in a very surprising prediction.

Although it may pass unnoticed, this paragraph also contains an image akin to that of the Aristotelian Prime Mover: "il se sent un point d'appui pour son levier." As a metaphorical expression of a potential inherent in Rastignac, like the potential Balzac felt in himself, this image of the fulcrum for whatever action his lever would propose may make the reader think of Archimedes' boast that he could move the earth, given a lever long enough and a place to stand. Rastignac's place to stand occurs at the end of this novel; the accomplishments of his career in other novels, the lever, contribute to the changes in French society, the displacement of the world so obsessively charted by Balzac.

Goriot's maxims also express the centrality of money: "L'argent, c'est la vie. Monnaie fait tout" [Money is life. Cash does everything] (3: 242). Vautrin emits another concise expression of the primacy of money in the often-quoted observation, "Si jamais vous fouillez des cœurs de femmes à Paris, vous y trouverez l'usurier avant l'amant" [If you ever dig into the hearts of women in Paris, you will find a usurer there before a lover] (3: 86). And Delphine de Nucingen, in a tirade of contained fury against her faithless lover de Marsay, confirms Vautrin: "L'argent ne devient quelque chose qu'au moment où le sentiment n'est plus" [Money becomes something only after sentiment is no longer] (3: 173). These one-liners about money also confirm the place of *Le père Goriot* at the center of *La Comédie humaine,* as others have noted, for instance Rose Fortassier in the preface to the Pléiade edition: "En somme, *Le père Goriot* aimante, annexe tout ce qui a été écrit ou va s'écrire. . . . Ce roman [était] destiné à être au centre de son œuvre par le nombre d'intrigues qui en rayonnaient" [In short, *Le père Goriot,* like a magnet, draws to it and annexes everything that has already been written or will be written. . . . This novel [was] destined to be in the center of his opus by the number of plots that radiated from it] (3: 27, 33–34). More recently, Arlette Michel reaffirms this centrality of *Le Père Goriot,* and hence of money: "Tous les commentateurs s'accordent pour voir dans *Le père Goriot* un archétype du roman balzacien. C'est à juste titre" [Critics all agree that *Le père Goriot* is an archetype of the Balzacian novel. They are right] (*Le réel* 136).² And with the novel's place at the archetypal center, money and love take center stage.

One of the radiating narratives stemming from *Le père Goriot* is *Gobseck*. Devoting a chapter to the central role of Gobseck in *La Comédie humaine*, Jean-Joseph Goux writes: "Le roman réaliste dans sa possibilité la plus intense, serait concomitant à l'émergence de celui que Balzac appelle parfois le 'capitaliste' ou le 'financier,' comme personnage central-intitulant" [The realistic novel, in its most perfect realization, is concomitant with the emergence of the character Balzac sometimes calls the "capitalist" or the "financier" as a central title character] (89). Goux notes that the novel genre becomes realistic at the same time as money takes on a dominant role: "Non seulement Balzac n'épargne au lecteur aucun détail sur les manipulations touchant l'argent, mais il situe au centre de la scène, des personnages dont l'activité principale est cette manipulation, et il noue une intrigue dont les fils se concentrent autour de ses enjeux" [Not only does Balzac spare the reader none of the details about manipulations concerning money, he also situates characters at center stage whose principal activity is such manipulations, and he devises plots whose threads converge on their actions] (87). Nothing is more "realistic," it seems, than matters that can be expressed in terms of their cost, where a financial number solidifies the concrete nature of the human interactions.

It is easy to assume that Love, as a motivation for the characters' actions, is opposed to Money. Love may sound like the antithesis of money, as in the expression "for love or for money" which places the terms in the position of alternatives, and one finds a sense of this idea in the critical literature. Raymond Mahieu for instance describes *Eugénie Grandet* as built on the interaction of the "principes antagonistes qui gouvernent le monde" [the antagonistic principles that govern the world] (49), which he calls Capital and Eros. (According to *La Maison Nucingen*, the "fusion" of love with money would have been considered dishonorable for Delphine and Eugène: "tout intérêt matériel est en dehors des sentiments" [any material interest lies outside sentiment] [6: 335].) Such an opposition could be made to account for the antagonisms, contraries, oppositions, dualities, and so on, that characterize the essence of the Balzacian conception. But from opposition Balzac draws unity. As Arlette Michel has written, "La poétique et la rhétorique de *La Comédie humaine* tendront à être unitaires parce que fondées sur la

---

2. In addition: "Ce roman peut ainsi être lu comme une ouverture à l'univers romanesque balzacien" [This novel can thus be read as an opening to the world of the Balzacian novel], proposes the introductory matter by Olivier Bara in the Bibliothèque Gallimard edition of *Le père Goriot*, aimed at students (14).

Introduction: The Prime Movers

coexistence des contraires"; "il s'agit de maintenir en présence des postulations antagonistes . . . pour qu'il résulte de leur mise en relation non un moyen terme rassurant par sa stabilité, mais une réalité radicalement neuve parce que née d'une tension, d'un déséquilibre corrigé" [The poetics and the rhetoric of *La Comédie humaine* will tend to be unitary because they are founded on the coexistence of contraries]; [he maintains antagonistic postulations together . . . so that their encounter results not in a middle term reassuring in its stability but in a radically new reality born from tension, from a corrected disequilibrium] ("Balzac et la rhétorique" 257). The interconnectedness of Love and Money forges this reality founded on a corrected disequilibrium; the unloved and unloving Gobseck's passion for gold is a question of Love as well as of Money. By means of this interconnectedness, what Balzac invented was precisely a world in which Love needs Money and vice versa; neither ever works alone, and it is the powerful interaction between them that defines *La Comédie humaine*. On such a basis, Balzac builds his particular brand of realism.

In *Le père Goriot,* the connection of Love to Money is Delphine de Nucingen's problem. Rastignac has just won seven thousand francs by proverbial beginner's luck at the gambling tables; the money acts on Delphine as if a dam had burst, and she launches into a two-and-a-half page paragraph about her money-and-love problems. Of course the problem is that Nucingen does not give her enough money, and that to obtain money from him implies giving her "love" to him: "Je suis trop fière pour l'implorer. Ne serais-je pas la dernière des créatures si j'achetais son argent au prix où il veut me le vendre!" [I am too proud to beg. I would be the lowest of the low if I were to buy his money for the price he wants to sell it to me!] (3: 172). Marriage is a disappointment; out of delicacy, Delphine will only tell Eugène: "qu'il vous suffise de savoir que je me jetterais par la fenêtre s'il fallait vivre avec Nucingen autrement qu'en ayant chacun notre appartement séparé" [know only that I would throw myself out of a window if I had to live with Nucingen in any way other than having separate bedrooms] (3: 172). Clearly money can be traded for love, even within a marriage.

Or outside a marriage. And here the relation of love and money becomes more complex, when we learn that de Marsay, Delphine's former lover, gave her money. On the one hand, she needed money to show herself worthy of his pride: "j'ai voulu répondre à l'amour-propre de quelqu'un que vous connaissez" [I wanted to satisfy the pride of someone you know] (3: 172). This causes her to go into debt. On the other hand, de Marsay gives her money, which she then has to return when his "love" ceases:

> *On* ne devrait jamais abandonner une femme à laquelle on a jeté, dans un jour de détresse, un tas d'or! *On* doit l'aimer toujours! . . . Mon Dieu! n'est-il pas naturel de tout partager avec l'être auquel nous devons notre bonheur? Quand on s'est tout donné, qui pourrait s'inquiéter d'une parcelle de ce tout? (3: 172–73)

> [*One* should never abandon a woman to whom one has thrown a pile of gold in a moment of misery! *One* should love her forever! . . . Goodness! Isn't it natural to share everything with the one to whom we owe our happiness? When we have given everything, why should anyone be concerned about a small part of this everything?]

With consummate irony, Delphine treats money as a small parcel of the complete package, the "everything" that includes, according to the laws of the language of sex in Balzac, sexual love. The topic of Love embraces the range of human sentiments. Delphine has a husband, a former lover, and a future lover. In all three cases, the relation of love (if we can include the rejected sexual relation with Nucingen among the forms of love) to money determines the nature of the relationship. A telling symbol in the opening pages of *Le père Goriot* taints love from the start: it is a statue of Eros found in the garden of the pension Vauquer whose flaking varnish indexes Parisian love as an illness that needs to be treated at the nearby Hôpital des Vénériens. This is the entry of love into this central novel, a cynical portrait and a forewarning.

The novel nevertheless produces a potent analysis of the many aspects of love in the liaison that will become one of the longest lasting in *La Comédie humaine,* described in *Le père Goriot* as "une passion véritable" for Eugène and "le véritable amour" for Delphine (3: 181, 182). Holding the watch Delphine has sent him, Eugène says, "Ah! ce soir je serai donc heureux! . . . Tout m'a réussi! Quand on s'aime bien pour toujours, l'on peut s'aider, je puis recevoir cela. D'ailleurs je parviendrai, certes, et pourrai tout rendre au centuple" [Ah! so I will have love tonight! . . . Everything is working out for me! When you love one another forever, you can help each other. I can receive this. Besides, I will surely succeed, and I can return everything a hundred times over] (3: 216). The watch, a love token, indicates the moment when, for the first time, Delphine and Eugène will sleep together, but it also becomes the focus of Eugène's reflection about how love motivates him to succeed, and to return everything to Delphine multiplied by a hundred. The suspicion of a numeration attaches to the pure expression of sentiment. If there are some moments of sincere appreciation for love as a full and complete sentiment uniting two beings—moments that follow the satisfaction of the sexual desire of the couple and where Balzac suspends his otherwise pervasive irony—much of the analysis instead ties love to money, especially in the form of power:

> L'amour à Paris ne ressemble en rien aux autres amours. . . . En ce pays, une femme ne doit pas satisfaire seulement le cœur et les sens, elle sait parfaitement qu'elle a de plus grandes obligations à remplir envers les mille vanités dont se compose la vie. Là surtout l'amour est essentiellement vantard, effronté, gaspilleur, charlatan et fastueux. . . . L'amour est une religion, et son culte doit coûter plus cher que celui de toutes les autres religions. (3: 236)

> [Love in Paris isn't anything like love elsewhere. . . . In this place a woman is expected to do more than satisfy the heart and the senses; she knows perfectly well that she must fulfill greater obligations to the thousands of vanities that compose a life. Here especially love is essentially boastful, shameless, wasteful, deceitful, and sumptuous. . . . Love is a religion, and its practice should cost more than that of all the other religions.]

It is right, in Balzac's analysis, that love should cost a lot. Delphine exemplifies this practice of a cult as she uses excessive language to describe the power of love: "Il n'est plus aujourd'hui qu'une seule crainte, un seul malheur pour moi, c'est de perdre l'amour qui m'a fait sentir le plaisir de vivre. En dehors de ce sentiment tout m'est indifférent, je n'aime plus rien au monde" [For me, now, there is only one fear, only one misfortune: to lose the love that has made me feel the pleasure of living. Everything else is indifferent to me; I love nothing else in the world] (3: 255). Even love can be expressed as a possession, an object to love, with the power to give pleasure to life.

And love is also a powerful motivator for Eugène. In the moral struggle depicted in *Le père Goriot,* the temptation of money takes the form of Vautrin's machinations with Victorine Taillefer and her brother, and it is this motivation that his love for Delphine will eventually overcome. Later Balzac will turn to delicate language to describe the sexual pleasure that cements the love between Eugène and Delphine, language I analyze in chapter 18. But until that chimerical moment of the magical union of physical desire with ideal sentiment, Eugène sees the love of a woman as the entry into the domain of power and seeks to combat Paris armed to the teeth. It is both love and money that give Rastignac power.

For Love or for Money
The Prime Movers of *La Comédie humaine*

This book brings together published and unpublished studies I have written on Balzac. The roots of my Balzac readings reach deeply into the geological layers of my professional life: all the way to graduate school and a course on Balzac taught by Peter Brooks. Out of these roots grew the first article I published on Balzac, "*La Maison Nucingen,* ou le récit financier," whose acceptance by Michael Riffaterre for publication in *Romanic Review* was one of the gratifying highlights of the probationary period of my professorship at the University of Illinois at Urbana-Champaign.

The reader will not find here anything like a complete interpretation of *La Comédie humaine*. I do not discuss every work in the ensemble, nor do I offer a full treatment of those I do discuss. My focus is specific, even narrow. For specific and sometimes contingent reasons, these are the Balzac titles that offered me the promise of the particular sort of pleasure that reading in depth affords; and that pleasure pointed to the aspects of each text that needed interpretation and analysis. Quite often these interpretations arose during the close reading one does to teach a novel or story, whether to undergraduates or to graduates. Now these readings have brought me to a certain remove from the geological origins of this fascination with Balzac, at which point it has become clear to me that everything happens in *La Comédie humaine* because of love and money. I call Love and Money the Prime Movers.

A few words follow to introduce this perspective on Balzac, but the real meat of the matter lies in the following chapters: this book is not only about love and money in Balzac (both of these topics have been treated in the critical literature), but about the interlacing network of images that give structure and meaning to *La Comédie humaine*.

Aristotelian causality reigns throughout *La Comédie humaine;* things move, but what moves them? What is the primary cause, the original impetus that gives rise to causality? In a given universe (the Aristotelian *ousia*), the social and physical world of Balzac's creation, the Prime Movers set matter into motion; Love and Money act both singly and together. I think of them as the motor that puts the whole narrative system into motion, that makes the spheres revolve, rotate, and orbit. Emblematic of this identification of the Prime Movers is the well-known introduction to *La fille aux yeux d'or,* where Balzac waxes horribly eloquent about gold and pleasure—"l'or et le plaisir"—in Paris. Pleasure is, after all, a form of love, even if it is assimilated into the populace of a Paris seen as an inferno à la Dante. The beginning and end of all feelings, beliefs, and mores are gold and pleasure (5: 1040); gold has a natural movement of ascension (5: 1046); the entire population of Paris, from the bottom to the top, is moved by gold and pleasure.

The importance of love and money has not gone unnoticed in the enormous body of critical literature on *La Comédie humaine*—it is scarcely necessary to inventory the list. Some of the notable Balzacian readers of the twentieth century brought the role of money to the fore, and critical discussions of money are more prevalent than analyses of love. Jean-Hervé Donnard's *Les réalités économiques et sociales dans La Comédie humaine* links the forces of money to the social situation of the characters. André Wurmser's diatribe against what he wittily calls *La comédie inhumaine* also addresses the harsh realities of material life in the times depicted in Balzac's immense fresco. Other writers have given their attention to banking, like Bertrand Gille in *La banque et le crédit en France, de 1818 à 1848,* and one also finds shorter articles about how money functions in the work.[3]

René Guise ends his introduction to *César Birotteau* with these words: "Il fut un temps où, dans les romans, l'amour était le mobile majeur des actions héroïques, nobles, vertueuses . . . Avec *César Birotteau,* Balzac nous peint un monde où l'amour et la vertu se prouvent en gagnant de l'argent" [There was a time when love was the major motivation of heroic, noble, and virtuous actions in novels . . . With *César Birotteau,* Balzac paints for us a world in which love and virtue are proved by gaining money] (6: 34). Gérard David writes quite similarly about Balzac:

> Il fut d'abord le premier écrivain à prendre aussi nettement conscience de l'importance et parfois de la prépondérance des réalités économiques sur les sentiments ou les idées. Il eut ensuite l'audace de mettre en scène dans le roman ces préoccupations financières en montrant leur influence sur le comportement des individus et des classes constitutives de la nation. (322)

> [To begin with, he was the first writer to take cognizance so distinctly of the importance and sometimes the preponderance of economic realities over feelings or ideas. Then he had the audacity to narrate these financial preoccupations in the novel by showing their influence on the behavior of the individuals and the classes that constitute the nation.]

---

3. An interesting complement to studies of the fictions is the analysis of Balzac himself as a businessman, in Bouvier's *Balzac homme d'affaires.*

Perhaps because Balzac was both first and audacious in writing money into his novels, readers of *La Comédie humaine* have been drawn to its manipulations. One of the most complete explanations of money manipulations is found in Hélène Gomart's book, *Les opérations financières dans le roman réaliste*. Her extensive, detailed analysis of the instruments of money in *César Birotteau* illuminates the mysteries of the pathetic industrialist and his bankruptcy. Allan H. Pasco, in "Process Structure in Balzac's *La Rabouilleuse*," remarks that "Balzac repeatedly returned to the dangers of a society ruled by money" (28). Christopher Prendergast, in writing about *Splendeurs et misères des courtisanes,* observes that "the form of paper that most completely [summarizes] the circulating and self-dissipating energies of the society is paper money. The passing of bits of paper from hand to hand in connection with Lucien's forged bills of exchange is described by Balzac as generating 'capitaux fictifs.' ... Paper money is 'unsound' money" (114). The view of money as merchandise, as opposed to "money-as-sign (as a token whose representative value is determined by consent)," is consistent with the political right of Balzac's time after the Revolution and the theoreticians on whom Balzac leaned (114). Prendergast also notes that the emptiness of money as sign is dangerous; "its circulation promotes an expansion of the system of credit that is without secure foundations in 'real' property and wealth" (115).

Others, but not as many, have focused on love. Arlette Michel's indispensable study of love and marriage, a monumental thesis, exhaustively examines all the male–female relations in *La Comédie humaine*. The same critic devotes a section of *Le réel et la beauté* to defining and distinguishing ideal love and absolute love, with an illustration from *Massimilla Doni*.

Love leading to marriage is the classic plot line of literature, and Balzac is in some respects at his most classic, as opposed to modern, in following this tradition. Many are the plots in which marriage is the end point, like *Modeste Mignon,* or some semblance of marriage, such as the long love affair of the princesse de Cadignan with d'Arthez. Other plots build out from the classic design to form variants. Sarrasine's love for La Zambinella, the love of half-sister and half-brother for one woman in *La fille aux yeux d'or,* the unequal love of Agathe Bridau for her two sons in *La Rabouilleuse,* the unrequited, hidden love of Paz in *La fausse maîtresse,* a panther's love in *Une passion dans le désert*—these are some examples of situations in which love as Prime Mover motivates variants of the classic plot. Of course adultery has pride of place, and it is with typical self-mocking humor that Balzac has one of the bourgeois characters in *La muse du département* speak about love and Parisian women: "depuis quelque temps, les livres que vous faites, messieurs les écrivains, vos revues, vos pièces de théâtre, toute votre infâme littérature, repose sur l'adultère" [for some time now, dear authors, the books you are writing, your reviews, your plays, all your infamous literature, has been based on adultery] (4: 680).

In the following chapters, a variety of reading strategies pertains, and the focus is adaptable to the objective. Yet always in the background one will find what I am calling the Prime Movers, and in the foreground, the overall objective of describing Balzacian realism.

The methodology that I have found the most persuasive addresses the constant interaction of levels of meaning that I call *rhetorical, mimetic,* and *semiotic*. The details, the plot, what is being conveyed to inform the reader constitute the mimesis; the semiosis concerns the methods for conveying that information; rhetoric (taken broadly) provides the tools for mimesis and semiosis and in a sense subsumes both mimesis and semiosis. What is happening on the level of the story being invented, the conception of content or the mimesis, seeks matching signs to execute the story, a symbolic language. Or, put differently, a structure or a form in Balzac's prose mirrors a structure of its content; the symbolic language matches the creation of content, which is the business of Balzacian realism. I have chosen to use *semiosis* and *mimesis* as the terms designating these two forms in interaction. The example I gave at the beginning of this introduction—the effect of money on Rastignac—shows how the mimetic and the semiotic work together: Balzac's rhetoric of realism rises up to match the growth of new power in Rastignac.

To draw out the distinction would be to reach for far-ranging explanations, as these two terms highlight the fundamental axes of signification through language. The semiotic concerns the activity of the signs, in particular the relations among them; the mimetic concerns the relation of the signs to what they represent. C. S. Peirce initiated the term semiosis to designate the formation and development of the linguistic sign and the movement toward another sign. Applying this general concept, I use semiosis to designate a form of expression, which relates to a form of content, mimesis. To distinguish between forms of expression and forms of content, the Danish linguist Louis Hjelmslev, writing in 1966, defined the sign as the unit constituted by the form of expression and the form of content, established by the solidarity of the semiotic function (77). Forms of content are the place where, in this study, we will find the mimetic expression of semiosis. There is always a double level of analysis.

In its rhetorical, semiotic, and mimetic aspects, Balzac's language provides the structures that create realism. I have grouped the following chapters under these three descriptors of Balzacian writing, which however point to phenomena that interact in such a way that all are present to some degree at all times. In the first part, I examine rhetorical forms such as doubleness, interest, unity, identity, and representation, which guide us into a method for reading out the realism of the Balzacian narrative according to its language. For the second part, I have grouped analyses that focus on in-dwelling sign systems, such as myth in *Pierrette,* the corset of the prose in *La vieille fille,* voyages in several narratives, and genealogies (one of Balzac's most consistent approaches to realism). In part three, the focus is on structures of mimesis such as magnetism, chemistry, medicine, historical present, and closure, narrative structures that create meaning. All these readings aim to reveal the interlacing network of narrative devices, in the author's strategies and choices of language, that express his world. The concluding chapter assesses Balzac's invention of realism in *La Comédie humaine.*

Rhetorical Forms of Realism

Mimetic Figures of Semiosis

Mémoires de deux jeunes mariées
Duality

Balzac's only epistolary novel in *La Comédie humaine, Mémoires de deux jeunes mariées,* serves to inaugurate the reader into the general problematic of reading a Balzacian narrative. It exposes and explicates how to understand the mimetic world the writer creates, and because it lacks the familiar narrator who explains everything, the novel raises this problematic in a particularly pointed way.

Written in 1841, the first of the novels in *La Comédie humaine* as it was published poses problems of interpretation arising in differing points of view, like *Les liaisons dangereuses.* Unlike Laclos's novel, however, the difficulty of interpretation concerns so fundamental a matter that an essential question remains without a satisfactory answer: what Balzac thinks about his characters. Louise and Renée, the two heroines, present widely divergent images of the role of love in a woman's life. As an immediate consequence, the reader seeks to understand the ethos that each represents. Since only Louise and Renée tell each other their stories, no single voiced narration guides our reading or helps us decide between their conflicting fundamental philosophies of life; direct authorial interventions are entirely lacking. That this is so defies convention: one might expect at least a framing narration, such as one finds in classic epistolary novels of the eighteenth century, disingenuously explaining the existence of these letters, commenting on them, or describing an editor's role. Usually such a prefatory text is motivated by a moral purpose (whether sincere or ironic) or serves as an interpretive guide. Yet, from the Furne edition on, remarkably, such mediation was limited to the hand that apparently numbered each letter and added the names of sender and receiver. A short preface in the first edition, however, sketchily followed convention—except that even it gave no hint of a moral interpretation.

Since there are for the most part only two letter writers, unlike *Les liaisons dangereuses,* this largely dual rather than multiple point of view combined with the more relaxed pace and longer time frame maintains a balanced focus on the stories of Louise de Chaulieu and Renée de Maucombe (although Louise occupies 108 pages and Renée 69, according to Pich [17]). Nor do other stories intervene, except as anecdotes. The correspondence begins at the moment the two young women leave their convent school, and it continues at first frequently, then more rarely, during their entire young adulthood, through marriage, Renée's motherhood, and Louise's widowhood and remarriage. Louise's quasi-suicidal death closes the correspondence. The problems of point of view, in short, are not those that stem from the accidental, obstacle-strewn structure of letters in *Les liaisons dangereuses.* Rather, as two lives diverge, the reader falls between them and very likely finds it difficult to choose. A rigorous dialogism rejects dialectical synthesis and sustains opposed values: Paris and the provinces, Society and Nature, aristocrat and bourgeois (Renée, though not strictly speaking a *bourgeoise,* makes a bourgeois marriage), illicit passionate love vs. legitimate conjugal love, two parallel but antithetical destinies, a chiasmic outcome (the *provinciale* finishes in Paris, the *Parisienne* in Nature), and a double morality. Louise's passionate life full of movement, uncertainty, and change contrasts wildly with Renée's calm, secure, but dull existence whose course is traced in advance. Louise clearly represents a Balzacian Ideal, the temptation of the absolute—where danger and death lie too. Renée stands for the Family, often proclaimed by Balzac as the only solid foundation for society, and some of the warmest pages defend this view—but how proper and insipid! Renée preaches those deep-seated values, while Louise wants excitement and risk. Philippe Berthier metaphorically speaks of two "instruments à la sonorité complémentaire, mais irréductible à toute fusion" [instruments whose sound is complementary but irreducible to any fusion] ("Accoucher au masculin" 294).

All commentators on the novel necessarily seek to elucidate the philosophies implied by the two life stories, but readers find it difficult to assert unequivocally which of the women conveys Balzac's thought. It is interesting that George Sand suffered little such doubt and indeed assumed Balzac wanted to promote the values represented by Renée. Sand wrote: "Je n'arrive pas à vos conclusions, et il me semble au contraire que vous prouvez tout l'opposé de ce que vous voulez prouver" [I don't come to your conclusions, and it seems to me on the contrary that you prove exactly the opposite of what you want to prove]; "J'admire celle qui procrée, mais *j'adore* celle qui meurt d'amour. Voilà tout ce que vous avez prouvé, et c'est *plus* que vous n'avez voulu" [I admire the woman who procreates, but I *adore* the one who dies of love. That is all you have proved, and it is *more* than you wanted to] (quoted in Michel, ed., *Mémoires* 306, 308). Sand's significant reading against Balzac offers a model for the reader's freedom to choose.

Yet what *did* Balzac think of the two "solutions" to the "problem" of passion in marriage? Every writer about this novel who has wrestled with those dialogic poles I have mentioned must resort to some affirmation of both, to avoid misrepresenting Balzac's thought.[1] As Arlette Michel postulates, Balzac is attracted by both Renée and Louise, excluding neither opposed term and trying to operate a mediation between them (Introduction 32). Michel also writes, in a study of passion in marriage, that for all the seriousness of the Bonaldism Renée represents, Balzac does not give her a triumphant position in the narrative: "Mais qu'il serait faux de voir dans les succès de Renée le triomphe du mariage de raison!" [How wrong it would be to see in Renée's successes the triumph of the marriage of reason!] ("Balzac juge du féminisme" 187). No more can Louise's failure be taken to invalidate the morality she represents. It is typical of the results of such analyses of the novel that Michel must resort to the following interesting formula to position the novelist with regard to his creations: "[Renée] offre ainsi l'exemple d'un personnage que Balzac 'philosophe' approuve et que, romancier, il déteste" [[Renée] thus offers the example of a character that Balzac as a "philosopher" approves of and that, as a novelist, he detests] ("Balzac juge du féminisme" 192). Only a split subject can hold both sides of the story in his hands, it would seem.

I feel the question of Balzac's philosophy has been adequately dealt with in the critical literature on *Mémoires de deux jeunes mariées* (mainly in the prefaces of different editions), and my purpose is not to bring another brick to that edifice. Rather, I would claim that this duality, this scarcely under-

---

1. That is not the case with Edgard Pich, who writes: "De là la préférence affichée de Balzac pour Louise, malgré sa folie, parce que ce qui l'oppose à Renée n'est pas au fond son enthousiasme pour les délires romantiques de la passion, mais son choix de l'absolu" [Hence Balzac's stated preference for Louise, in spite of her folly, because what opposes her to Renée is not so much her enthusiasm for the romantic deliriums of passion as her preference for the absolute] (19).

standable affirmation of doubleness, stands, for Balzac's writing, in the position of obstacle, of stumbling block—and hence of a creative prod. It may well be that Balzac the philosopher casts his vote with Renée, while adoring, like George Sand, a life like Louise's, but I suspect that the novelist is no less involved in this dilemma. It is not so clear that as a novelist he hates Renée and all she represents, because on her opposition with Louise depends the very existence of the novel. In this I am in disagreement with Edgard Pich who, motivated by the genetic record of the text, believes that "Balzac ne semble donc pas avoir maîtrisé une évolution qui allait à l'encontre de ses plans, qui aboutissait, contre son gré, à un parallélisme entre deux conceptions sociales et qui débouchait sur une sorte de symétrie de la construction" [Balzac does not seem to have mastered an evolution that contradicted his plans, that concluded, against his will, in a parallelism between two ideas of society and that ended in a sort of symmetry of construction] (19). Not symmetry, but duality, and a fruitful, productive one; it is an opposition (a schizophrenia, Pich does allow [20]), that is put relentlessly to good use by the master novelist. It is the figure of his semiosis.

The idea of a double woman initially proposes a vision of unity made from duality; it represents a potentially complete being made of contrary parts, but the image lies in the past and survives, artificially, only a short time. On the first page we find Louise and Renée compared to Siamese twins, an apt symbol of their girlish intimacy in the convent (1: 196). Through their letters, now separated by more than geography, Louise "lives" with Renée in her Provence valley, while Renée "lives" with Louise in Paris (1: 197). They agree to a division of labor. Renée writes, "Tu seras, ma chère Louise, la partie romanesque de mon existence. . . . Tu seras deux à écouter, à danser, à sentir le bout de tes doigts pressé" [You, my dear Louise, will be the romantic part of my existence. . . . There will be two of you, listening, dancing, feeling the tips of your fingers pressed] (1: 222). It is up to Louise to weave "some fine passion"—and she does!—"dans l'intérêt bien entendu de notre double existence" [in the interest, to be sure, of our double existence] (1: 240), while Renée knows all the joys and anguish of having children.

Philippe Berthier stresses the porosity, the mutual contamination, and the exchange that characterizes the relation between the two women, rather than binary differences, and concludes on the copula, rather than the disjunction, between them ("Frauenlieben" 158–59, 170). Edgard Pich similarly writes: "On peut poursuivre l'analyse pour montrer l'acharnement de Balzac à montrer que Renée et Louise ne sont qu'une seule et même personne, alors que la géographie, la maternité, le milieu, l'idéologie semblent les opposer point par point" [One could continue the analysis to show Balzac's determination to show that Renée and Louise are one and the same, whereas geography, maternity, social milieu, and ideology seem to oppose them point by point] (27). But the double woman figure is merely a configuration from the prenovelistic past (the convent school, of which there is properly nothing to be recounted); it is a deceptive misguidance for the reader, an initial condition of unity destined to be upset. Significantly, the Siamese twins of the first page are mentioned in their *death* ("nos âmes soudées l'une à l'autre, comme étaient ces deux filles hongroises dont la mort nous a été racontée" [our souls fused to each other, like those two Hungarian girls whose death was recounted to us] [1: 196]); what the comparison gives, it immediately takes away. Repeatedly, Renée and Louise accentuate their differences, sometimes in strong language. Each envies the other, but each also writes freely of her contempt for the life the other has chosen. Never does one change in response to the other's exhortations. No letter mediates between contraries.

Because writing has a double origin in the two correspondents, it readily construes these relentless conflicts; the necessary condition of letter-writing, physical separation, provides a mirror of the unrealizable union. The correspondence accentuates unmediated opposition, and since it is virtually limited to the two writers, their opposition is sustained rather than diffuse or multiple: "Le propre de l'idée, pour Balzac, est de mettre en présence les contraires, elle procède par dépassement des apories, jouant le jeu contrasté de l'analyse et de la synthèse" [The essence of the idea, for Balzac, is to confront contraries; it proceeds by overtaking aporias, playing out the contrasting game of analysis and synthesis] (Michel, "Balzac ou l'idée" 39). (In a different form, that contrasting game will again be seen in *La recherche de l'Absolu*.) In the mimetic realism of this correspondence, the conflicts and contrasts portrayed or staged for the benefit of Balzac's reader are left entirely up to the writers and readers of the correspondence to express, to resolve, or to reaffirm.

This is the very condition of Balzac himself before his writing: his narratives usually flow from and depend on the oppositional. It is the well-known "secret" of his composition, and the foundation of his philosophy: the only way to obtain wholeness and completeness is to add two conflicting parts together. Unity passes through duplicity. The complete being is made of contrary parts and is naturally, profoundly double, as attested by figures of the androgyne, the transsexual or the ambisexual, and the angel (see *Séraphîta*). The irreconcilable nature of the two writings expresses the nostalgia for the whole and the tragedy of incompletion in Balzac's work. Henri Gauthier has noted the desire for a monological system: "Balzac en effet, découvrant l'unité du multiple et la complémentarité des contraires, tend à transformer la triade structurelle et la dyade vitale dont les manifestations paraissent imposer un dualisme de fait, en un monisme conceptuel" [Balzac, then, discovering the unity of the multiple and the complementarity of contraries, tends to transform the structural triad and the vital dyad whose manifestations seem to impose a de facto dualism into a conceptual monism] (26). Or Pich notes: "On a affaire à une écriture de la gémellité où la répétition et la différence se confondent: l'homogénéité de l'écriture est absolue, à l'inverse de ce qui se passe dans l'écriture théâtrale" [We are dealing with a writing of twinhood in which repetition and difference are conjoined: the homogeneity of the writing is absolute, as opposed to what happens in theatrical writing] (35–36).

The unity Balzac finds lies less in the writing than in the reading; only then is there "copula" and not "disjunction," in the terms Berthier opposed: "indémêlable mixage . . . qui . . . cherche toujours obscurément à surmonter la loi de la coupure pour rêver la suture, à inscrire au cœur de la dualité le filigrane tantalisant de l'unité" [inextricable mixing . . . that . . . always tries mysteriously to overcome the law of separation and imagine the suture, to inscribe the tantalizing filigree of unity in the very heart of duality] ("Frauenlieben" 170). If, as Berthier eloquently states, each term of the diverging pair remains "intrinsèquement habité et fragilisé par l'autre" [intrinsically inhabited and made fragile by the other] (159), it is because of the activity of the reading. The reader who is presumed ignorant, though not the first receiver of the letters, is forced to participate in their interpretation and supplements the absent "explications nécessaires," potentially to combine writing and reading and make the work whole. Through the direct address to its two alternating receivers, the writing portrays the drive to reach the real reader, whose activity is interpretation. Alternately taking the place of Renée and Louise as letter *readers,* reading over their shoulders, as it were, the interpreter each time completes the fullness of the figure, unites the contraries, and operates the complementariness that the two opposed positions of writer and reader configure. Renée and Louise, in their primary semiotic activity, are our mimetic guides into semiosis. To be the reader presumed ignorant is to undertake the semiosis that supports interpretation: let us not be either Louises or Renées, but a successful combination of both in their semiotic roles. That combination occurs only in the outside writer (Balzac) and reader (us). Each woman by writing places herself with Balzac; each when she reads is an ever-contemporary reader. Anne-Marie Baron remarks that "Balzac est présent . . . en Louise et Renée, incarnations féminines du moi-plaisir et du moi-réalité" [Balzac is present . . . in Louise and Renée, female incarnations of the pleasure-self and the reality-self] (*L'auguste mensonge* 70). More philosophically, following Arlette Michel's analysis in "Balzac et la rhétorique," we can think of the letter reading as the "threshold" where contrary realities blend together in an absolute in which all antagonism is resolved (258–59).

The lesson, then, concerns how to interpret writing, with what knowledge and with what strategy, to grasp Balzac's stance. Forcing the reader to stand alternately with his two narrators, Balzac uses the epistolary form to problematize realism. If we read with a simple, straightforward, perhaps naive notion of realism, we simply identify with the letter writers, whose writing serves the direct function of presenting and re-presenting their selves, again and again. If we follow the rhetorical schema laid out in the semiotic figure of Balzac's mimesis, we recognize in this alternating, doubled identification the reader's guide to the essential fact of Balzac's realism, that a creation of the whole is to be won over its conflicting parts by dint of constant writing.

La Maison du Chat-qui-pelote
Ellipsis

In *La Maison du Chat-qui-pelote,* Balzac's realism relies on an elliptical narrative device, centered on a painting; the elliptical story of the painting, an element of the mimesis, becomes a figure for the semiosis of the novella.

Anne-Marie Meininger, introducing the story in the Pléiade edition, describes it as a "drame familial" founded on the reality of the disastrous marriage of Balzac's cherished younger sister Laurence to M. de Montzaigle, a ruined nobleman and faithless husband. Laurence dies in sorrow in 1825 at age twenty-three, tragically misunderstood by her family, neglected even by her loving brother, for he is otherwise occupied with the duchesse d'Abrantès and his social and amorous ambitions (Introduction 1: 32). The social background skillfully recreated in the story is that of the merchant family Guillaume, similar to the milieu of Balzac's parents, grandparents, and cousins. The moral background stems from Balzac's childhood as well. His mother and grandmother laid down draconian rules of work, strictly curtailed his sisters' activities, imposed exaggerated economies, and disallowed poetry and intellectual activity. Such is the upbringing Balzac supplied for the fictional incarnation of his sister, Augustine Guillaume, a draper's daughter. In this story, to which Balzac gave the unique role of opening *La Comédie humaine,* realism borrows much of its reality from the real.

Augustine's marriage to a romantic nobleman, the painter Théodore de Sommervieux, is a misalliance—of upbringing, temperament, social background, birth—that nevertheless thrives on love for three years before coming to a tragic downfall. Augustine's complete lack of ideas, her narrow experience of life, and her miseducation ill suit her to the stimulated life of an artist, and Sommervieux soon tires of his wife and takes several mistresses. Chief among these is the duchesse de Carigliano, a beautiful, enchanting siren, a "célèbre coquette" (1: 76) (apparently modeled on the duchesse d'Abrantès).

Still in love with her husband, Augustine takes the desperate step of visiting the duchesse de Carigliano herself, naively hoping to learn from that skilled practitioner of feminine wiles just how to win back her husband's affections. The duchess had demanded Sommervieux's portrait of Augustine as a proof of his love, and she takes the occasion of Augustine's visit to return the portrait to her lover, a perfectly unmistakable signal that she is through with him. To the innocent Augustine, she pretends that repossessing the painting will give her a hold over her husband; he will tremble to think that his secret love affair will be discovered: "je vais vous donner un moyen de mettre votre mari à la chaîne" [I am going to give you the means to put the chain on your husband] (1: 90). She adds: "Si, armée de ce talisman, vous n'êtes pas maîtresse de votre mari pendant cent ans, vous n'êtes pas une femme, et vous mériterez votre sort!" [If, armed with this talisman, you are not master of your husband for a hundred years, you are not a woman, and you will deserve your fate!] (1: 91).

This story about the painting pretends to endow it with a symbolic power of accusation: Augustine may use it to blackmail her husband. But in fact this story is designed to mislead the naive Augustine, uneducated in the realities of aristocratic social life. Balzac has underscored her simple-mindedness: when she arrives in the duchess's living room, "elle tâcha d'y deviner le caractère de sa rivale par l'aspect des objets épars; mais il y avait là quelque chose d'impénétrable . . . et pour la simple Augustine ce fut lettres closes" [she attempted to guess at her rival's character from the appearance of the scattered objects; but there was something impenetrable about this . . . and for poor Augustine it was a closed book] (1: 85). For the full effect of the irony, for the requisition against the miseducation of young women, for the commemorative portrait of his own sister, Balzac cannot bring the story to a happy ending. There is no such thing as a "talisman" that will overcome the errors of her marriage motivated by love, and the second message the portrait represents also remains *lettres closes*. The second symbolic function of the portrait signifies that the duchess no longer accepts the painter's homage, but it has to be read in the hints that only a better reader than Augustine will grasp.

Of course Sommervieux is that better reader, and when the artist sees Augustine's portrait once again in his home, he instantly recognizes the second message it conveys: "Cela est digne d'elle, s'écria l'artiste d'une voix tonnante. Je me vengerai" ["That is worthy of her," cried the artist in a thunderous voice. "I will get revenge"] (1: 92). As the unknowing bearer of this sentence of "death," Augustine has transmitted a message that the receiver does not wish to hear. At eight o'clock the following morning Mme Guillaume finds Augustine weeping over the portrait torn into fragments, its gilded frame in pieces. Sommervieux has thus killed if not the messenger of death, at least her image. And when Augustine does die, the destruction of the painting, a symbolic anticipation of her death, stands as its only cause, for there is never any other explanation of her death. Immediately after the scene of the fragmented painting comes the description of her tombstone, written in the historical present (see chapter 19). No romantic illness, languor, sorrow, or moral suicide intervenes to explain the message on her grave. In this significant ellipsis, the typically full explication of the Balzacian text stands out for its absence.

Three or four years pass between the destruction of the painting and Augustine's death, leaving the skilled reader to fill in the missing causes. A "friend" standing before her grave sees in it "la dernière scène d'un drame" [the last scene of a tragedy] (1: 93). Like the friend (an image of Balzac himself), the reader must supply these last events, ultimately, perhaps, imagining a direct attack on the living portrait of Augustine. The reader fills the gap between the destruction of the painting and the inscription on the tomb.

There is a very important variant that may serve as a guide. In the manuscript version, there was no dialogue between Augustine and Théodore around the painting; Théodore did not become angry, nor did he destroy the painting and its frame. All of this was added later. Instead, after the scene at the duchess's house the text continued: "Cette scène était la ruine du caractère d'innocence et de candeur d'Augustine" [This scene was the ruin of Augustine's innocent and ingenuous character] (1: 1207, variant). Thus began a final summarizing paragraph that told of Augustine's grave and described her as a flower too gentle to survive the burning embraces of a man of genius—the explanation of her death according to the familiar terms of Balzacian philosophy. The grave stands as a possible solution to "le problème de l'existence d'Augustine postérieure même à cette scène" [the problem of Augustine's existence, subsequent even to this scene], according to this original final paragraph (1: 1208). In writing "cette scène," Balzac clearly had in mind the encounter between Augustine and the duchesse de Carigliano in her boudoir, since these lines immediately followed that scene.

Any "dernière scène d'un drame," then, as Balzac later wrote in the revised version, would come *after* "cette scène." In writing the last paragraphs of the new version, therefore, Balzac could have been thinking of the scene he had just then invented *last,* the one where she discovers Théodore has destroyed the painting, which is effectively last in the writing, if not in the chronology of Augustine's life. At the level of dramatic structure, if not of diegetic chronology, since she did not die until a few years later, this "dernière scène d'un drame," the destruction of the painting, might actually be considered the last scene of Augustine's drama, which would naturally be equivalent to her death. Dramatically speaking, therefore, the last scene around the portrait appears as the actual cause of Augustine's death, an effect of Balzac's rhetorical realism.

In the final version, the few lines of dialogue following the scene of the painter's anger, the short conversation between Augustine and her mother as she discovers the torn painting, supply the *coup de grâce.* Mme Guillaume's continuing lack of compassion turns the knife in the wound, reminding us of the ultimate and initial cause of Augustine's death: the total incomprehension of her family, especially her mother, and the narrow education of which she was a victim. This completes the requisition against the miseducation of girls, and the story returns in its closure to the Balzac family drama.

Thus the original version neglected the symbolic role of the painting; it was neither an indirect message from the duchess to Sommervieux, nor a symbol of the "power" a wife can have over her wayward husband. The return of the painting to Augustine's home was not even mentioned. The narrative moved from the scene in the duchess's boudoir to Augustine's grave, without transition. In changing the ending, Balzac oriented the reading toward the discovery of the ellipsis, which tells us not only that Théodore is thrown out by the duchess in favor of the "petit colonel de cavalerie" [little cavalry colonel] but also, beyond that indirect message of the painting, the story of Augustine's death at Sommervieux's hands.

Parenthetically, a possible explanation for the text's use of this elliptical construction might lie in Balzac's own emotions. Perhaps he himself felt so much pain at the memory of his sister's death that he could not bring himself to recount it even in fictional form. He remains silent, incapable of writing it, possibly because of his own feeling of guilt with respect to his sister. In 1835, six years after the initial writing of *La Maison du Chat-qui-pelote* and ten years after Laurence's death, he will minutely describe the death of Mme de Mortsauf in *Le lys dans la vallée,* perhaps as a compensation for his silence on Augustine's death, as if to produce a belated act of repentance. *Le lys* offers an important correction to the earlier tableau of the life of a woman in love and sadly misunderstood, with an appropriate punishment falling on Félix de Vandenesse, a character whose childhood resembles Balzac's. In the last sentence of *La Maison du Chat-qui-pelote,* the description of Augustine as a flower too fragile to survive the passions of an artist brings to mind the flower symbolism of *Le lys.*

Whatever personal or biographical reasons there may have been, what makes the story important is that it functions very much like the painting. Like the second message of the painting, the one the duchesse de Carigliano sent, disguised with false meanings, Augustine's death occurs indirectly, by symbol. Her death is buried in silence, encoded in other symbols that must be unearthed from the subcodes of the text. The too naive or too hasty reader will not grasp it, or will say that Augustine died of sorrow or the conventional "broken heart." It is clear that one must not be naive like Augustine; one must not be content with the overt story, nor the first communicative function of the painting.

If Augustine had been a better reader, if she had understood, like a clever woman skilled in the relations between the sexes, the second message the painting obviously conveyed, she would certainly have hidden the painting and its message to Théodore, saving him from the shame, the fallen self-respect, the wounded vanity he would inevitably suffer. Théodore would not have become angry, the "dernière scène" would not have taken place—but then how would the story have ended? Not unlike the original version, which flatly misconstrued its own meaning and ended by petering out, with the inconclusive and inexplicable simple extinction of a sad life. The accusation against the painter is, in the final version, much more insinuating. So incomplete is the story without the portrait device, in fact, that I would conjecture that Balzac had planned to include it, and that he simply did not have time to write it until making additions to his original version.

The ultimate message of the novella is centered on Théodore's portrait of Augustine, but another painting mentioned at the beginning of the story, as part of one of those archeological, anthropological, and sociological descriptions that give the Balzacian decor such significance, alerts the reader to the deeper theme signaled by the elliptical construction. There is a strong link, via contrast, between the two paintings. The first two paragraphs, a typical Balzacian opening, detail the zoological and archeological significance of Augustine's family home above her father's fabric store, seen through the amused eyes of the young aristocratic painter, disdainful of the style of the bourgeois merchant class. The house is old and old-fashioned, rooted in bourgeois mentality, whimsical and frail, and opposed in all ways to the house where Augustine will later live after she marries Théodore and especially to the elegant salons and sumptuous boudoirs of the duchesse de Carigliano, spaces characteristic of Balzacian noble dwellings. The story's ultimate title (Balzac changed it from *Gloire et malheur* in the Furne edition), by its very oddity, focuses the reader's attention on the second paragraph (four pages long) which describes the painter observing the shop sign that hangs from the house. The sign depicts a cat engaged in the aristocratic *jeu de paume* or *pelote*, a game forbidden to commoners.[2] The cat holds a racket as large as he is in one of his forepaws, while standing on his hind legs to aim for an enormous ball sent his way by a nobleman in an embroidered costume. By its design, colors, and accessories, the painting is immediately interpreted as intending to mock the merchant and the passersby, and it provokes the painter's hilarity.

As a painting and as a shop sign, it contrasts with the portrait of Augustine (shown at the salon). This ironic juxtaposition of the merchant's sign with Augustine's portrait encapsulates the central purpose of the entire story: the merchant class errs in taking on aristocratic airs just as Augustine was mistaken to marry Sommervieux. Balzac weaves enough symbolism around this sign in the beginning pages, while focusing our attention through the painter himself, that the connection to the story's elliptical closure will become clear. When in addition we read in the opening that such store signs replicate devices that, in the past, rhetorically connected the living with the dead, we are, without knowing it, close to the other painting whose destruction is a metonym for Augustine's death: "ces enseignes ... sont les tableaux *morts* de *vivants* tableaux à l'aide desquels nos espiègles ancêtres avaient réussi à amener les chalands dans leurs maisons" [these street signs ... are the *dead* paintings of the *living* tableaus with which our clever ancestors had succeeded in attracting customers to their shops] (1: 41; emphasis added). Contrast is the chief quality of the archeological beginning, a separation of two worlds, and it is in that abyss of misunderstanding that Augustine will founder. If her death is not actually narrated in the closing pages, one could say it is because the narration itself stumbled into the abyss. The beginning of the story, one finds on second reading, contains a powerful clue to Augustine's end, by preparing the destruction of the painting as symbolic of her death.

In *La Maison du Chat-qui-pelote* the tragic ending can be explained only by the necessary insertion of the second story into the space of the ellipsis. This second story can be compared to what Umberto Eco has called a "ghost

---

2. On this and other games in Balzac's time, see Corry Cropper's *Playing at Monarchy*. Muriel Amar points to the irony of the relation between the sign and the commerce it represents, saying that the *pelotes* were made of torn pieces of fabric (145).

chapter," which the reader tentatively writes, and which the text implicitly validates (214). What is elided in this story is the death narrative and even the preparation for that death in any but symbolic form. Only the painting stands as a major, symbolic clue to her death. The portrait is part of what Barthes called the symbolic code (see *S/Z*). Sommervieux kills Augustine in slow motion by tearing her apart, emotionally and morally, the way he had, in fast motion, torn apart the painting. No detail at all is supplied in the elliptical story, suggesting that the story fails narrative etiquette (which can be compared to narrative convention) because it gives too few clues to the known outcome (see Eco 255). As a supplement to that blank center, or to that blank which stands off-center in one focus of the ellipse, there is only the painting as the figure in the tapestry (with the Chat-qui-pelote shop sign at the second focus of the ellipse). The painting thus stands as a necessary element for the completion of the design.

Ellipsis as a figure gives meaning through emptiness; it makes present what is absent, but only after the fact, when it has been recognized from its borders. In the case of a narrative with ellipsis, the action of making present occurs in the actualization of the story by the reader, just as the conjoining of duality in *Mémoires de deux jeunes mariées* takes place because the reader is the receiver of letters from both writers.

Une fille d'Ève
Interest

Une fille d'Ève offers one of the most explicit and concise expressions of the intimate link between Love and Money—or Money and Love, as I feel one should say in the case of this novel, where love is largely ironic and money only too brutal. The irony about love extends to the author's view of a woman's desire which, as Isabelle Hoog Naginski notes, is briefly exhibited but does not upset the social structure (147).

In the perfection of a uniformly happy and monotonous conjugal life, the countess Marie-Angélique de Vandenesse, wife of Félix, has nothing to wish for: "Vandenesse . . . avait supprimé le Désir" [Vandenesse . . . had eliminated Desire] (2: 294). "L'histoire des bons ménages . . . s'écrit en deux lignes et n'a rien de littéraire" [The story of good marriages . . . can be written in two lines and is in no way literary] (2: 293), for it is a Balzacian truism that there would be no story to tell if there were not a breach in paradise. Money indexes desire and unleashes the narrative, when, in the opening scene, Marie-Angélique asks to borrow 40,000 francs from her sister Marie-Eugénie du Tillet to pay the writer Raoul Nathan's debts. A particular conduct is needed to remedy the lack of money, and narrative interest follows the fortunes of this need. Love, "ces vivantes richesses du cœur" [those living riches of the heart] (2: 286), is also expressed in terms of interest: "Quel bonheur . . . que d'avoir à toute minute *un intérêt énorme* qui multiplie les fibres du cœur" [How fortunate . . . to have *an enormous interest* at every moment, which multiplies the fibers of the heart] (2: 285; emphasis added). Never mind that the interest rate is usurious!

A complicated round dance of *lettres de change* (bills of exchange) figures the circulation of interest and corresponds to the economy of the narrative. Christopher Prendergast spells out such narrative economy, in general terms: "Novels and bills of exchange have metaphorically something in common: they are a form of contractual note, promises to pay the bearer; they assure a system of credit" (102). Each monetary instrument represents a narrative potential, retaining value or detaining the reader's attention, but as long as money keeps passing from hand to hand, no result is certain. When each value returns to its emitter, narrative interest ceases. Similarly, when love can no longer be expressed in terms of interest, the narrative ends with the return to the conjugal paradise: "Mme de Vandenesse eut un mouvement de honte en songeant qu'elle s'était *intéressée* à Raoul" [Mme de Vandenesse, remembering that she had been *interested* in Raoul, felt a pang of shame], we learn on the last page (2: 382; emphasis added).

Interest motivates three intrigues: du Tillet conspires to ruin Nathan, get elected, and obtain the peerage; the two sisters plot to obtain money from Delphine de Nucingen; and Félix intrigues to extricate his Eve from the serpent's charms. The complex interweaving of love, desire, politics, ambition, money, and hatred structures these plots, each anchored in the story by an exchange of equal values, swapping *lettres de change* for cash, cash for love, love for politics, politics for hatred. Du Tillet maneuvers to discredit Nathan by forcing him into prison for his debts. Nathan borrows from du Tillet, then from Gigonnet to pay off du Tillet, not realizing that Gigonnet is du Tillet's straw man. Marie-Angélique obtains 40,000 francs from Delphine in exchange for four 10,000-franc *lettres de change* which have been signed by Schmucke, the sisters' piano teacher; Nathan uses this money to pay off Gigonnet, but now Marie is indebted to Delphine. Her signature on a promise to pay, "dans le portefeuille de la maison Nucingen" [in a portfolio in Nucingen's bank] (2: 371), attaches her honor to du Tillet's maneuvers, creating the potential for a plot in which she becomes his victim. The passage from this intrigue, with its possible catastrophic outcome, to the next and last (which prepares the happy dénouement) occurs as Marie-Eugénie retells the sisters' plot to Félix.

This puts narrative interest now in *his* hands, and while Marie-Eugénie goes off reassured, Félix buys back his wife's signature. He pays Delphine and destroys the *lettres de change,* but obtains from Nathan a "contre-valeur" for Schmucke in the same amount, to get the 40,000 francs back from Nathan. Félix gives this final *lettre de change* to Florine, the actress Nathan lives with, in exchange for the letters Marie had written to Nathan; the writer is now indebted to Florine. Vandenesse has admirably exploited the exchangeability of *lettres de change.*[3] Nathan forfeits his part in their newspaper to du Tillet, who gets elected. The Vandenesse are never reimbursed for *their* 40,000 francs, which is the price of compromising letters and the value of a thank-you note, so to speak, to Florine, who deserves it in untold ways. Just as each loan is converted into another, while power, knowledge, and interest move from person to person, just as three major plots (with subplots) succeed each other, so the narrative structure moves from one potentiality to another, until ultimate knowledge remains with Félix and Marie de Vandenesse and ultimate power with du Tillet, Nucingen, and their associates. The changing fortunes formulate a method for constructing intrigues: how to write a plot.

Of course none of this narrative interest would occur without what one might call the initiating plot, which is Raoul Nathan's, but this intrigue remains in the background and is no more focused than is the word that always applies to it, the polyvalent word *fortune.* However, Balzac exploits its ambiguous meanings to unite these semiotic structures, like a Riffaterrian matrix which linguistically cements love to money and thence to political power. "Tenu de produire par son manque de fortune" [Forced to produce [i.e., to write] by his lack of fortune] (2: 303), Nathan lacks and borrows and loses a financial fortune that signifies his political fortune or ambition, which he has invested in his newspaper: "La Presse avait été le moyen de tant de fortunes faites autour de lui" [The Press had been the means of so many fortunes made all around him] (2: 323). The word resonates with at least two meanings in the following sentences: "Si Nathan avait mis sa fortune dans son journal, il périrait bientôt" [If Nathan had put his fortune into his newspaper, he would soon perish] (2: 350); "Une arrestation tuait ses espérances de fortune politique" [An arrest would kill his chances of a political fortune] (2: 353). Moreover, the worldly love affair with a countess comes to Nathan by an effect of fortune, as the wisecracking Blondet punningly counsels him not to neglect "une bonne fortune aussi capitale" [so capital a good fortune]

---

3. As Nicole Ward Jouve has shown, Marie-Angélique's letters and *lettres de change* symbolically imprison her: "Retrieving the compromising trail of letters left by his wife, Félix is both freeing her from symbolic gaols . . . *and* removing her from circulation. He signals that from now on she will remain in his possession" (43).

(2: 308). The matrix compels us to reflect how "faire fortune" and "fortune politique" cluster with "une bonne fortune," an almost untranslatable expression euphemistically referring to a man's success in seducing a woman (see chapter 18 on the language of sex). Just as the events of the mimetic plot concur in the outcome, so these multiple senses are resolved in the chances that determine results ("un jeu du Hasard qui modifie tout ici-bas" [an act of Chance that modifies everything here below] [2: 373])—the narrative. Balzac shows his hand: follow this precarious fortune, this pile of *billets de banque*, this trail of *lettres de change*, and you will discover how the narrative arrives at its fortunate end, dispelling ignorance all around.

A dictum from the preface to *Le Cabinet des Antiques* lends moral authority to Balzac's realism: "Le vrai souvent ne serait pas vraisemblable, de même que le vrai littéraire ne saurait être le vrai de la nature" [The truth would often not be plausible, just as the truth of literature cannot in any way be the truth of nature] (4: 961). Balzac's constant effort to motivate the "vrai littéraire," directed toward the reader presumed ignorant, in Martin Kanes's term, leads him to marry mimetic and semiotic themes, in an economy of means dependent on a double use of signs.[4] Christopher Prendergast has written that the novel comes into being through a circuit of exchange which "turns on a circular principle of reciprocity at the level of the symbolic, whereby the text acts as the locus in and through which signs and meanings are exchanged; the reader gives credence to the mimetic claims of the text in return for confirmation by the writer of the reader's expectations" (37). Something like this happens when mimesis figures semiosis, provided we distinguish between naive representation ("the mimetic claims") and a "vraisemblable," a plausibility, found in the semiotic structures of realism. At crucial moments in Balzacian mimesis, the writing conforms to the composed realism of *La Comédie humaine*: the society of which Balzac is the historian is not "real" French society but the shadowy double he offers us

---

4. Kanes writes that there is "a spectrum ranging from a reader presumed totally ignorant to a reader presumed totally knowing. In the first case the novel would be impossible, since it would entail the establishment of a whole conceptual world. . . . In the second case the novel would be unnecessary, since the presumed reader already knows everything. In the former instance the product would be endless language; in the latter it would be silence. In practical terms, the pole of ignorance is characterized by language that is sequentially minute, painstaking, and highly explicative. As it moves toward the assumption of a knowing reader, language tends to lose its explicative qualities, to short-circuit logic and sequentiality, until at the theoretical extreme nothing is left" (191).

2: Mimetic Figures of Semiosis

as real. As Butor simply states: "Balzac, pour faire connaître le réel, raconte des histoires qui n'ont pas eu lieu" [Balzac makes us know the real by telling stories that didn't take place] ("Balzac et la réalité" 89). Signs created that realism, through the efficacy of semiotic verisimilitude, and thence the "reality" words imitate.

Semiosis configures the moral purpose of Balzac's mimetic realism. We are made to believe as true something that is demonstrably fictive; this practice is fundamentally deceptive, a necessary fraud and a manipulation. If we do not take offense and instead willingly submit to the "deceit," it is because semiosis is always real. While none but the naive may think of the mimetic story told as real, every reader must accept the reality of the semiosis. And from that reality, Balzac drew the moral truth of his mimesis. Balzac understood that what happened, as it were, *to* his stories—the semiotic structures that brought them to his readers—was a true expression of his moral-esthetic purpose. While he defended himself in several prefaces by proclaiming the ultimate aim of his complete, truthful portrayal of French society, better and more voluminous defense lies in the semiosis of his texts themselves, provided we bring it to the fore. The ever more knowing reader of Balzac comes to know a reality progressively closer to literary truth and farther from the truth of nature. No less is the paradox: reading Balzac implies an increasing "ignorance" of French society; we approach the pole of knowledge by accrediting the writing at the cost of a belief in naive representation.

I have been flirting with the notion of the *explication nécessaire,* the largely unsaid mimetic figure of my own semiosis. Apparently mere mortar to his bricks, Balzac's necessary explanations justify and motivate novelistic realism; as Gérard Genette writes in "Vraisemblance et Motivation," "elles bouchent toutes ses fissures, elles balisent tous ses carrefours" [they fill in all its cracks, they signal all its intersections] (81). These examples may help to suggest, on the contrary, that the mortar is the essential, not the accessory.

3

From Heteronomy to Unity
Les Chouans

Les Chouans is the only novel of the *Scènes de la vie militaire,* and it earns its right to inhabit that classification of the *Études de mœurs* because it depicts the conflict between the forces of the Republic and the Chouans, insurgents loyal to the exiled royal family, in the last year of the eighteenth century. In parallel with the military plot which sees the Republican effort to infiltrate the loosely organized Chouans and capture the marquis de Montauran, their charismatic leader, a love plot develops and challenges the "scène militaire" designation. Elements of the story serve both plots. This inherent generic instability is the primary mimetic characteristic of the novel. Its realism is grounded in history, but the union of this history with the love plot characterizes its rhetorical realism.

A thread of symbolism ties together the shapes of this realism according to a general semiotic pattern that progresses from the *heterogeneous* to the *uniform*. This movement, which may produce harmonious uniformity out of ill-sorted elements, acts like a formula for the production of the novel; there are small and large versions of it, in descriptions, in the love story, in the military plot, in the geography, and in knowledge. It is a motif that is present in a literal manner starting with the first words of the novel, with the opening description of the conscripts; this literal motif, the initiator of the military plot, then leads to a more metaphoric version by the end of the novel, represented by Marie de Verneuil's marriage with the marquis de Montauran. Heteronomy, disparity, and disjunction on the one side, present

3: From Heteronomy to Unity

in many forms, arrive or fail to arrive at a desired uniformity and unity on the other.

As the powerful opening of the novel shows, disparity characterizes everything on the side of the non-Republican elements, where a military uniform would be the desired symbol of a uniformity of sentiment and destiny. The novel plunges immediately into heteronomy; here are the opening words:

> Dans les premiers jours de l'an VIII . . . une centaine de paysans et un assez grand nombre de bourgeois, partis le matin de Fougères pour se rendre à Mayenne, gravissaient la montagne de la Pèlerine. . . . Ce détachement, divisé en groupes plus ou moins nombreux, offrait une collection de costumes si bizarres et une réunion d'individus appartenant à des localités ou à des professions si diverses, qu'il ne sera pas inutile de décrire leurs différences caractéristiques pour donner à cette histoire les couleurs vives auxquelles on met tant de prix aujourd'hui. (8: 905)

> [In the first days of year VIII . . . about a hundred peasants and a rather large number of bourgeois, having left Fougères in the morning to make their way to Mayenne, were climbing the mountain of la Pèlerine. . . . This detachment, divided into smaller and larger groups, offered a collection of costumes so bizarre and an assembly of individuals belonging to localities and professions so diverse, that it would not be unprofitable to describe their characteristic differences to give this story the vivid color that people prize so much today.]

The "characteristic differences" give a certain cachet to the story that begins with these words, which immediately stress the value Balzac places on the heterogeneous, under the concept of vivid color; Arlette Michel speaks of "la bizarrerie insolite de cette foule hétéroclite" [the exceptional bizarreness of this heterogeneous crowd] (*Le réel* 38). A terminology of differences rich in variations already marks these two sentences of the first paragraph: the peasants set apart from the bourgeois; the adjective "divided"; the different numbers within the groups and the approximations of the phrases "about a hundred" and "a rather large number"; the "collection of costumes" and the "assembly of individuals" that are "so bizarre" and "so diverse." In the following four pages, Balzac describes in detail this heterogeneous group of conscripts who will be recruited for the Republican side in Mayenne, "où la discipline militaire devait promptement leur donner un même esprit, une même livrée et l'uniformité d'allure qui leur manquait alors si complètement" [where military discipline was to promptly give them a single sentiment, a single livery, and the uniformity of bearing that was now lacking so completely] (8: 909). The commandant Hulot hopes to fill the ranks of his demi-brigade with these Breton conscripts.

But, in opposition to this desired uniformity, which is salutary to the Directoire government that has taken over the rule of the Republic, disparity reigns—not without a degree of conflict with the realistic aims of the novel. For there always exists in Balzac's work a tendency toward the *type*, a zoological classification, and this tendency enters into conflict with the insistence on the diverse. Thus the descriptions whose purpose is to detail the disparity of the band of conscripts follow in orderly fashion, depicting five categories or classes presented in order from the lowest to the highest, in such a way that to a certain extent the organized progression of these categories works against the disparity that nevertheless is present on several levels.

The first class or group, that of the peasants, goes barefooted and wears long-haired goatskins with which the peasant's own hair is intermingled. These poor men could be mistaken for animals, but they each carry a large stick made of oak from which an almost empty bag is suspended. Their distance from humanity contains, in the manner of a disorganized or badly composed tableau, all the absence of harmony and unity with which one could tax an entity that is missing a uniform—although a military uniform alone would probably not be enough to make them into a harmonious unity. In the second category, another group of peasants, we find those who dress themselves entirely in the coarse cloth from which the first group's pants were fashioned and a large felt hat above the "sale toque" [dirty cap] that those near-animals from the first group wore. Once again rather far from the human categories, "[ils] n'offraient presque rien dans leur costume qui appartînt à la civilisation nouvelle" [they offered almost nothing in their costume that might belong to the new civilization] (8: 906). All the details of their clothing—pants, jacket, clogs, or shoes held in their hands, felt hat with wool chenille—produce a rhetorical effect of accumulation; the heterogeneous operates especially in the details.

With the third class, it is again the clothes but also placement that accentuate the disparity: they are "quelques hommes qui, dispersés çà et là, au milieu de la troupe, y brillaient comme des fleurs" [a few men who, scattered here and there in the middle of the throng, shone like flowers] (8: 906). Their blue pants, their red or yellow waistcoats with copper buttons "tranchaient aussi vivement sur les vêtements blancs et les peaux de leurs compagnons, que des bleuets et des coquelicots dans un champ de blé" [stood out as sharply from the white clothes and the skins of their companions as cornflowers and poppies in a field of wheat] (8: 906)—a painterly effect where the eye is attracted by what is set off from the background. The contrast between the clogs on some of their feet and the solid hobnailed shoes of the majority also introduces variation within the group, and the number and precision of details of clothing, down to the buttons in the shape of hearts or anchors, exaggerate the absence of uniformity with the first two classes. Also, their sacks are "mieux fournis que ne l'étaient ceux de leurs compagnons" [better filled than those of their companions] (8: 907).

With the fourth class, a distinct social promotion is introduced: "Quelques citadins apparaissaient au milieu de ces hommes à demi sauvages, comme pour marquer le dernier terme de la civilisation de ces contrées" [A few town-dwellers appeared in the middle of these half-savage men, as if to mark the last footing of civilization in these parts] (8: 907). Here Balzac introduces some subcategories: "ils présentaient comme les paysans des différences remarquables dans leurs costumes. Une dizaine d'entre eux portaient cette veste républicaine connue sous le nom de carmagnole. D'autres, de riches artisans sans doute, étaient vêtus de la tête aux pieds en drap de la même couleur" [they presented, as did the peasants, noticeable differences in their costumes. Around ten of them wore that Republican jacket known as the *carmagnole*. Others, rich artisans without a doubt, were dressed from head to foot in a cloth of one color], and the ones with the most recherché apparel distinguish themselves with frock-coats and "portaient des bottes de diverses formes" [wore boots of diverse shapes] (8: 907). Among these "véritables personnages" [notable figures] can be found a few "têtes soigneusement poudrées" [carefully powdered heads] and well-braided pigtails, the indicators of good fortune or education. If all of this seems "ramassés comme au hasard" [gathered as if randomly together]—and the march of this heterogeneous mob along a single road gives the best image of such an assemblage of random elements—it is for political reasons, and there also Balzac stresses the heterogeneous: "Un observateur initié au secret des discordes civiles qui agitaient alors la France aurait pu facilement reconnaître le petit nombre de citoyens sur la fidélité desquels la République devait compter dans cette troupe, presque entièrement composée de gens qui, quatre ans auparavant, avaient guerroyé contre elle" [An observer initiated into the secrets of the civil discord that was afflicting France at the time could have easily recognized the small number of citizens in this band on whose fidelity the Republic could count, almost entirely composed of people who, four years earlier, had warred against it] (8: 907). In the phrasing of "almost entirely composed" can be found an ironic unity that is not the unity to which the absent military discipline would promptly have led them: "Les républicains seuls marchaient avec une sorte de gaieté. Quant aux autres individus de la troupe, s'ils offraient des différences sensibles dans leurs costumes, ils montraient sur leurs figures et dans leurs attitudes cette expression uniforme que donne le malheur" [Only the Republicans walked with a sort of gaiety. As to the other individuals of the troop, if they offered palpable differences in their costumes, they showed on their faces and in their posture the uniform expression that misfortune gives] (8: 907–8). Such ironic uniformity is not the desired one. The bourgeois and the peasants seem "courbés sous le joug d'une même pensée" [bent under the yoke of the same thought] (8: 908), and we have an idea of what that rebellious thought might be—one that cannot constitute a real unity for France, on the contrary.

So much for the first four categories. The difference between the fifth group and the four others is clearly marked at the outset by the only paragraph indentation of these four pages, forming a separate paragraph for the fifth category alone. "La marche de cette colonne sur Mayenne, les éléments hétérogènes qui la composaient et les divers sentiments qu'elle exprimait s'expliquaient assez naturellement par la présence d'une autre troupe formant la tête du détachement" [The march of this column toward Mayenne, the heterogeneous elements from which it was composed, and the diverse feelings that it expressed were explained naturally enough by the presence of another group forming the head of the detachment] (8: 908). These regulars from a demi-brigade of infantry are called the "Bleus," like all the soldiers of the Republic: "Ce surnom était dû à ces premiers uniformes bleus et rouges dont le souvenir est encore assez frais pour rendre leur description superflue" [This nickname was due to those first blue and red uniforms, the memory of which is fresh enough to render their description superfluous] (8: 908). Differentiated from the four other types of men by their function as escort to the conscripts, but assembled with them in the same detachment, and differentiated also by their uniformity denoted by precisely this uniform, this fifth category has the effect of emphasizing the heterogeneous nature of the four others and of stressing the conflict inherent in this random gathering.

This remarkable depiction inaugurates the novel as if with an explosion, which must be compressed into the narrow part of a funnel, forcing out a single form. As Arlette Michel has written,

> La description de la colonne des conscrits bretons qui ouvre le roman n'est pas un encadrement pour un drame à venir, elle en est déjà la manifestation, elle le porte comme en abîme. . . . Alors la masse opaque de ses "détails" révèle son étrangeté et, par décantations successives, laisse déposer dans

l'imagination du lecteur le principe d'unité qui en assure à la fois le sens et la beauté originale. La description . . . est exemplaire de la méthode que Balzac est en train de découvrir. (*Le réel* 38)

[The description of the column of Breton conscripts that opens the novel is not a frame-setting device for a drama to come; it is already a manifestation of the drama, it carries it *en abyme*. . . . Thus the opaque mass of its "details" reveals its strangeness and, by successive decantings, deposits in the reader's imagination the principle of unity that provides both its meaning and its original beauty. The description . . . is exemplary of the method Balzac is in the process of discovering.]

How can these men, representing opposite interests, be made to act as a single unit? Not only is that the problem Balzac poses for his novel, but on a larger scale, this is exactly France's problem.

The same can be said of the reiterated spectacle that is presented at the castle of la Vivetière. After the Chouans massacre the Bleus, these soldiers of a new species amuse themselves by throwing their victims' bodies into the pond. "Ce spectacle, joint aux différents tableaux que présentaient les bizarres costumes et les sauvages expressions de ces gars insouciants et barbares, était si extraordinaire et si nouveau" [This spectacle, joined with the different tableaus presented by the bizarre costumes and the savage expression of these heedless and barbarous lads, was so extraordinary and so new] (8: 1060) in comparison to the troops of the Vendée that "avaient offert quelque chose de noble et de régulier" [had offered something noble and regular] (8: 1060) that one wonders how such undisciplined soldiers could act as one in a unified action. And in fact they will not be able to. In the last quarter of the book, here is how the five to six thousand Chouans who are at Saint-James appear, during a strange war scene:

> Leurs costumes, assez semblables à ceux des réquisitionnaires de la Pèlerine, excluaient toute idée de guerre. Cette tumultueuse réunion d'hommes ressemblait à celle d'une grande foire. Il fallait même quelque attention pour découvrir que ces Bretons étaient armés, car leurs peaux de bique si diversement façonnées cachaient presque leurs fusils. . . . Il n'y avait aucune apparence d'ordre et de discipline. (8: 1122–23)

[Their clothes, rather similar to those of the requisitioned men from la Pèlerine, excluded all thought of war. This tumultuous assemblage of men resembled that of a large fair. Some attention was needed even to discover that these Bretons were armed, for their goatskins, so diversely shaped, almost hid their guns. . . . There was no appearance of order and discipline.]

Each time the Chouans' clothing is discussed, and even that of the counter-Chouans who are actually the Bleus disguised as Chouans, it is the absence of uniformity in their uniform that is stressed.

As with clothing, buildings can be burdened by the disorder of the heterogeneous. The castle of la Vivetière is nothing but a ruin, quite like the gothic buildings one finds in Edgar Allan Poe, as in "The Fall of the House of Usher." The main house is surrounded by two ponds whose abrupt banks mark the limits of the courtyard:

Ces berges sauvages, baignées par des eaux couvertes de grandes taches vertes, avaient pour tout ornement des arbres aquatiques dépouillés de feuilles, dont les troncs rabougris, les têtes énormes et chenues, élevées au-dessus des roseaux et des broussailles, ressemblaient à des marmousets grotesques. . . . La cour entourée d'herbes hautes et flétries, d'ajoncs, d'arbustes nains ou parasites, excluait toute idée d'ordre et de splendeur. (8: 1026)

[These wild banks, bathed by waters covered with large green spots, had as sole ornament some aquatic trees divested of leaves, whose stunted trunks, whose enormous and hoary tops, elevated above the rushes and underbrush, resembled grotesque urchins. . . . The courtyard, encircled by high, withered grasses, by gorse bushes, by dwarf or parasitic shrubs, excluded all thought of order and splendor.]

The house is in such disorder that it resembles something other than what it is; made of stone, it is nonetheless animal and vegetable: its roof is broken open under the weight of the vegetation that grows there; the cracked walls seem to be made of ivy; the granite and schistose stones create a dark and empty carcass: "Ses pierres disjointes, ses croisées sans vitres, sa tour à créneaux, ses toits à jour lui donnaient tout à fait l'air d'un squelette; et les oiseaux de proie qui s'envolèrent en criant ajoutaient un trait de plus à cette vague ressemblance" [Its disjointed stones, its casement windows lacking panes, the tower with its embattlements, its gaping roof gave it absolutely the appearance of a skeleton; and the birds of prey that flew off with a cry added another feature to this vague ressemblance] (8: 1027). In addition to its disorder in space, the chateau incarnates a temporal disorder: "Enfin, la forme des portes, la grossièreté des ornements, le peu d'ensemble des constructions, tout annonçait un de ces manoirs féodaux . . . des temps nébuleux qui précèdent l'établissement de la Monarchie" [Finally, the shape of the doors, the coarseness of the ornamentation, the lack of ensemble in the construction, everything announced one of those feudal manors . . . from the nebulous times that precede the establishment of the monarchy] (8: 1027). Symbolically, the castle represents this ill-defined, disorderly time from before the monarchy. Yet for Mlle de Verneuil, the word castle "réveillait toujours les formes d'un type convenu" [always awakened the forms of a conventional type]. In front of la Vivetière, she instead finds herself thrown back into that indecision that existed before historic time, when the heterogeneous elements of society were not yet united under one central authority.

This symbolism is continued within: the interior rooms are "en harmonie avec le spectacle de destruction qu'offraient les dehors du château. Les boiseries de noyer poli, mais de formes rudes et grossières, saillantes, mal travaillées, étaient disjointes et semblaient près de tomber. . . . quelques meubles séculaires et en ruine s'harmoniaient avec cet ensemble de débris" [in harmony with the spectacle of destruction that the outside of the castle offered. The walnut woodwork, polished but made into shapes that were primitive and coarse, jutting out and badly formed, was disjointed and seemed about to fall. . . . a few centuries-old, decayed pieces of furniture were in keeping with this ensemble of debris] (8: 1031). Lucienne Frappier-Mazur, in her edition of the novel, finds that by employing the word "tableau" for the scene that Mlle de Verneuil is contemplating, Balzac shows the need to "redonner au tableau son unité en dégageant, grâce au regard d'un personnage, une impression d'ensemble, qui résume ce que suggérait chaque détail" [return unity to the tableau by delineating, by means of a character's gaze, an impression of ensemble that sums up what each detail was suggesting] (8: 1748). Although I am generally in agreement that Balzacian descriptions can function as a unifying stratagem, I think that here the tableau remains one of disparity in spite of being told through a single character's gaze. Whatever unity there may be in the description, such as the use of the word "harmony," is ironic, and it is not enough for Balzac to use the word "tableau" for the disharmony to dissolve into unity.

For what is happening at la Vivetière? The two enemy camps are there together: the marquis de Montauran and Mme de Gua on one side, backed up by some eighty-seven Chouans, and Marie de Verneuil with her escort of sixty-five Bleus on the other. On behalf of these Republican soldiers, Marie de Verneuil solicits and obtains a solemn promise that they will be safe in the castle; but the Chouans will massacre them nonetheless. What is more, Marie and the marquis are simultaneously lovers and enemies, thrown together by chance or by passion in this dead-end shelter far from the road. Their union at la Vivetière is brought about by war and by passionate love, but the harmony is temporary and factitious—so precarious that it is soon destroyed, because it is not yet solidly established on a true acquaintance based on their real identities. Too often, Marie is still "l'inconnue" [the stranger] for Montauran. Anne-Marie Baron observes that Balzac uses a device of crystallization, the process of love analyzed by Stendhal, along with "les erreurs qu'elle provoque sur le compte de l'être aimé et du monde extérieur. Dans la malle qui les emporte vers Fougères, Montauran transfigure Marie de Verneuil en imagination" [the errors it provokes as concerns the loved one and the external world. In the carriage that takes them to Fougères, Montauran transfigures Marie de Verneuil in his imagination] (*L'auguste mensonge* 99). And as their relationship continues, through successive encounters often clouded with fog, the possibility of union is threatened by these differences, emphasized by the heterogeneous nature of the opposing troops. When the Bleus take off their uniforms to don the various costumes of the Chouans, disguising themselves as counter-Chouans, Marie and Montauran find themselves in the cottage of Galope-Chopine: "Une même espérance unissait leur pensée, un même doute les séparait, c'était une angoisse, c'était une volupté" [The same hope united their thoughts, the same doubt separated them, it was a single distress, it was a single pleasure] (8: 1165).

Geography plays a very large role in the military plot of *Les Chouans* and eventually affects the love plot. The spectacle of Fougères seen from the mountain of la Pèlerine is a scene of diverse features brought together only in the gaze that embraces the entire site (8: 912–14). Those many different features of Fougères are described in detail in the opening of the third chapter (8: 1069), one of the longest, most elaborate, and most important descriptions of an outdoor location in *La Comédie humaine*. The description contributes to the sense of the heterogeneous, which is also the sensation of the actors in the drama that takes place along the Promenade in Fougères or the gorge of the Nançon and the valley of the Couesnon. After three and a half pages of the most intensely diverse written geography, describing mountains, gorges, rivers and branches of rivers, valleys, craggy rocks, plateaus, churches, ramparts, castles, tortuous paths, bridges, towers, prairies, cottages, and houses, the reader can only hope to have formed a vision of a multifarious, acci-

3: From Heteronomy to Unity

dented site of many levels, directions, and terrains. Balzac summarizes by emphasizing the contrasts and randomness:

> Tels sont les traits les plus saillants de cette nature dont le principal caractère est une âpreté sauvage, adoucie par de riants motifs, par un heureux mélange des travaux les plus magnifiques de l'homme avec les caprices d'un sol tourmenté par des oppositions inattendues, par je ne sais quoi d'imprévu qui surprend, étonne et confond. (8: 1072)

> [Such are the most salient features of this natural setting whose principal character is a savage harshness, tempered by gay scenes, by a happy mixture of the most magnificent works of man with the caprices of a terrain tormented by unexpected oppositions, by heavens knows what unforeseen quality, which surprises, astonishes, and confounds.]

As for the Breton countryside, its geography forbids uniformity and unity. The Bretons live in isolated dwellings lacking the unification of a village: "Chaque famille y vit comme dans un désert" [Each family lives there as if in a desert] (8: 919); each flowered hedge hides invisible aggressors (8: 920). One of the reasons the Chouans hold off their pursuers for so long around Fougères is that their fields are cut up into separate pieces like the squares of a chessboard, outlined by impenetrable hedges planted with tall trees; tortuous paths border each field, but to go from one to the other, a complicated gate fixed partly into the hedge has to be maneuvered; and only the Chouans know where the openings are. "Ces haies et ces échaliers donnent au sol la physionomie d'un immense échiquier dont chaque champ forme une case parfaitement isolée des autres, close comme une forteresse, protégée comme elle par des remparts. La porte, facile à défendre, offre à des assaillants la plus périlleuse de toutes les conquêtes" [These hedges and these gates give the land the physiognomy of an immense chessboard in which each field forms a square perfectly isolated from the others, enclosed like a fortress and protected like one by ramparts. The gate, easy to defend, offers attackers the most perilous of all conquests] (8: 1114). The symbolism of this disjoined landscape echoes that of the novel's opening scene.

The heterogeneous also characterizes knowledge, particularly in the form of identity. By the end of the opening scene, when the Chouans have dispersed after attacking the band of conscripts and the Republican troops, the commandant Hulot is wondering about the identity of their leader, called "le Gars," and conjectures that a royalist with a white hat and black tie briefly glimpsed is he (8: 939, 940). But before Balzac allows his characters to be sure of this identity, he parades the reader through several different identifications of the man, each time with a different name or designation. As for Marie de Verneuil, who is she really, and when is she playing a part? She is called "cette mystérieuse personne" (8: 990), and Montauran wonders whether she is the queen or the slave of her Republican escort at Mortagne (8: 985). Similarly, who is Mme du Gua, really? Can she really be the marquis's mother, or his mistress? In short order we read "la dame inconnue" and "C'est sa mère" and then "Est-ce bien sa mère?" [the unknown woman; it's his mother; is it really his mother?] (8: 1019). The Chouans call her "la Grande Garce" (8: 1082) and "la Jument de Charrette" (8: 1085). Nearly every character, when first introduced, is called "l'inconnu" or "l'inconnue," like Marche-à-terre (8: 916). Both the marquis and Mlle de Verneuil are called "inconnu" repeatedly, as is Mme du Gua; the text insists on pretending not to know who they are until their union in marriage establishes the truth of their character once and for all. Montauran has been known by two other names, le Gars and du Gua, pronounced the same except for the article; before arriving at la Vivetière, he has sworn that his real identity is vicomte de Bauvan (8: 1009) (not to be confused with the real comte de Bauvan). The hearts of Mlle de Verneuil and Montauran have spoken, and Marie is called his mistress and he her lover, but Mlle de Verneuil is still guessing that he is the dangerous chieftain of the Chouans (8: 1023–24). But knowledge given can be taken away: "l'inconnu" applies to Montauran after he has already been identified, such sleight of hand being fostered by Balzac's manipulation of point of view. If Montauran is known to some, he is unknown to others; our knowledge depends on the perspective we are given, and the reader will be plunged again into ignorance when it serves the rhetorical realism of the plot, but at the cost of some verisimilitude. Even in a very late scene, at the ball in Saint-James, Marie de Verneuil, long since identified and her history given, becomes once again "l'inconnue," as if her ball gown were a disguise. The heterogeneous is expressed here in terms of the stark opposition between "fille" and "femme vertueuse" [courtesan and virtuous woman] (8: 1146), a disparity in her identity that will be settled only after her marriage. In such conditions, uniformity will consist in reaching a state of knowledge, symbolized by the lifting of the fog on the eleventh and last day of the love plot (8: 1208).

3: From Heteronomy to Unity

This structure that represents unstable unity constantly threatened by the heterogeneous is prevalent in the present time frame of the novel, but there is also a version for the future whose stakes are higher: to reunify France, by uniting France's noble past to a future just as noble. Within the strange personal history and destiny of Marie de Verneuil herself, there is a reunion of disparities: from illegitimate daughter to marquise, she unites the two contrary poles of the novel, history and sentiment, military politics and love. "Êtes-vous fille ou femme, ange ou démon?" [Are you courtesan or lady, angel or demon?], wonders Montauran (8: 1005). Her assignment, to seduce Montauran, contains the heterogeneous elements: handled like a marionette by Corentin, she uses love to effect a change in politics. Corentin's methods make him feel like God:

> Employer habilement les passions des hommes ou des femmes comme des ressorts que l'on fait mouvoir au profit de l'État, mettre les rouages à leur place dans cette grande machine que nous appelons un gouvernement, et se plaire à y renfermer les plus indomptables sentiments comme des détentes que l'on s'amuse à surveiller, n'est-ce pas créer, et, comme Dieu, se placer au centre de l'univers? (8: 1148)

> [To cleverly use the passions of men or women like springs that one activates for the profit of the State, to put the wheels into place in this great machine we call government, and to take pleasure in locking into it the most unconquerable feelings like triggers that one toys with and subjects to surveillance, is that not to create and, like God, to place oneself at the center of the universe?]

The machine creates uniformity—a universe with a center.

At the end of the novel, the priest, performing the marriage ceremony of Marie and Montauran in Marie's house, carries out the symbolic marriage of the two enemy factions and embodies the future union of Republican ideas with an enlightened monarchy (8: 1205). The marriage, a calm at the center of the tempest that makes the union a success on a personal level and in the love plot, forecasts the union of opposing parties in the future. If the priest must work in secret for now, as Balzac specifies, he assures us that such marriages will be recognized in the future: "L'union du marquis et de Mlle de Verneuil allait être consacrée, comme tant d'autres unions, par un acte contraire à la législation nouvelle; mais plus tard, ces mariages, bénis pour la plupart au pied des chênes, furent tous scrupuleusement reconnus" [The union of the marquis and Mlle de Verneuil would be consacrated, like so many other unions, by an act running counter to the new legislation; but later, these marriages, mostly blessed at the foot of oak trees, were all scrupulously recognized] (8: 1205). In this marriage, a conflation of home and church, royalist and Republican, religion and politics anticipates the future unity of France.

To better prepare for such happiness, Marie obtains an effect of unity by arranging the furniture in her room before Montauran's arrival. Balzac's penchant for interior decoration is well known; here he worked to make all the details of this scene stress the importance of unity. Marie de Verneuil has rented a house in Fougères abandoned by an émigré noble, a "maison nationale." In contrast to the harmonious unity she achieved for her love, she had settled into the house after escaping from la Vivetière with only the thought of revenge on her mind, and she takes possession of every last piece of décor as if it belonged to her, with a sudden appropriation of the furniture as if it were familiar to her. "Il semblait qu'un rêve l'eût familiarisée par avance avec cette demeure où elle vécut de sa haine" [It seemed as if a dream had prepared her in advance to know this dwelling, where she lived off her hatred] (8: 1065). But when vengeance has at last settled permanently into love, Mlle de Verneuil carefully makes harmony in her décor. First she has everything that is superfluous removed: "ôte ces babioles qui encombrent la cheminée, et n'y laisse que la pendule et les deux vases de Saxe. . . . Sors toutes les chaises, je ne veux voir ici que le canapé et un fauteuil" [take away these knick-knacks that are cluttering the mantel, and leave only the clock and the two Dresden vases. . . . Take out all these chairs, I only want the sofa and an armchair here] (8: 1181). Then, studying the tapestries on the walls, "elle sut trouver, parmi les brillantes nuances de la haute lisse, les teintes qui pouvaient servir à lier cette antique décoration aux meubles et aux accessoires de ce boudoir par l'harmonie des couleurs ou par le charme des oppositions. La même pensée dirigea l'arrangement des fleurs" [she was able to find, among the brilliant nuances of the yarns in the tapestry, the hues that could serve to tie together this antique decoration and the furniture and accessories of this boudoir through the harmony of the colors or the charm of contrast. The same thoughts directed the arrangement of the flowers] (8: 1182). Everything will be harmonious, balanced, linked, and symmetrical, organized according to a unified idea.

Connecting such unity contrasted with heteronomy to the larger frame of France's history, Balzac recalls for us the unusual word "nébuleux," the adjective he had used to characterize the disunity of France in times before the monarchy: "une espèce d'histoire monumentale des temps nébuleux qui précèdent l'établissement de la Monarchie" [a kind of monumental history from the nebulous times that precede the establishment of the monarchy] (8: 1027). In that earlier use of the symbolism of the nebulous, the context was also a house: the manor of la Vivetière. As Mlle de Verneuil prepares her randomly decorated rental house for her marriage, she says: "Ce jour est le dernier de mes jours nébuleux, il est gros de ma mort ou de notre bonheur" [Today is the last of my nebulous days; it is heavy with my death or our happiness] (8: 1181)—and she comments on the hateful fog. The lifting of the fog allows her at last to know the uniformity of her thought and Montauran's.

One could say that this thought of unity is the feminine equivalent of the desire the marquis will articulate as he is dying, when he tells his enemy, the commandant Hulot: "je compte sur votre probité pour annoncer ma mort à mon jeune frère qui se trouve à Londres, écrivez-lui que s'il veut obéir à mes dernières paroles, il ne portera pas les armes contre la France, sans néanmoins abandonner le service du Roi" [I am counting on your integrity to report my death to my young brother, who is in London. Write him that if he will obey my last wishes, he will not take up arms against France, without for all that abandoning the service of the King] (8: 1210). Solemn and ultimate words of the head of the Chouans and a clotural expression of the ideal of unity, this promise for the future lends grandiose dimensions to this motif of union extracted from separation: to reunite France. The union of contraries in the marriage envisions the future reunification of the French.

At the level of the novel, disparity is found in the elements that compound it: venerable history as well as the daily life of society, Brittany as well as Normandy, politics and private life, literature (Walter Scott, Chateaubriand, Cooper) and geography. There is fluidity in the use of narrative point of view, with freely flowing changes of perspective provoked by mere proximity, giving another image of the disparate in the rhetoric of this realism. Without transition, and without authorial commentary, the point of view can change from the Chouans to the Bleus, from Marie to the marquis, from victim to aggressor, and so on.

From this diversity, Balzac forges a uniform and homogenous composition. Uniformity wrenched from the heterogeneous: that is the essential trait of composition in Balzac and a lesson for the reader about how to read a Balzac novel. Lucien Dällenbach's classic two-part vision of what he eventually calls the "chaosmos" of *La Comédie humaine* remains powerfully expressive of the two conflicting tendencies in the work as a whole. What *Les Chouans* shows us, I think, is "un Système de fragments conçu, en définitive, comme totalité organique. Inessentiel et provisoire, le chaos est de toujours voué à se muer en cosmos. Pas de débris non totalisables chez Balzac; pas de pièces irrémédiablement détachées et disjointes" [a System of fragments definitively designed as an organic totality. Inessential and temporary, chaos is from the start destined to mutate into cosmos. No debris that cannot be totalized in Balzac; no pieces irremediably detached and disjointed] ("Du fragment au cosmos" 428).

Several similar comments are found in the copious notes to *Les Chouans* in the Pléiade edition by Lucienne Frappier-Mazur, who observes that "Le regard donne son unité à cette succession de notations fragmentaires" [The gaze gives its unity to this succession of fragmentary notations] (8: 1766). Dällenbach tells us how the success is only partial by showing that Balzac,

> d'avoir résolument opté à la fois pour l'Inconnu, le Tout et le désordre, et d'avoir su tirer de ce choix les conséquences structurelles qu'il fallait pour que son Grand Œuvre ... devînt *mosaïque*—mosaïque inachevée et en un certain sens, interminable—plutôt que *pyramide,* [a pu] manifester avec le plus d'éclat possible l'apanage du roman: rendre visible ce que nous ne verrions pas sans lui. (*La canne de Balzac* 69)

> [from having resolutely opted at the same time for the Unknown, the Whole, and disorder, and from having extracted from these choices the structural results that were needed for his Grand Work ... to become a *mosaic*—an unfinished mosaic and in a certain sense an interminable one—rather than a *pyramid,* [was able] to reveal with the greatest possible brilliance the prerogative of the novel: to make visible what we would not see without it.]

Through the conflicts and tension that set Marie and the marquis against each other, then allow their marriage; in the marriage of a novel of romance with a historical or political novel; in the outcome in a unified future for France beyond the final words, Balzac composes the only form capable of achieving unity in the story.

According to this idea of unity, the future union will be realized in the evolution toward realism in Balzac's writing. The union of history takes place in fiction, and Balzac strives to realize this union by writing, always writing, obsessively.

4

Tenebrous Affairs
and Necessary Explications

> Ce style ne suggère pas, ne reflète pas: il explique.
> [His style does not suggest, does not reflect—it explains.]
>
> —Marcel Proust

One of the strongest claims to realism lies in the desire or need to explain; at the same time, the novelist puts his creative power at risk. Commenting about the secret the novelist purports to convey, Chantal Massol writes: "En s'affirmant détenteur de secrets, le romancier s'arroge un pouvoir-dire. En les divulguant, il s'expose à être décevant—à affaiblir lui-même le pouvoir dont il se targue" [Asserting that he is the keeper of secrets, the novelist claims to have the power-to-tell. In revealing secrets, he runs the risk of being disappointing—of weakening the very power that he boasts of] (119). Balzac, the great explicator, proves his mettle in the novel that some readers have described as the first mystery novel in French,[1] *Une ténébreuse affaire,* a political novel written with passion and penetration. In this "affair" so dark as to earn the description "tenebrous," something visible and apparent obscures from view something that an explanation will uncover: the real story. The attractive underside, the "envers," gave Balzac the power to expose, to reveal. But the relation of fact to fiction is complex, and the layers of meaning reveal how the novel creates realism.

---

1. René Guise quite rightly opposes this designation in his introduction in the Folio edition (9); not a "roman policier," it is "le roman de la police" (11).

In *Une ténébreuse affaire,* Balzac postures as the one who knows the answer to the question his novel poses—what really happened and why?—for if ever an *explication* was *nécessaire,* it is in this "impure fiction" (one that has strong referentiality to history or philosophical reflection, according to Genette [*Seuils* 305]). The real event of the kidnapping of the senator Dominique Clément de Ris in 1800 underlies Balzac's story, a murky business of multiple royalist and republican conspiracies set in three moments of the Consulate and early Empire. History thus apparently comes first, but Balzac claims to prove what really happened by retelling the story in a fiction; facts will be learned via fictions. André Wurmser appreciates this subtle relation to history: "Parce qu'il dit l'essentiel: la bassesse de la police, les rivalités des ambitieux, la vacillation des destins individuels, tout grand homme pouvant à tout moment disparaître dans une trappe—et la continuité de l'histoire, que les grands hommes sont impuissants à dévier de son chemin" [Because he says what is essential: the despicable acts of the police, the rivalries of ambitious men, the vacillations of individual destinies, when any great man may disappear through a trap door—and the continuity of history, which great men are impotent to deviate from its path] (*La comédie inhumaine* 283). In its relation to history, the novel engages in *hysteron proteron,* which is not only a figure of speech in which natural or rational order is reversed, but also a figure in logic: the fallacy of assuming as a premise a proposition following something yet to be proved (for hysteron proteron, see Lukacher 262). This apparently simple yet devious rhetorical device is the brilliant invention of this novel.

To begin with, the title contains a striking reversal that strategically controls meaning and direction from the outset. Prosaic word order would call for "Une affaire ténébreuse," two anapests with the stressed syllables at regular intervals. Instead, the adjective placed abnormally before the noun forces equal accentuation on the three syllables of "ténébreuse." Thus foregrounded, "ténébreuse" alerts the reader to a potential for mystification and intrigue, which naturally provokes the desire to find out the truth. Richly signifying, the adjective "ténébreux" means dark, sinister, gloomy, dismal; secret, hidden, covered, obscure, mysterious, impenetrable, difficult to elucidate (the Petit Robert dictionary cites Balzac's title for the sense "obscur pour l'esprit," and the expression "ténébreuse affaire" has come to mean, since Balzac, a conspiracy). "Ténébreux" also means perfidious, unavowable, dishonest ("qui fait le mal en se cachant; qui se cache, se trame dans l'ombre" [which hides the evil it does; which hides, plots in the shadows], according to the Robert); and melancholic. In the novel, "ténébreuse" occasionally alludes to the atmosphere both meteorological and moral. The obscure and impenetrable, in sum, readily become perfidious. Such is the "tenebrosity" of the political story told by the fiction that the reader, confused and distressed, also craves explication.

For the question the novel poses on behalf of the reader—what really happened and why?—authorizes us to also ask about the novel: "what *really really* happened?" In other words, it is pertinent to comment on Balzac's narrative strategies. *Une ténébreuse affaire* has the advantage of including in its mimetic narrative a semiotic model for each of the terms or limits between which the novel lies: tenebrosity and explication. The "cachot" [dark prison cell] in the impenetrable center of the forest of Nodesme figures its tenebrous affairs, while the interpretive reading of the "procès politique" [political trial] gives consistency to the idea of necessary explications. I suggest that the novel also illustrates the precarious posture of all Balzacian narratives between tenebrous affairs and necessary explications. The outer limits of any narration are the secrecy of its affairs and the necessity of unfolding them. In *Pierrette* we will also see a criminal trial that purports to bring truth to light in the face of the forces of obscurity (see chapter 8).

Balzac believed he alone could tell the real story of the kidnapping of Clément de Ris because he had inside information from his father and from Mme de Berny, whose knowledge of the facts came from her lover André Campi, involved in the case. Balzac presumes to correct mistakes in other accounts, such as the *Mémoires* of the duchesse d'Abrantès, which had already added a layer of mediation between story and event. (The duchess retells the history because she also thinks she can "correct" it.) In a long preface later suppressed, Balzac claimed that his novel answers a question that remains unanswered to this day about the historical event of the kidnapping: who did it? On the stage of real history, the novel purports to play the historian's role; as Marthe Robert writes, "ce ne sont pas les hommes politiques, *mais les personnages de Balzac* qui ont fait l'Histoire du pays" [it is not the politicians, but *Balzac's characters* that made the country's History] (258). An additional layer of "correction" is added by the editors of the novel in the Pléiade edition, Suzanne-J. Bérard and Pierre-Georges Castex, who cite archives that disagree with contemporary written accounts.

What Balzac "knows" and tells us is that his character Malin de Gondreville (or the real senator Clément de Ris) acted in concert with a secret party born of the Revolution, opposed to Bonaparte and conspiring to create a new government. In Balzac's account, Talleyrand, Fouché, Sieyès, and Carnot, joined by Malin as factotum, plot against the Premier Consul on the eve of the battle of Marengo, on June 13, 1800. If Napoleon is defeated, the conspirators intend to exploit popular disappointment to take power; if victorious, they will rally round the Consulate. Fouché has forced Malin to print and stockpile the documents needed for the "gouvernement inédit" (8: 1501) in sufficient quantities for distribution. When news of Napoleon's decisive victory reaches Paris, Malin hastens to conceal the compromising papers in his château at Gondreville, a "bien national" [national property] filched from the Simeuse family, and returns to Paris in time to congratulate the Premier Consul. Six years later, the distrustful Fouché, to bury the conspiracy more surely, secretly sends his police, led by Corentin, to Gondreville, to seek and destroy any evidence. To cover their actions, five policemen disguised as the four noble Simeuse and d'Hauteserre brothers and their faithful follower Michu kidnap and sequester the senator. Fouché pretends to investigate the kidnapping and has the four aristocrats and Michu arrested; they are tried and convicted. Thus is consummated an official crime, in which the guilty punish the innocent. Not unlike a La Fontaine fable, the moral of the story is something like might makes right: "La raison du plus fort est toujours la meilleure."[2] As Bérard writes, "Balzac croyait savoir que, dans la véritable affaire, des agents mandatés par Fouché et le secrétaire de préfecture lui-même, Sénéchal, avaient aidé, organisé l'erreur judiciaire et n'avaient pas reculé devant l'irréparable: la condamnation à mort" [Balzac believed that, in the real affair, agents under Fouché's orders and the secretary of the prefecture himself, Sénéchal, had helped and organized the judicial error and had not retreated in the face of the irreparable consequence: the death penalty] (8: 1456). So convinced was Balzac of the truth of his story that he told it a second time, as part of the muddy past of the character du Bousquier in *La vieille fille*.

To be clear about this: the answer Balzac gives in his impure fiction may or may not be the truth of history. Taken with respect to facts, the story of the novel stands in an awkward and uncertain relation as to revealing or hiding. It may darken or eclipse the story of Clément de Ris, in altering it for fiction's purposes, or reveal something hitherto unknown about it.

The change of title from the first draft's "Une affaire secrète" (8: 1495) concisely indexes how what was merely secret became tenebrous, in all the senses cited above. The draft began by portraying the five conspirators in dialogue in a certain boudoir, this conspiracy being the cause of the events the novel was to recount. Between the first draft and the later manuscript version, a major reordering of the novel's parts resulted in a tenebrous reading effect: Balzac moved these necessary explications to the last few pages of the novel

---

2. Michu is blamed by public opinion for cutting off heads during the Terror, "lui ou son beau-père" [he or his father-in-law] (8: 640), quite like the guilt by association that concludes La Fontaine's fable "Le loup et l'agneau," whose first line, which Balzac quotes, gives its moral.

(making at the same time several smaller changes which contribute to entenebrating causes; for instance, while the first version immediately identifies Talleyrand, the second resorts to various enigmatic but colorful periphrases, such as "Celui qui marchait difficilement" [He who walked with difficulty] [8: 689]). Hysteron proteron begins to overtake narrative logic: the telling of the cause now follows the telling of its complex effects. The last chapter of the Souverain edition of 1842 (chapter divisions have been retained in the Folio edition), is called "Les ténèbres dissipées" [Darkness Dissipated], an apt name for the place of necessary explanations; but would the sky have been so dark if the explanations had come in chapter 1? The life of the plot now depends on the final scene of explication without which the story would remain entenebrated. Yet, instead of one of those assertive, informative, airless explanations by the familiar, all-knowing narrator, the one Proust chided for striking but disharmonious images (270), the "secret de l'affaire" (8: 695) comes mediated by a secondary narration. Now an aged and wizened Henri de Marsay tells the story at a classic gathering of duchesses and princesses in 1833, decades after the event, to reveal why the countess Laurence de Cinq-Cygne leaves in a huff of *ancien régime* disdain when the comte—*d'Empire*—Malin de Gondreville arrives. This genteel mediation necessitates, as a trait of verisimilitude, the frequent use of phrases like "je crois" [I believe] or "il a dû dire" [he must have said] and several other markers of hearsay knowledge—and of taking a safe political distance.

Putting the necessary explication after the tenebrous affair mirrors the psychological effect that receivers of the event experience; the story remains inexplicable until all the facts are in. When we read the cause in the last chapter, we must mentally retell everything that has been recounted, not unlike those who would interpret evidence for the trial. Intelligence comes only when the novel is done and the chronology made whole again. Having forced us to seek explanations, the novel turns the reader into something like the Proustian character, one who says "plus tard j'ai compris" [later on I understood]. This characteristic choice for complication defines *Une ténébreuse affaire* and the character Malin, "l'un de ces personnages qui ont tant de faces et tant de profondeur sous chaque face, qu'ils sont impénétrables au moment où ils jouent et qu'ils ne peuvent être expliqués que longtemps après la partie" [one of those characters who have so many faces and such depth behind each face that they are impenetrable when they are playing and cannot be explained until long after the game] (8: 523). Another example of this delay in the ability to understand: "La présence [du duc d'Enghien] sur le territoire de Bade . . . donna *plus tard* du poids à ces suppositions" [The presence [of the duc d'Enghien] on the territory of Bade . . . *later* gave weight to these suppositions] (8: 538; emphasis added). Complication precedes explication.

The premise according to which personal or small history unfolds from prior cause to later result functions, microscopically, in the narrative of the hatreds and alliances among the characters Malin, Marion, Michu, Laurence de Cinq-Cygne, the Simeuse twins, and others. The novel proposes to do what Balzac's necessary explications do: explaining or unfolding personal history replicates, in small, the macroscopic unfolding of past causes in history. (A great deal of *La Comédie humaine* owes its existence to the productivity arising from the political instability from 1789 to 1830, or from what Taylor calls the "trajectoires aberrantes" of the players of the period [4].) A typical introduction of a necessary explication reads: "Peut-être n'est-il pas inutile de raconter les circonstances" [Perhaps it is not unnecessary to explain the circumstances] (8: 520). Speaking of himself in an almost pompous third person, Balzac writes in his preface: "Il a changé les lieux, changé les intérêts, tout en conservant le point de départ politique; il a enfin rendu, littérairement parlant, l'impossible, vrai" [He changed the locations, changed the interests, while conserving the political starting point; finally, literarily speaking, he made the impossible true] (8: 493). So much and no less does the fiction claim for itself; making real history into literary fiction, he has made it "true." In retelling the story, Balzac's hysteron proteron makes it possible to "know" much more about history than his suppressed preface recounted, for the fabulation in *Une ténébreuse affaire* retells a "secret" deeper and greater than the truth about the kidnapping.

The *cachot* in the Nodesme forest is also a *cachette* [hiding-place]; it is plurivalent and expressive, natural and symbolic. Hard to find, difficult to get to, invisible from the outside, the prison suggests a crypt that protects the aristocrats but also situates danger. It emblematizes tenebrosity. It represents the heart of darkness of the story as it lies in the heart of the dense forest, unknown, implausibly, to Laurence de Cinq-Cygne, who spends entire days riding in the woods. The space of this hiding place defines its location in a historic past as the secret prison of a monastery eight centuries old, for the relation of space to time is archeological (8: 565). Of the five avenues that once led to the monastery, several are nearly effaced, symbolizing incomplete and difficult access to the secret. The "bords inaccessibles" [inaccessible boundary] and the "épais buissons impénétrables" [thick, impenetrable shrubbery] that surround the cave naturalize the allegory of the inaccessible (8: 564,

565). In telling how Michu guides Laurence to the *cachot,* "en faisant des détours, des retours, coupant son propre chemin à travers des clairières pour y perdre la trace" [by taking detours, turning back, cutting across his own path through the clearings to hide his tracks] (8: 563), Balzac provides a fine metaphor for how the characters experience events and for how knowledge is encrypted in his narrative.

Once inside, characters are in the dark, figuratively and literally (8: 526), for people in the midst of actions do not know what they mean: "Marthe, épuisée, tremblante, s'attendait à un dénouement quelconque après une pareille course. A quoi devait-elle servir? à une bonne action ou à un crime?" [Marthe, exhausted and trembling, was waiting for some sort of outcome after such a journey. What was its purpose? Was it for a good action or a crime?] (8: 532). If the notion of a dénouement implies seeing clearly, with the characters, actions in the meantime are enshrouded in tenebrosity. By the same logic an essential element of the power of the police lies in avoiding darkness, for instance by reconnoitering hiding places: "Corentin reçut de Fouché l'ordre d'explorer le château de Gondreville, d'en inscrire le plan dans sa mémoire, et d'y reconnaître les moindres cachettes" [Corentin received from Fouché the order to explore the castle of Gondreville, to commit its layout to memory, and to locate its smallest hiding places] (8: 554). The novel also develops the "buried treasure" theme (à la Poe). A document indexes the location of the aristocrats' fortune which Michu buried in the forest (8: 568–69). As in Poe's "The Gold Bug," one has to know how to interpret a coded map to arrive at wealth, happiness, and possibly marriage.

While de Marsay eventually explains the conspiracy that secretly initiated the entire sequence of events in the novel, not all of its proliferating tenebrosity is assigned to revelation by a knowledgeable informer. Laurence de Cinq-Cygne, bearer of all past generations of her family's history, including its political secrets, reinvents herself in the text in a way that keeps her secret stance intact and throws up obstacles to revisions of her history. The virility of her character masks a heart of excessive sensitivity; the comparison to the "buried treasure" motif is explicit: "mais cette sensibilité gisait, chez elle, comme un trésor caché à une profondeur infinie sous un bloc de granit" [but in her this sensitivity lay like a treasure hidden at an infinite depth under a granite rock] (8: 588). Large stone blocks are precisely what cover the opening of the *cachot.* Laurence's behavior and speech are determined by what Esther Rashkin has called a phantom: her unstinting devotion to the legitimist cause. So adamant is her refusal to recognize any but *ancien régime* royalty that well into the July Monarchy she continues to refer to Louis-Philippe as "monseigneur le duc d'Orléans" (8: 686). All the aristocrats are too unyielding in their pretensions based on inheritance and a dead past ("Nous sommes de vrais chevaliers du Moyen Âge" [We are true knights of the Middle Ages], says the elder Simeuse [8: 620]); they are the victims of "la fierté de leurs sentiments" [the haughtiness of their views] (8: 670). Laurence, however, not only appears in the story as the exemplary heroine of chivalric romance, but she covers another archeological figure and its secrets. In tandem with this secret of the old aristocracy, which is meant to be found out just as the police must find the *cachot* for the story to go forward, the novel unfolds another secret. When de Marsay explains what happened, at the end, he clears a path, in our later retelling, to a tenebrosity of the highest stature, which the novel encodes. It is Napoleon's secret that the novel tells and repeats, a secret preserved in the family of France in the generations preceding the July Monarchy. To bring us to that deeper hidden meaning, Balzac employs devices signifying darkness and explication.

The *cachot* provides a powerful model for writing or encrypting the story, which remains in a state of tension with the reading or decrypting exemplified in the judicial trial. Christopher Prendergast's useful term "extended structural metonymy" applies well to the function of the trial in the narrative discourse (90). Like the model of composition in *Le chef-d'œuvre inconnu*, the trial creates "truth" by addition, fabricating it out of the fragments of evidence—the "remains" or "fossils." Tiny details in the writing lend convincing complication to the story; variants reveal, moreover, that for Balzac to revise is to complicate (see 8: 1569). The notion of a proof is the very meat of a trial, and of an interpretation; a proof bolsters. One reasons on the basis of testimony and evidence; reasoning leads to the truth (8: 646). Reasoning, however, may fail; proofs may be absent or incomplete; they may lie; they may even be manufactured to suit a political interest: the five disguised men contrived by the police are taken as proof, a duplication that prevents the introduction of accurate evidence. For although in principle a judicial trial tests guilt by uncovering the truth, in Balzac's emplotment formulating the events for the retelling during the trial primarily puts into question credibility. As elsewhere, Balzac here deploys his intrigue to speculate on the paradoxical relation between "le vrai" [what is real] and "le vraisemblable" [what is plausible], and, once again, the truth is not plausible.

The defense attorney Bordin, who judges the defendants' case indecipherable for the accusers and the court (8: 647), gives a fascinating performance as an interpreter of facts. After listening to the defendants recounting the events we know from Balzac's narration (the truth), the attorney interprets them according to plausibility. Bordin demonstrates how justice, which will not be just (8: 643–44), will badly explain actions. No one on the side of the defense understands how the senator was kidnapped, and plausibility is put into play to cast light on this still tenebrous action. What plausible reason could there be for five men to disguise themselves as the four noblemen and Michu, to the extent of procuring identical horses and shoeing them identically? Surely they would not go to all that trouble "exprès pour perdre Michu, messieurs d'Hauteserre et de Simeuse" [on purpose to condemn Michu, the Hauteserres and the Simeuses], the defense opines (8: 645); that would be implausible. And yet that is exactly what did happen. Similarly, the presumption of guilt taints neutral and insignificant events with telling significance because they fit the plausible account the accusation composes. The "vrai de la nature"—the fact that the aristocrats had spent the day in the forest recovering their secret treasure—would be "invraisemblable," and on no account should the jury be told such a truth, Bordin holds. Either it would be laughed out of court, or it would condemn them more surely. The truth would convince the jury (and the public) that the cousins are lying, since they would be seen as having resorted to inventing such an implausible story to support their claim. Or it would make them appear guilty of a theft, because no one would believe the preposterous reality: that Michu, whom everyone takes for a revolutionary, had protected the Simeuse treasure during the years of their emigration.

Three times Balzac tells us that people habitually judge events "sous une présomption arrivée à l'état de certitude" [through a presumption that has reached a state of certainty] (8: 625, 628, 640). Public accuser, jury, judges, audience, and all France would "know" with the certitude of presumption that the Simeuse brothers had kidnapped Malin to steal his money. Balzac chooses a most paradoxical way of saying the truth may cause the greatest harm: "En admettant l'accusation telle qu'elle est en ce moment, l'affaire n'est pas claire; mais, dans sa vérité pure, elle deviendrait *limpide;* les jurés expliqueraient par le vol toutes les parties ténébreuses, car royaliste aujourd'hui veut dire brigand!" [If we accept the accusation as it stands right now, the affair is not clear; but, in its pure truth, it would become *limpid;* the jury would explain all the obscure parts as theft, because people today take royalists for thieves!] (8: 644; emphasis added). And yet, for all its limpidity, that explanation would be false. Among the acts and words that the jury would unfailingly interpret to condemn the accused, Bordin lists "les mots dits à Beauvisage" [the words said to Beauvisage], a farmer (8: 619), and "les paroles dites dans la cour" [the remarks said in the courtyard], overheard by a man from the village (8: 616). Bordin's reading thus forces the reader to remember these details where they occurred in the novel, or, failing that, to seek out the sentences in which those events were narrated; the call to memory resembles the tenebrous effect that putting the cause last has on the reading.

No surprise, then, that the text explicitly compares the trial to all the dynamics at play in reading a novel: "L'innocence doit un compte claire et plausible de ses actions. Le devoir de la Défense est donc d'opposer un roman probable au roman improbable de l'Accusation [qui] devient une fable" [Innocence owes a clear and plausible account of its actions. The duty of the Defense is to offer up a probable story to oppose the Prosecution's improbable story, which then becomes a fable] (8: 656). The facts be damned. Plausible lies told by the defendants during the trial, the "roman probable," nearly bring their acquittal (an example concerns their use of the plaster [8: 657–58]). As the narrator observes, "Si, en justice, la vérité ressemble souvent à une fable, la fable aussi ressemble beaucoup à la vérité" [If, in courts of justice, truth often resembles a fable, fables also closely resemble the truth] (8: 657)—expressing in a nutshell the credo of the realistic author. In his suppressed preface, Balzac recounted in passionate detail the visit of the judge who presided at the first trial of Clément de Ris's kidnappers, one Viriot, who claims to have learned "le secret du mystère," Balzac triumphantly reports, by reading the pre-publication of his novel in Le Commerce (8: 499). The novel as creator of truth . . . or was Balzac still writing fiction? When truth is not believed, it loses its ethical value.

In all, the trial suggests that explication saves, while inexplicability, or the failure to explicate, is fatal, for the noblemen's inability to explain that they spent the day of the crime recovering buried treasure causes their condemnation. Not all complication admits explication. Implausibility requires them to keep it a secret that they were digging up their own money—1,100,000 francs buried seven feet deep, two feet from the foot of eleven old oak trees scattered in an obscure part of the forest, their locations indicated by a ciphered map (8: 568–69). Innocence means clarity (8: 641), and "Avec le temps, les innocents éclaircissent les affaires" [In time, the innocent make matters clear] (8: 645), but the "circonstances inexplicables" [inexplicable circumstances], the "parties ténébreuses" [obscure parts] (8: 665) make victims, for this "affaire" remains "indéchiffrable," "inexplicable," for the accused and accusers, for justice and the public (8: 665, 645, 647). The crime seems obscure, the outcome of the trial muddy at best, and above all, the true story cannot be unfolded for justice; it is tenebrous. Yet if the "real" true story is saved at all, it is because Balzac recasts it into his fiction.

The historical truth that Balzac writes, obeying the "devoir d'un historien" [historian's duty] (8: 564), is embedded in the complex verisimilitude of the plot: it is Fouché himself, he claims, who ordered the kidnapping and framed the noblemen and Michu by disguising five men as the accused. As history, this is not credible—it is a fable; yet it stands in the structural position of history, and that is how we are intended to read it. Verisimilitude mediates between history and the reader, to whom is granted that safe political distance that the story's tenebrosity vouchsafes. The text would force the reader to follow in the great explicator's wake and to use plausibility to explicate tenebrosity, to pursue our trial reading into deeper crypts.

A broader perspective connects the narrow story of the kidnapping to the general history of France during the Consulate and the start of the Empire. The political history underlying the story implies that the author may not monkey with the relation between causes and effects, but Balzac plays fast and loose. "Le style est tellement la marque de la transformation que la pensée de l'écrivain fait subir à la réalité," wrote Proust, "que, dans Balzac, il n'y a pas à proprement parler de style" [Style so clearly marks the transformation that the writer's thought imposes on reality that, in Balzac's case, one cannot truly speak of style] (269). Was Proust so taken in by the reality claims of the Balzacian text that he failed to see in what multiple ways Balzac does impose style on reality? Hysteron proteron in the narrative logic shows that it is fallacious to assume as a premise that a cause can be uncovered for the puzzling events the characters undergo (and for the incoherencies of the narrative). It is not simply that the cause remains untold until the end; it also remains to be proved what did indeed cause the events. And Balzac did much to obscure the relation to history when he suppressed his preface with its parallel account of the historical events: pulling a "coup," he effaced the pathways. He thus acted on his premise that Malin represents a type—"un personnage qui résume en lui-même les traits caractéristiques de tous ceux qui lui ressemblent plus ou moins" [a character who sums up in himself the traits that characterize all those who more or less resemble him]—and reaffirmed his claim that he had transposed a most implausible event into "un milieu vrai" [a real environment], the transposed version being the only true story (8: 492–93).

In effect, the stance of the novel in the face of the historical event is tenebrous. As a reader of the tenebrous affair of the trial, Napoleon holds the key to its explication. With a single stunning sentence, the third in the novel, Balzac inaugurates a governing metaphor that connects sunshine dissipating darkness to the prestige Napoleon enjoys for bringing prosperity to France: "Aussi le peuple commençait-il à établir entre le ciel et Bonaparte, alors déclaré consul à vie, une entente à laquelle cet homme a dû l'un de ses prestiges; et, chose étrange! le jour où, en 1812, le soleil lui manqua, ses prospérités cessèrent" [Thus the people had come to believe there existed between the heavens and Bonaparte, now declared consul for life, an agreement to which this man owed some of his prestige; and, strange to say, the day when, in 1812, the sun failed him, their prosperity ceased] (8: 501). Balzac may well have borrowed the metaphor from Napoleon himself, who wrote in his *Pensées politiques et sociales* in 1801: "Le gouvernement est au centre des sociétés comme le soleil: les diverses institutions doivent parcourir autour de lui leur orbite, sans s'en écarter jamais" [The government lies at the center of societies like the sun: the various institutions must run their orbit around it, without ever diverging from it] (65). Max Andréoli, in a detailed commentary on Balzac's opening lines, points out the miracle accompanying this alliance; he also underscores the contrast of the sun with the significant obscurity throughout the novel: "La présence du soleil est d'autant plus prégnante qu'elle marque le seuil d'un texte où règne l'obscur; les personnages se meuvent dans les ténèbres, celles de la nuit ou celles des machinations nouées par le hasard et par les hommes" [The sun's presence is all the more telling that it marks the threshold of a text where obscurity reigns; the characters evolve in darkness, either of the night or of the machinations wrought by chance or by men] ("Sur le début" 96). Interestingly, justices of the peace were required as of 1796 to display a symbol of their policing authority consisting of an eye surrounded by rays, poetically suggesting the clarity that comes with seeing well in sunshine, as if in an equation: eye plus sun equals power (8: 1505–6). And one might suggest that the resetting of the events in the department of Aube, meaning Dawn, is poetically justified.

The suggestion that a mystique hovers about this "entente," placing Napoleon above mere mortals, contributes to the mystical comprehension of history ("chose étrange") that Balzac proposes in this novel. Folding the time of the writing, the July Monarchy, onto the period of the events, the era of Napoleon, in a narrative that oscillates between entenebration and explication, Balzac teaches that the connections between facts or events—the causes—and their atmospheric effects are obscure, concealed, mysterious. He gives us to understand that the tenebrosity Napoleon most feared is represented by Fouché, described twice as possessing a "génie ténébreux" [obscure genius] and as a "singulier génie qui frappa Napoléon d'une sorte de terreur" [singular genius who struck Napoleon with a sort of terror] (8: 552, 553, 692). Balzac writes:

> Certes l'amour-propre excessif de Napoléon est une des mille raisons de sa chute qui, d'ailleurs, a cruellement expié ses torts. Il se rencontrait chez ce

défiant souverain une jalousie de son jeune pouvoir qui influa sur ses actes autant que sa haine secrète contre les hommes habiles, legs précieux de la Révolution. (8: 553)

[To be sure, Napoleon's excessive pride is one of the thousand reasons for his fall, which incidentally has cruelly atoned for his wrongs. In this defiant sovereign, there was a jealous guarding of his young power that influenced his acts as much as his secret hatred for capable men, the precious legacy of the Revolution.]

The minister of police acting behind the scenes insures that what is (merely) obscure, impenetrable, or secret becomes perfidious, that the hidden acts are also the evil ones. Fouché is the only character in the action who stands to explicate the story better than the narrator can: "Fouché se réservait ainsi une grande partie des secrets qu'il surprenait, et se ménageait sur les personnes un pouvoir supérieur à celui de Bonaparte" [Fouché kept for himself a large part of the secrets that he uncovered, and he held over people a power superior to that of Bonaparte] (8: 554); he plans "absolument comme" [utterly like] Napoleon at Austerlitz; he is the Napoleon of police. In the chapter of "ténèbres dissipées," de Marsay observes about Fouché, Masséna, and Talleyrand, with some exaggeration: "si Napoléon les avait franchement associés à son œuvre, il n'y aurait plus d'Europe, mais un vaste empire français" [if Napoleon had freely associated them with his work, there would no longer be a Europe, but rather a vast French empire] (8: 692).

On a deeper level, therefore, the ultimate tenebrous affair explicated only for a reader of genius is that Napoleon's fear of Fouché represents the central Balzacian theme of the harm caused by mediocrities and the failure of government to make a place for capable men. In an uncanny repetition, this huge defect of France since the July Monarchy, in Balzac's analysis, stems from Napoleon's tenebrosity and undermines the potential of France for greatness since his fall. Napoleon's secret defect has played out over time and several governments, as if a germ has spread from one to many, from the unique to the general.

What Balzac the explicator unfolds therefore has stature, not only as a reading out of history but also in bolstering the fundamental stance of *La Comédie humaine* as both social document and narrative model. The flaw that Napoleon expiated in exile, a secret fear of superiorities, is the very defect that permanently undermined the July Monarchy *and* that had such a large role in the existence of *La Comédie humaine*. "1830 fut pour Balzac une sorte de mort du père—à la fois deuil et libération" [1830 was for

Balzac a sort of death of the father—both a loss and a liberation], writes Nicole Mozet ("Temps historique" 241). This archeological family secret of a nation motivates Balzac's political writing (however the novels are classified in *La Comédie humaine*); it is the well-known secret of the Balzacian novel, a motive force that makes stories happen. Moreover, scarcely has one opened the book when a Balzac family secret parades before our eyes: Jean de Margonne, to whom the novel is dedicated, was Mme Balzac's lover and the father of younger brother Henri. More overt than covert, like a perverse secret that reveals by hiding, and like many supposedly secret details of the Clément de Ris affair, Mme Balzac's adultery can qualify as tenebrous in its effects on our author. Proust alludes to causes of which Balzac has never spoken: "Là, sous l'action apparente et extérieure du drame, circulent de mystérieuses lois de la chair et du sentiment" [There, beneath the apparent, external action of the drama, mysterious laws of the flesh and of the senses circulate] (277–78). If it is virtually certain that Proust had homosexuality in mind, it is also possible to think about the relation between revealing and concealing in writing a narrative. Perhaps the quality of Mme Balzac's secret was particularly on Balzac's mind as he wrote *Une ténébreuse affaire*, because in October 1840 he was moving from les Jardies to Paris, and his mother was to move in with him in November. Was the absent father, dead since 1829 but the source of the writer's exceptional knowledge about the historical tenebrous affair, to be enveloped in darkness?

Politics imposes a way to run the country: it represents order, meaning, and direction, in both senses (to direct the country, to go in a certain direction); power invested in authority; a use of history dependent on knowledge thereof; the march of time to the future; and progress. As Lukacher writes, Bonapartism reintroduced hierarchy reversing anarchic republicanism (266), and therein lay its value and its harm. According to *Une ténébreuse affaire*, Balzac's assessment of Napoleon remains dark, hidden, or contradictory, the verity of his pro-Napoleonic sentiment apparently conflicting with the verisimilitude of his monarchical intention. If the four *ancien régime* aristocrats (but not Michu) are saved from condemnation, it is only because Napoleon grants them amnesty. Heaping paradox upon paradox, Balzac gives us to understand that the figure of a lost aristocracy whose nobility is yet imperishable (also illustrated by the Chouans who are serving both sides in the affair) stands in apparent conflict but secret affinity with Napoleon the Emperor. When the plausible fables recounted by the accused noblemen fail to prevent their conviction, only the majesty of Napoleon's nobility and grace saves them. The grandeur of the accord Laurence wins, in the memorable scene at Napoleon's bivouac at Iéna (a scene Balzac added on proofs), plays out and projects onto the metonymic narrative line a metaphoric replication of the old and the new aristocracies. "Comprenez-vous ce que doit être l'Empire français? . . .," the emperor asks [Do you understand what the French Empire is to be?]. "Ah! je ne comprends en ce moment que l'Empereur, dit-elle vaincue par la bonhomie avec laquelle l'homme du destin avait dit ces paroles qui faisaient pressentir la grâce" ["Ah! at this moment I understand only the Emperor," said she, vanquished by the good-heartedness with which the man of destiny had said these words that hinted at the granting of clemency] (8: 681). The novel displays at once the arrogance of telling the *real* story and the assurance that it is impossible to do so except by narrating the plausible. Following the plausible, the "it-must-have-been-this-way," Balzac's narrative eschews hierarchy, ascribing no certain historical cause; it buries sense and direction, disseminates the power of authority; it looks backward to an archeological present-in-the-past.

What makes this novel especially compelling is that the tensions between hiding and revealing exemplify those of realistic writing in general. In other words, not only does the novel include in its story the structure of its own semiotic processes, the strategies by which it makes meaning and guides the reader, but it can also stand as a general reader's guide to Balzac. The processes of the events that entenebrated history, on the referential level, and the narrative events that entenebrate the story, which constitute the mimetic level, are analogous. This is not surprising; it is the common business of mimesis to pretend to imitate, in a narrative, what happened in the world, even if it does so by convention. That is, although we know that mimesis is a *composition*, not a *reflection*, of reality, we agree that in mimesis narrative imitates reality. It is less of a common business that a further analogy governs the hiding that happens in the story and the structure of Balzac's writing, which creates and hides secret motivation. The events of the writing, on the semiotic level, replicate those of the story, the mimetic level. Everywhere there are "mechanisms of concealment and dissembling that thwart readability" (Rashkin 33)—which are in fact the essential strategy for awakening and sustaining interest. Although Balzac most characteristically fulfills his mission to describe when he obeys what Genette has called his "démon explicatif" [explanatory demon] ("Vraisemblance et motivation" 79), paintings that obscure the message abound in La Comédie humaine. To paint is to cover over as well as to depict; in *Le chef-d'œuvre inconnu*, the creation of the masterpiece obscures what it intends to show; it reveals instead an unintended message (there are messages loaded with death, like *Le message*, as Ross Chambers has shown in a brilliant reading ["Reading"]). A writer cannot show too little, or understanding fails; or too much, for then interest flags; as Lucien Dällenbach writes, the text that fills all the holes loses interest ("Du fragment au cosmos" 430). The ideal would lie somewhere between tenebrous affairs and necessary explications—the equilibrium also struck in this novel between noble sentiment and base dealings.

One may thus take *Une ténébreuse affaire* as a model for many other novels and especially for a certain kind of reading that Balzac's novels require of us. Reading is an affair of genius, and it is significant that "le génie du mal" [the evil genius], the police who incarnate evil, read according to the political process of the trial. Describing the devious policemen Corentin and Peyrade as "impénétrables," Balzac compares them to reasoning canines:

> Mais, pour qui eût suivi les effets du flair moral de ces deux limiers à la piste des *faits inconnus et cachés,* pour qui eût compris les mouvements d'agilité canine qui les portaient à trouver *le vrai* par le rapide examen des *probabilités,* il y avait de quoi frémir! Comment et pourquoi ces hommes de génie étaient-ils si bas quand ils pouvaient être si haut? (8: 579; emphasis added)

> [But, for anyone who had followed the effects of the moral flair of these two bloodhounds on the track of *unknown and hidden facts,* for anyone who understood the agile canine movements that led them to find *the truth* by quickly examining the *probabilities,* there was something worth shuddering about! How and why were these men of genius so low when they could be so great?]

When Corentin and Peyrade find the *cachot,* the heart of the darkness, they guide the reader to the Kurtz-like evil of Fouché. It is the reading of the probabilities, the plausible in the domain of fiction, and not of the real facts, that uncovers the secret horror in this history. Reading is "un procès politique," fraught with murkiness, fringing the horrible. Balzac's preposterous claim that the truth would not save the story, that he tells the "vraisemblable" because the truth would not be convincing, deviously lends an excessive degree of truth to the truth when mediated by his narration, and only then. Explication, finally, constitutes Balzac's greatest presumption to an aristocracy of realistic writing.

5

Self-Narration and the Fakery of Imitation

Although Balzac wrote only a small portion of La Comédie humaine using first-person narration, there are several stories in which the topic of identity dominates and self-narration occurs via third-person narrative. Balzac embodied his own self in so many of his characters that self-narration can only be a central topic of the work as a whole. His portrayal of himself in numerous characters has attracted a great deal of critical attention literally from the very beginnings of Balzacian criticism, as the necrologies collected by Stéphane Vachon in his *1850 Tombeau de Balzac* eloquently testify. Pierre Citron's *Dans Balzac* from 1986 is a classic study of the doubles or partial doubles of the author among his characters, which he calls "sosies," "homologues," or "doubles." Anne-Marie Baron, in her *Balzac ou l'auguste mensonge* of 1998, brings a Freudian perspective to her analyses that examine the family dynamics of the author's life in conjunction with the structures of relations among characters in several novels, among them *Louis Lambert, Mémoires de deux jeunes mariées,* and *Les Chouans*. She notes: "Nécessairement narcissique, l'œuvre romanesque démultiplie l'image de son auteur sous une forme savamment déguisée" [Necessarily narcisisstic, the fictional work multiplies the image of its author in a brilliantly disguised form] (58); and "Son roman familial . . . se décline à l'infini dans La Comédie humaine" [His family romance . . . is infinitely conjugated in La Comédie humaine] (148).[1]

---

1. Baron's *Le fils prodige* also uses the Freudian perspective to illuminate the novels by casting on them the light of Balzac's unconscious.

The connection to "real life" distinguishes all such analyses, smaller parcels of which are nearly ubiquitous among the vast territories of critical writing on Balzac.

But while Balzac often put himself into the fictions as a "phantom of the mirror," to use Pierre Abraham's phrase, borrowed from Cervantes and quoted by Citron in *Dans Balzac* (33), there are also several cases of characters who, within the diegetic fiction, engage in self-narration. The problematic of self-narration is less the object of critical attention than the matter of the autobiographical connection. Jacques-David Ebguy inventoried the many forms of the composition and decomposition of identity in "Description d'une (dé)composition de quelques modalités de la construction balzacienne des personnages."[2] His argument underscores the overwhelming force of uncertainty and changeability in the constitution of characters, both as a general feature of *La Comédie humaine* and in particular cases. My focus in this chapter is on identity and the self-narration of it within the diegetic universe, not on the link of self-narration to Balzac's insertion of himself into his narration (except partially in the case of *Albert Savarus*). Yet, indirectly, the characters do resemble Balzac: like Balzac writing his *Comédie humaine* and peopling it with doubles for the purpose of narrating himself in his multiple images, certain characters use narration to produce images of themselves. And what is interesting is how often self-narration stumbles, meets obstacles, or fails.

Among those instances of self-narration, certain characters engage in misrepresentations, for good or ill; they act out and masquerade; they fake it. Just as the semiotic figures arise in the mimesis, what happens in these stories conveys information about how the stories are written. Extending the concept of representation to misrepresentation, one can see that Balzac, writing his novels and stories, employs strategies of narration, in the mimetic creation, that represent by misrepresenting: by strategies of phoniness. In short, I am suggesting a parallel between what characters do when they are being phony and what Balzac does in creating his novelistic world.

Thus I propose to discuss the rhetorical schemes that structure several stories where self-narration and mimesis are problematic.

In the brilliant opening pages of *Madame Firmiani*, the narrator provides eighteen different answers to the question of the identity of Mme Firmiani, and the entire plot arises from and plays on this uncertainty about what one can know. The opening is famous for its unique strategy of introducing the

2. The headings of Ebguy's sections read as follows: *l'identité ex-posée, l'uniformisation des identités, l'identité instable, l'identité discordante, une identité relativisée, l'identité construite, l'identité énigmatique, l'identité mystérieuse,* and *l'identité multiple.*

title character. Establishing the identity of the central characters is the typical task of Balzac's openings—or if not openings, those flashbacks following the beginnings where it becomes necessary to explain the character to make the events of the story intelligible. The city, the street, the house, certain rooms, the furnishings, the dress, the stature, corpulence, and coloring, the age, civil status, past history and so on are the typical topics of these character analyses. In *Madame Firmiani,* however, a temporary abeyance of such narrative/descriptive authority, or more exactly a *dispersal* of narrative authority, introduces the heroine's identity: sixteen types of Parisians, plus two more, speak in the style and manner of their places in the Balzacian zoological taxonomy and successively build a description of Mme Firmiani, until the narrator (who does exist) must conclude, "il y avait enfin autant de madames Firmiani que de classes dans la société" [in all there were as many Madame Firmianis as there are social classes] (2: 147). The entire opening is a tour de force that portrays distinct social types and simultaneously serves to introduce the main character by successive approximations, doing duty as the necessary description of the character but doing so in an already narrative manner. It is a narration brilliantly designed to establish the self of Mme Firmiani, and it incidentally confirms Allan Pasco's thesis, in *Balzacian Montage,* that narration is description.

The story's title seems to proclaim the subject, but her identity is immediately in question: who is Mme Firmiani, really? The question "Connaissez-vous Mme Firmiani?" [Do you know Mme Firmiani?] (2: 142) launches multiple answers given by the narrator in the manner of the eighteen different types. They begin with the type of the Positifs, who explain everything by numbers, income, and real estate, and continue with the Flâneurs, the Personnels, the Lycéens, and so on. M. de Bourbonne receives these accounts as *médisances, vérités,* and *faussetés* [slander, truths, and falsehoods] (2: 148), a mixture of viewpoints that prompts him to seek out their subject, for Mme Firmiani is reputed to have ruined M. de Bourbonne's cherished nephew Octave de Camps. Not content to show off his dazzling wit and expertise, the narrator himself describes Mme Firmiani when at last M. de Bourbonne sees her for the first time, and he seems to claim final, complete identification of the person when he says: "Vous connaissez alors Mme Firmiani" [Now you know Mme Firmiani] (2: 151). Speaking in his own supposedly neutral voice, the narrator claims an authority that the dispersed narration does not. It is at this point that a *récit* has been unleashed which will in due course, when fully played out, provide the complete and final answer to the identity question.

This narrative concerns love and money: in brief, to deserve Mme Firmiani's love, Octave de Camps must honorably restore to the rightful owners the fortune his father had appropriated from another family by means of a dishonest proceeding. As Guy Sagnes writes in the Introduction in the Pléiade edition, "Au contraire de ce qui se produit souvent dans *La Comédie humaine,* ce n'est pas ici l'argent qui corrompt l'amour, mais l'amour qui purifie l'argent" [Here it is not that money corrupts love, but that love purifies money, as opposed to what often occurs in *La Comédie humaine*] (2: 139). At the moment M. de Bourbonne and the reader with him will begin finding out what this story is, the narrator comments on his own strategy as follows: "Les observations par lesquelles cette histoire commence étaient donc nécessaires pour opposer la vraie Firmiani à la Firmiani du monde" [The remarks by which this story begins were therefore necessary to contrast the true Firmiani woman with the Firmiani known to the world] (2: 152), but it is a deconstructive moment, since it is hard to believe at this moment that there is a "vraie Firmiani." There follow additional multiple visions of this "femme inconnue" [unknown woman] (2: 152), so that, in fact, only the narration about Octave de Camps's love for Mme Firmiani and the money he must return to reverse his father's greediness will actually reveal the true person.

To advance that revelation, Octave gives his uncle a letter from Mme Firmiani which, he says, will portray "une Mme Firmiani inconnue du monde" [a Mme Firmiani unknown to society] (2: 156). The letter provides an intimate view of her character; indeed, this well-worn device which relies on the authenticity claimed by the actual words of the letter-writer does much to promote the reality of this finally "real" Mme Firmiani. The reader, like M. de Bourbonne, is expected to trust the veracity of a self-narration so heartfelt. Mme Firmiani writes: "viens à moi pauvre, mon amour redoublera si cela se peut" [come to me poor, my love will redouble, if that is possible] (2: 157). Because of this narrative, narration of the self does finally arrive at a description of the person whose identity was doubtful, and if there is a happy ending, it is because self-narration achieves its ends.

In contrast to such purity of character, Balzac created quite a few "phonies." Some people really are not what they seem. In the almost too obvious example of la Zambinella in *Sarrasine,* the masquerade bears on the gender, or perhaps one should say it hides the lack of one of the usual genders. In *Maître Cornélius,* d'Estouteville acts the role of a new apprentice for Cornélius as part of a complex strategy to obtain a rendezvous with his mistress, Marie de Sassenage. I have already discussed the uncertainties that cloud the self-representations of Marie de Verneuil and the marquis de Montauran in *Les Chouans* (see chapter 3). As for the insouciant Vautrin of *Le père Goriot*, what is he if not an elaborate phony? This master at playing parts carries his fake identities through five names and countless pages. Another example is the Napoleon of finance, master of deception and misrepresentation, the baron de Nucingen, who adjusts the mask and manipulates the financial world from behind it, in several novels. Misrepresentation has a financial value which also has meaning for the narrative.

This is precisely the situation in *La bourse*. Fearing she is a phony, the painter Hippolyte Schinner mistrusts Adélaïde Leseigneur until the ultimate moments and then only realizes her true identity because of a device external to her self-narration, the purse of the title. Schinner first meets Adélaïde and her mother at a crepuscular moment that Balzac takes pains to instill with illusion, magic, reverie, poetry, play of light and shadow, imagination, dream, fantasy, meditation, and vagabond thoughts (all terms present in the opening), a moment when, on top of such an overdetermined predisposition to being incapable of recognizing reality, he has just hit his head in a fall and is prey to "le vague." The two women who run to help him are "inconnues"; there is an aura of uncertainty about their identities. They are "neither . . . nor"; or they are both noble and simple; the mother only resembles a marquise of the old aristocracy. Inquiry produces more mystery: "Nous ne savons pas encore ce que font ces dames" [We don't know yet what these women do] (1: 418), the concierge reveals, but in the evenings they are visited by gentlemen, at least one of whom is wealthy. Are they "kept" by these visitors, or cheating at cards, or are they poor, honest women? Speculation runs to extremes: "ou ces deux femmes sont la probité même, ou elles vivent d'intrigue et de jeu" [either these women are probity itself or they live on intrigue and gaming] (1: 423). The truth of these women is as contestable as the d'Aisnon mother and daughter in Mme de La Pommeraye's tale in *Jacques le fataliste*. Why does the daughter have a different last name than the mother (1: 419), and why does the narration nevertheless sometimes use the daughter's name, Leseigneur, for the mother (1: 423, 424)? Every element of decor perpetuates the ambiguity; signs of luxury conflict with misery; misery is "fardée" [beautified] (1: 423). Like the apartment, the mother's face is a sign with conflicting interpretations: "Ces traits si fins, si déliés pouvaient tout aussi bien dénoter des sentiments mauvais, faire supposer l'astuce et la ruse féminines à un haut degré de perversité que révéler les délicatesses d'une belle âme" [These features, so fine, so open, could just as well denote evil sentiments, suggest feminine chicanery and ruse at a high degree of perversity as to reveal the delicacies of a fine soul] (1: 425).

From the beginning to nearly the end, Balzac insists on this system of uncertain signs and the painter's suspicions about them (1: 434, 436). Judging on the basis of "une foule d'observations, légères en apparence, mais qui corroboraient ses affreux soupçons" [a myriad of observations, apparently slight, but which corroborated his horrible suspicions] (1: 436), like the mother's shawl, the daughter's dress, their way of walking (1: 438–39), and the apartment "sale et flétri, . . . la représentation d'une vie intérieure sans noblesse, inoccupée, vicieuse" [dirty and worn, . . . the representation of a private life without nobility, unoccupied and full of vice] (1: 437), Schinner concludes beyond a doubt that Adélaïde has stolen his purse left on the card table, and that the rich old visitor must be Adélaïde's protector (1: 440). It is typical of Balzac's narration that characters interpret signs, just as Balzac prepares signs for the reader to interpret, and that the signs are overdetermined: Schinner in agonies of doubt turns into Schinner overwhelmingly certain of the immorality of the woman he loves. Interpreting the signs leads the painter to conclusions he is sure of even though they are in fact erroneous; the story could have finished in an "affreux dénouement" [atrocious ending] (1: 440). Only the return of his gold coins in a new purse skillfully embroidered by Adélaïde turns the outcome to the opposite certainty and provokes the painter's request in marriage, bringing the narration of Mlle Leseigneur's self to permanent morality—a morality to be sanctioned by marriage like the Marquis des Arcis's with Mlle d'Aisnon in *Jacques le Fataliste*. But the self-narration cannot achieve this reality without the final sign, a device I called external: the new purse. Until a second reading, the hapless reader is no more able to interpret the signs correctly than Schinner; and if, retrospectively, it becomes clear that the title was an indication of the centrality of the purse for the conduct of the narration, still its valence can as easily be negative as positive. Who Adélaïde really is cannot be found out on the basis of the self-narration.

Albert Savarus puts the hero's identity *en abyme,* in an embedded narrative, when he publishes a short story, and the self thus exposed to Rosalie de Watteville's eyes will provoke her to destroy the writer of the story. Not unlike *Madame Firmiani,* Balzac resorts to a device to complete the presentation of his title character: the embedded narration of his love for the duchesse d'Argaiolo disguised in a *nouvelle à clés*. This Parisian, set down among Besançon society, appears to the *Bisontins* of variable name (Albert Savaron, Albert Savarus, Albert *de* Savarus, Savaron de Savarus); of unknown origin

("Il est si peu de quelque part, qu'on ne sait pas d'où il est"; "Mais qu'est-il?" [He is so little from someplace that no one knows where he's from. But what is he?] [1: 916]); of dubious birth (although "le bâtard d'un comte de Savarus est noble" [the bastard of a Count de Savarus is noble] [1: 926]); identified with the devil but also, on the same page, with Saints Paul and Peter; having a neck like a woman's and hands like a prelate's (1: 928);[3] sporting a mask to hide secrets (1: 929) and offering an enigma to be deciphered (1: 930), like Thaddée Paz in *La fausse maîtresse*. The nobles and magistrats of Besançon do not know how to fit him in. Albert Savarus is a phony partly because of his bastard birth, but it is a phoniness that is successful (not unlike Vautrin's). To all these defects of identity, the embedded narrative, "L'ambitieux par amour," brings explanation and illumination, and for Rosalie as reader, a degree of satisfaction.

Savarus particularly resembles Balzac in two respects: he is writing a story and he is ambitious because of love. Savarus's novella disguises him under the name of his character Rodolphe, just as Balzac creates Savarus as a model for himself. Introducing the embedded novella, the narrator stresses the autobiographical nature of this new kind of literature, this "nouvelle école littéraire" [new literary school] (1: 938). Both Balzac and Savarus thus produce a written misrepresentation of the self in a hopeful version, a fiction. Not only does Savarus recount his life, in the novella about Rodolphe intended for the duchesse d'Argaiolo, the woman he loves, but Balzac thereby recreates his life, addressing, via this narrative, a self-portrait in gold to Ève Hanska.

Because of that high noble plane, one would expect Savarus's story, "L'ambitieux par amour," to extol sincerity in love, and so it does, thematically; and yet the self-narration of this embedded tale admits of fakery. Multiple disguises make the heroine of Savarus's tale if not exactly a phony, at least a deceptive creature. The mask of an Englishwoman named Miss Fanny Lovelace is the first to go, followed by that of the Milanese Francesca Colonna, wife of the librarian signor Lamborini, which will later turn out to be only a cover for the princess Gandolphini of Rome. From the perspective of the embedding tale, in which Albert Savarus is the hero, the Gandolphini name and position mask those of the duchesse d'Argaiolo, of Florence, the woman whom Savarus loves. The prince in the novella, a man of sixty-five "encore vert" [still youthful], uses makeup to give him the air of a doddering ninety-year-old, and the Sicilian maid Gina plays the part of a deaf-mute.

---

3. "Il semblerait en effet, d'après ce passage, qu'Albert soit dominé par une dualité où coexistent le diabolique et la sainteté" [It would indeed seem, according to this passage, that Albert is dominated by a duality in which the diabolical and the saintly coexist], observes Andrew Oliver (98).

These multiple disguises within the embedded story configure the Italian characters as enigmas, which serve to fire up the hero's imagination and enthusiasm. The enigmas also stimulate Rosalie de Watteville's intense interest as she reads the novella, and beyond her, Balzac hoped, the interest of his reader, beginning with Mme Hanska. The entire embedded tale serves as a masquerade for Albert Savarus, replacing a declaration of love, and on another level as a cover for a devious Balzac, using his story to describe his ambition to Mme Hanska. But for both of these "ambitieux par amour," there is a risk of being misrepresented as the "amoureux par ambition," especially if we read Balzac as a model for Albert Savarus.

Savarus's self-narration remains incomplete, without closure, because, unlike a well-designed short story such as Balzac might have written, his novella is made to serve another, external purpose: the narrator's purpose of bringing Savarus's story just up to the point of his studiously ambitious activities in Besançon (like Balzac's in Paris), which are all aimed at deserving the exalted woman he loves. Encouraged by the lack of closure in Albert's story, Rosalie strategizes and maneuvers to manipulate the narrative direction toward an ending according to her desires. Unlike Andrew Oliver, I give Rosalie complete agency in these actions rather than seeing her as fulfilling "un destin déjà déterminé par l'auteur postiche" [a fate already determined by the artificial author] (101). Savarus's political ambitions have already led him to the brink of self-destruction:

> Ce combat avec les hommes et les choses, où j'ai sans cesse versé ma force et mon énergie, où j'ai tant usé les ressorts du désir, m'a miné, pour ainsi dire, intérieurement.... je me sens ruiné.... Je n'ai plus de force et de puissance que pour le bonheur, et s'il n'arrivait pas ... le moi que je suis n'existerait plus, je deviendrais une chose détruite ... je ne voudrais plus rien être. (1: 976)

> [This struggle with men and things, into which I've continually put my strength and my energy, where I've worn out the sources of desire, has undermined me internally, so to speak.... I feel ruined.... I have strength and power left only for my happiness, and if it did not come about ... the self that I am would no longer exist, I would become a destroyed thing ... I wouldn't wish to be anything anymore.]

As his plans fail, he describes himself as dying (1: 1000) and "comme un mort" [as if a dead man] (1: 1007), and once he disappears from Besançon, he also disappears from the *Bisontins'* narratives about him: "il n'était plus question d'Albert de Savarus" [Albert de Savarus was no longer mentioned] (1: 1008). The closure of Savarus's self-narration is death to the world at the Chartreuse convent near Grenoble: "tout meurt sur le seuil de ce cloître" [everything dies at the threshold of this cloister] (1: 1015). However one construes Rosalie de Watteville's agency, Balzac brought this story of a self-narration to failure.[4]

Creativity relates to another of Balzac's phonies and his deception. In *La fausse maîtresse,* comte Thaddée Paz plots an elaborate masquerade as a cover for his real love for his best friend's wife, comtesse Clémentine Laginska. After recognizing in Clémentine "cette femme que tout homme doit aimer exclusivement" [the woman whom every man is to love exclusively] (2: 214) with a unique, ideal passion, he retreats into the role of the stiff, distant manager of the family affairs, but the mask of deceit threatens to crack under the constant presence of Clémentine and her provocative manner, for she accuses him of being "sournois et cachottier" [underhanded and secretive] (2: 219). To keep himself from yielding to this love, nothing less than an "héroïque mensonge" [heroic lie] (2: 221) will do: he fakes a mistress, the circus performer Malaga, so that none will suspect his love for his friend's wife—starting with that wife herself. Thus he has to go far in his fakery, far enough to earn her contempt, not just her indifference. The fakery also completely deceives Malaga herself. As Jacques-David Ebguy puts it, "*La fausse maîtresse* oppose ainsi fréquemment ce que semble être un personnage et ce que le récit nous révèle sur lui" [*La fausse maîtresse* thus frequently opposes what a character seems to be to what the narrative reveals about him] ("Ce que racontent" 185).

Love here is like Honorine's love for the man who abandoned her in that novella and Claudine's for La Palférine in *Un prince de la bohème.* But Clémentine is the wife of Adam Laginski whom Paz will not betray. The price of letting Clémentine see his love for her is the fabrication of a false self destructive to the real one. In spite of the count's necessary explanations narrating Paz's life, apparently justifying his presence in the Laginski household, and

---

4. Massol writes: "*Albert Savarus* ne se contente donc pas d'exprimer la crainte que l'action d'un désir étranger ne vienne ravir à l'auteur sa 'prérogative . . . d'omniscience' (L. Mazet). Il montre ce désir à l'œuvre, et en consacre la victoire" [*Albert Savarus* does not stop at expressing the fear that the action of an outside desire may steal from the author his "prerogative . . . of omniscience" (L. Mazet). It shows this desire in action and consecrates its victory] (195).

in spite of Paz's own description of his role as financial guide and controller, Paz is a mystery (2: 206), skilled at hiding (2: 211), full of *stratégie, tromperie,* and *énigme* [stratagems, deceit, and enigmas] (2: 215). And those are the qualities that allow him to conceive the heroic lie about Malaga and to give it an air of reality—chiefly by spending madly and visibly on her behalf. As part of the artifice he lets a real letter from Malaga fall into Clémentine's hands. The ironic success of this self-narration shows in Clémentine's utter scorn and disdain, as Paz sadly says to himself: "Tu t'es rendu toi-même indigne d'elle" [you have made yourself unworthy of her] (2: 230). To complete his false identity ("achevons mon ouvrage" [2: 233]), he puts on a display of himself and Malaga wildly dancing at a masked ball, and Clémentine asks him to leave her house. The letter he leaves behind reveals the truth about his false self-narration, plunging Clémentine into despair at her loss of such a love. To this irony Balzac added a few short paragraphs brightening her loss with a glimmer of hope, but he allows us no assurance that this love will ever be mutually acknowledged; as far as the narrative is concerned, Paz's self-narration condemns him permanently to the false self he created. *La fausse maîtresse* could just as well have been called *Le faux moi.*

Behind the plot lies a plea from Balzac to Mme Hanska not to misrecognize true love, as many Parisian women do: "Oui, plus d'un Paz est méconnu" [Yes, more than one Paz remains misunderstood] (2: 243). But true love requires a *mise en scène* of fakery: "La femme la plus simple du monde exige encore chez l'homme le plus grand un peu de charlatanisme" [The simplest woman in the world yet demands of the greatest man a little charlatanism] (2: 243)—hence the risk for any lover, even one who is a genius at forging new realities out of mere nothings. Early in the relationship between Thaddée Paz and Clémentine, Balzac allows the Polish count access to the rank of true poets, the creators: "En proie à des joies de créateur indicibles, Thaddée était en amour ce que nous connaissons de plus grand dans les fastes du génie" [In the throes of the unspeakable joys of the creator, Thaddée was, in love, what we recognize at the highest level among the splendors of genius] (2: 216); but only three pages later the narrator says: "mais le don de création qui fait le grand homme, il ne le possédait point" [but the gift of creation which makes a man great was not in his possession] (2: 219). Only love carries him to the sublime. The ultimate purpose of the story is to justify the most contemptible lies if they are made in the name of this sublime cause—and especially if a good narrative of its effects arises out of the fakery. Thus the count's letter to Clémentine revealing his true love buried under all his phoniness, "griffonnée pendant la nuit" [scribbled during the night] (2: 240) just the way Balzac wrote his novels, stands as a symbol of the kind of creation this sublime lover could cast into words like a true poet. And again we have the image of Balzac as inspired creator exploiting phoniness. The moment when Paz completely removes the mask resembles Balzac showing his hand, as he so often does, by embedding in his narratives the explanation of how they come to us. If that letter can also be called a written confession, as Véronique Bui has noted (129), it would best be considered a confession of narrative strategy rather than of a forbidden desire.

Le bal de Sceaux turns on the unknown qualities of a man misidentified for lack of self-narration. Emilie de Fontaine's intense vanity molds a mental image of the man she would accept to marry (Balzac's term for it is "le type" [1: 134]); her "programme" (1: 123) for her ideal mate provides an outline, a skeleton to be fleshed out: young, svelte, noble, and a peer. The unknown man she sees at the ball at Sceaux and falls in love with is certainly young and svelte, and he seems noble, but the peerage is "invisible": it requires a self-narration that is lacking. Maximilien Longueville—or *de* Longueville, as it will turn out—simply will not explain his rank and station to Emilie, in spite of their growing intimacy. Like the outside observers' comments on Mme Firmiani, several bits of information accumulate, beginning with the noble family name, and yet Maximilien does not answer direct questions and the text repeatedly calls him "l'inconnu" and "le bel inconnu" (1: 134, 156), in echo of a famous medieval poem of that title.

In spite of the ancient nobility of the Longueville family, in spite of the uncle's information that Max will one day be a *pair de France,* these promises of a whole identity cannot lead to certain identification of the peer or son of a peer, because Maximilien does not indulge in self-narration and the peerage is invisible, except perhaps for a certain "je ne sais quoi," as Emilie's uncle says: "Quoique aujourd'hui rien ne marque le haut rang, ces jeunes gens-là auront pour toi, peut-être, un *je ne sais quoi* qui te les révélera" [Although nothing signals high rank today, these young men will perhaps have for you a certain *je ne sais quoi* that will reveal them to you] (1: 130). But the *je ne sais quoi* is lacking, and other signs would contradict it. When Emilie sees Maximilien selling cloth in a lingerie store, she scathingly remarks on the invisibility of the peerage: "À l'entendre, peut-être était-ce un malheur pour la monarchie qu'il n'y eût aucune différence visible entre un marchand et un pair de France" [Hearing her speak, one would think it was a disaster for the monarchy that there was no visible difference between a merchant and a peer of France] (1: 158). A merchant can look like a peer, and vice versa.

But of course she is wrong; it is just that, unlike *La bourse,* the narrative fails to make the difference visible to her. The telling *particule,* possibly hidden under Emilie's uncle's thumb when he shows her Maximilien's card, belongs instead to Max's older brother, a chatty, pompous, self-centered diplomat who does nothing but talk about himself. The full form of the name, M. *de* Longueville, designates only the nobleman with the fortune and the complete self-narration, namely the older brother, while the absent *de* reveals the one without either. The promise of a fulfilled "programme" is there and in fact will be realized by the end of the story, when Maximilien becomes vicomte de Longueville at his brother's early death. Too late for love: the absence of self-narration by Maximilien aborts the love story; Emilie marries her seventy-three-year-old uncle and loses the love of her life.

Le colonel Chabert famously rises as a resurrected man out of the ground, but his long self-narration is thrown out of "court"—out of the realm of credibility—and he too will finish "dead to the world," not in a convent like Albert Savarus but in an old-age hospice. At his first appearance in the narrative, still unnamed, elements of his story pop into the clerks' witty but unwitting dialogue: *crâne, déterré, colonel, noble* [cranium, dug up, colonel, noble] (3: 316, 317). In not one but two dialogues, Chabert confirms that he is the very colonel Chabert who died at Eylau (3: 317, 322), an improbable opening for a self-narration, and the joke continues: it is "le feu colonel" and "le défunt" [the late colonel; the dead man] (3: 323) who now tells the story of "l'événement qu'il faut bien appeler ma mort" [the event I am obliged to call my death] (3: 324) to the lawyer Derville.

Here is a case of a first-person self-narration embedded in a third-person narrative, of which the function is to determine the veracity of the claim that this man found naked in a soldiers' grave is, as he remembers six months later, in fact the colonel Chabert who died at Eylau. Elements of that proof include his own written attestations and those of a German doctor, but he does not have these papers (3: 327) and, as Vachon has observed, a declaration of identity, *récit* or fiction, is nothing unless confirmed by a piece of writing ("Chabert" 223, 227). Life itself he can claim only by not claiming the "vie sociale" [social existence] of colonel Chabert (3: 327), so that to have any self at all, he has to cease narrating his own adventure; and it is by *not* narrating his self that he has stayed alive until this moment of narration to Derville. When at the end of the transaction that his wife imposes on him he abandons his claim to be colonel Chabert, it is at least in part

5: Self-Narration and the Fakery of Imitation

because judicial procedure will not recognize the truth of his narration, and the attempt to be Chabert is doomed. And so he renounces Chabert and substitutes a different self-narration: "Je ne réclamerai jamais le nom que j'ai peut-être illustré. Je ne suis plus qu'un pauvre diable nommé Hyacinthe, qui ne demande que sa place au soleil" [I will never claim the name that I have perhaps made illustrious. I am nothing but a poor devil named Hyacinthe asking only for his place in the sun] (3: 367). Nothing in this new self-narration conveys any other information than that the man is a fake. He purchases life as Hyacinthe at the price of a false self-narration that means death of the real self.

Real, physical death is the outcome of *Adieu*. This much analyzed and psychoanalyzed story contains a theatrical representation, the cinematic re-enactment of a past. Philippe de Sucy seeks to restore his mistress Stéphanie de Vandières's identity by means of an extremely elaborate false construction that succeeds only for the length of a line or two of text. In a sense, de Sucy imposes this identity on Stéphanie when he literally constructs or reconstructs the passage of the Berezina before her eyes, with such attention to realistic detail, as Balzac did for the reader in the stunning second part (and like his narratives in general), that Stéphanie has no choice but to see it as the continuation of her own self-narration, the outcome of which must be fatal.

Like a Hollywood director overseeing a complete location constructed on the back lot of a studio, Philippe de Sucy builds a realistic set in the park of his country home. This setting and the scene to be enacted have just been described, in intense and indeed cinematic detail, in the preceding part of the story: it is the passage of the Berezina by the routed troops of Napoleon on November 29, 1812. During the real event, that is, the event as described in part two, Stéphanie de Vandières lost her reason. She should have died then and there, at the passage of the Berezina; only madness preserved her body in life, though not her spirit. In a Freudian move that predates Freud by almost a century, Philippe de Sucy conceives (during a dream) the incredible idea of replaying that trauma to snap Stéphanie out of her psychosis and return her to mental health. The set copies and imitates the original setting, until, nature helping, Philippe sees the Berezina: "Vers les premiers jours du mois de décembre, quand la neige eut revêtu la terre d'un épais manteau blanc, il reconnut la Bérésina. Cette fausse Russie était d'une si épouvantable vérité, que plusieurs de ses compagnons d'armes reconnurent la scène de leurs anciennes misères" [Toward the first days of the month of December, when snow had clothed the earth in a thick white mantle, he recognized the Berezina. This fake Russia was so horribly real that several of his companions in arms recognized the scene of their former misery] (10: 1011). The success of the fakery provides one of the most intense pages in *La Comédie humaine*:

> Le beau visage de Stéphanie se colora faiblement; puis, de teinte en teinte, elle finit par reprendre l'éclat d'une jeune fille étincelant de fraîcheur. Son visage devint d'un beau pourpre. La vie et le bonheur, animés par une intelligence flamboyante, gagnaient de proche en proche comme un incendie. Un tremblement convulsif se communiqua des pieds au cœur. . . . Elle vivait, elle pensait! . . . La volonté humaine vint avec ses torrents électriques et vivifia ce corps d'où elle avait été si longtemps absente. (10: 1012–13)

> [Stéphanie's beautiful face took on a faint color; then, from tone to tone, she regained the splendor of a young woman sparkling with freshness. Her face became a beautiful crimson. Life and happiness animated by the flames of intelligence spread from place to place like a fire. A convulsive trembling flowed from her feet to her heart. . . . She was alive, she could think! . . . Human will came with its electric torrents and vivified this body from which it had so long been absent.]

Stéphanie is utterly transformed in a single page that equals the intense drama of the real Berezina scene in the second part. The proto-Freudian cure eliminates the countess's madness, which is signified by the fact that she recognizes Philippe, and the suspended story of the horror recounted in the second part rushes to its inherent end: the countess immediately dies. "Tout à coup ses pleurs se séchèrent, elle se cadavérisa comme si la foudre l'eût touchée" [All of a sudden her tears dried up, she turned into a cadaver as if struck by lightning] (10: 1013).

What is happening here serves as an interesting metaphor for Balzac's writing. A grand fakery consisting of a natural geographical setting (stream, town, swamp) enhanced by artifice; characters depicted by peasants disguised in tattered soldiers' uniforms (a cast of thousands); newly built structures artfully made old by fire and destruction; a hero made up to look like the defeated Napoleonic officer that he was; action begun on signal. If it weren't a movie, it would be a Balzacian novel. The irony is that representation fails in its intended effect—no doubt because Philippe de Sucy was not the genius Balzac was. Stéphanie's unexplained death and her lover's suicide return the reader to the story's middle section, the incredible description of the scene at the Berezina, the "real" scene which is Balzac's success after all. In all, there

5: Self-Narration and the Fakery of Imitation

is a realism that arises in the most grandiose fakery with an effect as piercing as if the battle were real.

No other novels indulge in so well constructed cinema, but other elaborate schemes, plots, and deceptions are everywhere. *Béatrix* includes a plot devised by Camille Maupin, the writer, to make Béatrix fall in love with Calyste, and another very complex one involving several layers of fakery to make her fall out of love—and bring an end to the story. Like all-seeing novelists plotting the destinies of their characters, and like Claudine the countess in *Un prince de la bohème,* the two plot-makers forge new realities out of fakes.

In *Honorine,* Maurice de l'Hostal's fakery is theatrical. As Maurice introduces his narration of the story, he calls it "une histoire dans laquelle je joue un rôle" [a story in which I play a part] (2: 531), which modestly understates his position. Playing the part of a friend to Honorine, he leads a double life, his every move robotically controlled by Honorine's husband, comte Octave. More than a mere role, Maurice assumes an entire false persona, turning himself into a keen gardener disinterested in women: "je me fis fleuriste jusqu'à la manie, je m'occupai furieusement, en homme que rien ne pouvait distraire, de défoncer le marais et d'en approprier le terrain à la culture des fleurs. De même que les maniaques de Hollande ou d'Angleterre, je me donnai pour monofloriste" [I became a florist with a mania, I occupied myself with a vengeance, like a man whom nothing could distract, with draining the swamp and preparing the land for the cultivation of flowers. Like those maniacs of Holland or England, I gave myself to be a monoflorist] (2: 560–61). He employs ruses; he dirties his hands and clothes. His false self includes misanthropy, because "Les fous tranquilles sont les seuls hommes de qui les femmes ne conçoivent aucune méfiance en fait de sentiment" [Peaceful madmen are the only men of whom women conceive no mistrust as regards feelings] (2: 562). False wounds to the heart are artfully simulated to draw Honorine's pity and thus confidence. Like a double agent's cover, Maurice's masquerade incurs the risk that he will be discovered as a liar, and this makes him unhappy. When the phoniness is revealed, Maurice says, "J'irai jusqu'au bout de mon rôle" [I will play my part to the end] (2: 585) and asks comte Octave to obtain for him a consulate in a foreign country so that Honorine will never have to realize that the mad *fleuriste* was Octave's secretary. In this self-exile he continues to play a part—the false part of the happily married man, the price he has to pay for taking his role as friend to Honorine too much to heart. The risk of being found out as a phony lies under the surface of *Honorine*.

Every one of these cases claims our attention for the problematic way the self is narrated—the private life made public at some cost, the self-reflexive self-destroying portrait, the questioned identity ironically confirmed and sometimes lost. Unlike the princesse de Cadignan, Maurice de l'Hostal, or the comte Paz, colonel Chabert did not choose a double identity, but his two names indicate it: his "real" self, the colonel who died at Eylau, and the one forced upon him, the beggar Hyacinthe. In *Adieu,* Philippe de Sucy's fake cinema has the most real of effects, whereas Chabert's narrated reality is taken for fake. For Chabert the failure is in the telling; his creation does not win the prestige of reality and does not restore him to his unique identity. Two of these examples arrive at happy endings (*Madame Firmiani, La bourse*), when the self-narration finishes in the fullness of a self recovered or regained, because the self-narration finds a symbolic crutch, a semiotic device in Balzac's narration, to bring it to truth. One, *La fausse maîtresse,* neither destroys nor gratifies the self, ending in suspension. The others end with loss, death to the world, or death.

Whatever the outcome, these problematic self-narrations are figures for the narrative: self-narration and phoniness are rhetorical expressions of Balzac's realism. Like the colonel Chabert's self, which has to remain buried, narrative is fragile because the realities it contains may not reach the surface, and if they do, they may destroy the organism: "il suffirait d'un obstacle nouveau, de quelque fait imprévu qui en romprait les ressorts affaiblis et produirait des hésitations, ces actes incompris, incomplets" [some new obstacle would be enough, some unexpected fact that would break the weakened springs and produce hesitations, those misunderstood, incomplete actions] (*Chabert* 3: 344). Such a sentence applies just as well to the narratives Balzac produced. He often wrote about his difficulties in letters and prefaces, but it is strikingly characteristic of *La Comédie humaine* that such a fundamental preoccupation finds its way into the narratives as well: as I have said before, the narratives always tell us about their own writing. Like poor befuddled Schinner in *La bourse,* the reader has to work out the truth from whatever clues are present, and the reader could be mistaken. In presenting reality in minute detail before the reader's eyes as Philippe de Sucy does for Stéphanie de Vandières, the creator risks being taken for a liar. The claim that "all is true" is always under attack and always must be defended, and as Balzac multiplies the details to prove his system, the very multiplicity of information, like the multiple observations on Mme Firmiani, paradoxically threaten the wholeness of the creation.[5] There is always the risk that narration, like Albert Savarus's narrative, will not achieve the desired end. And even when the signs are there, and a certain *je ne sais quoi* may possibly reveal the truth, Balzac's success or failure as a creator lies entirely in the hands of his reader, who must be less blinded than Emilie de Fontaine. Balzac can only hope that, like the comtesse Clémentine, when we arrive at the end, we will have had a glimpse into this reality so painstakingly conceived and executed and recognize it as true.

Pierre Grassou, the mediocre painter of fake artworks, exemplifies the successful practice of the art of imitation: the bourgeoisie reward him well for his skill. To indulge in the pleasure of making copies of real art while gaining fame and fortune, consideration and credit, a wife, a decoration, and a title (even if the title is fake) would seem to describe Balzac's goals as well. Balzac often said that truth would not be plausible; it is the fiction that wins our belief. Yet he shows us, indirectly, what artfulness it takes to make the fiction credible, by showing us failures.

---

5. For a curious commentary on the "all is true" cited in *Le père Goriot*, see Franc Schuerewegen's chapter "All Is False" in *Balzac suite et fin* (71–83).

The Double Representation of the History of César Birotteau

In Dreams Begin Representations

Broadly speaking, illusion and reality—terms used with some caution—are the two modes by which César Birotteau's history is represented.[1] The novel begins impressionistically with Constance Birotteau awakening in fear from a dream in which she has seen herself doubled—an old woman in rags begging alms from her younger self sitting at the counter in the store. The dream is as real as her panic at not finding César in bed (6: 38). In several other Balzac novels, dreams and illusions are opposed to the harsh realities, such as *Illusions perdues, Modeste Mignon, Splendeurs et misères des courtisanes,* or *Albert Savarus.* Illusions and harsh realities in those novels concern love; in *César Birotteau,* illusions and reality generally line up on an axis of money. The key moment of crisis that precipitates Birotteau into bankruptcy opposes illusions—"mon neveu, plus d'illusions! On doit faire les affaires avec des écus et non avec des sentiments" [my dear nephew, no more illusions! Business is done with money, not with feelings]—to the cold hard facts of his real financial situation (6: 252). But the "real" assets are "non réalisables" (6: 249), and the arrival at the fatal moment is described as waking up from a dream of twenty-two years (6: 260).

---

1. The heading is modeled on W. B. Yeats and Delmore Schwartz's "In dreams begin responsibilities."

The rarest of Balzacian titles inaugurates this double representation. In its full form: *Histoire de la Grandeur et de la Décadence de César Birotteau, marchand parfumeur, adjoint au maire du deuxième arrondissement de Paris, chevalier de la Légion d'honneur, etc.* And the novel is divided into two chapters: "César à son apogée" [César at his peak] and "César aux prises avec le Malheur" [César at grips with Misfortune]. But which chapter recounts his grandeur, which his decadence? Where is the reality and where the illusion of this representation? The answer is not the obvious one, and we can generally read the novel ironically. Thus when on the fifth page Constance accuses César of dreaming as he announces they will give a grand ball, the representation of *grandeur* begins to be tied to the mode of dreaming. Hélène Gomart, throughout her fine analysis of the perfumer's financial dealings, underscores the illusions and dreams, the irrationality and the desire that undermine his ability to make real financial decisions.

For the reader, the protagonist poses a basic problem of interpretation: Are Birotteau's actions exemplars of *probité* or *bêtise*? *Grandeur* or *décadence*? Is the implied author's attitude one of mockery or empathy? Does he treat his character with sincerity or irony? These and other questions undermine the reader's comfortable relation to the story throughout, in a challenge that echoes the reading effect of *Mémories de deux jeunes mariées*. Only naive readers would take mentions of Birotteau's *probité* at face value, failing to see that, at thirty-five repetitions of the word, Balzac's narrative doth protest too much. Most readers have indeed noticed, and some go very far: André Wurmser in his preface to the Folio edition skewers Birotteau's morality altogether. Others compare this "martyr de la probité" [martyr of integrity] (which is the last use of the word *probité*), explicitly likened to Christ (6: 260, 312), to the "Christ de la Paternité," le père Goriot. Any reader can be convinced of one view, and my intent is not to argue the merits of either side or decide between them. Rather, I am struck by how contradictory the representation is; elements of the answers to these questions line up either on the side of illusion or on the side of reality.

This doubleness is expressed in a variety of ways. In the *explication nécessaire* of the Birotteau past, Constance and César *represent* the opposite of what they actually *are*; César evolves in the virtual, whereas Constance is characterized by realism and the reality of her desires, as Gomart has put it (35). Thus:

> Ayant apprécié César durant les trois premières années de leur mariage, sa femme fut en proie à des transes continuelles; elle *représentait* dans cette union la partie sagace et prévoyante, le doute, l'opposition, la crainte; César

y *représentait* l'audace, l'ambition, l'action, le bonheur inouï de la fatalité. Malgré les apparences, le marchand était trembleur, tandis que sa femme avait en réalité de la patience et du courage. (6: 70–71; emphasis added)

[Having appreciated César during the first three years of their marriage, his wife was prey to continual fears; she *represented* in this union the sagacious and far-sighted part, the doubt, the opposition, the dread; César *represented* audacity, ambition, action, the unheard of good fortune of fate. In spite of appearances, the merchant was a timid, apprehensive person, while his wife actually had patience and courage.]

In this passage the repeated verb *représenter* is theatrical, each character taking on a role before the public. Similarly, the "commercial drama" of bankruptcy is described as a "double spectacle" where "il y a la représentation vue du parterre et la représentation vue des coulisses" [there is the performance seen from the stalls and the performance seen from the wings] (6: 272)—the latter being the hidden devices set off stage as opposed to the public presentation. Repeatedly, representation is shown to sit on the side of illusion, as opposed to reality. At the moment of the fall, near the start of part two, Birotteau will not let his wife see the disaster: "Birotteau se faisait gai, jovial pour sa femme" [Birotteau acted gay, jovial for his wife] (6: 203), another illusion.

Adjectives on opposite ends of various scales describe César Birotteau throughout, lining up on the poles of reality and illusion (or appearance). He *is* simple, gross, of limited intelligence, but he *appears* intelligent, clever, sharp. As a merchant and judge of the tribune of commerce, he appears honest, fair, and just, but (as Wurmser has hammered it home) his business dealings are based on dishonest speculation, abusive profits, lies, deceitful advertising, and unfair competition. He appears modest but he is ambitious, in the first chapter; the terms could easily be reversed in the second. At the moment of the fatal ball (first chapter), whose excessive cost contributes to his bankruptcy, Birotteau thinks about being modest (6: 168) by reminding himself of his origins, but what stands instead for the modest origin he does not think about is the oft-repeated sentence by which he explains to others why he was decorated: "Peut-être . . . me suis-je rendu digne de cette . . . insigne . . . et . . . royale . . . faveur . . . en siégeant au tribunal consulaire et en combattant pour les Bourbons sur les marches de Saint-Roch au 13 vendémiaire, où je fus blessé par Napoléon" [Maybe . . . I have made myself worthy of this . . . signal . . . and . . . royal . . . favor . . . by serving on the bench of the consular tribunal and by fighting for the Bourbons on the steps of Saint-Roch on 13 vendémiaire, where I was wounded by Napoleon] (6: 101). This formulaic sentence is characterized as Birotteau's attempt to "apprendre avec modestie ses grandeurs au prochain" [modestly inform his fellow-creatures of his importance] (6: 101), but for the fellow-creatures, the ball represents ambition and political pretensions, not modesty.

Once bankrupt, Birotteau is driven by a real ambition so overwhelming that, like many a passion-driven Balzacian character, he dies from the expenditure of his vital energy—and that ambition is to return every penny to his creditors, giving proof of humility and honor beyond all expectation or necessity. His real probity is often the greatest when the word is not being used in the text ("Je connais ton père, il ne soustraira pas un denier" [I know your father, he will not subtract a single farthing] [6: 237], as Constance tells her daughter). Neither brave nor politically astute, he represents political bravery for those around him, and he is named captain in the national guard (6: 63): "Le coup de feu qu'il avait reçu sur les marches de Saint-Roch lui donna la réputation d'un homme mêlé aux secrets de la politique et celle d'un homme courageux, quoiqu'il n'eût aucun courage militaire au cœur et nulle idée politique dans la cervelle" [The gunshot wound he had received on the steps of Saint-Roch gave him the reputation of a man involved in political secrets and that of a courageous man, although he had no military courage in his heart and no political ideas in his brain] (6: 62). Stupid in reality according to the first chapter, Birotteau appears as if he is acting stupid: "Quoique Birotteau n'eût pas joué sa bêtise, on lui donna le talent de savoir faire la bête à propos" [Although Birotteau had not played at being stupid, they assumed he had the talent of knowing how to pretend stupidity at the right moment] (6: 65). It is precisely his upright, truthful, honest nature that makes du Tillet hate him (6: 219).

So do we find César admirable or contemptible? On the side of admirable actions we find real, stated facts about Birotteau in which his honesty and good qualities are visible; for instance, he enjoys good social credit (in a highly appropriate metaphor) because he is regular in his business affairs and correct in his dealings and never has any debt (6: 68–69). As commerce judge, his sense of justice, his rectitude, and his good will make him "un des juges les plus estimés" [one of the most highly valued judges] (6: 67). He shows himself an astute and intelligent negotiator with François Keller, but his apparent successes with the banker are then called illusions (6: 209–12). Concrete, measurable indicators of Birotteau's real grandeur can be undermined, precisely because reality is constantly challenged by illusion: "Ses défauts contribuèrent également à sa réputation" [His faults likewise contributed to his reputation] (6: 67). The irony is patent throughout and is expressed from the detached vantage point of the intelligent observer of bourgeois limitations. In a witty paragraph, whose manner is close to the indirect free style more frequently used by Flaubert in his ironic treatment of the bourgeois mentality in *Madame Bovary,* the Balzacian narrator enumerates "le langage, les erreurs, les opinions du bourgeois de Paris" [the language, errors, opinions of the Parisian bourgeois] (6: 69) with evident sarcasm, even scorn, accumulating the examples of ignorance and stupidity. The passage ends with this pointedly ironic statement: "Ces points lumineux de leurs connaissances en langue française, en art dramatique, en politique, en littérature, en science expliquent la portée de ces intelligences bourgeoises" [These luminous examples of their knowledge in the French language, in the dramatic arts, in politics, in literature, in the sciences explain the extent of this bourgeois intelligence] (6: 70). The relation between illusion and reality is doubly devious: "[Birotteau] avait sur les lèvres le sourire de bienveillance que prennent les marchands quand vous entrez chez eux; mais ce sourire commercial était l'image de son contentement intérieur et peignait l'état de son âme douce" [on his lips, [Birotteau] had the benevolent smile that merchants put on when you enter their store; but this commercial smile was the image of his interior contentment and painted the state of his gentle soul] (6: 78). The actual, real smile on Birotteau's lips is the same as the fake one that merchants use to cover their eagerness for your business, but in Birotteau's case, although reality is expressed in terms of image, its origin in the depths of his soul guarantees its authenticity. What a doubly devious maneuver in Balzac's representation of realism!

César's identities are also double. What is he? *Marchand parfumeur* [perfume merchant] or *adjoint* [assistant mayor]? *Parfumeur* [perfumer] or *spéculateur* [speculator]? Constance will keep reminding him that he is a *parfumeur;* César keeps dreaming that he will become a *député de Paris* (6: 48). From a quite different perspective, Graham Falconer comments that the cause of Birotteau's end is the series of difficult passages "entre ces différentes strates sociales, mondes parallèles où règnent des attitudes, des croyances et des systèmes de valeurs tout à fait différents, sinon contradictoires" [among these different social strata, parallel worlds where completely different, if not contradictory, attitudes, beliefs, and value systems reign] (58). It is a question of titles. One of the possible interpretations of the *etc.* at the end of the book's title would maintain that there are additional identities one can ascribe to César. At the Restoration, "Il fut nommé chef de bataillon dans la Garde nationale, quoiqu'il fût incapable de répéter le moindre mot de commandement" [He was appointed major in the national guard, although he was incapable of repeating the least word of command] (6: 77). A short-lived *etc.,* this *chef de bataillon,* because Napoleon divests him in 1815. Balzac's text uses a vast variety of terms to designate the man. Aside from the omnipresent *parfumeur* (an amazing 205 times in 276 pages) and the frequent *négociant* [trader] and *marchand*, we find *paysan parvenu* [newly-rich peasant], *royaliste, chevalier de la Légion d'honneur* [knight of the Legion of Honor], *ange* [angel], *adjoint, juge, le pauvre homme* [the poor man], *généreux martyr* [generous martyr], *homme politique* [politician], *ce pauvre niais* [that poor fool], *vieux juge consulaire* [aged consular judge], *ancien négociant* [former trader], and finally, *martyr*. Not to mention comparisons and periphrases like "comme un héros de Plutarque" [like a hero in Plutarch] (6: 94) or "la machine inerte qui avait nom César" [the sluggish contraption which had César as a name] (6: 189) and "une ganache royaliste près de faire faillite" [a royalist blockhead close to bankruptcy] (6: 214)—and afterwards: "ce noble cadavre commercial" [that noble commercial cadaver] (6: 279).

In sum, the double representations produce a history that cannot be settled: the image is disparate, the presentation duplicitous.

A Calculable Duplicity—or Duplicitous Calculations

The double representations of Birotteau are numerated: how this novel is understood depends on how we read the structures of money in it. There is a parallel between the elaborate financial dealings on the one hand and the narrative structure on the other (as is often the case in *La Comédie humaine*). *César Birotteau* is a "financial narrative" as I called *La Maison Nucingen,* the novella with which this novel is paired in Balzac's structural design (see chapter 7). Not unlike the tone of persiflage in that novella, Balzac will indulge us in a wonderfully comical description of the new structure of capital under the name of "la Spéculation," as narrated by the amoral operative Claparon; it is the poetic scaffold for the concrete realization of the novel (6: 241–42). Speculation was a new way to make money at the time the novel took place, between 1818 and 1820, and to underscore the novelty of this approach, Balzac shows us Birotteau wide-eyed with bewilderment when Claparon tells him: "Ne carottez pas avec des pots de pommade et des peignes: mauvais! mauvais! Tondez le public, entrez dans la Spéculation" [Don't fiddle around with pots of pomade and combs. Bad! Bad! Shave the public, get into Speculation] (6: 241). Wurmser, in his introduction to the novel in the Folio edition, characterizes speculation as fraud (22). But Claparon calls it "le commerce abstrait" and predicts that it will remain secret for another ten years or so; certainly it remains a mystery to César, until Claparon finds a useful but utterly comical metaphor to concretize the abstract:

Écoutez . . . de semblables coups veulent des hommes. Il y a l'homme à idées qui n'a pas le sou, comme tous les gens à idées. . . . Figurez-vous un cochon qui vague dans un bois à truffes! Il est suivi par un gaillard, l'homme d'argent qui attend le grognement excité par la trouvaille. Quand l'homme à idées a rencontré quelque bonne affaire, l'homme d'argent lui donne alors une tape sur l'épaule et lui dit: Qu'est-ce que c'est que ça? Vous vous mettez dans la gueule d'un four, mon brave, vous n'avez pas les reins assez forts; voilà mille francs, et laissez-moi mettre en scène cette affaire. Bon! le Banquier convoque alors les industriels. Mes amis, à l'ouvrage! des prospectus! la blague à mort! On prend des cors de chasse et on crie à son de trompe: Cent mille francs pour cinq sous! ou cinq sous pour cent mille francs, des mines d'or, des mines de charbon. Enfin tout l'*esbrouffe* du commerce. On achète l'avis des hommes de science ou d'art, la parade se déploie, le public entre, il en a pour son argent, la recette est dans nos mains. Le cochon est chambré sous son toit avec des pommes de terre, et les autres se chafriolent dans les billets de banque. Voilà, mon cher monsieur. Entrez dans les affaires. Que voulez-vous être? cochon, dindon, paillasse ou millionnaire? Réfléchissez à ceci: je vous ai formulé la théorie des emprunts modernes. (6: 242)

[Listen . . . such actions need men. There is the idea man who hasn't got a bean, like all the men with ideas. . . . Picture him like a pig that roots around in the truffle wood! He is followed by a strong fellow, the money man, who awaits the grunt occasioned by the discovery. When the idea man has come upon some good deal, the money man gives him a tap on the shoulder and says: "What's this? You are putting your head into a gaping oven, my good man, you haven't got strong enough shoulders; here is a thousand francs, and let me do the staging of this business." Okay! The Banker then calls in the industrialists. Friends, to work! Prospectuses! What a joke! They get some hunting horns and they shout like trumpets: "A hundred thousand francs for five sous! Or five sous for a hundred thousand francs, gold mines, coal mines." Anyway all the finagling of commerce. They buy the opinions of the men of science or art, the show takes shape, the public comes in, they get to keep their money, the income is in our hands. The pig is boxed in under his own roof with potatoes, and the others are contented with banknotes. There you have it, my dear sir. Go into business. What do you want to be? Pig, turkey, doormat, or millionaire? Think about it: I've outlined for you the theory of modern borrowing.]

What is most suggestive about this lesson in the new finance is the relentlessly concrete nature of its grotesque imagery. In *César Birotteau*, real money means cold hard cash, not speculation. Claparon indulges in this comical extended metaphor—a parody of an allegory—precisely because he wants to justify and drive home his refusal to lend real money when Birotteau needs it. Instead, the speculator's purpose to make money out of money undermines the real, and the absence of solid instruments of credit make real money as illusory as speculation, as Gomart has shown.[2] Her analysis of the complete picture of money in *César Birotteau* is based on the most careful reading of the actual financial operations and in particular emphasizes the monetary and semiotic concept of *circulation*.

The sums of money, in each case, appear to indicate a reference to reality (in Balzac's world, nothing is deemed more real than money), but in effect they are figments of writing. Money refers us to semiosis—the action of signs—not to mimesis. The factual, concrete nature of money ought to make real calculations possible, and by the same token verifiable, but this reality is not operable. Balzac's maneuvers with money are in general products of writing and not of brute factual reality; they cannot exist in the real world, and yet Balzac acts as though the financial calculations of his narrative are the most grounded in reality. Just as the speculator "écrème les revenus avant qu'ils n'existent" [skims the income off the top before it exists] (6: 241), the calculations by which Balzac restores Birotteau to probity have no foundation in real money; they are dreams and illusions. Try to reproduce the calculations and the financial deals, try to operate this reality, and one sees that it does not work. One cannot, as a reader, actualize those moments in the text, in spite of Balzac's apparent certainty that nothing is more real.

Nevertheless, a few determined readers have attempted to operate these financial manipulations. Pierre Laubriet and René Bouvier have both written extensively about the calculations in *César Birotteau,* and Jean-Hervé Donnard (282–83) also examines Birotteau's business dealings, to conclude that they fail only because he cannot obtain credit. But such verifications work only at the price of slight modifications to Balzac's text. It is rather the connections among the words, among the parts of the text, that determine the

---

2. See also Péraud, who describes how the lack of credit gave rise to fake monetary instruments: "Billets à ordre et lettres de change deviennent ainsi une sorte de monnaie-bis, mais une monnaie extrêmement volatile dont la valeur nominale n'abuse personne et dont le pouvoir d'achat réel peut, selon la conjoncture et la *fiabilité* du porteur, passer du simple au double.... De la chute de l'Empire à 1848, 'l'argent [...] fai[t] défaut, en face d'une infinité de titres trompeurs, de billets de complaisance'" [Promissory notes and bills of exchange thus become a sort of parallel currency, but an extremely volatile currency whose nominal value fools no one and whose real purchasing power can go from the single to the double, depending on the circumstances and the *reliability* of the bearer.... From the fall of the Empire to 1848, "money ... is lacking, as opposed to an infinity of fake securities and obliging drafts"] (152).

numbers and amounts Balzac mentions, which correspond to a need of the writing, not of the invented reality. For instance, somehow Birotteau's need for ten thousand francs' credit suddenly becomes a need for thirty thousand francs; not long afterward, it is forty thousand. After his *faillite,* within a matter of pages, César goes from *owing* hundreds of thousands of francs to *owning* ten thousand francs of income, as trickles and streams unite to form an improbable river of cash, in a narrative device quite common in Balzac's writing about money. The function of the writing is to bring César Birotteau to the ending in death as a martyr of probity, debts paid, wife and daughter well off, and himself rehabilitated at the price of his life.

Financial success came to Birotteau with the invention of *La Double Pâte des Sultanes,* a "double cosmétique" capable of both tightening loose skins and loosening tight ones (6: 64), which certainly sounds double in the duplicitous sense I am examining. The novel's title reads like a prospectus for such a beauty product, full of duplicitous claims: it too is on the side of theatrical representation, not humble reality. *Le Figaro,* in its issue of 17 December 1837, announced Balzac's novel as a free premium for people who subscribe for three months in terms that read just like such a prospectus.[3] This promise of publication, the last in a series, was the one that was eventually fulfilled, the genesis of *César Birotteau* being among the most difficult in *La Comédie humaine.* But the interesting thing is that the publicity for the novel resembles the publicity for Birotteau's cosmetics: it is a financial success only on the level of the writing. I want to show the narratological implications of this duplicity.

When grandeur, probity, or high morality are the subject of sarcasm and scorn, irony and mockery, the obvious values are reversed; Birotteau is apparently decadent or fallen in his grandiose phase, and he becomes grand and admirable only because he has lost his grandeur. A graduate student

---

3. The text of the announcement is found in a footnote to a December 20 letter to Mme Hanska (1: 426), and it is interesting for the variation on the novel's title: "Avis, en souscrivant pour trois mois (20 fr) au *Figaro* on reçoit gratuitement à titre de prime: l'*Histoire de la grandeur et de la décadence de César Birotteau,* parfumeur, chevalier de la Légion d'honneur, adjoint au maire du 2e arrondissement de la ville de Paris, nouvelle *Scène de la vie parisienne,* par M. DE BALZAC, 2 volumes in-8o, entièrement inédits" [Notice: by subscribing for three months (20 fr) to the *Figaro,* you'll receive free, as a premium, the *History of the grandeur and of the decadence of César Birotteau,* perfumer, Knight of the Legion of Honor, assistant mayor of the 2nd arrondissement of the city of Paris, a new *Scene of Parisian Life,* by M. DE BALZAC, 2 volumes in octavo, never before published].

reading this novel had the excellent insight that perhaps we should not take the *grandeur* and *décadence* of the title as an outline of the narrative to come, but rather see them as simultaneous. Grandeur and decadence acting together produce a tension of duplicity. That duplicity then casts its shadow on the Balzacian project.

Thus the *etc.* of the title can further be interpreted as commenting on the title itself: the title could continue, becoming a story in itself. Beyond the story of Birotteau, seen as going from organization to disorganization (a structure opposite to the desired unity of *Les Chouans*), Balzac adumbrates the history of far vaster organizations. The trailing *etc.* propels us toward a larger application of the system of grandeur vs. decadence, of apogee vs. the fall, and that is precisely what Balzac develops in an extremely important passage where he applies this system to nothing less than "tout ce qui s'organise ici-bas" [everything that has existence here below] (6: 81)—death, our terrestrial globe, History with a capital H, sovereigns, politics, nations, even pyramids. The rest of my analysis will be about this passage:

> Toute existence a son apogée, une époque pendant laquelle les causes agissent et sont en rapport exact avec les résultats. Ce midi de la vie, où les forces vives s'équilibrent et se produisent dans tout leur éclat, est non seulement commun aux êtres organisés, mais encore aux cités, aux nations, aux idées, aux institutions, aux commerces, aux entreprises qui, semblables aux races nobles et aux dynasties, naissent, s'élèvent et tombent. D'où vient la rigueur avec laquelle ce thème de croissance et de décroissance s'applique à tout ce qui s'organise ici-bas? car la mort elle-même a, dans les temps de fléau, son progrès, son ralentissement, sa recrudescence et son sommeil. Notre globe lui-même est peut-être une fusée un peu plus durable que les autres. L'Histoire, en redisant les causes de la grandeur et de la décadence de tout ce qui fut ici-bas, pourrait avertir l'homme du moment où il doit arrêter le jeu de toutes ses facultés; mais ni les conquérants, ni les acteurs, ni les femmes, ni les auteurs n'en écoutent la voix salutaire.
>
> César Birotteau, qui devait se considérer comme étant à l'apogée de sa fortune, prenait ce temps d'arrêt comme un nouveau point de départ. Il ne savait pas, et d'ailleurs ni les nations, ni les rois n'ont tenté d'écrire en caractères ineffaçables la cause de ces renversements dont l'Histoire est grosse, dont tant de maisons souveraines ou commerciales offrent de si grands exemples. Pourquoi de nouvelles pyramides ne rappelleraient-elles pas incessamment ce principe qui doit dominer la politique des nations aussi bien que celle des particuliers: *Quand l'effet produit n'est plus en rapport direct ni en proportion égale avec sa cause, la désorganisation commence?* Mais

ces monuments existent partout, c'est les traditions et les pierres qui nous parlent du passé, qui consacrent les caprices de l'indomptable Destin, dont la main efface nos songes et nous prouve que les plus grands événements se résument dans une idée. Troie et Napoléon ne sont que des poèmes. Puisse cette histoire être le poème des vicissitudes bourgeoises auxquelles nulle voix n'a songé, tant elles semblent dénuées de grandeur, tandis qu'elles sont au même titre immenses: il ne s'agit pas d'un seul homme ici, mais de tout un peuple de douleurs. (6: 80–81)

[Every existence has its apogee, a period during which the causes act and are in direct relation with the results. This prime of life, where the lively forces reach equilibrium and are present in all their glory, is not only common to organic beings, but also to cities, nations, ideas, institutions, businesses, enterprises, which, like the noble breeds and dynasties, are born, rise, and fall. Whence comes the rigor with which this theme of growth and decline is applied to everything that has existence here below? For death itself has, in times of plague, its progress, its slowing down, its renewed outbreak, and its sleep. Our globe itself is perhaps a flare lasting a little longer than others. History, by retelling the causes of the grandeur and the decadence of everything that has existence here below, could warn a man of the moment when he should bring an end to the action of all his faculties; but neither conquerors, nor actors, nor women, nor authors listen to its salutary voice.

César Birotteau, who should have considered himself at the apogee of his fortune, took this pause as a new point of departure. He did not know, and moreover neither nations nor kings have attempted to write in indelible characters the cause of these reversals of which History is full, of which so many sovereign or commercial families offer such important examples. Why shouldn't new pyramids ceaselessly call to mind this principle that must dominate the politics of nations as well as of individuals: *When the produced effect is no longer in direct relation or equal proportion to the cause, disorganization begins?* But these monuments exist everywhere, they are the traditions and the stones that speak to us about the past, that sanctify the whims of indomitable Destiny, whose hand erases our dreams and proves to us that the greatest events are summed up in one idea. Troy and Napoleon are but poems. May this story be the poem of the bourgeois vicissitudes that no voice has dreamed of, since they seem to be so devoid of grandeur, while they are by the same claim immense: this is not about a single man, but about an entire populace of suffering.]

Balzac quickly makes the connection whereby a particular history, the first word of the title, can represent all History. From the story of one man, a bourgeois merchant during the Restoration, to the history of many: an entire populace of suffering. And we are justified in understanding that general History as the one Balzac sought to contain in La Comédie humaine. *Décadence, croissance, décroissance, renversements, apogée, chute, fin, début* [Decadence, growth, decline, reversals, peak, fall, end, beginning], organization, disorganization—all these things enabled La Comédie humaine. Everything rises or falls or grows and diminishes.[4]

What is more, this passage reveals that Balzac perceived he would not finish his great work. The words Balzac himself italicized contain the key terms *cause* and *effet*. As is well known, the Études de mœurs were to be the *effects* visible in the organization, the Études philosophiques the *causes,* the Études analytiques the principles. This three-part logical structure is weakest on principles—few titles, little ground covered; the structure functions rather as if it were a two-part one, with causes underlying and explaining effects. But there are far more effects than causes.

The effects are the observable elements, the actions, decors, events, characters, and plots whose details make up the world we call Balzacian. They correspond to the tendency for Balzac's novels to create and put forward vast quantities of information. The causes of these effects are the machinery of desires, the passions, the will, and the visions that motivate action in the real world. Narratologically speaking, the twenty titles in the *Études philosophiques,* in addition to narrating stories of the human mind, erect the signifying structures into which the myriad observable details can be agglomerated until the whole takes on a meaning; the Études philosophiques are the narratological causes, or forms, for the myriad effects, or facts, of the Études de mœurs. But there is a disproportion: there are far fewer of these signifying structures and they cannot accommodate everything Balzac's fertile pen captured (or more accurately created); as a result, like the italicized phrase on this page of *César Birotteau,* the effect is not in direct connection with the cause, and disorganization ensues.

How could it have been otherwise? Characters, plots, events, decors and so on are not limited to the novels of the Études de mœurs; effects and the tendency to overload on information are necessarily out of proportion to the structures of imagination on which they rely for intelligibility; and those

---

4. Butor considers the rise and fall of the French and writes: "Si la bourgeoisie évolue du côté d'Anselme Popinot, la France ira vers son salut, vers la grandeur; si elle se laisse tromper par du Tillet, elle ira vers la catastrophe, la décadence" [If the bourgeoisie evolves in the direction of Anselme Popinot, France will go toward salvation, toward grandeur; if it lets itself be fooled by du Tillet, it will go toward catastrophe, toward decadence] (*Paris* 176).

structures of imagination are certainly not limited to the *Études philosophiques*. As Balzac wrote to Mme Hanska in 1834, "à mesure que l'œuvre gagne en spirale les hauteurs de la pensée, elle se resserre et se condense" [as the work spirals to the heights of thought, it tightens and condenses] (*Hanska* 1: 204). In enunciating this principle, Balzac is admitting that as he writes, *he himself goes toward disorganization.*

Notice that dreams—"songes"—are what our monuments (stones and traditions) erase, and that (even) the greatest events can be reduced to an idea—events in their massive quantity being the detailed information Balzac's novels supply and the ideas to which they can be reduced being the themes and motifs of their narrative structure. Eventually, only the reality, not the dream or illusion, will remain; dreams are crushed by the sheer weight of the massive monuments. "Ces monuments existent partout" [These monuments exist everywhere], Balzac writes: these new pyramids—almost inconceivable acts of labor—represent Balzac's very novels, "qui nous parlent du passé" [that speak to us about the past]. Grandiose audacity lies in these words. Balzac posed himself as the mere secretary taking down the stories written by History, but neither nations nor kings have succeeded in the effort to "écrire en caractères ineffaçables" [write in indelible characters] the mammoth events of History; only Balzac will do so, we are to believe. The humble realities of bourgeois fortunes are not "dénuées de grandeur" [devoid of grandeur], they are "immense," and César's history equals in importance, as an IDEA, the mammoth events of History that are represented by the two names, Troy and Napoleon.

This important passage occurs quite early in the novel, and Balzac uses it to explain the notion of apogee—which is also in the title of the first chapter, "César à son apogée." Balzac was at his height when he wrote *César Birotteau* starting in 1834. Like his perfumer, he took it for the moment to make a new departure, toward the wonderful organized disorganization that is *La Comédie humaine*. Was he using this passage and this plot to hint at an unconscious anxiety about his future? Was he poised at his apogee, without apparently knowing it—as a slight syntactical anomaly highlights: "il ne savait pas" [he did not know]—and sensing that he should admonish himself to "arrêter le jeu de toutes ses facultés" [bring an end to the action of all his faculties] while at the same time confessing that "ni les conquérants, ni les acteurs, ni les femmes, *ni les auteurs* n'en écoutent la voix salutaire" [neither conquerors, nor actors, nor women, *nor authors* listen to its salutary voice] (emphasis added)? Yet he writes to Mme Hanska: "Quelque jour, *quand j'aurai fini,* nous rirons bien" [Some day, *when I am finished,* we will have a good laugh] (*Hanska* 1: 205; emphasis added). Working on *César Birotteau,* he tells his mistress that he is motivated by his desire to appear grander to her, that *César Birotteau* and *La Maison Nucingen* "vous feront arriver mon nom à vos oreilles plus grand que par le passé" [will make my name reach your ears grander than in the past] (*Hanska* 1: 371). But Balzac like Birotteau is double, representing himself writing as both illusion and reality, appearing only as a dream in the never written *Essai sur les forces humaines,* which was to be "l'ouvrage de toute ma vie" [the work of my whole life] (Vachon, *Les travaux* 144). This system works only because we, his willing readers, grant to his duplicitous representations the credit that, unlike Birotteau, keeps Balzac safe from bankruptcy and the martyrdom of his probity.

La Maison Nucingen, *A Financial Narrative*

> Les romans de Balzac n'auraient pas lieu si la question de l'argent ne se posait pas.
> [Balzac's novels would not take place if the question of money were not an issue.]
>
> —Wurmser, *La Comédie inhumaine* 106

The principal theme of *La Maison Nucingen,* belonging to the *Études de mœurs,* is high finance, but this short novel or long novella also provides one of the best illustrations of the semiosis of narration. A story about a financial coup as well as about a narrative in the process of creating itself, the novella includes an elaborate commentary on its own narration. The artifice of an external narrator lends importance to the act of narration: an anonymous listener, who speaks in the first-person singular, eavesdrops through the thin partition of a private restaurant dining room on a witty dialogue among four friends, Bixiou, Finot, Blondet, and Couture, who become progressively intoxicated. To explain the origins of Rastignac's fortune, Bixiou, Balzacian wit par excellence, launches into a convoluted account of the baron de Nucingen's skillful and deceptive financial maneuvers, which also determine the form of the story line. (For an interesting discussion of the conversational maxims governing this story and Balzacian narration in general, see Barel-Moisan and Déruelle, "Balzac et la pragmatique.")

Although the device of an external narrator is not rare in Balzac (see Conner; Madden), in this case the frame is largely limited to the opening portion; while we see (or more exactly hear) the narrator depart at the end, he does not add his commentary or a moral. But until the fifth set of proofs, the frame had ended with a short speech by the narrator decrying the journalistic wit that has corroded the intelligence of youth and criticizing their inattentiveness to art (see chapter 20 for a fuller analysis of the ending). More of a prologue than an embedding structure in the final version, the external frame serves to describe the narrator as a secretary (not unlike Balzac). To say that the conversation he hears "fut sténographiée par ma mémoire" [was taken down by my memory] (6: 331) is perhaps a necessary justification, for he claims to reproduce textually and in full detail an extremely complicated conversation.

The task of framing is taken up by the continuous commentary of the four friends both on the events they are relating and on their manner of telling them, providing a sort of internal frame. The spoken form naturally permits digressions, during which the four friends discourse about society, history, politics, or morality. They explain the term "coup de Jarnac" and the English notion of "improper"; they compare material happiness and moral happiness; they debate the meaning of love and the politics of the bank. These more or less lengthy digressions furnish the principal moral descriptions of the four speakers who "slander" themselves (6: 337), framing them in a social and historical reality that confers on them a certain credibility as the product of this civilization, as "*condottieri* de l'Industrie moderne" [*condottieri* of modern Industry] (6: 330). Digressions also serve to add to the suspense by interrupting the course of the narrative, and they are the occasion for Balzac to discourse on subjects dear to his heart (among which an important instance, near the end of the novella, on the law).

Within these two framing structures that frame one another, the account of Rastignac's fortune takes the form of a series of successive narrative branchings. Each branch appears as the opening of a new story, to which a conclusion can be expected in a corresponding order after further interruptions, in the manner of many an eighteenth-century memoir novel. But Balzac invented instead an artful rhetorical device: a kind of aborted chiasmus structure. No principle of order governs the narration in the last third of the novella, and this disorder in the continuity of the stories represents a state of confusion in the minds of the listeners. The threads of the narration are tangled in a common conclusion where the distinction between branches is lost. In short, the novella is structured as a succession of beginnings which then converge into one large finale of twenty-two pages. Like the truncated external frame, the stories telescope at the end into a conclusion that does not maintain the structures set in place at the beginning.

After being asked six times, Bixiou launches into his explanation of the mysterious origin of Rastignac's fortune of 40,000 *livres* of annual income. A clearly announced "Je vais vous raconter l'origine de sa fortune" [I am going to tell you the origin of his fortune] (6: 334) marks the beginning of the first narrative branch; others too will begin with similar questions and responses, forming an interior framework that will determine the structure. We learn three details: Rastignac's fortune concerns "circumstances" rather than absolute virtue; there were shareholders involved; and Nucingen helped him. But just as Bixiou is about to elaborate, the thread of the tale is interrupted by the necessary explanation of the origin of Nucingen's fortune, in many respects the essential topic of the novella.

This second beginning is introduced by a question from Blondet: "Tu ne sais seulement pas . . . un mot de ses débuts?" [Don't you even know anything about his beginnings?] (6: 338), which he himself answers. Nucingen's first two liquidations are quickly sketched out (6: 337–38); the baron is rapidly compared to du Tillet (6: 338–39). But hardly has it begun when the Nucingen story is interrupted by the narrative about Beaudenord, which seems to be an integral part of it (Bixiou says: "Je reviens à nos moutons" [Getting back to our story] [6: 340]).

The question that introduces this third story, asked once again by the character who will answer it, is "Connaissez-vous Beaudenord?" [Do you know Beaudenord?] (6: 340). A physical and moral description (6: 340–41) is followed by a digression on "Paddy, Joby, Toby (à volonté)" [as you will], Beaudenord's "tiger" or groomsboy who gives him a certain renown in Parisian society ("il fut connu par son tigre" [he was known for his tiger]). Bixiou returns to Beaudenord's material happiness, then to his moral happiness—his love for Isaure d'Aldrigger—and once again the story is interrupted, this time for an account of the d'Aldrigger family.

Bixiou begins to tell this fourth story in response to the request: "massenous des tableaux" [pile up some pictures]: "voilà, messieurs, le tableau demandé" [here, gentlemen, is the requested picture] (6: 353, 354). The description of baron d'Aldrigger's family and his funeral ceremony is interrupted by a two-page digression on the lawyer Desroches, who is courting Malvina d'Aldrigger, accompanied by a discourse on the solicitor's life. This dynamic tableau—comedy aside—reveals in a few words the characters of some of the participants; makes the plot move forward (we learn that Nucingen wants to have Malvina marry du Tillet to indirectly acquire du Tillet's fortune, and Desroches is jealous of du Tillet); and specifies the circumstances of d'Aldrigger's two daughters. But Desroches is also wooing the Matifats' daughter, and the d'Aldrigger story is interrupted by one last major narrative branch, concerning the Matifats.

The presentation of the Matifat family completes the series of beginnings of stories that constitute the opening of the chiasmus structure. The reader notices only one link between all these stories, which is that each of these families has invested its funds in Nucingen's bank. With the end of this scene, the chips are down: all the accounts have been opened and more or less developed. From this point forward, events will multiply wildly until the end.

In short, besides a few of the digressions, the structure of the novella up to this point (6: 368) has appeared largely like a series of story openings, well differentiated one from the other. Each interruption or new story is necessary as an explanation of the story that precedes it, and the ensemble is formed by multiple embedded narratives. Each story adds a few details to those that came before, but the ties among them are not at all evident. The reader, like Bixiou's impatient friends, awaits the conclusion of each tale. One manages to glimpse a few more or less apparent connections among the characters, in the absence of connections between each tale and the whole, but these facts have accumulated without allowing the reader to conceive how they will serve in the conclusion of the tale, since there are no intermediary conclusions. Without knowing it, the reader is nevertheless in possession of all the facts that will serve to create a complete and meaningful ensemble. The evident pleasure with which Bixiou leads his hearers in this act of narration is doubtless similar to Balzac's pleasure, who, though offering the details necessary for the conclusion to his readers, toys with them by refusing to explain their significance.

To achieve the financial coup described as his third liquidation, Nucingen had to prepare it well in advance; similarly, this tale about the 1827 "puff financier" goes back some distance in the form of all the stories begun in the aborted chiasmus. The words "Nous y sommes" [Now we're there] (6: 369) proclaim the start of a conclusion where the principal actors are Rastignac and Nucingen. The former holds in his hands all the strings—people and fortunes—that the latter is secretly pulling. Here the barely begun stories about Rastignac and Nucingen are concluded. We finally learn, in minute detail and with precise values in francs, the origin of Rastignac's fortune, and we discover at last the moral or immoral methods that Nucingen employed to create sums of money. With the exception of a polemic digression on the financial laws of the time that is longer and weightier than all the others and that slows the flow of the story almost to a standstill, where Balzac allows himself to be more of a political observer than a story-teller (6: 373–79), the various scenes in the last twenty-two pages follow one another very rapidly, and the events quickly result in the anticipated outcome. Bixiou's tale in the last pages is as complex, but also as well oiled, as the elegant machinery Nucingen devised for his third liquidation, which also liquidates the incomplete stories. The results are given in a few words by Bixiou in a sort of epilogue (6: 389–91): Desroches loses both of the dowries he had aimed at; the Beaudenord and d'Aldrigger families are reduced to poverty; Matifat loses his fortune; Rastignac and Mme de Nucingen are enriched; and Nucingen will become a peer and an officer of the Légion d'honneur ("toute fortune implique mérite" [any fortune implies merit], wrote Félicien Marceau [9]).

The fact that such a list of outcomes is possible shows that each individual story does come to a conclusion. However, one retains a strong impression of confusion, and the muddle is such that the reader can scarcely tease out the narrative threads that would conclude each story. Unlike the enigmas created intentionally by Bixiou to build suspense, the conclusion is confusing because the narratives, each influencing one another, telescope and combine. Thus, rather than a dénouement, one could say that the ending functions more like a "nouement" [knotting together]; knots begin to form only when Bixiou announces the ending. Rather than undoing combinations formed throughout the story to explain each of the elements in detail, here the ending creates combinations, in the process adding new characters, some of which, like Palma and Werburst, are essential to the success of the financial operation. Thus the account of Nucingen's third liquidation, which enriches him along with several others, has a complicated structure that closely resembles the complexity of Nucingen's maneuvers. It is nevertheless possible to extricate several internal rhetorical structures, designs that belong as much to the area of finance as to narration. It is in this knotting of the conclusion that one sees financial genius draw nearer to narrative genius.

One of the maxims about money in the universe of *La Comédie humaine* is that those who have little spend much. This general rule also applies to the conversation of the four men; just as they are money spenders, Bixiou and his friends are generous with their words, caring little where they come from. (It is Finot the parvenu who has the most money and the most words, since he was the owner of newspapers, but it is he who speaks the least.) Words can be bought: "—Cinq cent francs pour les rendre à Finot, afin de dégager ma langue et déchirer ma reconnaissance" ["Five hundred francs to return to

7: La Maison Nucingen, *A Financial Narrative*

Finot, to free up my tongue and tear up my IOU"] (6: 337), Bixiou demands. Money structures the tale in the same way that it structures the Balzacian society seen in the novel. In this "narré d'un tripotage financier" [narration of a financial manipulation] (Marceau 5), each tale has a certain value in francs that will be combined with other sums to produce the conclusion. The meeting-place for all the sums of money is the house of Nucingen; similarly, the assemblage of the four men's words constitutes the narration of *La Maison Nucingen*. The use of theatrical vocabulary and the description of high finance as an art (6: 372) contribute to forming the ties between the mimetic realism of finance and the narrative semiosis of the discourse and lead to the interpretation of several images according to both finance and narration.

In the frame, the external narrator characterizes this narrative structure, with its interruptions and detours, as "une de ces terribles improvisions" [one of those terrible improvisations], "interrompue, prise et reprise" [interrupted, taken up, and taken up again]; it is "un pot-pourri de choses sinistres" [a potpourri of sinister things] (6: 331–32). This negative description (at least as concerns literature) makes of it a tale comparable only to *Le Neveu de Rameau,* a book the narrator calls "débraillé" [untidy, barely decent]: "ce pamphlet dit sans aucune arrière-pensée, où le mot ne respecta même point ce que le penseur discute encore, où l'on ne construisit qu'avec des ruines, où l'on nia tout, où l'on n'admira que ce que le scepticisme adopte: l'omnipotence, l'omniscience, l'omniconvenance de l'argent" [this pamphlet pronounced without any reflection, where the words did not even respect what the thinker is still discussing, where they constructed only with ruins, where they denied everything, where they admired only what skepticism adopts: the omnipotence, the omniscience, the omni-suitability of money] (6: 331). Ruins, the negation of everything, the skepticism, the irony, and the sarcasm define as negative the attitudes, the tone, the style, and the language of the dialogue. Blondet accuses Bixiou of anti-literature: "tu ne racontes pas, tu *blagues*" [you're not telling a story, you're *kidding around*] (6: 363). But Bixiou defends his negativity in a witty paragraph (6: 363–64). He admires the "imagination française" symbolized by *Candide* and by its satirical author with his mocking wit. He pronounces a brilliant tirade, an impassioned attack against "l'entassement des faits" [the accumulation of facts]—which explains the interruptions and narration by means of allusion or irony, but does not explain the order of the narrated stories, which does appear as an accumulation. He refutes the "cannon-ball" style—which explains or excuses the slowness of the narrative and the carelessness of its form. He denounces the "sotte allure d'un livre" [idiotic manner of a book], of "la critique de la raison pure" [the critique of pure reason], of systems. If the critic next door is censorious, the reader is rather in Bixiou's anti-literary camp, entertained by Balzac's animated narrative sparkling with sarcasm, irony, jokes, puns, and comedic allusions.

This palace built on the tip of a needle (6: 363), this elaborate story based on a single premise—the question of Rastignac's fortune—corresponds to the mysterious, almost magical creation of money by Nucingen. His tactic is not to "épointer les aiguilles" [blunt the needles] of the French imagination, but to avoid "spiritual sterility" in finance the same way Bixiou avoids it in narration. His banking methods are "en dehors des conditions littéraires" [outside literary conditions] (6: 331–32), that is to say, speaking plainly, they do not strictly obey the rules of high finance (the way Bixiou does not obey literary decorum), and the illegality or "meta-legality" of his financial methods is reflected by the negativity of Bixiou's narrative.

Thus various descriptions of narration apply well to finance and vice versa. "*La loi punit de mort le contrefacteur*" [*The law punishes the counterfeiter with death*] (6: 335); but just as Nucingen escapes the law by fabricating "de jolies petites actions à placer" [pretty little shares to negotiate] and "ses millions faits d'une main de papier rose" [his millions made from a quire of rose-colored paper] (6: 380), the four friends, and most of all Bixiou, escape from literary laws while counterfeiting the language. What is implied in passing is a criticism of the weakness of the conventions—financial as well as narrative.

But the stylistic and narrative images are not all negative. Some are merely descriptive. Speaking of the narrative he hears, the external narrator uses the words "tableaux" and "pantomimes." Allusions to Molière and the use of the verb *marivauder* [to banter in the style of Marivaux] strengthen the comparison of this jesting tale to the comedic tradition, with Bixiou in the role of the buffoon and the stage monkey. Painter and dramatist, Bixiou is a spokesperson for Balzac, who, through the person of the listening narrator, makes his character speak and move, all the while refusing responsibility for his words and his actions.

The three listeners sometimes accuse the storyteller of using procedures that slow down the development of the story and increase their impatience: "—Et allons un peu plus vite! dit Blondet, tu marivaudes" ["Let's go a little faster!" said Blondet, "this is mere banter"] (6: 351). Couture shows the same impatience at the end of the narration of the "beginnings" when he says: "Je ne vois, dans toutes ces toupies que tu lances, rien qui ressemble à l'origine de la fortune de Rastignac" [In all these tops that you have set spinning I see nothing that resembles the origin of Rastignac's fortune] (6: 369). Further on, the narration seems like a riddle or a practical joke; Finot says: "je n'entrevois pas le mot de cette énigme" [I cannot imagine the answer to this enigma] (6: 369). Slowness and secret in the preparation of the conclusion resemble Nucingen's machinations aided by his "pistons." Nucingen's coup has been prepared for six months, and no one but he can see how each stage and each new situation at the bank help his operation to advance. Nucingen's third bankruptcy is a sleight of hand, an enigma understood after the fact only by Palma, du Tillet, and Werbrust, who, like well-informed critics, have in their hands the necessary documents to "analyze the text."

Nucingen appears to treat his creditors with scorn, but the false assets he gives them will end up having a real value; in the same way, the listeners accuse Bixiou of making fun of them (6: 337) and of only producing an immense spoof (6: 334), in short, of lying to them—whereas his stories eventually have a value or a place in the account of the origins of Nucingen's fortune. Thus the form of Bixiou's tale is a verbal machine misunderstood by his audience, who see only afterwards the reasons for the accumulation of the various stories.

Three images of the accumulation of money and its increase at the bank can also describe the style of Bixiou's tale. The first is that of a river of money: "Vous avez suivi le cours de tous les petits ruisseaux qui ont fait les quarante mille livres de rente auxquelles tant de gens portent envie!" [You have been following the flow of all the little streams that formed the forty thousand pounds of income that so many people envy!] (6: 369). Each person mentioned and each tale told by Bixiou corresponds to a certain numerical amount, and the streams united in a river of francs are like the tales united in the end in a complete story about the origin of Rastignac's fortune.

A second metaphor for Nucingen's operations is taken from a work of art, and notably from a vocal art (like the art of tale-telling)—an aria from the opera *The Barber of Seville*:

Les loups-cerviers exécutaient, financièrement parlant, l'air de la calomnie du *Barbier de Séville*. Ils allaient *piano, piano,* procédant par de légers cancans, sur la bonté de l'affaire, dits d'oreille à oreille. Ils . . . exploitaient le patient, l'actionnaire . . . par cette rumeur habilement créée et qui grandissait jusqu'au *tutti* d'une cote à quatre chiffres. (6: 372–73)

[The lynxes were performing, financially speaking, the calumny aria from *The Barber of Seville*. They went *piano, piano,* proceeding with airy rumors on the excellence of the business, which were passed from ear to ear. They . . . exploited the passive partner and the shareholder . . . by this ably created rumor that grew to the *tutti* of a four-figure share price.]

To represent the accumulation of the money, this metaphor evoking Rossini's famous crescendos is particularly fitting. The word *tutti* will occur again later to describe the strongest moment of the financial manipulations (6: 388). In a parallel way, the conclusion to Bixiou's tale is a sort of *tutti* where the voices heard separately until now (the telling of each story) create an ensemble where they are superimposed.

The third image of Nucingen's machinations takes up a metaphor already mentioned: "Mais quand un écheveau a tant de fils, il s'y fait des nœuds" [But when a skein has so many threads, knots form] (6: 381). The knots are the complications and the elaborations in Bixiou's many threads that make up the "knotting" of the conclusion.

This relationship between words and money becomes tighter precisely because the complexity of the financial activity creates the necessity for a complex form of narration, as much in the syntax of the sentences as in their organization. Confusion reigns at the bank, "les choses les plus contradictoires se disaient" [the most contradictory things were being said] (6: 386), "la question se compliqua bien plus encore" [the matter became even more complicated] (6: 388); a little more and the reader would be like Rastignac, who "n'y comprit rien" [didn't understand a thing] (6: 388), and we would agree with Bixiou when he says of Nucingen: "Il est impossible à qui que ce soit au monde de démontrer comment cet homme a, par trois fois et sans effraction, voulu voler le public enrichi par lui, malgré lui" [It is impossible for anyone in the world to explain how this man, three times and without committing burglary, tried to rob the public that he managed to enrich, in spite of himself] (6: 391). Given the complexity of the text, we are in danger of falling asleep like the Matifats, at whose house Bixiou tells his "aventure à tiroirs" [episodic narrative] from nine o'clock in the evening until midnight, and thus to miss the ending. Here is the passage that describes this scene: "J'en étais à l'introduction de mon vingt-neuvième personnage (les romans en feuilletons m'ont volé!), quand le père Matifat . . . a ronflé comme les autres, après avoir clignoté pendant cinq minutes. Le lendemain, tous m'ont fait des compliments sur le dénouement de mon histoire" [I was just introducing my twenty-ninth character (the serials stole from me!), when old Matifat . . . snored like the others after having blinked for five minutes. The next day, all of them complimented me on the ending of my story] (6: 367). The appearance of this adventure novel in the novella is one of the most curious commentaries on its narration. The elements in common are the large number of characters (fifty-five reappearing characters in *La Maison Nucingen*); a large number of ill-matched stories without any apparent ties, with false starts, etc.; the important element of suspense; the sudden break in the middle of a story leaving things unexplained (the aborted chiasmus); the riddle-like aspect; and finally a (potential) conclusion that takes up all the broken threads and ties them back together without leaving any loose ends. This story-within-a-story is thus a final image of the structures of this novella. The great literary man, like the great financier, "a ses stratagèmes à combiner, ses embuscades à tendre" [has his strategies to arrange, his ambushes to set up] (6: 340). It is noteworthy that this "aventure à tiroirs" does not seem to have a conclusion; the dénouement is lost in sleep.

These are the ties between the two themes of this work—the financial theme and the narration theme. Let me look a little closer at the theme of money.

In relation to other novels in *La Comédie humaine*, *La Maison Nucingen* plays two important roles: it fills the gap between the poor and young Rastignac and the Rastignac who is a minister and peer of France; his 40,000 pounds of income oiled the machinery that raised his worldly stature. In addition, the story develops and defines the character of Nucingen, one of Balzac's men of passion and a financial genius (Napoleon or elephant of finance, according to this tale [6: 339]), by showing us the underside of his operations. To tell the origin of Nucingen's fortune is to discuss his questionable morality: his morals are based on pacification, which consists in giving little *pâtés* for gold *louis*. Rastignac's morals are a little different; "il ne croyait à aucune vertu, mais à des circonstances où l'homme est vertueux" [he did not believe in any virtue but in circumstances where men are virtuous] (6: 381), where one can see the dénouement of Vautrin's lessons in *Le père Goriot*. According to Balzac's metaphor, Rastignac is just a little fly—not big enough to create his fortune by himself—who consents to fasten like a parasite on the back of a large fly and whose involuntary toy he almost becomes. One cannot describe him as "honnête homme, mais bête" [an honorable man, but stupid], like the baron d'Aldrigger; Rastignac has accepted the immorality of a society that defines Being with Having, and he will use his relatively feeble strength to make money for himself, as a means to prove himself against society, to "jouer tout ce monde" [outmaneuver all these people] (6: 381). In Nucingen's morality, on the other hand, money is an end in itself; he wants to have more in order to make even more; the peerage and the Légion d'honneur are simply accessories, and men are the means he employs.

To escape the spider web of laws, Nucingen hides behind a veil of confusion and contradictions. He intentionally creates a state of disorder at the bank to produce the desired results and to facilitate his manipulations, which will seem legal in the end. This confusion is reflected in the disorder in the narrative, which opens with teasing and false starts, proceeds by irony and interruption, and concludes with the superimposition, combination, and interweaving of the stories introduced earlier.

The comparison between literary words and money is social. Barbéris observed that money is the sign and the instrument of a new world (*Mythes* 159), of a society where modern industry will be fully developed. The role of the banker is to make the money circulate, to amass capital that, placed back into production companies or exploitation companies (such as the Wortschin mines), will permit the development of progress. Since Nucingen "invents" capital, he is a creator of progress—he announces a new vision of a capitalist world. The role of Bixiou's words is similar. Creative genius and enunciator of a new sort of narration, he invents a new form that fits his subject. Barbéris also notes that this parody of an intimate conversation, in another century, would have been on a sentimental subject (*Mythes* 135). But the secret overheard by the narrator, who takes on the role of a revealer to the general public, is here the more modern subject of a new sort of literature—money. It is a new literature whose frames and expressions are more scientifically true (Barbéris, *Mythes* 135). The narrative technique reflects this scientific subject.

Henceforth the intimate threads of words and money have been knotted together. Every remark made about the circulation of money is also about the circulation of words; they both make up signifying systems that have an ultimate meaning in the capitalist/literary world of *La Comédie humaine*. This meaning, it must be specified, has to do with genius: genius in finance, genius in literature. In the semantics of a Balzacian work, there are two signs, that of natural language and that of economic or financial language. In the same way that words have significance with respect to other words, within structures established by linguistic rules and literary conventions, money, as a sign, has significance within another system, that of the economic world, which also has its rules and conventions. But the most characteristic form of this world is illegality. The success of Bixiou's narrative for his listeners is paralleled by the success of Nucingen's third bankruptcy, which reaffirms his greatness in illegality. For Balzac, then, according to this tale, greatness consists in being illegal under the laws; it means that the laws are not good. The entire novella has served to demonstrate the logic of this thesis, summed up by Blondet at the end of the novel:

—Où veux-tu donc en venir? dit Finot à Blondet.—Au gouvernement absolu, le seul où les entreprises de l'Esprit contre la Loi puissent être réprimées! Oui, l'Arbitraire sauve les peuples en venant au secours de la justice,

7: La Maison Nucingen, *A Financial Narrative*

car le droit de grâce n'a pas d'envers: le Roi, qui peut gracier le banqueroutier frauduleux, ne rend rien à la victime dépouillée. La Légalité tue la Société moderne. (6: 391–92)

["What are you getting at?" said Finot to Blondet. "Absolute government, the only one where the ventures of the Mind against the Law can be repressed! Yes, Arbitrariness saves the people by coming to the aid of justice, for the right of pardon has no reverse side: the King, who can pardon the fraudulent bankrupt, gives nothing back to the deprived victim. Legality is killing modern Society."]

In this ideal world of absolute government—an inevitable world, according to Blondet ("la royauté est éternelle" [royalty is eternal] [6: 392])—high finance would be governed by an exterior force. If *La Maison Nucingen* is the explanation, the justification, the instruction of a new system of speculation, the basis of the renovation of industry, it is also the teaching of a new form of literature. In the same way that the banker of genius teaches the timid in matters of speculation (Donnard 323–24), the narrator of genius is the founder of a social teaching, of a socially engaged literature, realistic in the sense of paying homage to the reality of life. If the new literature can go beyond the rules and the conventions, it is because there is an "absolute government" that allows it to do so, an Arbitrariness that is represented in this novella by the narrator-recorder, the secretary who reveals secrets. Nothing justifies better the role of the omnipresent, omniscient, omnipotent auditor—that is to say the reader—whose power Balzac obligingly recognizes: "Il y a toujours du monde à côté" [There are always people next door] (6: 392).

II

Semiotic Images of Realism

Myth and Mendacity
Pierrette *and* Beatrice Cenci

No tale is too slight, in *La Comédie humaine,* to bear a political burden, and *Pierrette,* as slight as its pitiful heroine, shoulders a disproportionately weighty charge. In this short novel of 1840, an innocent young girl dies, not just because of neglect and abuse by her hateful unmarried cousins, but also because of politics. Certainly Balzac intended to expose the harm caused by the *célibataires,* Sylvie and Jérôme-Denis Rogron, "célibataires sérieusement célibataires," as Balzac called them in his preface to the first edition (4: 24), but through their story his narrative emphasizes the fateful connection between Pierrette Lorrain's private story and the larger social theater. In the provincial town of Provins to which circumstances bring her, political passions rage, fueled by petty private ones. It is to these furious and devious party politics that Pierrette falls victim. Just before the end, the guilty partisans turn her story into a lie, first through a judicial *non-lieu,* dismissing the case, which is unjust, then by mendacious retellings. In the final paragraphs, Balzac turns her story into a myth.

Pierrette is one of the novels of *La Comédie humaine* in which the personal history of an individual is inflected toward myth, the enduring history of a type. Lise Queffélec's strong analysis of the mythic dimension of *La vieille fille,* which dominates the summary ending of that novel, connects myth with anthropology, the Balzacian science that allows us to make sense of a story. (According to *La vieille fille,* the lack of instruction in anthropology for all its people led France into the error of the July Monarchy.) In *Pierrette,* the key to this anthropology is the story of Beatrice Cenci, treated by Balzac as a mythic figure of innocence and purity sullied by political passions.

Pierrette's genealogy, shown schematically in figure 8.1, makes her a victim from the start. By virtue of M. Auffray's two marriages separated by fifty years, the family divides into two camps, which are diametrically opposed along several axes. On the side of the first Mme Auffray, mother of the ugly Mme Rogron and grandmother of the noxious *célibataires,* there is age, malice, avarice, hatred, health, longevity, and strength, while on the side of the second Mme Auffray, mother of the charming Mme Lorrain and grandmother of the adorable Pierrette, one finds youth, kindness, generosity, love, illness, mortality, and weakness. Even in the first description of Pierrette, as Véronique Bui has shown, she appears so ill and pale that she is compared to a funerary statue of marble (241). Rogron the father practiced usury and supplies his children with apprentices in what Bui has called a slave trade (242). His children, the retired mercers Sylvie and Jérôme-Denis, are narrow, cold, heartless, greedy, and stupid. At forty Sylvie looks like fifty. She especially is characterized by her implacable hatred, while Pierrette, "un de ces enfants de l'amour, que l'amour a doués de sa tendresse, de sa vivacité, de sa gaieté, de sa noblesse, de son dévouement" [one of those love children whom love has endowed with its tenderness, its vivacity, its gaiety, it nobility, and its devotion] (4: 77), "ne savait qu'aimer" [knew only how to love] (4: 79). She incarnates love and would, if she lived, make a marriage of love like her mother. On the Rogron side greedy business succeeds, whereas the Lorrain family goes bankrupt and lives at the mercy of others in an old-age hospice; all the Rogrons live long, while the second Mme Auffray dies at forty, her daughter Mme Lorrain dies the same year at about twenty-two, and Colonel Lorrain dies when Pierrette is only fourteen months old. Pierrette too will die young, as a teenager. In its systematic antithesis, this genetic structure, like most of Balzac's genealogies, is overwhelmingly significant, figuring both character and destiny. As an indicator of character, one can hardly fail to notice the roguish, grasping ill-humor suggested by the sonority of the name Rogron. Pierre Citron in the Preface to the Garnier-Flammarion edition unfolds Rogron into "le ton rogue d'un ogre qui gronde" [the arrogant tone of a scowling ogre] (36). Jean-Louis Tritter for his part hears in it "la grognerie, la rogne et le grondement" [growling, crossness, and snarling] (Introduction, 4: 18). Finally, Jean-Hervé Donnard speaks of "Rogron, ce sinistre crétin, qui étale sa vanité" [Rogron, that sinister moron who displays his vanity] (293).

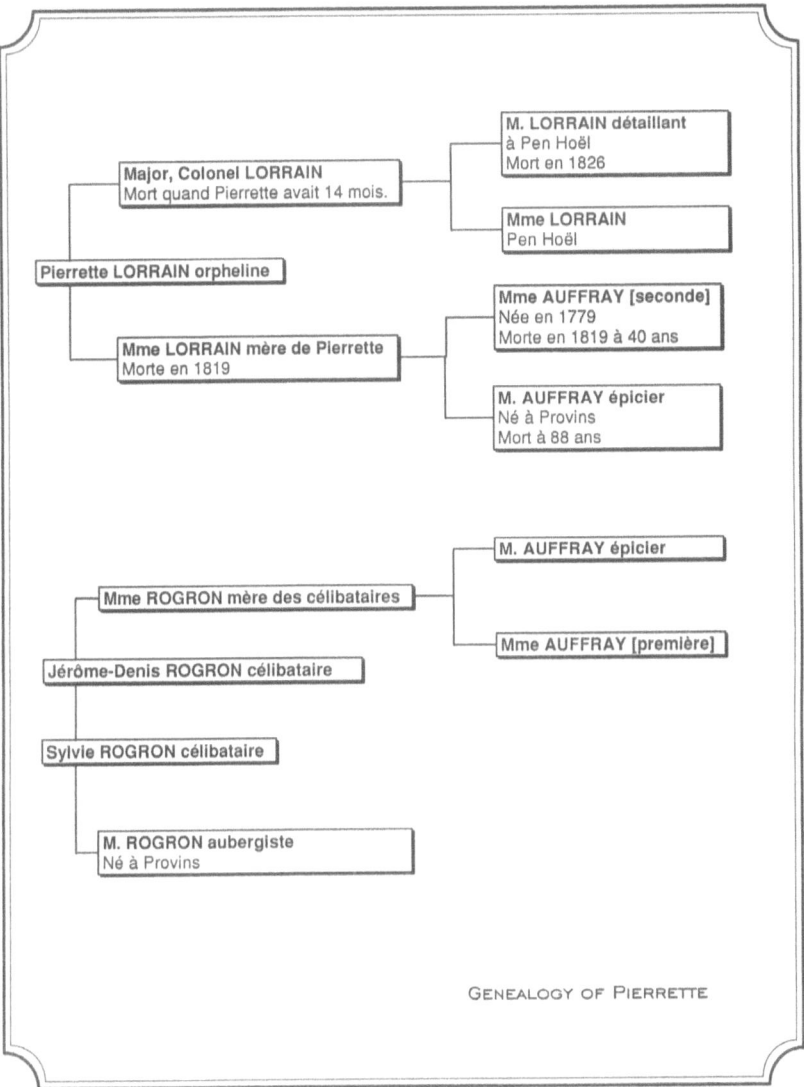

Figure 8.1 *Pierrette* genealogy

Orphaned at an early age, raised by her grandparents on her father's side, Pierrette resembles the chaste and virginal Virginie in *Paul et Virginie*, a comparison Balzac twice brings to our attention. Nicole Mozet, however, calls *Pierrette* the anti-*Paul et Virginie*, "la revanche brutale du social sur la nature" [the brutal revenge of the social on nature] (*La ville de province* 212). But I believe Bernardin de Saint-Pierre's novel already represents the brutal revenge of the social on nature. *Paul et Virginie* contains this very thesis in its ending: Virginie dies because she has been sent away to France and has lost the natural innocence of her childhood. In Balzac's novel, Pierrette's native Brittany stands for her primitive, innocent life, full of natural affection, as the Ile de France (her island home) does for Virginie. Brittany is Pierrette's lost paradise. Pierre Citron describes it as "une province reculée, peu atteinte par la civilisation, et où se conservent des traditions de naturel, de simplicité et de générosité" [a remote province, scarcely touched by civilization, where traditions of nature, simplicity, and generosity are preserved] (Preface 23). Everything that comes from this distant and utopian province is charming, gay, natural, beautiful—like the song Brigaut sings, Pierrette's Breton bonnet, her manners, and even her silvery voice. The sixteen-year-old Jacques Brigaut, who follows her to Provins, is her Paul (one who eventually seeks but cannot find the romantic death of his model), while Provins figures the regulated society that imposes other rules upon Pierrette (such as the need to learn what a young woman should know). Her half first cousin Sylvie, like Virginie's aunt in France, represents the social ethos, an influence contradicting nature in this case as in the earlier novel, and for very similar reasons—primarily celibacy, misplaced pride, and greed.

As long as Sylvie is compared to Virginie's unmarried aunt in France and not to her mother Mme de la Tour or Paul's mother Marguerite, both ideal Balzacian maternal figures, *Pierrette* is a *Paul et Virginie* for the 1840s. Just as Virginie dies because of the inflexible social and colonial forces still powerful at the end of the eighteenth century, overwhelming the gentle qualities of nature, Pierrette dies the victim of forces characteristic of the time when the novel takes place—near the end of the monarchy. These forces are money fueling political ambition, born of materialism and "l'empire accordé par les lois à l'argent" [the power granted by laws to money] (4: 94). As Citron notes: "L'important est le pouvoir, lequel s'obtient par l'argent, lequel à son tour ne s'obtient vite que par le mariage ou l'héritage" [The important thing is power, which is obtained by money, which in turn is obtained quickly only through marriage or inheritance] (Preface 45).

As the first of the three novels grouped in *Les célibataires*, *Pierrette* paints the moral portrait of a particular social segment and its effects in the context where it occurs. The portrait of the *célibataires* is set amid a generalized lowering of social rank in Provins. There is no viable aristocracy except as a bourgeoisie with pretensions ("l'aristocratie bourgeoise et ministérielle de la ville haute" [the ministerial bourgeois aristocracy of the upper section of the city] [4: 72]), while the Rogrons' post-mercantile rank is lower yet, symbolically set in the "ville basse" [lower section of the city]. Jean-Louis Tritter, in his introduction to *Pierrette* in the Pléiade edition, notes that the party in power scuttles itself, and that in a sense Provins represents "le symbole de la France royaliste en décomposition" [the symbol of a decomposing Royalist France] (4: 14). Having left behind the world of commerce and returned to Provins, Rogron brother and sister represent the nefarious class of the idle former merchant. Stupidly believing that they can now "be" bourgeois because they have amassed enough wealth to stop working, they incarnate the maxim "Tout marchand aspire à la bourgeoisie" [Every merchant aspires to join the bourgeois class] (4: 46), by which Balzac early suggests a source of the harm to be done to Pierrette. The Rogron house apes bourgeois style in comic exaggeration; it is the old maid's mania, the "affection factice" [artificial attachment] that replaces natural affections for the *célibataires* (4: 78–79). With nothing to do, excluded from the bourgeois salons, Sylvie and Jérôme-Denis are easily snatched up by the loosely grouped liberals, cunning schemers with shady pasts. When the Rogrons acquire Pierrette, they happily return to their old cruel habits as despots of their apprentices, when they were mercers, and their boredom vanishes.

Shaped by this social climate, the political drama around Pierrette starts in 1824 when she is sent to live in Provins at the end of her eleventh year; she dies in March 1828, at Easter, and the novel closes with the political destinies of the town's bourgeois forces after 1830. In its narrative design and chronology, the novel links Pierrette's story tightly with the political one: events of Pierrette's life are simultaneous with political events, and the narration alternates between political episodes and episodes concerning Pierrette. Not only do political explanations intervene in the narration of Pierrette's story, but, moreover, Pierrette's story serves political interests directly. Provins had never had a liberal party of any consequence until she came. Her arrival in Provins is the object of careful study by the scattered elements of the opposition, to which the new situation at the Rogrons' house gives the consistency it lacked. To show this connection between the personal and the political, a paragraph describing the beginnings of intrigues immediately follows the short summary of the first of three phases in Pierrette's life (4: 83). With Rogron as their moneybags, Vinet, Gouraud, and others form a liberal party which figures the forces of greed and hatred in the political arena as much as the *célibataires* represent cruelty and malice in the genealogical sphere. (Jean-Louis Tritter ranks the novel among those where "Balzac attaque le plus violemment les libéraux" [Balzac attacks liberals the most violently] ["A propos des épreuves" 29].) Even as the party is just being constituted, as the political intrigues are just starting to ferment, Pierrette is already described as its victim. Because Mme Tiphaine's salon scorns Sylvie while admitting the charming Pierrette, Sylvie becomes the implacable enemy of the established party headed by the Tiphaines. The wily lawyer Vinet exploits Sylvie's hatred and founds a newspaper paid for by Jérôme-Denis Rogron. Balzac's text repeatedly emphasizes how tightly the formation of the liberal party is linked to Pierrette: "Au moment où, pendant que sa femme donnait les cartes, l'avocat expliquait l'importance que Rogron, le colonel et lui, Vinet, acquerraient par la publication d'une feuille indépendante pour l'arrondissement de Provins, Pierrette fondait en larmes" [While his wife was dealing the cards, at the moment when the lawyer was explaining the importance that Rogron, the colonel, and he, Vinet, would acquire through the publication of an independent newspaper for the Provins arrondissement, Pierrette was bursting into tears] (4: 87). Vinet's ambitions against the rich and powerful have a horrible influence on Pierrette's destiny comparable to the malignant mercantilism of her cousins.

The political rivalry fatefully predestines Pierrette to harm, like the predetermined outcome of a myth: "Provins ne devait pas moins être funeste à Pierrette que les antécédants commerciaux de ses cousins" [Provins would not be less fatal to Pierrette than her cousins' commercial background] (4: 50). She becomes the token shifted about on the game board by the several squabbling interests, the pieces thrown down as the stakes in the game. By the time the drama reaches its crisis, Pierrette's destiny has become inextricably embroiled in politics, and Balzac insists on reminding us of it, underscoring the simultaneity of Pierrette's illness and the most recent developments in the partisan war (4: 143); describing political events that have a great influence on the trial concerning Rogron's guardianship of Pierrette (4: 152); pithily condemning Vinet's lies: "Le procès se plaidait. Pendant que la victime des Rogron se mourait, Vinet la calomniait au tribunal" [The case was being heard. While the Rogrons' victim was dying, Vinet was slandering her before the court] (4: 157). The maneuvers of the opposed camps both exploit and depend on Pierrette's martyrdom. André Vanoncini calls this chillingly effective source of evil a dramatic, multidimensional machine (262). Lying, betrayal, and deceit are the hallmarks of the multidimensional political action as it takes the young girl into the teeth of the machine. The play could hardly be more somber, a tenebrous *Scène de la vie politique*

Balzac could have added (along with others) to that much under-populated rubric.

As the liberal party is planted in the fertile soil of Sylvie's hatred, the political passion feeds and is fed by private ones centered on Pierrette. Balzac carefully makes the connection: "La prochaine arrivée de Pierrette hâta de faire éclore les pensées cupides inspirées par l'ignorance et par la sottise des deux célibataires" [Pierrette's imminent arrival hastened the hatching of covetous thoughts inspired by the ignorance and stupidity of the two bachelors] (4: 69). By a law of his world, every *célibataire* wants a spouse, and that impulse toward marriage figures the passion driving all movement in this novel, where the comedy of marriage exactly aligns with the political comedy. Balzac engages in some of his most tortuous language to describe what must be taken as the desire of the *vieille fille*. Here is a sample:

> Ces calculs profonds ne parlent pas aussi brutalement que l'histoire les exprime. Vouloir rendre les circonlocutions, les précautions oratoires, les longues conversations où l'esprit obscurcit à dessein la lumière qu'il y porte, où la parole mielleuse délaie le venin de certaines intentions, ce serait tenter un livre aussi long que le magnifique poème appelé *Clarisse Harlowe*. (4: 101)

> [These deep calculations do not speak as brutally as the story expresses them. To want to express the circumlocutions, the oratorical precautions, the long conversations where the mind purposefully obscures the light it brings to it, where honeyed speech dilutes the venom of certain intentions, would be to attempt a book as long as the magnificent poem called *Clarissa Harlowe*.]

Intrigues link the private politics of an inheritance to be won, if not stolen from its deserving owner, to the public politics in which power depends on connections. Marriages are plotted like political alliances, for purposes of power and not for love, affection, or family (in truth, somewhat business as usual). In her maniacal urge to marry, Sylvie casts her eye on colonel Gouraud and absurdly finds a rival in Pierrette. Such a rivalry recalls one of the stock situations of the comic theater, here strangely distorted and deviously twisted by Sylvie's atrocious hatred. Only Sylvie could imagine the misalliance of the fourteen-year-old Pierrette with the blustery colonel more than three times her age. As for Gouraud, eager for the old maid's money, he thinks nothing of blaming Pierrette (while at the same time thinking of marrying her in case she should inherit): "Le colonel Gouraud, jaloux de plaire à Mlle Rogron, lui donnait raison en tout ce qui concernait Pierrette. Vinet appuyait également les deux parents en tout ce qu'ils disaient contre Pierrette" [Colonel Gouraud, eager to please Mlle Rogron, agreed with her in everything concerning Pierrette. Vinet also supported the two siblings in everything they said against Pierrette] (4: 89). Exploiting these marital intrigues, both Vinet and Tiphaine, on opposite sides of the political fence, play Pierrette for their strategic purposes: "[Vinet] eut bientôt trouvé le moyen de perdre à la fois Pierrette et le colonel, espérant être débarrassé de l'un par l'autre" [[Vinet] had soon found the means of destroying both Pierrette and the colonel, hoping to be rid of one through the other] (4: 104); "Ainsi le Président [Tiphaine] vit dans la cause entre Pierrette et les Rogron un moyen d'abattre, de déconsidérer, de déshonorer [l'Opposition]" [Thus the President saw in the case between Pierrette and the Rogrons a means of demolishing, of discrediting, of dishonoring [the Opposition]] (4: 143). Pierrette is truly "cette enfant broyée entre des intérêts implacables" [this child crushed between implacable interests] (4: 96).

In such a way does the bourgeoisie of the town acquire a guilty conscience—and so it will retell Pierrette's story to suit itself. As Balzac pithily writes, "L'intérêt général exigeait l'abaissement de cette pauvre victime" [The general welfare called for the abasement of this poor victim] (4: 96). Sylvie's mounting jealousy has boiled over the political pot. Sent away by the furious old maid, Pierrette walks into a door in the dark, strikes her head at the temple and develops a subdural hematoma (Van den Doel 1291); at the same time, suspected of receiving a love letter from Gouraud, she is attacked by Sylvie, who bashes her hand to a bloody mess. The injuries compound her chlorosis (greensickness), an enfeebling anemic illness of adolescent girls that fascinated Balzac, and lead to the melodramatic arrival of her grandmother, Mme Lorrain, the mother of Pierrette's father. With her "colère divine" [divine fury] and her visionary ability to "read" Pierrette's entire story (4: 140), Mme Lorrain appears as a mythological figure, an intervention of a force of good. The doctors too, including Bianchon and Desplein, are on the side of truth—a constant in *La Comédie humaine*. Toward the end, while the waning life in Pierrette's fragile body depends on a final heroic medical operation, trepanation or trephining, the demonstration of the harm caused by the two *célibataires* is summarized in several restatements. These results are announced in logical fashion with a phrase beginning "Ainsi, l'épouvantable martyre exercé brutalement sur Pierrette par deux imbéciles tyrans" [Thus the dreadful martyr brutally exercised upon Pierrette by two imbecilic tyrants] (4: 152). The true account Pierrette tells her grandmother, the first of the several retellings, is nevertheless powerless in the face of those that follow, narratives of mendacity and myth.

The revisions of Pierrette's story arise in a number of legal proceedings that stem from the crisis—appropriately so, to the extent that they are trial testimony, but they also occur as rumors and innuendoes. Although for the most part the struggle goes in Pierrette's favor, when she dies, the last legal action, a criminal trial against Jérôme-Denis Rogron, ends officially in a *non-lieu,* and no one is left to counter the lies that follow. From the start, Balzac had announced, as is his wont, a "drama" (by which he often meant a tragedy), and clearly this concerns Pierrette's present life in Provins, just as the expression "son histoire" [her story] (4: 36) signifies her past. By the end, both the story and the drama have been taken over by the political forces of the town—and of the narrative. The retellings are all that will remain of the plot.

What makes the lies insidious is that they are not entirely fiction. It is a matter of verbiage masking the truth, and this structure of mendacity is anchored in the character of the two bachelors. From the start, Denis Rogron's stupidity is "parleuse" [talkative] (4: 44). Thus is established in the story an exemplar of speech unhinged from a content; his verbiage is empty, not to say false. Even though Rogron has little role in the retelling, which is given to third parties, empty verbiage is an ingredient in the mendacity that reigns at the end, for which the reader has been well prepared. Similarly, Sylvie has, since adolescence, two masks: the face she makes up to show her clients in her fabric store, and the real face, which is natural to old maids (4: 45). In like manner, her hideous behavior toward Pierrette is now masked by the lies others tell. Balzac thus establishes a semiotic system giving consistency and presence to mendacity. As the novel approaches its end, the retellings of Pierrette's story perpetuate this system. After the judge pronounces an order in Pierrette's favor, Vinet inaugurates a mendacious version of her story: "Et tout ce bruit pour une petite fille qui entretenait une intrigue avec un garçon menuisier!" [And all this fuss for a little girl who was having a romantic intrigue with a carpenter boy!] (4: 149). He goes around explaining to his political cohorts: "Sylvie, fille éminemment sage et religieuse [and that is her mask], avait découvert une intrigue entre la pupille de son frère et un petit ouvrier menuisier, un Breton nommé Brigaut. Ce drôle savait très bien que la petite fille allait avoir une fortune de sa grand-mère, il voulait la suborner" [Sylvie, an eminently decent and religious woman [and that is her mask], had uncovered an amorous intrigue between her brother's pupil and a little carpentry worker, a Breton named Brigaut. The rascal knew perfectly well that the young girl was going to inherit a fortune from her grandmother; he wanted to suborn her] (4: 149).

This version lies at a considerable distance from the truth we have been told throughout the story. The Conseil de Famille, another legal proceeding with testimony, hears the same story: that there was an amorous intrigue between Pierrette and Brigaut (4: 150–51).

To one particular character belong the most important retellings, including the last one: the magistrate Desfondrilles. He is first described as a "juge-suppléant" [surrogate judge], "plus archéologue que magistrat" [more of an archeologist than a magistrate] (4: 64). Studying the past and seeking to restore it in the present, on the one hand, and making judgments and promulgating legal opinions, on the other, Desfondrilles serves as the perfect figure combining myth and mendacity: he is one who can make a lie into a vital, enduring, and signifying story. Desfondrilles is an "homme fin . . . qui avait fini par s'amuser de tous les intérêts en jeu dans Provins" [astute man . . . who had come to enjoy all the interests at play in Provins] (4: 123). He has no serious role until the last pages, when his double authority as judge and archeologist will bring to Pierrette's life, beyond her death, a closure without appeal. At the moment he is introduced in the novel, he is acting like an archeologist, calling for a bas-relief to commemorate Provins's glorious past as a capital (4: 65). (The mention of the bas-relief, as a symbolic representation of history, foreshadows the portrait of Beatrice Cenci, which follows upon Desfondrilles's retelling of Pierrette's story.) By the time Rogron is being tried, Desfondrilles has become the *juge d'instruction* (investigating magistrate) in Provins, and three pages before the end, when he reports to the court, "le Tribunal rendit un jugement de non-lieu parfaitement motivé" [the Court rendered a perfectly justified judgment of case dismissed] (4: 160).

By then, no one who has dabbled in Pierrette's death admits the least remnant of guilt, and Desfondrilles caps the general amnesty of the bourgeoisie with this astonishing, brilliant retelling:

> —Affaire de parti, répond le président Desfondrilles. On a voulu faire croire à des monstruosités [on the part of the Rogron bachelors]. Par bonté d'âme, ils ont pris chez eux cette Pierrette, petite fille assez gentille et sans fortune; au moment de se former, elle eut une intrigue avec un garçon menuisier, elle venait pieds nus à sa fenêtre y causer avec ce garçon qui se tenait là, voyez-vous? Les deux amants s'envoyaient des billets doux au moyen d'une ficelle. Vous comprenez que dans son état, aux mois d'octobre et de novembre, il n'en fallait pas davantage pour faire aller à mal une fille qui avait les pâles couleurs. Les Rogron se sont admirablement bien conduits, ils n'ont pas réclamé leur part de l'héritage de cette petite, ils ont tout abandonné à sa

8: Myth and Mendacity

grand-mère. La morale de cela, mes amis, est que le diable nous punit toujours d'un bienfait. (4: 162)

["A partisan affair," answers president Desfondrilles. "They wanted to make people believe there were monstrosities [on the part of the Rogron bachelors]. Out of the kindness of their souls, they took in this Pierrette, a rather nice little girl without a fortune; as she was becoming a young woman, she had an amorous intrigue with a carpenter boy, she would come to her window in her bare feet to chat with the boy who stood over there, you see? The two lovers sent each other love letters by means of a string. You understand that in her state, during the months of October and November, little else was needed for such a pale-colored girl to go bad. The Rogrons behaved themselves admirably; they did not claim their part in this little girl's inheritance; they gave up everything to her grandmother. The moral of all this, my friends, is that the devil always punishes us for a good action."]

None of the events is actually changed, but, like the other retellings, *everything* is slanted to protect the guilty. The "épouvantable vérité" [dreadful truth] is known only to Brigaut and the doctor Martener (4: 162), after Mme Lorrain has died. In the lines that follow this retelling, myth joins these lies to further obscure the truth.

For Balzac too retells Pierrette's story in the penultimate paragraph, balancing mendacity with a powerful myth: he compares her to Beatrice Cenci, hoping to grant a mythic dimension to his less famous story and to compel the reader's involvement in making his delicate narrative more significant than mere history, drama, or story: "Pour donner à ceci d'immenses proportions, il suffit de rappeler qu'en transportant la scène au Moyen Âge et à Rome sur ce vaste théâtre, une jeune fille sublime, Béatrix Cenci, fut conduite au supplice par des raisons et par des intrigues presque analogues à celles qui menèrent Pierrette au tombeau" [To give immense proportions to this, it suffices to remember that, transporting the scene to the Middle Ages and to the vast theater that was Rome, a sublime young girl, Beatrice Cenci, was led to her execution for reasons and intrigues almost analogous to those that led Pierrette to her grave] (4: 162). The sixteen-year-old Beatrice Cenci was condemned by the pope to be beheaded in 1599 for having her father killed, after he had long abused her. But the comparison is troubling. Little of Beatrice's story explains Pierrette's. There are some elements in common: the suffering of the heroine, the injustices and the persecution by judicial forces of which she was victim, her calm stoicism and her resistance to pain, and a wound to the head (Count Cenci is said to have stomped on his daughter's head). Yet, while the Cenci story involves evil, private passions, and politics, all of which do occur in *Pierrette,* it tells us nothing about the evil that Balzac specifically castigates while exposing it in horrifying detail: celibacy. More important, the key terms determining Beatrice's guilt and innocence are absent from Pierrette's life and death. Nothing resembling rape, incest, parricide, or execution by beheading occurs in *Pierrette,* and the moral ambiguities that make the Cenci story both fascinating and disturbing would seem to make Beatrice ill-suited to confer on Pierrette a quasi-divine aura. Furthermore, although Balzac claims that now "l'histoire et les vivants . . . condamnent le pape, et font de Béatrix une des plus touchantes victimes des passions infâmes et des factions" [history and the living . . . condemn the pope, and make Beatrice one of the most moving victims of infamous passions and factions] (4: 162–63), it is not certain that the living and the dead have so universally condemned Beatrice Cenci's punishment by the forces of the pope. The two important nineteenth-century versions of the story by Stendhal and Percy Bysshe Shelley are less partisan.

Long before Balzac mentions it, the Cenci story had achieved a kind of mythic quality, partly because it existed from the start in several narrations, which were produced for particular purposes to persuade people, and partly because it involved archetypal family relationships. As Antonin Artaud wrote of his play *Les Cenci,* "le père est destructeur. Et c'est par là que ce sujet rejoint les Grands Mythes" [the father is destructive. And that is the reason this subject belongs with the Great Myths] (cited in di Maio 161). Derrida in his study of Artaud also mentions parricide as a mythic origin of theater: "Un meurtre est toujours à l'origine de la cruauté, de la nécessité nommée cruauté. Et d'abord un parricide. L'origine du théâtre, telle qu'on doit la restaurer, c'est une main portée contre le détenteur abusif du logos, contre le père, contre le Dieu d'une scène soumise au pouvoir de la parole et du texte" [A murder is always at the origin of cruelty, of the necessity named cruelty. And above all a parricide. The origin of theater, such as we should understand it, is a hand raised against the abusive detainer of the Logos, against the father, against the God of a stage subject to the power of speech and of the text] (350).

Clearly for Balzac too the central figure had the quality of myth. It is virtually certain that Balzac knew Stendhal's narrative "Les Cenci," published in *La Revue des deux mondes* in 1837. In addition to the circumstantial proof of chronology and Balzac's interest in Stendhal, both Stendhal and Balzac consider the 1500s part of the "Moyen Âge";[1] this usage is all the more aberrant in that Beatrice Cenci died in the last year of the sixteenth century; if Balzac too speaks of "Moyen Âge," it is likely he borrowed this detail from Stendhal. Several readers have shown the influence of Stendhal on *Pierrette,* particularly in the description of the love between Pierrette and Brigaut. "Les Cenci" was published among the *Chroniques italiennes,* eight narratives Stendhal borrowed and retold from manuscripts obtained in Italy. In translating and adapting the account found in the manuscript, he both omitted some of the most gruesome and obscene particulars and added to the original, especially to contribute psychological motivations and to clarify points of detail; he also elaborated on the portraits of both father and daughter. Unlike Shelley's play, Stendhal does not give us to understand that Francesco Cenci actually raped his daughter. In any case, those who tried to save Beatrice from capital punishment argued self-defense, and Stendhal added a considerable paragraph on this topic.

Alexandre Dumas also retold the Cenci story based on similar manuscripts, and unlike Stendhal did not stint on the description of the gruesome murder of Francesco Cenci and the official tortures of Beatrice and her family. Like Stendhal's *Chroniques italiennes,* Dumas's "Les Cenci" was published in 1839, the first of his *Crimes célèbres,* just when Balzac was writing *Pierrette;* it too was based on Roman manuscripts that Dumas probably saw when he traveled to Rome in 1835 (Del Litto 230–32). It is very likely that Balzac read Dumas's account as well.

Shelley too was given a manuscript "copied from the archives of the Cenci Palace at Rome" early in his self-exile in Italy, in Livorno in 1818 ("Preface" to *The Cenci* 2). Stephen C. Behrendt observes about Shelley's tragedy,

> *The Cenci* is the record of a failed revolution, a rebellion that proceeds to its catastrophe from that most traditional, mythic spring: the conflict between generation and generation, between parent and child. . . . Beatrice's dilemma parallels those both of women during Shelley's era . . . and of the British populace generally. . . . Hence her situation and the choices she makes are invested with a significance far greater than the merely historical. (218)

The story assumes the nature and significance of myth, Behrendt believes, because it follows the Aristotelian precept of reducing the events to univer-

---

1. Quoted in a note to *La physiologie du mariage* (11: 1830, note 3), Geneviève Delattre observes that "Balzac inclut assez volontiers le XVIe siècle dans le Moyen Âge" [Balzac quite habitually includes the sixteenth century in the Middle Ages] (*Les opinions littéraires* 7).

sal form; the thing that has happened becomes the thing that might happen (224). Balzac claims something like this when he speaks of granting immense proportions to his fable. It would then become "une histoire, une fable symbolique, simple et frappante, résumant un nombre infini de situations plus ou moins analogues" [a story, a symbolic fable, simple and striking, summing up an infinite number of more or less analogous situations], according to the broad definition of myth proposed by Denis de Rougemont (cited in Brunel, "Mythanalyse" 41).

Myth redefines the drama of the present as a story of the past. When Balzac replaces the lies of the Provinois with the "touching" story of the "sublime" Beatrice Cenci, who was martyred for reasons and intrigues "presque analogues à celles qui menèrent Pierrette au tombeau" [almost analogous to those that led Pierrette to her grave] (4: 162), we are obliged to consider how Pierrette's drama is transformed. It is strange that Balzac chose the Cenci story to orient the reader toward a wider interpretation of his not immense story ("Pour donner à ceci d'immenses proportions" [To give immense proportions to this]), where earlier allusions to *Paul et Virginie* and to Cinderella (4: 121) had already provided closer mythological models.

Like Bernardin de Saint-Pierre's Virginie, the universal Beatrice stands for a childlike innocence and purity, but she is tainted by guilt. Shelley writes in his preface: "Beatrice Cenci appears to have been one of those rare persons in whom energy and gentleness dwell together without destroying one another: her nature was simple and profound" (7). He claims she maintains her innocence in the face of the blight, poison, and corruption around her. Crimes and evil were merely the mask and mantle of circumstances. As Laurence S. Lockridge has written, "Shelley has used the strongest possible images of violation and contamination to make vivid the fact of evil having been forced upon her from without. . . . *The Cenci* portrays a world so evil that it can tragically infect the innocent" (98). For Stuart Curran, "As a work of the theater *The Cenci* stands today where Artaud left it [after adapting Shelley's play], capable of that 'unrelenting incandescence' of psychological truth he envisioned, the mythic record of an innocence resolutely reduced to despair and redeemed by the human power to accept the absurd and thereby triumph over it" (280). Balzac's view of Beatrice is similar to these. The Stendhalian coloration of the heroine may also have contributed to the entirely sympathetic notion Balzac had of her. Moreover, the fact that Beatrice was tortured by the pope's judges may have been in Balzac's mind as he evoked the mythic dimension; the Cenci story ends in a case of *official* torture, ordered by the pope. Judging from the use Balzac makes of the Cenci story, he must have believed that infamous passions and political factions made a victim of Beatrice; it was of secondary importance that she had her father killed. It is as if he neglects all but the rape and the trial phase of her story, in which she is, in small part, the game piece shifted on the playing field of interests barely related to her actions. In short, the mythic dimension of Beatrice Cenci's drama, which many writers since Balzac have also observed, works its primary effect on Balzac. It is this rather than the historical image that must have captured Balzac. (Among his *Pensées, sujets, et fragments* was the plan to write a five-act drama on Beatrice's fate.)

Of great significance in this mythological reading of the Cenci story is the painted portrait of the heroine (see figure 8.2). As Balzac wrote: "Aujourd'hui l'histoire et les vivants, *sur la foi du portrait de Guido Reni,* condamnent le pape, et font de Béatrix une des plus touchantes victimes des passions infâmes et des factions" [Today, history and the living, *on the strength of the portrait by Guido Reni,* condemn the pope and make Beatrice one of the most moving victims of infamous passions and factions] (4: 162–63; emphasis added). Louise Barnett, among others, informs us that the portrait thought to be by Guido Reni was considered the high point of a tourist's visit to Rome by the early nineteenth century. Poorly executed copies were to be found in every shop. "Their purchasers were attracted not by art but by the titillating Cenci history which the portrait mediated" (170). Shelley had such a copy, and he comments on its fame by noting that his servant instantly recognized its subject ("Preface" 3). The cloth draped on Beatrice's body and the turban from which her blond hair escapes suggest the dress she designed for her execution, according to Stendhal's narrative. Trollope, Taine, and Dickens wrote about the portrait, Stendhal too. A contemporary account written in 1838 by one Valery glowed with admiration:

> La pathétique tête de la Cenci, coiffée avec élégance et coquetterie, ouvrage présumé de la première jeunesse du Guide, aurait été faite de mémoire après avoir vu l'héroïne monter à l'échafaud. . . . La Cenci . . . était le vrai type de la jeune fille italienne, et la tête attribuée au Guide a merveilleusement exprimé ce caractère ardent, naïf et tendre. (cited in *Chroniques italiennes* 1: 479–80)

> [The Cenci girl's pitiable head, dressed with elegance and affectation, the presumed work of Guido's earliest period, was thought to have been painted from memory after having seen the heroine mount the scaffold. . . . The Cenci girl . . . was the true type of a young Italian girl, and the head attributed to Guido marvelously expressed this ardent, naive, and tender character.]

Nathaniel Hawthorne waxed rhapsodic about the portrait in his journal in 1858:

> its spell is indefinable, and the painter has wrought it in a way more like magic than anything else I have known. . . . It is the very saddest picture that ever was painted, or conceived; there is an unfathomable depth and sorrow in the eyes; the sense of it comes to you by a sort of intuition. It is a sorrow that removes her out of the sphere of humanity; and yet she looks so innocent. . . . It is the most profoundly wrought picture in the world; no artist did it, nor could do it again. Guido may have held the brush, but he painted better than he knew. (cited in Barnett 168)

Shelley wrote with a similar fervor in his preface to *The Cenci,* describing the portrait as

> a just representation of one of the loveliest specimens of the workmanship of Nature. There is a fixed and pale composure upon the features: she seems sad and stricken down in spirit, yet the despair thus expressed is lightened by the patience of gentleness. Her head is bound with folds of white drapery from which the yellow strings of her golden hair escape, and fall about her neck. The moulding of her face is exquisitely delicate; the eyebrows are distinct and arched; the lips have that permanent meaning of imagination and sensibility which suffering has not repressed and which it seems as if death scarcely could extinguish. Her forehead is large and clear; her eyes, which we are told were remarkable for their vivacity, are swollen with weeping and lustreless, but beautifully tender and serene. In the whole mien there is a simplicity and dignity which united with her exquisite loveliness and deep sorrow are inexpressibly pathetic. ("Preface" 6–7)

In Hawthorne's *The Marble Faun,* in Melville's *Pierre,* and in two of Edith Wharton's novels, the portrait serves to evoke the theme of incest. Unfortunately, since late in the nineteenth century, art historians have known that it is neither of Beatrice nor by Guido Reni—unknown painter, unknown subject.

It is possible that Balzac first came to know the story of the Cenci because of the painting. He limns Pierrette's description in the manner of a painted portrait (4: 155) and describes her eyes in a language that echoes the enthusiastic descriptions of the painting: "avec des yeux d'une tendresse à réchauffer un cœur mort" [with eyes containing such tenderness as would warm up a lifeless heart] (4: 106). There is one other significant mention of Beatrice Cenci in *La Comédie humaine,* in *La femme de trente ans* (2: 1205): "le

Figure 8.2 Presumed portrait of B. Cenci

visage de Béatrice Cenci où le Guide sut peindre la plus touchante innocence au fond du plus épouvantable crime" [Beatrice Cenci's face, where Guido was able to paint the most touching innocence behind the most appalling crime]. Appropriate for *La femme de trente ans,* this description acknowledges the horror of Beatrice Cenci's crime, unlike the reference in *Pierrette.* Only by separating the notion of the "plus épouvantable crime" from Pierrette's actions, and setting her undeniable innocence against a *background* of the "crimes" committed around her and against her, would the portrait fairly symbolize Pierrette. Barnett writes that "to the nineteenth century, Beatrice Cenci was the embodiment of victimization and crime on the level of the most ancient and absolute taboos" (170–71). In this novel, for Balzac, the painting expresses the suffering of young innocence, the embodiment of victimization without the crime and without the ancient taboos.

Yet the fact is that the mythic transfiguration brings Balzac's story to a *non-lieu* (a dismissed case) also. Is it possible that this is the final effect he sought? André Vanoncini has recently written of "la dissolution de l'histoire sous le régime du non-lieu" [the dissolution of the story under the order of the case dismissal] (260). Beatrice Martina Guenther seems to accept Balzac's belief that alluding to Beatrice Cenci transforms Pierrette's story into "an immortal work." As she writes, "The story of Pierrette's life (and the injustice she has suffered) will never be allowed to stop, and [the uplifting example guarantees] the narrative's continued existence" (121). However, "[b]y decentering his conclusion through the reference to Béatrix Cenci, the writer implicitly reenacts the persecution of Pierrette" (123). Ultimately, I believe, more is at stake than is apparent at first glance.

What, after all, happened? A young girl died. When the immense proportions of myth take over from that simple story, its destiny changes, just as its *destinataire* changes: the story is destined (both meanings) to reveal a deep narrative truth of Balzac's creation. When Pierrette's drama resolves, like a fadeout, into Beatrice Cenci's portrait, the myth eclipses the tragic conflict that has been played out, just as the new, powerful destinies of the bourgeoisie of Provins camouflage their small-minded meanness. It is significant that, in the July Monarchy where the novel ends, the opposed camps have dissolved, and Provins and the Provinois have come to new prominence based on the success of their maneuvers. Washed of guilt, the city folk achieve their goals. Vinet becomes deputy and *procureur-général,* Rogron is *receveur-général,* Tiphaine *premier président de la Cour Royale,* Gouraud becomes a general and has the peerage and the Légion d'honneur, etc. The new regime has soothed the political passions that raged so violently and pulverized Pierrette in their machinery. Like Pierrette's drama, the historical guilty conscience dissolves into a *non-lieu*. The failure of justice in the plot—not only in the court but in the moral domain of the novel—figures the dismissal of the narrative, which evaporates. Under such a whitewash, rare is the archeologist who might uncover Pierrette's memory. If, like an ornamental lion in Sylvie's gaudy living room, the commemorative icon were only a constitutional myth (4: 61), if the idea of a symbolic meaning were to be treated only as parody, then the immense proportions of myth would not transport Pierrette to the universal. Guided by his sentimental attraction for the painting, Balzac let Pierrette's private drama disappear. Nothing will have happened here except politics—lies and myths.

But the politics we must read, as the story's *destinataire*, are newly defined. Politics can touch individuals and families intimately, a concept that constitutes a major element of the determinism that lies as a deep-seated belief in *La Comédie humaine*. Moreover, the political message about lies and myths applies as well to the art of narrative writing: narrative resembles the political in that it deals in lies and myths. "Politics" so understood is the ultimate meaning here: about a narrative art more significant than mere history or small story, the narrative art of *La Comédie humaine,* placed in the immediate context of "aujourd'hui" [today] and of "l'histoire et les vivants" [history and the living] (4: 162). Whether Balzac knew it or not, by turning Pierrette's story into myth and mendacity, he lent greater weight to this deeper purpose, which we can find in the ending if we are good readers of myths and lies. The *artist* is the one who saves the story in spite of all—it is because the artist acts that what may have dissolved, what may have "not taken place," remains for the world to contemplate again and again, that the mythic portraits of young, lovely innocence and of old, hateful malignancy remain on the stage of the vast theater of Balzac's world, transported from the Roman "Middle Ages." In this light, the most significant phrase in the penultimate paragraph (the one about Beatrice Cenci), which comes between the comparison of Pierrette to Beatrice and the mention of the portrait and the condemnation of the pope, is this short sentence: "Béatrix Cenci n'eut pour tout défenseur qu'un artiste, un peintre" [Beatrice Cenci had an artist, a painter, as sole defender] (4: 162). Identifying with him, Balzac could claim: "Je serai celui-là." [I would be that one.] "Celui-là"? A kind of god, without a doubt. Only now does the final one-sentence paragraph betray its meaning and purpose, which is to elevate the preserver of this small story to divine existence: "Convenons entre nous que la Légalité serait, pour les friponneries sociales, une belle chose si Dieu n'existait pas" [Let us agree that Legality would be, for the rogues of society, a beautiful thing if God did not exist] (4: 163).

The Corset of La vieille fille

> O Rose, thou art sick!
> The invisible worm
> That flies in the night,
> In the howling storm,
>
> Has found out thy bed
> Of crimson joy,
> And his dark secret love
> Does thy life destroy.
>
> —William Blake, "The Sick Rose," 1794

As a piece of underwear, a corset would seem to have no plausible connection to actual writing; but as a semiotic device of mimesis, the corset worn by Rose Cormon in *La vieille fille* calls attention to the rhetoric of realism in this novel. Being semiotic, it functions as a reading device and therefore contributes to the description that an action illustrates. *La vieille fille,* an exceptional novel in many ways, poses a problem of interpretation that the device of the corset helps to solve: does the novel portray the failure of a fat old maid to marry, or is it the story of a girl's marriage?

Set, by its title, *against* the familiar marriage comedy (found in the *Modeste Mignons,* the *Béatrixes,* the *Contrats de mariage*) a book called *La vieille fille* should illustrate the comedy of *no* marriage—or its tragedy. The arrival of the third pretender to Mlle Cormon's hand, the well-named vicomte de Troisville, precipitates the actions of the first two, the chevalier de Valois and du Bousquier—but Troisville has no such pretension; he is only a "prétendu prétendu" [pretended pretender] (4: 903) (as always, Balzac cannot resist the profound witticism when it falls under his pen). When

Rose learns that Troisville has a wife and daughter, she faints, and the broad-shouldered but impotent du Bousquier carries her to her bedroom. There, unfortunately, he sees what spills out of her corset when her maid cuts it away. Clearly the corset plays a controlling part in the shape of the action, even though it is mentioned only three times, since it forces Mlle Cormon's hand in accepting du Bousquier's marriage proposal the next day. More to the point, this high burlesque becomes the rhetorical image of Rose's essence and of the novel's purpose. Her corset, the corset of Balzac's prose, should give a metonymic identity to the novel, as the typifying illustration of the old maid. Instead, Rose's corset does not contain her too plentiful contours any more than Balzac's title contains his writing.

For the first-time reader, a surprise of ample proportions squeezes out of the covers of the book. The novel spills over its title and its apparent theme, stretching the characteristic Balzacian definition of the *célibataire* found elsewhere (for instance in *Pierrette, Le curé de Tours,* and *La Rabouilleuse*), just as Rose's body overflows both above and below the corset that cannot define her shape. Escaping the confines of its constricting type-narrative, the novel does not illustrate the sterile, unmarriageable *vieille fille* but something very different: the amorous desire of a *jeune femme*.[1] The announced topic does not contain the story. As Patricia Kinder speculates, about the *feuilleton* publisher Émile Girardin, "S'était-il fié au titre, croyant trouver dans *La vieille fille* ... une œuvre dans le genre d'*Eugénie Grandet?*" [Had he relied on the title, expecting to find in *La vieille fille* ... a work in the manner of *Eugénie Grandet?*], while a critic from *La Phalange,* a rival review, complained: "Nous attendions un pendant au *Père Goriot* ou même d'*Eugénie Grandet;* le sujet semblait le promettre ... mais nous avouerons que la manière dont il a esquissé cette étrange anomalie de nos sociétés a trompé notre attente" [We expected a companion piece to *Le Père Goriot* or even *Eugénie Grandet;* the subject seemed to promise that ... but we admit that the way he has sketched this strange anomaly of our society has deceived our expectations] (Kinder 195, 197).

With the aplomb typical of Balzac's vigorous statements of opinion, the narrator tackles the question of the *type* in an imaginary debate with looser women than Rose: "Ici quelques femmes légères essaieront peut-être de chicaner la vraisemblance de ce récit, elles diront qu'il n'existe pas en France de fille assez niaise pour ignorer l'art de pêcher un homme, que Mlle Cormon est une de ces exceptions monstrueuses que le bon sens interdit de présenter

---

1. In this focus on the woman's desire, I am taking a different perspective from Fredric Jameson's reading in *The Political Unconscious,* e.g., 156.

comme type" [At this point, some facile women will perhaps try to dispute the plausibility of this narrative; they will say that nowhere in France does there exist a girl who is so stupid as to not know the art of catching a man, that Mlle Cormon is one of those monstrous exceptions that common sense forbids us to present as a type] (4: 862). But these criticisms fail, Balzac says, because Rose is Catholic. Poor argument! If she is a monstrous exception, she is not out to land a husband; but if she is a type, then she wants a husband, for even if a *fille* is a *vieille fille,* then it follows by Balzacian necessity, no matter what the narrator may claim, that she desires a man. This is the conundrum signaled by the semiotic device of the corset.

I take Rose Cormon's corset as an emblem of metonymy understood partly as the container signifying the contained. Philippe Perrot writes of this essential undergarment, "Prendre la taille, soutenir les seins, faire rebondir la croupe, cambrer une silhouette selon les canons érotico-esthétiques du moment, constituent une de ses principales destinations" [To take in the waist, support the breasts, round out the buttocks, give camber to the silhouette according to the erotico-esthetic canons of the moment was one of its principal functions] (268). With the help of Rose's corset, paradoxically, *La vieille fille* profiles the hidden contour of sexual desire. To be sure, the word "désir" occurs freely in the text—but corseted, molded, reshaped to mean something else: desire for marriage, desire for children, desire for "le bonheur." These are some of the metonyms, which are clearly displacements, by which the subject of sexual desire escapes. The corset traces the action of this displaced discourse. I acknowledge Éric Bordas's warning that "Toute traduction de la métaphore est un appauvrissement, et l'érotique jouit des détours qu'elle impose aux discours conducteurs" [Any translation of a metaphor is an impoverishment, and eroticism profits from the detours it imposes on the conveying discourse] ("Ne touchez pas le H" 27–28). It is such detours that interest me, rather than the translation of the metaphor or metonymy.[2]

2. Bordas also comments that Balzac refuses indecent language: "Même certaines notations de *La vieille fille* (1837), pourtant fort orientées, comme celle dans laquelle il est dit qu'il 'fallait le silence de la nuit' à mademoiselle Cormon pour 'épouser en pensée' quelque sous-lieutenant, ce qui vaut à Pérotte de retrouver le lendemain 'le lit de sa maîtresse cen dessus dessous' (*VF,* IV, 860–61), relèvent du comique satirique et non de la gauloiserie paillarde: la représentation a une finalité de déconstruction critique, soupçonneuse, presque méchante" [Even certain remarks in *La vieille fille* (1837), although they are quite tendentious, like the one which says that Mlle Cormon "needed the silence of the night" to "marry in her mind" some second lieutenant, with the result that Pérotte finds "her mistress's bed all atumble" the next morning, are satirical comedy and not bawdy gauloiserie: such representation has a critically deconstructive, suspicious, almost unkind purpose] ("Ne touchez pas le H" 28–29).

9: The Corset of La vieille fille

Rose Cormon is defined by two qualities incompatible with the contour-giving task of a corset: "la force et l'abondance, les deux caractères principaux de sa personne" [heaviness and abundance, the two principal qualities of her person] (4: 857). With the years, we are told, fat had so badly distributed itself about her body that

> il en avait détruit les primitives proportions. En ce moment, aucun corset ne pouvait faire retrouver de hanches à la pauvre fille, qui semblait fondue d'une seule pièce. La jeune harmonie de son corsage n'existait plus, et son ampleur excessive faisait craindre qu'en se baissant elle ne fût emportée par ces masses supérieures; mais la nature l'avait douée d'un contrepoids naturel. (4: 857)

> [it had destroyed its original proportions. At present, no corset was up to the task of finding hips for the poor woman, who seemed to be poured in one piece. The youthful harmony of her bodice no longer existed, and its excessive volume made one fear that if she were to bend down, she would be toppled by those superior masses; but nature had endowed her with a natural counterweight.]

This tendentious text actually tones down the scathing description Balzac had first written, where one finds the suggestive expression "agreeable proportions" later replaced by "original proportions"; where "its excessive abundance" became the more neutral "excessive volume"; and "these floating masses" gave way to "superior masses." In addition, the adjective "énorme" occurred at the end of the original version to qualify the "natural counterweight" (see the Folio edition 247). Indeed, the narrator's attitude toward his subject deserves to be the object of a separate study; suffice it to say that it teeters on the border between sympathy and irony.

Alas, Rose's abundance naturally lends itself to jokes which the narrator indulges in at her expense: "'Je crois rêver,' dit Josette en voyant sa maîtresse volant par les escaliers comme un éléphant auquel Dieu aurait donné des ailes" ["I must be dreaming," said Josette, seeing her mistress flying about the staircases like an elephant to whom God had somehow given wings] (4: 890). At least her "embonpoint de nourrice" [wet nurse's bosom] (4: 857) approximates a bait, suitable for catching a husband: "Quand elle s'était ainsi mise sous les armes, il se glissait dans les ténèbres de son cœur un rayon d'espoir: une voix lui disait que la nature ne l'avait pas si abondamment pourvue en vain, et qu'il allait se présenter un homme entreprenant" [When she had dressed to the hilt, a ray of hope would slip into the darker regions of her heart: a voice would tell her that nature had not worked in vain to provide for her so abundantly, and that an enterprising man was going to present himself] (4: 869). Balzac maneuvers the rhetoric of his realism to accomplish that notion in the most literal fashion, when her *embonpoint* snares du Bousquier: "Elle avait été vue pour la première fois par un homme, sa ceinture brisée, son lacet rompu, ses trésors violemment lancés hors de leur écrin" [She had been seen for the first time by a man, her belt broken, her laces torn, her treasures violently flung from their coffer] (4: 907). Perrot contends that the "conception bourgeoise de la tenue" [bourgeois conception of clothing] heightens self-control, "self-maintien," and the "domination continue des affects" [continuous restraint of feelings] (243), so that the failure of Rose's corset implies failure to control emotions. While the corset signals matrimonial availability, according to Perrot—"Une des missions de ce modelage anatomique consiste en effet, en obtenant une taille fine et un beau maintien, à ce qu'il devienne sur le marché matrimonial une valeur érotique, un atout social et un gage symbolique" [One of the missions of this anatomical modeling, by obtaining a narrow waist and an attractive appearance, did consist in its becoming an erotic value on the matrimonial market, a social trump card and symbolic guarantee] (275)—its failure to contain and contour suggests overstepping the boundary of the social.

And indeed, a veritable metaphoric series of liquid images stems from—or rather flows from—the central passage about Rose's corset, the moment of crisis when du Bousquier, to revive her, "jeta brutalement des gouttes d'eau sur le visage de Mlle Cormon et sur le corsage qui s'étala comme une inondation de la Loire" [brutally sprinkled drops of water on Mlle Cormon's face and on her bodice which spread about like an inundation of the Loire] (4: 904). With comical medical precision Balzac had earlier described the "drowning" of her nerve endings in her fat (4: 895–96). Since neither excess nor abundance characterize Rose's intellect, "quand la pauvre fille voyait la conversation s'alanguir, elle suait dans son corset, tant elle souffrait en essayant d'émettre des idées pour ranimer les discussions éteintes" [when the poor girl saw the conversation languish, she suffered so much trying to put forth ideas to revive the extinct discussion that she sweated in her corset] (4: 870). Here the corset symbolizes the limits of her mental ability. At the thought of putting up the vicomte de Troisville for the night, "La vieille fille était inondée d'espérance" [The old maid was inundated with hopefulness] (4: 893). Even her mare Pénélope "en sueur" [sweating] (4: 893) and "en nage" [drenched] (4: 894) somehow suggests Rose's spilling out of her bounds. And a series of allusions to her "boiling blood" gives metaphoric consistence to the inundations of her not very "sage" "corps."

La vieille fille most narrowly skirts a woman's desire, I think, by assigning sex insistently to the domain of Nature. Good periphrases for sex are "les vœux de la nature" [yearnings of nature] (4: 860) and "les agitations de la Chair" [agitation of the Flesh] (4: 861). Rose promises ten *écus* to support the supposed maternity of Suzanne, the most she has ever given, and justifies her largesse with a sentence that stupefies her friend Mme Granson: "Mais, ma bonne, il est si naturel d'avoir des enfants!" [But my dear, it is so natural to have children!] (4: 885). This sentiment, characterized as immoral, stems from the heart; her desire overflows the strict contours of her own principled modesty. Combining this naive frankness with extreme innocence produces striking rhetorical effects—among them, apparently, what might be called a lightning rod function. Balzac thus pretends to cultivate delicate ground while warding off criticisms from the partisans of morality—virtue guardians among the press and among the aristocracy. In *Le lys dans la vallée,* both the framing device and Lady Dudley are lightning rods, while in *Béatrix* and in *Les secrets de la princesse de Cadignan,* woman's desire is so theatrical, so performed, as to approach parody and hence carry safely away the fury of the flash. In *La vieille fille,* the alliance of nature and ignorance functions in the adroit expressions of Rose's exacerbated desire for Troisville: "La vieille fille n'avait jamais rencontré d'homme aussi séduisant que l'était l'olympien vicomte. Elle ne pouvait se dire à l'allemande: 'Voilà mon idéal!' mais elle se sentait *prise* de la tête aux pieds, et se disait: 'Voilà mon affaire!' [The old maid had never met so seductive a man as the Olympian viscount. She couldn't say like the Germans do, "Here is my ideal!" but she felt herself *possessed* from head to toe, and she said to herself, "This is the one for me!"] (4: 898–99; emphasis added). The accent is on "possessed." While the corset of Balzac's prose purports to shape Mlle Cormon into a "vieille fille," she would rather feel like a "fille," a type notably represented in the novel by Suzanne.

Analyzing the many indirect languages for sex would produce a valuable study of this novel (see chapter 18 on the language of sex), but the metonym of happiness, with the repeated words "bonheur" and "heureux," is symptomatic of the rhetorical process involved. (And here I take metonymy chiefly as displacement.)

Happiness means either Love or Money. "Un heureux mariage" (4: 829) means additional wealth for du Bousquier (as for many of the suitors in *La Comédie humaine,* all, in this, avatars of Balzac himself), while for Mlle Cormon "heureux" is a euphemism for "sexual." When she turns forty-two,

> Son désir acquit alors une intensité qui avoisina la monomanie, car elle comprit que toute chance de progéniture finirait par se perdre; et ce que, dans sa

céleste ignorance, elle désirait par-dessus tout, c'était des enfants. Il n'y avait pas une seule personne dans tout Alençon qui attribuât à cette vertueuse fille un seul désir des licences amoureuses. (4: 859)

[Her desire then acquired an intensity close to monomania, because she understood that any chance for offspring would soon be lost; and what she desired above all, in her celestial ignorance, was children. There was not a single person in all Alençon who would have attributed to this virtuous maid a single desire for the licentious pleasures of love.]

—but among Balzac's readers there are such persons; at any rate, it is clear that Balzac's text seeks them. For instance, if Rose wishes God would send her a husband so she can be "chrétiennement heureuse" [happy in the Christian way] (4: 860), doesn't the adjective make it clear that any un-Christian happiness could only be immoral, "des licences amoureuses"? In typical fashion, Balzac treats the problem sociologically: the woman who would be virtuous must choose a "mari libertin" [libertine husband]. Rose little cares for the "vieille ruine" [old ruin] that is Valois, her other suitor, and she is anxious about his apparent indifference to marriage and the "prétendue pureté" [pretence of purity] of his morals. Her fears are rooted in an obscure private politics; how is it that no one has noticed, Balzac asks, that "ces nobles créatures, réduites par la rigidité de leurs principes à ne jamais enfreindre la fidélité conjugale, doivent naturellement désirer un mari de haute expérience pratique!" [these noble creatures, reduced to never breaking conjugal fidelity by the rigidity of their principles, must naturally desire a husband of considerable practical experience!] (4: 876). Sex and money, money and sex: the fact that the terms are reversed with Suzanne, who desires an "heureux mariage" in the sense of money, underscores the quid pro quo.

Indeed, the semiotic significance of *bonheur* and *heureux* slips along a slope from metonymy to metaphor. "Bonheur" stands for "child" from the start, as Suzanne fakes a pregnancy attempting to trick du Bousquier into marriage: "un bonheur que vous payeriez cher un jour" [a good fortune you would one day pay dearly for] (4: 833). Suzanne's *patronne* likes the chevalier de Valois and goes so far as to excuse him in advance in these terms: "Une de ses ouvrières aurait-elle été coupable d'un bonheur attribué au chevalier, elle eût dit, '*Il est si aimable!*'" [Had one of her working girls been guilty of a good fortune attributed to the chevalier, she would have said, *He is so attractive!*] (4: 821), where *bonheur* clearly means pregnancy. When after the fatal failure of her corset Rose asks du Bousquier to pretend that the marriage had been agreed upon for six months already, du Bousquier wonders: "Serait-elle comme Suzanne? . . . Quel bonheur!" [Could she be like Suzanne? . . . What good fortune!] (4: 908), where "like Suzanne" literally means pregnant, a boon for the impotent future husband. Of course society would call the unmarried mother's *bonheur* a *malheur* (4: 918)—which underscores the opposition of the private sexual desire, uncontainable by the corset of the prose, to the social sanction of marriage. Later, we learn that, for the first two years of marriage, Rose is "satisfaite" [satisfied] (4: 925) and that "Le sang ne la tourmentait plus" [Her blood had ceased to torment her]. Are we to believe she has obtained the *bonheur* she sought? The editor Philippe Berthier notes: "Balzac pouvait difficilement faire plus nettement entendre que, même si son mariage n'a pas été 'consommé,' Mlle Cormon a été initiée au plaisir par son mari" [It would have been difficult for Balzac to make it more clearly understood that, even if her marriage has not been "consummated," Mlle Cormon has been initiated into the pleasure of sex by her husband] (366). Here the reader may interrogate at once Rose's *bonheur* and her ignorance, for she bewails her "désespoirs périodiques" [periodical despair] (4: 929)—the monthly proof that she is not pregnant. Frankly, a reader may well ask: just what was du Bousquier doing? Suzanne metaphorically changes the bride's orange flowers into "fleurs de nénuphar" [lily-pad flowers] (4: 921), reputedly anti-aphrodisiac, and is the first to declare that "Mme du Bousquier ne serait jamais que Mlle Cormon" [Mme du Bousquier would never be anyone but Mlle Cormon] (4: 921)—i.e., never deflowered. Rose *married* best illustrates *la vieille fille*, and Balzac's text continues to call her so well beyond her marriage (4: 930). It is not until the secret of du Bousquier's failure to make Rose happy is revealed that we learn that "*Cette pauvre Mme du Bousquier* remplaça *cette bonne demoiselle Cormon*" [*The poor Mme du Bousquier* replaced *the good Miss Cormon*] (4: 932). As for Valois, intent on revenge, he asks: "Êtes-vous heureuse au moins?" [Are you happy at least?], but Rose's modest and completely dishonest "Oui" is countered by Mlle Armande: "Pour que votre bonheur fût complet . . . il vous faudrait des enfants" [For your happiness to be complete . . . you would need to have children] (4: 931). It is ironic that Rose remains a *vieille fille* precisely because that *bonheur* eludes her as a married woman, and in fact the word comes to connote its exact opposite, childlessness: "D'ailleurs quel bonheur pour cette pauvre femme, car à son âge il était si dangereux d'avoir des enfants! . . . ma chère, vous ne savez pas ce que vous désirez" [Besides, what good fortune for the poor woman, because at her age it was so dangerous to have children! . . . "my dear, you don't know what you want"] (4: 929).

Balzac makes no mystery of Rose's "désir de se marier" [desire to get married] (4: 890), her "monomanie," but encases her unavowable desire in the corset of her innocence and ignorance. Her common designation as "la bonne Mlle Cormon" signifies "qu'elle était ignorante comme une carpe" [as ignorant as a carp] (4: 870). It is up to Mme Granson to dot the i's of *bonheur*, while Rose's innocence and ignorance appear to contain it, the better to suggest that sexual desire is its subtext:

> —Chère cousine, vous épouseriez mon fils Athanase, il n'y aurait là rien que de très naturel; il est jeune et beau, plein d'avenir . . . seulement tout le monde penserait que vous avez pris un si jeune homme pour être très *heureuse*; les mauvaises langues diraient que vous faites vos provisions de *bonheur* pour n'en jamais manquer; il y aurait des femmes jalouses qui vous accuseraient de dépravation; mais, qu'est-ce que cela ferait? vous seriez bien aimée et véritablement. . . . Eh bien, changez les termes . . . il en est de même de du Bousquier par rapport à Suzanne. Vous seriez calomniée, vous; mais, dans l'affaire de du Bousquier, tout est vrai. Comprenez-vous?
>
> —Pas plus que si vous me parliez grec, dit Mlle Cormon qui ouvrait de grands yeux en tendant toutes les forces de son intelligence.
>
> —Hé bien, cousine, puisqu'il faut mettre les points sur les i, Suzanne ne peut pas aimer du Bousquier. Et si le cœur n'est pour rien dans cette affaire . . .
>
> —Mais, cousine, avec quoi aime-t-on donc, si l'on n'aime pas avec le cœur? (4: 885–86; emphasis added)

["Dear cousin, if you married my son Athanase, it would be the most natural thing; he is young and handsome, his future is bright . . . only everyone would think you had taken such a young man so you could be very *happy*; wicked tongues would say that you are stocking up on *happiness* so as to never be lacking; there would be some jealous women who would accuse you of depravity; but what of it? You would be well and truly loved. . . . Well, change the terms . . . it's the same for du Bousquier with respect to Suzanne. In your case, it would be slander; but in the du Bousquier affair, everything is true. Do you understand?"

"No more than if you were speaking Greek," said Mlle Cormon opening her eyes wide and straining all the forces of her intellect.

"Well, cousin, since you need me to dot the i's, Suzanne can't love du Bousquier. And if the heart has no part in this business . . ."

"But cousin, what does one love with, if not the heart?"]

This illuminating conversation expresses the encrypted topic of the novel: the sexual desire of a virgin woman. It is Mme Granson who thinks Rose could not possibly care about her *bonheur* in marriage, but it is Rose who somehow manages to say that is *exactly* what she wants. Were Rose Cormon as knowledgeable about relations between the sexes as Suzanne, this scene would lose its punch, naturally.

The corset of ignorance and innocence necessarily casts the body into the *vieille fille* from which the fluid expressions of sex overflow. Condemned nearly unanimously at publication for its unheard-of vulgarity, the novel proved it had reached those readers it sought by its simultaneous strategies of containment and overflow.

Like *Pierrette, La vieille fille* comes to an important anthropological conclusion, "une moralité bien plus élevée" [a much higher moral] than the lesson that sentimental objects should be bequeathed to friendly hands (4: 935–36). The moral concerns myths, like *Pierrette,* for which a chair in anthropology would be a good idea: "Les mythes modernes sont encore moins compris que les mythes anciens, quoique nous soyons dévorés par les mythes. Les mythes nous pressent de toutes parts, ils servent à tout, ils expliquent tout" [Modern myths are even less understood than ancient myths, even though we are being devoured by myths. Myths pressure us on all sides, they serve for every purpose, they explain everything] (4: 935). Balzac would arrive at an explanation for everything by turning his stories into myths, which function like a condensed history of humanity.[3] In these final paragraphs of analysis, the semiotic strategy of the corset takes the form of a larger political expression, in which empires and revolution are at stake. Massol calls the story an allegory and sees the marriage as an alliance of liberalism, revolutionary ideas, and France against the forces of the former monarchy (96). Mlle Cormon's personal story would have been saved by anthropology just as modern myths would save empires:

> [Si les mythes] sont . . . les flambeaux de l'histoire, ils sauveront les empires de toute révolution, pour peu que les professeurs d'histoire fassent pénétrer les explications qu'ils en donnent jusque dans les masses départementales! Si Mlle Cormon eût été lettrée, s'il eût existé dans le département de l'Orne un professeur d'anthropologie, enfin si elle avait lu l'Arioste, les effroyables malheurs de sa vie conjugale eussent-ils jamais eu lieu? (4: 935)

---

3. Lise Queffélec in an excellent article has given a strong political meaning to the allusion to myth at the end of the novel.

> [[If myths] are . . . the torch lights of history, they will save empires from all revolutions, if only history professors would instill the explanations they give of them into the masses of the department! If Mlle Cormon had been well educated, if there had been an anthropology professor in the department of the Orne, if, finally, she had read Ariosto, would the horrible misfortunes of her conjugal life ever have taken place?]

With such instruction, Rose would have known how to "read" the magnificent nose possessed by the chevalier de Valois, whereas du Bousquier would have been recognized as similar to Ariosto's Orlando, whose horse is dead and who represents "le mythe des révolutions désordonnées, furieuses, impuissantes, qui détruisent tout sans rien produire" [the myth of disordered, furious, and impotent revolutions which destroy everything and produce nothing] (4: 936). The code is given; Mlle Cormon misses it. As Queffélec observes, "La forme mythique est inapte à assurer l'ordre dans l'histoire, tant que la faculté d'interprétation mythique manque au peuple. L'œuvre balzacienne sera donc à la fois mythe et science du mythe, univers de symboles et code de déchiffrement" [The mythic form is incapable of assuring order in history as long as the people lack the faculty of mythic interpretation. Balzac's work is thus both myth and science of myths, universe of symbols and code of decipherment] (176). But Balzac addresses the myth to his reader, along with the semiotic code to decipher it, leaving Rose Cormon permanently in her error.

Genealogy and the Unmarried in La Rabouilleuse

The third novel in Balzac's trilogy against unmarried people, *La Rabouilleuse* (1842), contains one of his most complex genealogies, so complex that one cannot read the book without establishing its genealogical facts. René Guise devoted more than two dense pages of editorial material in the Folio edition to a concise accounting of all the characters, generation by generation (382–84). For my part, I drew several family trees. The complexity of the genealogy arises from the defects of love within the family, and those defects radiate from a symbolic core noxious in its effects: celibacy. Balzac minced no words in declaring his position on this class of human beings. He began the preface to the first edition of *Pierrette,* which illustrates a similar topos, with these words: "L'état du Célibataire est un état contraire à la société" [The condition of Bachelor is a condition harmful to society] and identified the principle behind this assertion as "la haine profonde de l'auteur contre tout être improductif, contre les célibataires, les vieilles filles et les vieux garçons, ces bourdons de la ruche!" [the author's deep hatred against all unproductive beings, against bachelors, old maids, and old unmarried men, those bumblebee workers of the hive!] (4: 21). When the social regulation afforded by family is lacking, celibates, those useless unproductive beings who consume without producing, whose jealousy and hatred arise from their false position against society, have a monstrous effect. The harm caused by the unmarried proliferates in this story of domination and submission, of controllers and the controlled, and Money, seen in the symbolic structures of the novel, takes the balance of power over Love. Where one character wastes love on her profligate son, who wastes money, characters maneuver around a misappropriated fortune in Issoudun. "Only money matters," Pasco observes, in placing the inheritance at the "essential nucleus" of the novel ("Process Structure" 23, 25). Love is corrupted by the manipulations around Money.

Schematically, the genealogy reveals these failures. Extending over four generations, the family tree includes an amazing array of problems: illegitimate births and suspicions thereof; repudiated children, grandchildren, mothers, brothers, and spouses; missing fathers; complicated remarriages; extramarital affairs; concubinage arrangements; phony relationships; and so on. Households of families constituted by error, passion, evil, or untimely deaths are the rule; healthy families simply do not exist. Pasco stresses the significance for this novel of the missing fathers: "Balzac was convinced that nothing but families governed regularly by fathers had the power to control self-centered individuals" ("Process Structure" 24). While across *La Comédie humaine,* bonds formed by love in the family remain an often unrealized ideal, no novel illustrates this pessimistic condition better than *La Rabouilleuse.* The genealogy contains and explains the symbolic structures of domination and submission and gain and loss that constitute the central conflict, and the family structure propels the story, built on the twin axes of Love and Money.

Figure 10.1 illustrates the handwritten draft of a genealogy I established while reading the novel, and figure 10.2 a computer-generated version of it, whose clean lines and clear presentation belie the elaborate, messy reality we are expected to follow in reading *La Rabouilleuse*. The computer's purpose is to make order out of confusion, which masks the complexity of Balzac's invention (but makes it easier to follow the story); Balzac on the contrary requires of his reader a willingness to build chaotic facts into structures that must be and remain irregular. The very interesting manuscript draft of the novel's opening pages (4: 1219–21) shows the extreme haste with which Balzac first couched the family tree on paper. The characters appeared in rapid succession in short phrases, as if to serve as placeholders for the entire set of family relations, fully formed in Balzac's mind with their genealogical relations. Reading like an outline to be fleshed out with further details, the draft reveals that the intention to build complexity into the family structures was present from the outset, just as it shows the "facilité déconcertante" [disconcerting facility] (Bodin 94) with which Balzac was able to set it down on paper without getting lost himself. One can say that Balzac's first draft and my hand-written genealogy are analogous; Balzac's rewriting and the computer software have the function of making the relations, the lines of filiation or absence thereof, more readily apparent.

The defects in the family tree of *La Rabouilleuse* concern Family, Maternity, and Love.

Family

All the families are incomplete. Widowed, Agathe Bridau raises her two sons without their father; she will not consider finding a second husband, which would conflict with her love for her sons and indeed for her dead husband (Agathe, like an Andromaque, "ne pouvait plus exister que pour ses enfants" [no longer had an existence except for her sons] [4: 285]), and she has what Balzac calls the contradictory obligations of motherhood and the exercise of paternal authority (4: 282). Mme Bridau is also frequently called "the widow" instead of by her name. Mme Descoings, twice a widow, is living with her niece, has lost her only son in battle, pretends out of vanity that her grandson Bixiou is her stepson, and is childless by her second marriage. The Hochon couple at Issoudun have lost all three of their children and have reconstituted a sort of family with three grandchildren from different families. Jean-Jacques Rouget marries only to die within months. And marriage to Philippe is a death sentence for Flore Brazier.

Agathe Bridau's mother's brother Descoings leaves Issoudun for Paris to make his fortune; in his absence, his brother-in-law, the doctor Rouget, takes control of the Descoings family fortune, which has gone entirely to Descoings's sister. The brother, having become a grocer, marries the widow of his employer, Bixiou, who has also lost her only son; beheaded during the Terror, Descoings leaves his widow bereft of family except her grandson, the journalist Bixiou.

Agathe Rouget Bridau, daughter of her mother and her father but resembling neither, though loved by her mother and her godmother Mme Hochon, is presumed illegitimate and repudiated by her father, sent away at seventeen to Paris, and disinherited. Her father, Rouget the doctor, maneuvers to give Agathe's share of her inheritance to her imbecilic bachelor brother Jean-Jacques Rouget. The doctor suspects his wife of sleeping with his former friend Lousteau (which would have made Agathe the half-sister of Maxence Gilet, according to popular belief), and until his death he persists in "sa haine contre sa fille Agathe" [his hatred of his daughter Agathe] (4: 391).

Maxence Gilet, perpetrator of vicious practical jokes in Issoudun, is appropriately enough the joker or wild card in this genealogy. Although

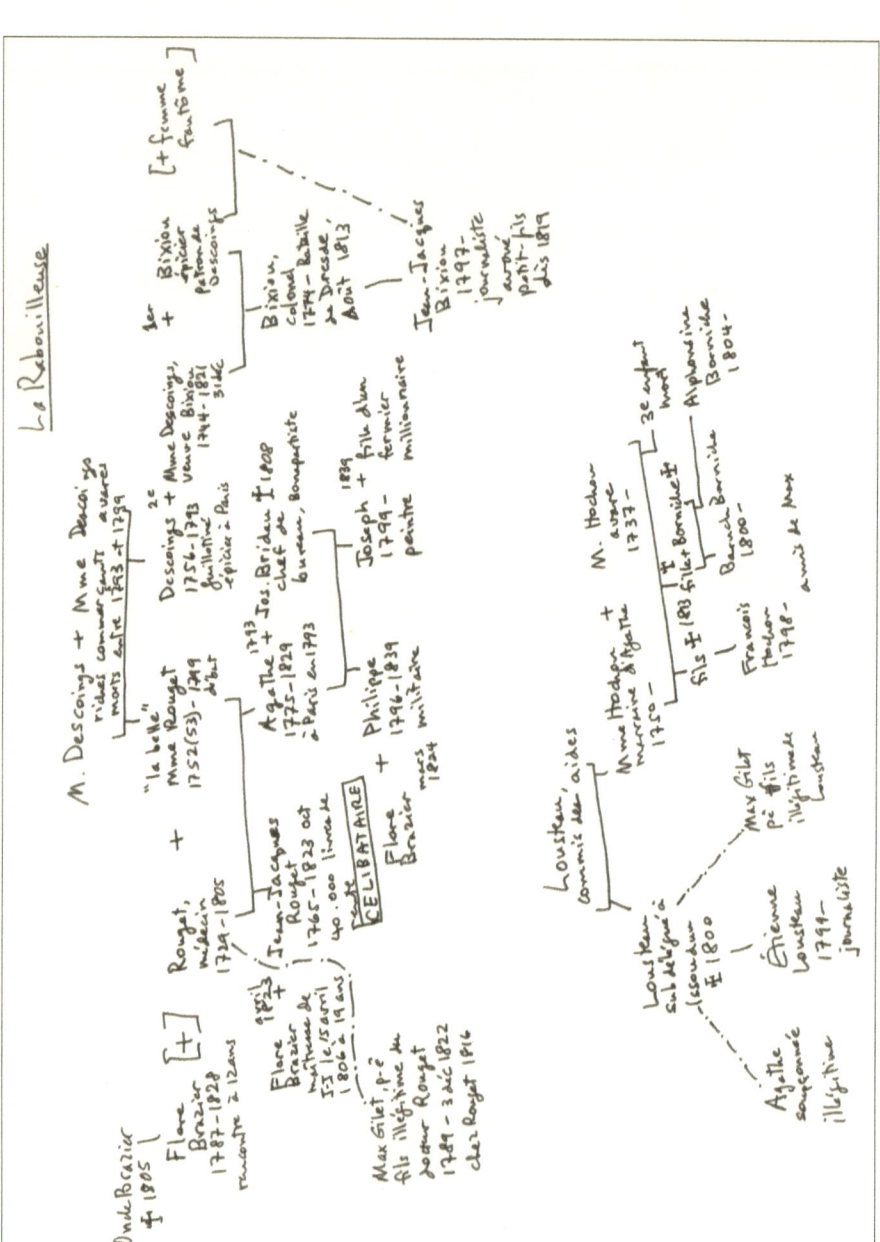

Figure 10.1 Handwritten *La Rabouilleuse* genealogy

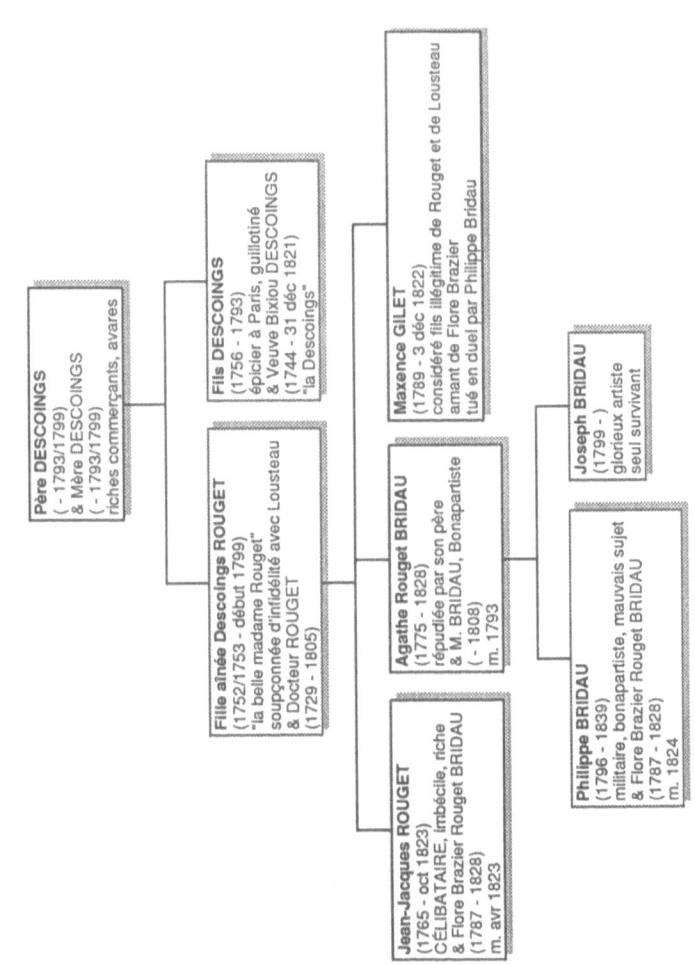

Figure 10.2 Computer-generated genealogy

illegitimate, he has an overabundance of putative fathers, so that placing Max on the family tree requires graphic ingenuity and a special kind of dotted line indicating "presumed son of" (see figure 10.1). People take him for the son of Rouget, the doctor (father of Jean-Jacques the bachelor and of Agathe, a man known for his vices), or the son of the doctor's accomplice in debauchery, the *subdélégué* Lousteau, Mme Hochon's brother. In fact, neither one is Max's father, nor is it old M. Gilet, who was his mother's husband (both Gilets die miserably, leaving Max an orphan); rather, Max owes his existence to "un charmant officier de dragons en garnison à Bourges" [a charming officer of the dragoons stationed at Bourges] (4: 367), who was a nobleman. The beautiful but unfaithful Mme Gilet financially exploits both of the presumed illegitimate fathers as well as her husband: "Pour procurer des protecteurs à son fils, la Gilet se garda bien d'éclairer les pères postiches" [To obtain protectors for her son, la Gilet took care not to illuminate the spurious fathers] (4: 367). Because people think the doctor fathered Max, Balzac calls him Jean-Jacques's "soi-disant frère naturel" [so-called bastard brother] (4: 407), putting a double doubt on the fraternal relation—not only illegitimate, but dubiously so. Flore takes advantage of this belief that Max is the son of old Rouget; she lies that Rouget *told* her Max was his son and claims that Joseph Bridau tried to kill Max to inherit from Jean-Jacques (4: 457). She calls Max "son parent par nature" [her natural relative] (4: 473) and accuses Jean-Jacques of fratricide, because Max is "un garçon que votre père a toujours pris pour son fils! . . ." [a boy that your father always took for his son! . . .] (4: 405).

Of course the lack of a father is often the intimate cause of disasters, in Balzac. Both Maxence Gilet and Philippe Bridau distinguished themselves in the Grande Armée but get into trouble in their lives because of the loss of their symbolic father, Napoleon (4: 369–70). As Mozet remarks, the unbalanced couple of the old man and the young girl is the exact negative of the couple in *Ursule Mirouët,* where the doctor Minoret exercises a "maternité scientifique et toute bénéfique" [a scientific and entirely beneficent maternity] (*Ville de province* 237, 238). Quite like that novel, three old gentlemen, Claparon, du Breul, and Desroches (ancient fathers of three notable actors of *La Comédie humaine*), constitute the regular society of the two widows Bridau and Descoings in their Parisian solitude, visiting every evening for a card game; but their factitious fatherhood is all that takes the place of the dead husbands, and it cannot prevent the disasters of the Bridau family. When Maxence moves into the Rouget household, Flore behaves like an orphan happy to make a family for herself (4: 401), and Rouget comments that the two of them constitute his family (4: 417): these families are constituted by compensating for what they lack.

Fraternal relations in the family do nothing to overcome the celibate core. "Les frères ennemis" would not quite do for the title of the first part, called "Les deux frères," but that is only because Joseph Bridau does not return his brother Philippe's enmity. Philippe rejects fraternal sentiment, in spite of Joseph's loyalty and care. Similarly, the fraternal relation between Agathe and Jean-Jacques is altogether severed by their physical separation when Agathe is seventeen: "il y avait, pour un frère, quelque chose d'un peu trop extraordinaire à rester trente ans sans donner signe de vie à sa sœur" [for a brother, there was something a little too extraordinary about not giving any sign of life to his sister for thirty years] (4: 358). Balzac blames their emotional separation on la Rabouilleuse. The only fraternal association that functions well is the "permanent conspiracy" of the Chevaliers de la Désœuvrance in Issoudun, whose evil actions define the association as the contrary of the nuclear family that for Balzac was always the foundation of a good society.

Flore Brazier, la Rabouilleuse, is, like Max, an orphan, or quasi-orphan: her mother is dead and her father is in an institution for the insane; her guardian, an uncle Brazier of disreputable aspect, sells her to old Rouget when she is twelve and he seventy, soon after Mme Rouget dies. The uncle sarcastically calls Rouget "digne père des indigents" [worthy father of the indigent] (4: 390)—meaning exactly the opposite, another defective symbolic fatherhood. For six years Flore lives with the doctor, some believe as his mistress. In April 1806, she becomes Jean-Jacques's mistress; in April 1823, forced by Philippe, she marries Jean-Jacques and is widowed the same year. Her next husband is the powerful dominator and manipulator Philippe Bridau, who repudiates her as soon as he has married her and drives her to her death within four years (after boasting that he has three ways to make a woman die [4: 499]).

Philippe also denies his birth family: "J'ai bien vu que ni vous ni mon frère vous ne m'aimez plus. Je suis maintenant seul au monde: j'aime mieux cela!" [I can clearly see that neither you nor my brother loves me anymore. I am alone in the world now—and I prefer it!] cries Philippe early on (4: 343), unfairly rejecting both his mother and his brother, who continue to love him in spite of his bad behavior toward them. And much later, when Philippe is aiming for power and rank: "Moins j'aurai de famille, meilleure sera ma position" [The less I have of a family, the better will my position be] (4: 531). Having obtained the title of comte de Brambourg, he attempts to bury his family name of Bridau. But when Philippe tries to buy his way into a noble family and status, by marrying Amélie de Soulanges, daughter of a count, Bixiou sees to it that he is exposed. Philippe will die in 1839 an unmarried man.

Maternity

Maternal relationships, always a very important part of the family in *La Comédie humaine,* are defective or distorted. This bad situation radiates throughout the genealogy, underscoring its persistence across the generations. The beautiful Mme Rouget, wife of the doctor, suffers in her motherhood of Jean-Jacques and Agathe; her son, "stupide en tout point, n'avait ni les attentions ni le respect qu'un fils doit à sa mère" [stupid in every way, gave neither the attentiveness nor the respect that a son owes to his mother] (4: 274). Agathe Bridau is similarly unhappy as the mother of Philippe and Joseph. Descoings the son of the Issoudun family is disinherited, like Agathe; the author of both financial repudiations is the doctor Rouget, father of Agathe and brother-in-law of the grocer Descoings: withdrawing love, he retains their money. Agathe perpetuates the withdrawal of love to the next generation: preferring Philippe, she "disinherits" Joseph of her love; her maternity is stupid, erroneous.

In particular, Agathe Bridau's unjust preference for Philippe seesaws through several crises. Her maternity is falsified by this unfairness to her younger son, the one who deserves maternal affection, and the reiterated horrors Philippe perpetrates destroy her maternal feeling. "Comment s'altère le sentiment maternel" [How the Maternal Sentiment Decays] was the title of the eighth chapter in part I. During one crisis, Agathe calls Philippe "monsieur," and he sarcastically accuses her of playing *Le fils banni,* a melodrama, to which she replies, "Vous êtes un monstre" [You are a monster] (4: 340). Philippe retaliates by accusing his mother of a mysterious crime, the cause of her own banishment from the paternal home: "Qu'aviez-vous fait à grand-papa Rouget, à votre père, pour qu'il vous chassât et vous déshéritât?" [What did you do to grandfather Rouget, your father, for him to banish you and disinherit you?] (4: 341). Thereupon Agathe "abdiqua sa pesante maternité" [abdicated her burdensome maternity] (4: 343). After Philippe steals a painting from his brother, Agathe sighs, "Je n'ai donc plus qu'un fils" [So I have only one son left] (4: 350). But Joseph observes that she is "mère comme Raphaël était peintre!" [a mother the way Raphael was a painter!] (4: 357), and so, with a passion comparable to an artistic genius, she continues to lavish love and money on Philippe, who wastes both and returns neither. When Philippe survives the duel in which he kills Max, "Cette pauvre mère . . . retrouva pour son fils maudit toute sa maternité" [The poor mother . . . found herself a mother again for her accursed son] (4: 512). When Philippe becomes a count and is employed by the royal family, "Agathe ne se sentait mère que pour l'audacieux aide de camp de S. A. R. Monseigneur le Dauphin!" [Agathe felt herself a mother only for the audacious aide de camp of His Royal Highness Monsignor the Dauphin] (4: 526), whereas for Joseph, still the unrecognized painter, she is only "une espèce de sœur grise dévouée" [a sort of devoted sister of charity].

The maternity of Mme Descoings is defective as well. Balzac's explanation is that her guilt in depriving Agathe's children of some of their money makes her love them: "Elle aimait les deux petits Bridau plus que son petit-fils Bixiou, tant elle avait le sentiment de ses torts envers eux" [She loved the two Bridau boys more than her grandson Bixiou, so great was her guilt about the harm she had done them] (4: 286). It is striking how love is determined by money, to bad effect. "Depuis onze ans, la Descoings, en donnant mille écus chaque année, avait payé presque deux fois sa dette [à Agathe], et continuait à immoler les intérêts de son petit-fils à ceux de la famille Bridau" [In eleven years, la Descoings had paid her debt [to Agathe] almost twice over, by giving a thousand *écus* each year, and she continued to sacrifice the interests of her grandson to those of the Bridau family] (4: 322). The alienation of funds from the direct line to the lateral line—la Descoings is Agathe's aunt not by blood but by marriage—works to Bixiou's detriment. Like money, maternal love is diverted from the direct to the lateral: until 1819, Mme Descoings refuses to admit that Bixiou is her grandson, son of her son the colonel who died on the Dresden battlefield in August 1813, and claims he is instead the son of her first husband Bixiou by his first marriage. But Bixiou senior did not have a first wife, so his widow is inventing not only a false relationship—another odd dotted line in the family tree—but a phantom family. On the other hand, Joseph Bridau, her grandnephew, is called "son enfant d'adoption" [her child by adoption] (4: 335). She is paradoxically much closer to Agathe, her niece by marriage, than to her grandson. Family relationships and financial interest both turn away from the straight, simple, and direct to the devious, complex, and detoured.

At the core of the genealogy are the distorted maternal relationships radiating from the celibacy of Jean-Jacques Rouget. Flore, eighteen years younger than the bachelor, becomes like a mother to him. Balzac pointedly describes this motherhood as vicious and dominating: "Ce grand enfant [Jean-Jacques] alla de lui-même au-devant de cette domination, en se laissant rendre tant de soins, que Flore fut avec lui comme une mère est avec son fils. Aussi Jean-Jacques finit-il par avoir pour Flore le sentiment qui rend nécessaire à un enfant la protection maternelle" [This grown child [Jean-Jacques] went after this domination himself, letting himself be looked after so much that Flore behaved toward him like a mother with her son. And so Jean-Jacques ended up having for Flore the feelings that make maternal protection necessary to a child] (4: 402–3). An interesting semantic effect stems from the constant use of the word "garçon"—and not just "vieux garçon"—for the bachelor; unmarried, he cannot reach the maturity of manhood and must have a mother, who frequently calls him "petit." This factitious maternity of la Rabouilleuse can be contrasted ironically to the "maternité factice" (4: 423) that Mme Hochon has always had for the disinherited, unloved Agathe Bridau. Balzac's use of the expression "factitious maternity" for Mme Hochon is remarkably ironic; it would apply to Flore in her relationship to the celibate Rouget, not to Mme Hochon, whose maternal feeling is about the only consistently positive such sentiment in the novel. If her maternity is factitious, not real, it is because it takes an indirect path: she is only Agathe's godmother; what is worse, she has outlived her own three children.

Love

Love is vitiated and cannot overcome the harm people do to one another. It is linked instead with vice, avarice, and death. Philippe reduces his mother and brother to poverty by spending their money on his love affair with the demimondaine Mariette. Agathe buries her conjugal life after Bridau's death. She is thunderstruck when Philippe rejects her request for money for Joseph in a letter "dont la concise brutalité venait de briser le cœur délicat de cette pauvre mère" [whose concise brutality had just broken the delicate heart of this poor mother] (4: 527), and she will die because he refuses to see her. Rouget's premarital relationship with Flore is sadomasochistic, leading directly to his death. Everywhere Money contaminates Love: greed destroys all the possible family bonds that love might make.

Joseph loves his mother Agathe, who loves Philippe: in such a schema, love is literally not returned, for Philippe loves only himself: "Joseph adorait sa mère, tandis que Philippe se laissait adorer par elle" [Joseph adored his mother, while Philippe let himself be adored by her] (4: 298); "Hélas! L'officier n'aimait plus qu'une seule personne au monde, et cette personne était le colonel Philippe" [Alas! The officer loved only one person in the world, and that person was colonel Philippe] (4: 303). In such a way, the energy of love dies, buried in the egoism of its self-circulation, a circle of vice if not a vicious circle. When Maxence Gilet arrives in Issoudun, Flore Brazier, object of Jean-Jacques's passion, falls in love with Max. Rouget's passion for Flore and her passion for Max, however vicious, are easy to represent with one-way arrows. But turn the arrows the other way, and they are labeled money. Max is attached to Flore because, as Balzac says emphatically: "D'abord, et avant tout, les quarante mille livres de rente en fonds de terre que possédait le père Rouget constituaient la passion de Gilet pour Flore Brazier, croyez-le bien" [To begin with, and above all, the forty thousand pounds of income in landed funds that old Rouget owned constituted Gilet's passion for Flore Brazier, better believe it!] (4: 384–85). He also says that Gilet "ne voulait pas Flore sans la fortune du père Rouget" [did not want Flore without old Rouget's fortune] (4: 501).

As for Flore, money is the only attraction Rouget possesses for her, not love. Among the melodramatic events during Philippe's reign in Issoudun is the flight of la Rabouilleuse, which leaves Rouget totally distraught and rushing off to bring her back. But Philippe brings *him* home and makes him write a simple letter to Flore: "Si vous ne partez pas . . . pour revenir chez moi, . . . je révoquerai le testament fait en votre faveur" [If you do not leave there . . . to return home to me . . . I will revoke the testament made in your favor] (4: 496). Money brings her back in four hours. Her two marriages also come about because of money. On his wife's death, Philippe keeps the money she inherited at Rouget's death, repeating in his generation the dishonest maneuver by which his grandfather disinherited his mother. Philippe Bridau is also, incidentally, the cause of all the deaths: Mme Descoings, Agathe, Max, Rouget, and Flore.

In the place of love, the celibate's passion is, as I said, noxious. When Flore talks to Rouget, he says: "elle me remue l'âme à me faire perdre la raison. Tiens, quand elle me regarde d'une certaine façon, ses yeux bleus me semblent le paradis, et je ne suis plus mon maître, surtout quand il y a quelques jours qu'elle me tient rigueur" [she stirs my soul so as to make me lose my mind. You see, when she looks at me in a certain way, her blue eyes seem like paradis to me and I am no longer my own master, especially when she has held me off for several days] (4: 488). The antidote to such loss of reason would be love within the functional family. Balzac gives the wit Bixiou the task of summarizing the examples of bad passions that cause deaths: "Ma grand-mère aimait la loterie et Philippe l'a tuée par la loterie! Le père Rouget aimait la gaudriole et Lolotte l'a tué! Madame Bridau, pauvre femme, aimait Philippe, elle a péri par lui! . . . Le Vice! le Vice! mes amis! . . . " [My grandmother loved the lottery and Philippe killed her by the lottery! Old Rouget loved debauchery and Lolotte killed him! Madame Bridau, poor woman, loved Philippe, through him she perished! . . . It's Vice! Vice, my friends! . . .] (4: 535).

But instead of love, it is money, principally the inheritance, that appears as the only positive value. Philippe's rotten character, destructive of love, is just what is needed to overthrow the domination of Maxence Gilet and Flore

Brazier over the holder of the fortune, Jean-Jacques Rouget. Not that Philippe undergoes a conversion, but all the qualities that were negative before have powerful positive effects once he is in Issoudun and regaining the family fortune is the chief objective: clever, devious, hateful, single-minded, deceitful, Philippe Bridau inspires fear in those to whom he threatens harm, and that is precisely what is needed to regain the fortune. At moments, he resembles the mythological character whose renunciation of love grants him power—in this case, power to obtain the fortune. The bourgeois of Issoudun go so far as to consider him "le digne colonel Bridau" [the worthy Colonel Bridau] (4: 503), and he achieves a kind of grandeur of the type Balzac granted to the corsaire, as for instance at the moment of the duel with Max (4: 509). This success of the money strain stands in ironic juxtaposition to the multiple failures of love.

In the end, the debris of Philippe's fortune will finally come to the one character who deserves it, Joseph Bridau (it is true that he is also the only one left alive), but only after the genealogy is almost completely voided by deaths. It is as if outliving this pernicious family structure is the only way to arrive at a happy ending. The novel achieves this gratification at the price of an extra effort: paragraphs Balzac added at the end, covering several years, bring Philippe to a horrible death in the Algerian war in 1839, only two years before the novel was composed. Emptied, the genealogy no longer contains any celibates, except on the fringes: Bixiou and Lousteau, both journalists. At about the same time, Joseph is married with the protection of the comte de Sérisy to a rich heiress, achieves the fabulous figure of sixty thousand pounds of income, and inherits Philippe's title. We can consider this the just reward that the gods of novel-writing grant to genius, when genius is so well seconded by tenacity.

The root cause of all these disasters of family, maternity, and love can be found in the changing political atmosphere so ripe with dramatic power for *La Comédie humaine*. The events of 1812, 1814, 1815, and 1816 bring confusion, sudden change, uncertainty, and errors (people believe they are following a good course, only to find that they are mistaken): thus is delineated the world in which the Bridau family functions (4: 296–301). It is a confused situation whose direct influence on the family takes it from bad to worse; Philippe is its victim and then its perpetrator. The Bridaus rant about the Bourbons whom they call "the foreigners" (4: 300, 313), and Balzac rants about the liberals (4: 304–5). Politics change Philippe Bridau's life by giving him a position on the newspaper (4: 314–15); conspiring with other Bonapartists against the Restoration government, Philippe is twice arrested or threatened with incarceration (4: 299, 353). As an image of the hazards and chances brought about by the political changes, gambling plays a large role in this novel. On one page, Philippe's luck at gambling reverses itself several times, mirroring the ups and downs of his fortunes linked to Bonaparte's (4: 320–21).

In Issoudun as well, the different political evolutions since 1787 are evoked in their relation to the characters' fates. The irregularity of the scandalous relations between Rouget and Flore is underscored in a newspaper article which finds the cause of this effect in the absence of religion under the effects of the Revolution (4: 515), and Napoleon's difficulty in reestablishing the church, due to the shortage of priests, is also mentioned (4: 392). The public and publicized dramas, the changing face of France, especially the fall of Napoleon (always a grandiose figure in Balzac) are the public reflections of the private events through which Balzac drags his characters, always keen to be the one who reveals the unknown, secret, hidden realities of human existence. As reflections of external events, these secret dramas are brought under the microscope, analyzed, dissected, augmented. Such is the story of Mme Hochon, for instance (4: 431).

La Rabouilleuse illustrates a theme found in several other texts of *La Comédie humaine:* after 1830, mediocrity reigns and artistic genius goes unrecognized, even scorned. Once again, that theme comes home to Balzac himself, primarily. Not only does the defective mother with the unbalanced love-hatred for the two sons recapitulate the family romance Balzac saw himself in, between his adulterous mother and his better loved half-brother Henri, but, more importantly, he portrayed in Joseph Bridau's character and destiny the role of the man of genius in saving France from bourgeois mediocrity.[1]

---

1. Anne-Marie Baron comments that the story of the Blondet family in *Le Cabinet des Antiques* shows "comment procède le romancier: il brouille les cartes, déforme une situation réellement vécue, punissant la mère adultère dans ce qu'elle a de plus cher et échangeant les destins de son frère Henry et de lui-même de manière à ce que l'enfant de l'amour soit évincé à sa place du paradis familial" [how the novelist proceeds: he shuffles the cards and deforms an actual lived experience, punishing the adulterous mother through what she holds the most dear and exchanging the destinies of his brother Henry and himself so that the love-child is evicted from his place in the family paradise] (*L'auguste mensonge* 148–49). The same can be said of the relations among Agathe Bridau and her two sons.

11

Ursule Mirouët
Genealogy and Inheritance

In this first novel of the *Scènes de la vie de Province,* written in 1841, a familiar picture of the provincial town emerges, one that is found in several other Balzac novels. Here Nemours is represented as a stifling, narrow-minded milieu in which a stupid, greedy, and powerful bourgeoisie smothers the good and the noble. As if to underscore the underlying dichotomy of Paris and the provinces, several escapes to the capital designate it as the place where one makes money (or spends it), and as the locus of illumination and knowledge. While money flows loosely in Paris, in Nemours it is as inbred as the social structure, in which pernicious ignorance breeds unchecked. The peasantry are exploited and cheated by the rising bourgeoisie, who hold all the positions in town, while the aristocracy stubbornly retains its *ancien régime* prejudices and falls by its own impoverishments under the determined attack of the bourgeoisie. The social picture is a standard in *La Comédie humaine,* as I've suggested, but two figures of semiosis particularize it: the omnipresent relations among the four families of Minoret, Levrault, Massin, and Crémière representing the pervasive extension of the bourgeoisie, on the one hand, and, on the other, the extraordinary coterie enfolding the heroine, uniquely identified by its belonging to no class and by its elite intellectuality. I characterize as genealogical the relations among the four bourgeois families, whereas the classless intellectuals are connected by inheritance, particularly in the case of the two central characters, Ursule Mirouët and her tutor. The pure and innocent Ursule is put in grave danger by the lowly evils of the triumphant bourgeoisie, as in *Pierrette,* but all nevertheless ends happily, with order, justice, truth, and light, thanks to spiritualism.

For a major effect of the novel is to demonstrate that spirituality triumphs over materiality. Balzac opposes these deeper themes of the novel in the same way as genealogy and inheritance, mimetic structures which these themes extend into the domain of ideas. The topic is central and vital to *La Comédie humaine,* but no subject however profound is immune to those puns and word games that Balzac can never resist. Consider this sterling example, in which lapidary wit puts spirituality and materiality momentarily on the same plane: "Croyez-vous aux revenants? dit Zélie au curé.—Croyez-vous aux revenus? répondit le prêtre en souriant" ["Do you believe in ghosts?" said Zélie to the priest. "Do you believe in gold?" replied the priest, smiling] (3: 976). The play on words is ironic: the materialistic Zélie speaks of spirits, while the priest reminds her of money. Like so many Balzacian novels, it seems, this one is built on series of oppositions, functioning in tandem.

The action begins in 1829 and turns repeatedly to near and distant past times to provide necessary explanations, until a return to the present. After a rich, enlightened life in Paris, the philosophically minded doctor Denis Minoret has returned in 1815 to Nemours, where he was born, to finish his life with his ward and three chosen friends: the abbé Chaperon, justice of the peace Bongrand, and captain Jordy. Together, these four men have been raising Ursule Mirouët, Minoret's deceased wife's half-brother's child, who in 1815 was an orphan of ten months. By 1829, Minoret's nieces and nephews in Nemours are fearful of losing their inheritance to Ursule. The striking opening pages portray their alarm when the doctor attends mass for the first time in his life (his conversion is the work of Ursule, who is now fifteen, and of animal magnetism). When the doctor dies, Ursule does not receive the fortune he left her, because Minoret-Levrault, the nephew, steals three "inscriptions de rentes en trois pour cent, au porteur" [government stock certificates at 3 percent, to the bearer] intended for Ursule and together worth 36,000 francs of income. For good measure, Minoret-Levrault also burns the doctor's will. In the purity of her spirituality, Ursule is visited by the doctor's image in her dreams. He shows her Minoret-Levrault's crime and the numbers of the *inscriptions de rente;* she recovers the fortune, marries the aristocrat Savinien de Portenduère whom she loves, and moves to Paris. Minoret-Levrault becomes an honest man, but his wife Zélie loses her mind when their son Désiré dies after an accident.

This astute narrative design thus combines an affair of succession with a story of animal magnetism: the stolen inheritance returns to Ursule only because she possesses somnambulistic powers. For Balzac, this combination whereby a spiritual faculty produces a material gain is not in the least contradictory. It is central to the effectiveness of the narrative semiosis of this novel.

Minoret at eighty-three can well be called an uncle to inherit from (3: 776): his nephew Minoret-Levrault, niece Mme Crémière-Crémière, and first cousin once removed Mme Massin-Levrault with their spouses expect to inherit the doctor's considerable wealth, and in fact they have virtually no other collective designation than "the heirs." Upon first arriving in Nemours, Minoret asks his nephew: "Ai-je d'autres héritiers?" ["Have I other heirs?"] (3: 786), and, henceforth, whenever they are collectively mentioned, that is the word for the Massins, Levraults, Minorets, and Crémières, almost exclusively. "Héritiers" is used 105 times in the 220 pages of the Pléiade edition—by far the greatest number of occurrences among the forty-nine novels included in an electronic concordance of *La Comédie humaine*. In addition, "héritier" occurs seven times in the singular and "héritière" five times in singular and plural forms. "Cohéritier" and "cohéritières" occur six times. "Héritier" applies to family members; the Petit Robert gives this definition: "relative designated by law to receive the succession of a dead person.... The *heirs* or blood heirs are distinguished from irregular *successors,* from *legatees*" (emphasis added). The term "héritiers" thus represents immense narrative potential or plot-value, which is only heightened when Balzac, in a sociological vein, uses instead the broader terms "bourgeois" and "bourgeoise" (twenty-nine times), and "bourgeoisie" (ten times). Savinien de Portenduère, referring to the heirs, will say, "Ces bourgeois sont comme des chiens à la curée" ["These bourgeois are like dogs going for quarry"] (3: 925). The strength of their evil lies partly in their common purpose as "cohéritiers." As Georges Poulet observes, "Conspiration, coalition, l'ensemble des convoitises se forme volontiers en une association des forces tendues vers un même but. Dans presque chaque roman de Balzac, autour d'une figure qui est à la fois une victime et un objet d'envie, se constitue un cercle de volontés avides" [Conspiracy or coalition, the instances of cupidity readily come together into an association of forces directed toward a single goal. In almost every novel by Balzac, around a figure who is both a victim and an object of envy, there forms a ring of greedy desires] (209).

Balzac often indulged in complex genealogies, notably in *Pierrette, La Rabouilleuse,* and *Les paysans,* but none is so relentless, so pervasive, so inescapable in its action as the one he created here. Thierry Bodin has sketched the development of Balzac's idea of the evil in bourgeois genealogies in the case of *Les paysans.* The unfinished *Les héritiers Boirouge* consists almost entirely of the family tree whose final version will end up in *Ursule Mirouët,* but Balzac complicated the genealogy so much that he had to abandon that novel. The genealogy in *Ursule Mirouët* is a mimetic figure of his semiosis. Madeleine Ambrière-Fargeaud writes, in notes to the novel: *"Ursule Mirouët, La Rabouilleuse et Les Paysans peuvent être considérés comme des avatars des Héritiers Boirouge, projet reparaissant, ondoyant et divers, mais toujours centré sur le grand thème du partage, de la succession"* [*Ursule Mirouët, La Rabouilleuse,* and *Les paysans* can be considered incarnations of *Les héritiers Boirouge,* a recurring project, undulating and diverse, but always centered on the vast theme of distribution, of succession] (3: 1524). The four indigenous families of Nemours—Minoret, Massin, Levrault, and Crémière—forge the links of a "zigzag" network; they are the four "shuttles" that weave the "lacework" of a "human cloth," the pieces configuring the "domestic kaleidoscope" of the bourgeois "cousinage" (3: 782, 783). The image of a kaleidoscope, in which the same few pieces taking different positions form a vast number of configurations, aptly figures the internal genetic crossings and the thousands of possible varieties stemming from them. Minutely, obsessively explicative, the genealogy of these families, which Balzac anchors in the time of Louis XI, is both an obstacle to reading and an excellent example of a text presuming ignorance. Its complexity would stump a genealogical scientist, Balzac writes: "Les variations de ce kaléidoscope domestique à quatre éléments se compliquaient tellement par les naissances et par les mariages, que l'arbre généalogique des bourgeois de Nemours eût embarrassé les Bénédictins de l'Almanach de Gotha eux-même" [The variations in this four-piece domestic kaleidoscope were becoming so complicated by births and marriages that the genealogical tree of the bourgeois of Nemours would have embarrassed the Benedictines of the Almanach de Gotha themselves] (3: 782). (My own response to such complexity, as with *La Rabouilleuse* and *Pierrette,* is to draw the family tree: see figure 11.1.)

Ubiquitous hyphenated combinations of the four names arise under Louis XIII, and arise in Balzac's text as an astonishing exercise in excessive, unreasonable writing:

> ces quatre familles produisaient déjà des Massin-Crémière, des Levrault-Massin, des Massin-Minoret, des Minoret-Minoret, des Crémière-Levrault, des Levrault-Minoret-Massin, des Massin-Levrault, des Minoret-Massin, des Massin-Massin, des Crémière-Massin, tout cela bariolé de junior, de fils aîné, de Crémière-François, de Levrault-Jacques, de Jean-Minoret. (3: 782)

> [these four families were already producing some Massin-Crémières, Levrault-Massins, Massin-Minorets, Minoret-Minorets, Crémière-Levraults,

Ursule Mirouët

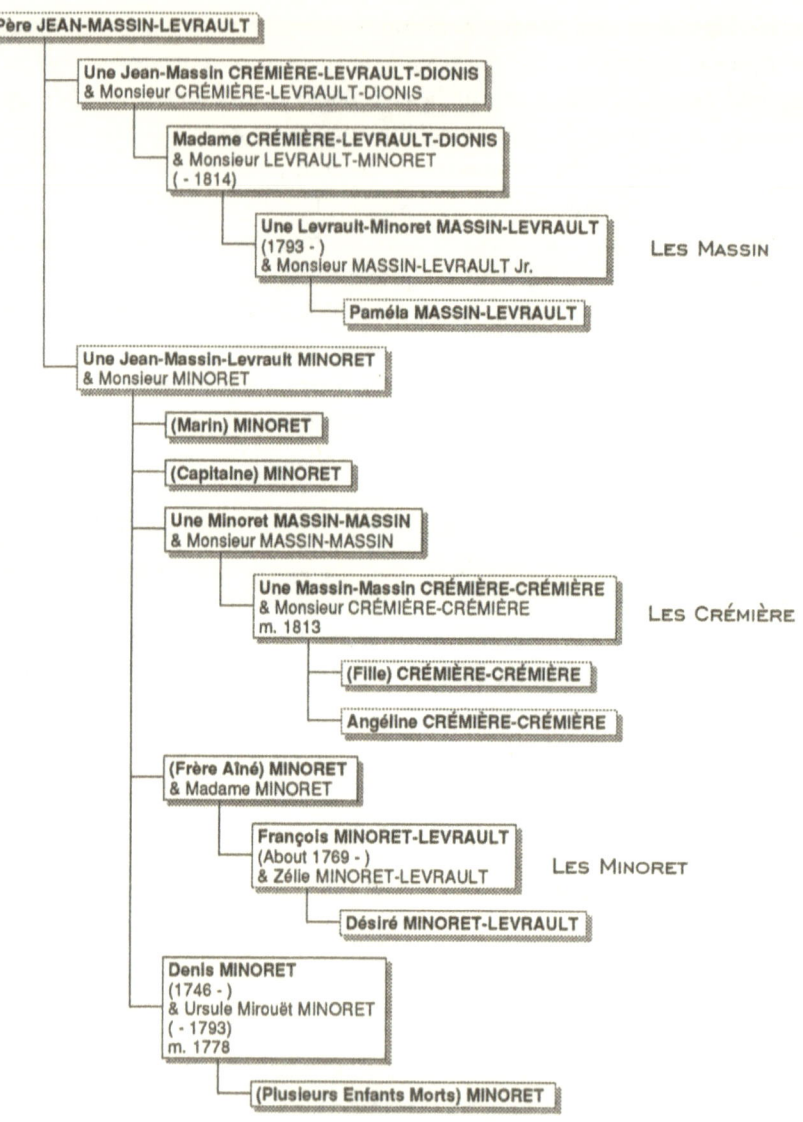

Figure 11.1 *Ursule Mirouët* genealogy

Levrault-Minoret-Massins, Massin-Levraults, Minoret-Massins, Massin-Massins, Crémière-Massins, all variegated with juniors, the firsts, Crémières-François, Levraults-Jacques, and Jean-Minorets.]

Surely this is Balzac at his most obsessive. These connections (to which are added a fifth name, the lawyer usually called Dionis whose full name is Crémière-Dionis, and who is associated with Massin-Levrault in usury) make it impossible to apprehend a character unless one also interrogates his relationships; in reading for knowledge, we read multiple relations, and thus we approach impossible closure and endless language. The hyphenated linkages signal the alliances that offer "le curieux spectacle de l'irradiation de quelques familles autochtones" ["the odd spectacle of the irradiation of a few autochthonous families"] (3: 782) and the "entrecroisements de races au fond des provinces" [intertwining of races deep in the provinces] (3: 781). One also finds this odd spectacle in the Swiss cantons, Balzac writes (3: 782). (The spectacle continues: in January 1996, in Saas-Fee in the Wallis canton, I saw the surnames of about ten families, often linked by hyphens, emblazoned on every hotel, restaurant, store, or service in town.) These hyphenated relations become emblems of the complex narration, mimetic figures of the plot and of the structure of writing. A further complication, for my reading at least, stems from a certain laxity in using the full versions of the names: Massin-Levrault is often called simply Massin; Crémière is actually Crémière-Crémière, etc. Balzac relies heavily on the reader's assiduity in acquiring knowledge. But this repeated mechanism also allows the name Minoret to apply equally to the two chief antagonists in the possession of the fortune, the doctor and his nephew Minoret-Levrault.

A second set of relations concerns what Balzac innovatively called "cognomonisme," the connection of a person's name to his work: the profession gives rise to the name. In the present case, cognomonism justifies designating the person by the profession; thus Minoret-Levrault is the "maître de poste" or captain of the post, Crémière is the "percepteur de Nemours" or tax collector, and Massin is the "greffier de la justice de paix," the clerk of the justice of the peace, and these designations are as likely to occur as the names, in Balzac's writing. The effect is to lend greater weight to the dominating forces of the bourgeoisie, which govern both the social and the narrative structures.

In juxtaposition to this semiotic structure of genealogy, excessive in its manifestations, Balzac places the harmonious unity of Ursule Mirouët. Several passages underscore this unity. For instance:

> Bientôt la mélancolie de ses pensées insensiblement adoucie teignit en quelque sorte ses heures, et relia toutes ces choses par une indéfinissable

harmonie: ce fut une exquise propreté, la plus exacte symétrie dans la disposition des meubles . . . une paix que les habitudes de la jeune fille communiquaient aux choses et qui rendit son chez-soi aimable. (3: 930-31)

[Soon the gently stilled melancholy of her thoughts colored her hours, as it were, and brought all these things together by an indefinable harmony: there was an exquisite cleanliness, the most exact symmetry in the position of her furniture . . . a peacefulness that the young girl's habits communicated to things and that made her home lovable.]

While the spider's web of the bourgeois genealogy surrounds the doctor's succession ("ils essayèrent d'entourer moins l'oncle que la succession" [they tried to surround not so much the uncle as the inheritance] [3: 790]) and nearly destroys the rightful heiress, the plot schemes to explain how the fortune comes to the central figure, Ursule Mirouët, after being lost among the collaterals. The circulation of money, never secondary or insignificant in Balzac, follows a complex structure analogous to the excessive complexities of the genealogy.

Autochthonous families thus form the bourgeoisie of Nemours, which is endogamous, materialistic, anti-intellectual, and anti-musical. The heirs fail to appreciate Ursule's piano-playing of Beethoven's seventh symphony ("Bête à vent" [Beet oven], says Mme Crémière, the Mrs. Malaprop of the *héritiers* [3: 871]). They want nothing so much as to demolish Minoret's exquisite library after his death. In contrast, Minoret's chosen company explicitly excludes the bourgeoisie and is exogamous, spiritual, intellectual, and musical. Ursule's upbringing reproduces the ideals of the Enlightenment, and the members of the minute society that separates her from the town are repeatedly characterized by their luminosity and illumination (3: 793, 794, 797). They constitute a "family of chosen minds," whose "fraternity" forms a "compact, exclusive society," an "oasis" (3: 798) in the doctor's living room. Under the effect of the light that streams forth from Ursule, the doctor's wall of incredulity cracks and crumbles (3: 837-38). From the opening pages, after Minoret's conversion, the mystical and the spiritual hold sway in his household, with the support of the priest. In the confrontation between the heirs and Ursule, these many structures of opposition repeatedly place Ursule outside the materialistic pathways by which a succession usually passes. The transfer of money to her is thus made problematic by the very semiotic structures of the novel.

As if to exacerbate this repudiation of bourgeois breeding and inbreeding, the novel, not without irony, is structured to bring about the passage of the succession through illegitimacy, for Ursule's father Joseph Mirouët is the illegitimate though recognized half-brother of the doctor Minoret's wife. (Nicole Mozet, in *Balzac au pluriel,* has called the novel "une véritable apologie de la bâtardise et de la mésalliance" [a veritable justification of illegitimacy and misalliance] [53]). It is useful to spell out this relationship (an *explication nécessaire*). Minoret's wife, also named Ursule Mirouët, was the daughter of Valentin Mirouët, an organist and builder of musical instruments. (Having left Nemours in his youth, Minoret did not take a wife from among the bourgeois cousinage.) This first Ursule Mirouët died in 1793, leaving the doctor childless after several of their children died. Ursule's father Valentin, meanwhile, had an illegitimate son in his old age, Joseph, whose mother he did not marry in order to avoid bringing dishonor to the legitimate Ursule. Joseph Mirouët, "excessivement mauvais sujet" [an exceedingly bad fellow] (3: 812), after an adventurous life, married Dinah Grollman in Germany, and the legitimate product of that union is the Ursule Mirouët who is the heroine of this novel, born in 1814 and costing her mother's life. Joseph Mirouët, "the natural brother-in-law" of the doctor and the half-brother of the doctor's wife, died soon after, leaving Ursule an orphan. Thus Balzac can describe her as Minoret's "natural niece" (3: 843), since her father is the illegitimate brother of his wife. It is to be noted that the blood relation, which is only half a blood relation, passes through the wife, not the doctor, and that the first Ursule Mirouët was dead twenty-one years before the heroine was born. There is, strictly speaking, no blood relation between Denis Minoret and Ursule Mirouët, and the text underscores this fact by calling him her godfather and her guardian, never her uncle.

Exogamy compounded by illegitimacy thus defines Ursule's distinctness from the bourgeois cousinage. In this matter the text exploits French law, which held that legitimization of bastards did not extend to the next generation: illegitimate descent does not continue beyond the first degree, according to notes by Madeleine Ambrière-Fargeaud in the Folio edition (389). The legitimate child of an illegitimate child can make no claim on its grandfather. Ursule, second-generation offspring of illegitimacy, is a stranger to Minoret (3: 851), "car on peut soutenir qu'il n'existe aucun lien de parenté entre Ursule et le docteur" [for one can maintain that there is no family relation between Ursule and the doctor] (3: 843), according to Dionis the lawyer. The text insists on this absence of relationship, and indeed depends on it. (Nicole Mozet's observation in *"Ursule Mirouët ou le test du bâtard"* is not entirely in agreement with Balzac. She writes: "De ce fait, au regard des lois et des mœurs de l'époque, elle n'est pour lui ni une parente ni une étrangère, et tout testament en sa faveur serait susceptible de faire l'objet d'un procès de la part des neveux et nièces en attente d'héritage" [Because of this fact, with respect to the laws and mores of the time, she is neither a relative nor a stranger to him, and any will in her favor would be susceptible of being the object of a lawsuit brought by the nephews and nieces awaiting their inheritance] [217].)

The legal situation is however complicated enough to require two sets of explanations in the novel (which are yet not adequate without the extensive additional information found in the editor's notes). The explanation Dionis supplies to the heirs, supplemented by information from Goupil the clerk and Désiré, newly become a lawyer (3: 843-48), favors the heirs, while justice of the peace Bongrand's detailed discussion with the doctor (3: 850-52) seeks Ursule's interest. Yet both come to the same conclusion, the gist of which is that Minoret cannot leave his fortune to Ursule by making a will in her favor. This is not strictly speaking the case, however. If Minoret were Ursule's natural (not legitimate) father, the law would prevent his leaving his entire fortune to her, for the spirit of the law is to prevent the natural parent's predilection for the illegitimate child from disinheriting the legitimate children. But, as Balzac wrote (in referring to an earlier version), "Ursule Mirouët est évidemment une étrangère pour le Dr Minoret" [Ursule Mirouët is obviously a stranger for Dr. Minoret] (3: 1533). In fact Minoret *could* write a will in Ursule's favor—just as he does write a will bequeathing 36,000 francs of income to Savinien. What really prevents the doctor from bequeathing his fortune directly to Ursule is quite precisely the greediness of the heirs and their very conviction that they deserve Minoret's entire fortune. So certain and predictable is this circumstance that both camps reach the same conclusion, that the doctor cannot bequeath his fortune to Ursule, and for the same reason: the heirs are sure to bring a lawsuit against Ursule, who would be, though legally in her right, too feeble to win. As Balzac wrote, "le docteur, justement effrayé de cette perspective, renonce à laisser à sa filleule sa succession par testament" [the doctor, justly alarmed by this perspective, abandons the attempt to leave his inheritance to his godchild by testament] (3: 1533).

In legal terms, then, there is no family relationship and thus no relation of genealogy between Minoret and Ursule. Instead, by a semantic turn of phrase, the doctor "inherited" her when Joseph Mirouët "légua sa fille au docteur" [bequeathed his daughter to the doctor] (3: 813). This welcome metaphor provides an excellent example of Balzac's supplying pointed markers for our guidance. Inheritance is the indicator of desire and preference: Minoret is father, mother, friend, doctor, and godfather to Ursule (3: 855); desire and preference characterize their relationship, whereas mindless and reiterated intermarriage produced the genealogy. One may say that interest governs the genealogy, desire the inheritance; or, in the basic terms of the prime movers, Money on the one hand, Love on the other. As Nicole Mozet writes, "Espace utopique dans une certaine mesure, le Nemours balzacien est le lieu d'une stupéfiante redéfinition de la filialité, conçue en termes d'amour et non plus en termes de sang" [Balzac's Nemours, a utopian space to a degree, is the site of a stunning redefinition of filiation, conceived in terms of love rather than blood] (*La ville de province* 219). We learn in detail about the disappointed paternity of the doctor (3: 813), who compensates for the loss of his several children by accepting "avec bonheur *le legs* que lui fit Joseph Mirouët" [with joy *the bequest* that Joseph Mirouët made him] (3: 813; emphasis added). (Just as the heir is distinct from the legatee, the "legs" or bequest is defined by the Petit Robert as "free disposition made by testament.") In Minoret's letter expressing his last wishes and telling Ursule where to find the stock certificates, he recalls her resemblance to the first Ursule Mirouët, his wife, which also motivates his paternal affection; and he mentions "le serment que j'ai fait à ton pauvre père de le remplacer" [the oath I made to your poor father to replace him] (3: 915). Through this metaphor of inheritance, Ursule replaces the doctor's wife and the doctor replaces Ursule's father, in a perfect, closed system, which also recovers lost time by superposing past and present. Attached to this letter is a testament granting 36,000 francs of income to Savinien de Portenduère, in case Ursule refuses to take the money herself. Indirectly, this provision shows how Ursule is defined by her refusal of greediness, her refusal to "salir par des pensées d'intérêt" [sully by thoughts of self-interest] (3: 930) her affection for her guardian, while thoughts of interest alone characterize the greed of the heirs. Most important, I take a key word from the short testament itself to characterize the essential nature of the relations of inheritance between Minoret and Ursule: preference. The doctor's money goes to Savinien "par préférence à tous mes héritiers" [in preference to all my heirs] (3: 917). (As a minor point contributing to the relations by inheritance, captain Jordy writes a touching will by which he bequeaths his 10,000 francs of savings to Ursule [3: 817].)

In short, Minoret chooses to pass the succession to Ursule by a mechanism that does not fall under the legality of the relationships defined by intermarriages and births. The fortune Minoret leaves to his cherished pupil in the form of the government certificates to the bearer is hidden in the pages of a folio volume of the *Pandectes* in his library. Not only is it worthy of Minoret's keen sense of fairness to place these writings in a volume of the Roman civil law which forms the basis for European law, but the wit in Balzac no doubt chose this title because it means, in Latin, "book containing everything" (*American Heritage Dictionary of the English Language*). Everything, indeed, for without the *inscriptions de rente* Ursule has a mere pittance; she is described as "sans aucune fortune" [with no fortune at all] (3: 925). The money that has been converted to these certificates no longer has any connection to the succession or the doctor's estate, any more than Ursule has to Minoret, legally speaking. Rather, these papers have value only for the hands that hold them. Because they are immediately related to their cash value, they can be removed from the succession both literally (as by robbery) and in terms of the financial portion they represent. This monetary document thus becomes an emblem for the position of the writing in this novel. Both the nature of the writing and its location are figures for how writing achieves significance and value by its location; eventually the position of the inscriptions will become the focus of spiritualism, the value of which resides specifically in its placement in the narrative. As for the doctor's will, once it is stolen and burned it has no value of any sort. The fact that both camps continue to look for a will as if it were merely unfound indicates that it too depends on position for value. As Balzac writes, "Pour les monuments comme pour les hommes, la position fait tout" [For monuments as for men, position is all] (3: 777).

By these mechanisms Minoret sees to it that his preferred relation will inherit most of his money. When Minoret-Levrault steals the money, and tells no one, the full value of the estate becomes moot. ("Et les valeurs?" ["And the shares?"] asks the priest. "Courez donc après!" ["See if you can catch them!"] says Bongrand [3: 926].) Those portions of Minoret's succession that are publicly known, including his house, are divided among three heirs, while Ursule receives nothing. Predilection characterizes the reader's desire to see the money returned to Ursule, but, true to her upbringing and her nature, Ursule refuses to employ the greedy strategies variously proposed to her by the townsfolk. The harmful actions of the domestic coalition, centered on Minoret-Levrault's theft of the government stock certificates, counteract the reader's desire until spiritualism, a concrete and active manifestation of a penetrating influence focused by will and desire, conquers materialism and brings the money to the unitary figure of composition, Ursule.

Just as somnambulism arises in a concentration of the will, the narrative's recourse to somnambulism indicates the concentration of unitary thought in the composition of the novel, seen in the genotextual process by which money enters the system of the spiritual. Somnambulism is the mechanism that transfers the certificates from the semiotic figure of genealogy to that of inheritance. A passing mention of Geoffroy Saint-Hilaire (3: 823) in the *explication nécessaire* that justifies the doctor's conversion by magnetism and mesmerism is no incidental reference but a precious guide to the structure of the plot and its unitary thought. Balzac is at his most fervent in his explanation of magnetism, which is anchored in its opposition to the materialism of eighteenth-century philosophy. What for Balzac is a misrecognized or badly exploited phenomenon of nature manifest not only in the inscrutable Orient but also in Jesus Christ was in the eighteenth century "repoussé par les doubles atteintes des gens religieux et des philosophes matérialistes également alarmés" [repulsed by the twin attacks from religious people and materialist philosophers both equally alarmed] (3: 822). Balzac compares this erroneous assessment of magnetism to the "sort qu'avait eu la vérité dans la personne de Galilée" [fate that truth had had in the person of Galileo] in the sixteenth century (3: 822). To Geoffroy Saint-Hilaire belongs the merit of the "immense progrès que font en ce moment les sciences naturelles" [immense progress that the natural sciences are now making] (3: 823), under the idea of unity. That such a unity takes the form, in this novel, of magnetism or mesmerism, in their somnambulistic version, stems from Balzac's profound belief in the "ancient human power" (3: 822) that allows one person to influence another by concentrating one's will.

Mesmerism underlies the novel as the principle of its effects. This science of imponderable fluids (3: 823) is profoundly rooted in the luminous figure of Ursule Mirouët; Balzac says it is "étroitement lié[e] par la nature de ses phénomènes à la lumière" [narrowly linked, by the nature of its phenomena, to light] (3: 823). Music, which plays a significant role (see also chapter 14), provides another expression of mesmerism:

> Il existe en toute musique, outre la pensée du compositeur, l'âme de l'exécutant [Ursule], qui, par un privilège acquis seulement à cet art, peut donner du sens et de la poésie à des phrases sans grande valeur. . . . Par sa sublime et périlleuse organisation, Ursule appartenait à cette école de génies si rares. . . . Par un jeu à la fois suave et rêveur, son âme parlait à l'âme du jeune homme [Savinien] et l'enveloppait comme d'un nuage par des idées presque visibles. (3: 890–91)

[One finds in all music, in addition to the composer's ideas, the soul of the performer [Ursule], who, by a privilege pertaining only to this art, can give meaning and poetry to phrases lacking much value. . . . By her sublime and perilous organization, Ursule belonged to this school of rarefied geniuses. . . . Through her at once suave and dreamy playing, her soul spoke to the soul of the young man [Savinien] and enveloped it, like a cloud, with nearly visible thoughts.]

Music and harmonic unity, genius, and the mesmeric concentration of thought all combine to elevate the composition of the novel to the level of the sublime.

Readers like Allan Pasco suggest it is necessary to recognize the part played by God in the symbolic or semantic structures of this novel ("Ursule"). The conversion of the deist but unbelieving (3: 826, 828) doctor Minoret to Christian religion motivates his faith in his ability to protect Ursule after his death. Yet, since this protection from beyond death takes the form of somnambulism, a science to which Balzac takes the trouble to provide its letters of patent, we should think of a God and a Christianity much secularized by these *explications nécessaires*. Significantly, it is to Chaperon the priest that Balzac gives the task of explaining Minoret's scientific understanding of somnambulism, as if to suggest that religion recognizes the superior ability of science to explain the occult:

> Il avait reconnu la possibilité de l'existence d'un monde spirituel, d'un monde des idées. Si les idées sont une création propre à l'homme, si elles subsistent en vivant d'une vie qui leur soit propre, elles doivent avoir des formes insaisissables à nos sens extérieurs, mais perceptibles à nos sens intérieurs quand ils sont dans certaines conditions. Ainsi les idées de votre parrain peuvent vous envelopper, et peut-être les avez-vous revêtues de son apparence. Puis, si Minoret a commis ces actions, elles se résolvent en idées; car toute action est le résultat de plusieurs idées. Or, si les idées se meuvent dans le monde spirituel, votre esprit a pu les apercevoir en y pénétrant. (3: 961–62)

> [He had recognized the possible existence of a spiritual world, of a world of thought. If ideas are a creation proper to the human being, if they subsist by living a life that is proper to them, they must have a shape that cannot be grasped by our external senses, but which is perceptible to our internal senses in certain conditions. Thus your godfather's ideas can enclose you, and perhaps you have clothed them in his appearance. Then, if Minoret performed these actions, they would resolve into ideas; for every action is the result of several ideas. And so, if ideas move about in the spiritual world, your mind, by entering it, was able to perceive them.]

Here Balzac offers the double guide of the converted non-believer, Minoret, and the intelligent, unbigoted priest, Chaperon, to make it possible for the reader to believe also—believe in somnambulism, that is. It takes very little reflection to extend this explanation to the process of composition, and to realize that Balzac grounds in a scientific vision of unity the spiritual basis of *La Comédie humaine*.

Although the powerful mesmerist, whose demonstrations in Paris convince and help to convert Minoret, may well describe his power as emanating from God (3: 827), although his power to heal may well be compared to the Savior's (3: 826), the narrative significantly elevates this power to the status of *science* and *principle*. Mozet also stresses the importance of science "behind" God and comments that Ursule's happiness was "indispensable au triomphe de la vérité scientifique" [indispensable to the triumph of scientific truth] (*"Ursule Mirouët"* 218, 225). Faith and unity are taken up by the scientific system of *La Comédie humaine*. Françoise Gaillard, in a rich commentary on unitary science in the *Avant-propos*, shows that for Geoffroy Saint-Hilaire, as for Balzac, the theory is one of analogy, which postulates a principle of resemblance and a principle of continuity among species ("La science" 64–65). Founded on analogy, the semiotic unity of the novel is represented by the transformation I have described from a system of relations based on genealogy (intermarriage) to one based on inheritance, desire, preference, and the generosity that consistently characterize Ursule Mirouët. (Arguing for a new form of nobility against his mother's prejudices, Savinien de Portenduère uses the telling metaphor "une chimère" [3: 885] to designate the old system. The monstrous, composite chimera symbolizes another contrast to the harmonious unity of Ursule.) Analogy underlies Minoret's love for Ursule, because she is like another Ursule Mirouët, but also, paradoxically, because she is a stranger to the doctor, and love arises where there is no genealogy. Analogy as a principle of composition lies in the semiotic structures based on preference and predilection. When the descendant of exogamous and illegitimate unions marries the only eligible aristocrat in town, the happy alliance reaffirms the inheritance against the harmful posterity of the bourgeois cousinage of Nemours.

Spirituality as it appears in *Ursule Mirouët* focuses on written texts, especially on their position. This necessary connection between the spiritual and writing has been well prepared in the novel. Ursule's visionary genius specifically includes the ability to see written texts: while Savinien is at sea in the marines, Ursule sees each of his letters in a dream before receiving them, and never fails to announce their arrival by recounting her dream (3: 900). Likewise, during the demonstration of mesmerism in Paris, what convinced the doctor of the real existence of magnetism was the mesmerized subject's ability to see Minoret's two bank notes stored between the two next-to-last leaves of the *Pandectes,* volume II, in Nemours (3: 831). The position of the 500-franc notes gives them their value in the narrative of the experiments, for the precision with which the subject locates them leaves the doctor thunderstruck (3: 832).

Connecting semiosis to mimesis, we can say that the passing of the fortune from a genealogy described as a pernicious system, mindless and materialistic, to an inheritance formed by love and preference provides both the mimetic frame of the narrative (the represented story) and the semiotic structure of our reading. The very materiality of money lends strength and consistency to the ideality of the moral plot here: while the money is lost among the collaterals, it figures error in the spiritual sense and failure of the narrative. When it is at last returned to Ursule, it figures the reward of spirituality and recovery from error. In like fashion, we are in error until we realize the power of spirituality to unify composition. That is the message of the unity of composition: the ideal is not contaminated by the real.

12

Un prince de la bohème *and* Pierre Grassou, *or* How Love Makes Money

Genius in spite of mediocrity, in a bourgeois context: this is what characterizes two novellas in which love and money determine the representation of reality and interact to the benefit of the mediocre.

In *Un prince de la bohème,* Claudine, a dancer known as Tullia, mistress of several rich important men, evolves into a *bourgeoise* by marrying the vaudeville writer du Bruel, which does not prevent her from falling madly in love with Charles-Édouard Rusticoli, comte de La Palférine, an impoverished but authentic nobleman. But La Palférine, the cynical, capricious prince of bohemia, is bored with her and, to get rid of her, pretends he would keep her only if she had a title and rode in a carriage equal to his rank. Not one to miss a hint, Claudine proceeds with alacrity to transform her *vaudevilliste* of a husband into a count, with his heraldic arms on a splendid carriage. In the process, her evolution from demi-mondaine to countess casts doubt on the real meaning of the name and insignia of a countess.

This short story puts into place a trio of characters tied together by love in one direction, because du Bruel loves Claudine in spite of her fickleness ("il portait à une femme de théâtre une de ces affections qui ne s'expliquent pas" [for this lady of the theater he bore one of those affections that cannot be explained] [7: 825]), and by money or its associated interests in the other direction. Like the "alte Geschichte" that Heinrich Heine put into a poem and Schumann set to music, like the formulaic round of love in a type of comic play, and like the situation of the Bridaus in *La Rabouilleuse,* none of the characters in this story returns the love they receive. Balzac dedicated the story to Heine, "à vous qui savez mieux que personne ce qu'il peut y avoir ici de critique, de plaisanterie, d'amour et de vérité" [to you, who know better than anyone what criticism, humor, love, and truth one might find here] (7: 807), thus alerting the reader to the motifs of the story. But the one-way arrows indicating Love become arrows of Money in the opposite direction, and the desire for love affects the action of money on the situation of the three characters. Balzac exploited such a premise more than once (see chapter 10).

Love as expressed in this story rests on the Balzacian theory of the unique, profound, unalterable love that only the fortunate will find once in their lifetime. Du Bruel loves Claudine like this: "le vaudevilliste . . . l'aimait de cet amour que l'habitude finit par rendre indispensable à l'existence" [the vaudevillist . . . loved her with the love that habit makes indispensable to existence]; he is "un homme lié, pieds et poings, cœur et tête" [a man tied up hands and feet, heart and head] (7: 829). This Balzacian theory of love also contributes to the contradictory portrait of La Palférine: "Charles-Édouard a sur l'amour les idées les plus justes. Il n'y a pas, selon lui, deux amours dans la vie de l'homme; il n'y en a qu'un seul, profond comme la mer, mais sans rivages. A tout âge, cet amour fond sur vous comme la grâce fondit sur saint Paul" [Charles-Édouard has a most appropriate understanding of love. In his opinion, there are not two loves in a man's life; there is only one, as deep as the sea but without shorelines. This love can descend upon you at any age just as grace descended upon St. Paul] (7: 818). Unfortunately for Claudine he feels neither the thunderbolt nor the slow revelation and recognition of attractive qualities that bind two people in a powerful crescendo—neither love at first sight, nor the gradual fusion of two beings into one. And in contradiction to his views, La Palférine has love affairs—practice belies the theory. Claudine however "éprouvait l'amour complet, idéal et physique, enfin La Palférine fut sa vraie passion à elle" [felt complete, ideal, and physical love—in all, La Palférine was the true passion for her] (7: 819). Such absolute love exists on a high moral plane when it is mutual, but when the arrows point in only one direction, as also happens to Thaddée Paz in *La fausse maîtresse,* the love thus illustrated can become a corrupted, degraded version of absolute love (see Michel, *Le réel* 246, for observations on absolute love). Du Bruel obeys Claudine, who obeys La Palférine, each a slave to love. Paul Gadenne coupled the slave metaphor to the tyrant: "Claudine, qui est tyran, se fera esclave mais pas pour le même homme. . . . Ange et démon, certes, mais ange pour l'un [La Palférinie], démon pour l'autre [du Bruel]" [Claudine, a tyrant, will make herself a slave, but not for the same man. . . . Angel and demon, to be sure, but angel for one [La Palférine] and demon for the other [du Bruel]] (638–39). Once Claudine has money, La Palférine loves her again, but in merely honoring his part in what is essentially a contractual agreement, he expresses cynicism: money corrupts what could have been absolute love, in this narrative design.

Here Money is expressed not in terms of how it can keep a family in food and furniture, which was the case for the Bridau family in *La Rabouilleuse,* but in terms of the social rank or status it can purchase. To have money, for a down-and-out aristocrat, is to have the external signs of status that accompany the inalterable internal ones of birth and ancestry. Hence La Palférine's desire to complete the fullness of the sign identifying him in his proper and full identity in the world. Gadenne wrote:

> la différence de race, d'origine, justifie la manière dont Claudine est traitée. Claudine a pu s'élever; ce n'est pas ce qui compte. La Palférine est une protestation vivante—faite, notons-le, moins au nom de la race elle-même que de *l'esprit* qui est attaché à la race—contre une bourgeoisie qui croit pouvoir se sauver par l'argent. L'ambition de Claudine du Bruel . . . est de devenir une bourgeoise; et l'on sait que cela s'achète. (635)

> [the difference in class, in birth, justifies the way Claudine is treated. Claudine was able to lift herself up; that is not what counts. La Palférine is a living protest against a bourgeois class that thinks it can save itself by means of money (a protest leveled, it should be noted, at the *spirit* of the class rather than the class itself). Claudine du Bruel's ambition . . . is to become bourgeois; and it is well known that that can be bought.]

The drive for money essentially characterizing the social-climbing lower class female constitutes a fundamental driving force of *La Comédie humaine.*

Yet money, or more exactly signs thereof, are what La Palférine requests of Claudine, and she will do everything to obtain it precisely by turning the same interest in the direction of her unloved husband. She drives her husband to wealth, just as she is driven by Charles-Édouard. The relation of love and money works by reverse psychology: La Palférine exploits Claudine's love, which expresses itself through complete obedience to his wishes, to demand that she obtain title, wealth, carriage, liveried lackeys, and horses, thinking she cannot reach such a level of money; that will be his plan to be rid of her; but when she succeeds, money turns into a form of love.

"Les Fantaisies de Claudine" was the original title of *Un prince de la bohème;* its focus on Claudine lent true measure to the psychology of the social-climbing "premier sujet" of the theater. "Fantaisies" refers not only to the expensive baubles she buys to furnish her home and impress others, but also to the demands she makes of her husband: exerting her will power, she launches him into writing vaudevilles at a ferocious pace, making pots of money that allow him to buy carriage and horses—whence his meteoric rise in the political sphere. Additionally, "fantaisies" implies capricious fancies, which describe not only Claudine's behavior with her husband but also La Palférine's with Claudine. But "fantaisie" also has the precise connotation of a lover, as in "On ne connaissait pas de fantaisie à l'ancien Premier Sujet" [The former Prima Donna was not known to have had any "fantasies"] (7: 830)—not, that is, until she meets La Palfèrine. Then her fantasy for the prince of bohemia must be turned into money to obtain the interest she hopes to gain.

Un prince de la bohème employs one of the most elaborate discursive structures found in *La Comédie humaine:* a doubly framed story within a story transmitted via two embedded manuscripts in which the authorial voice is split from the narrative voice, and whose ending lies outside the diegesis. Chantal Massol (185–88) has given an excellent analysis of this narrative design, whose ultimate effect makes itself felt in the closing lines, including the famous "je ne crois pas aux dénouements" [I don't believe in conclusions] (7: 838; see also chapter 20 on problems of closure). The diegetic story about Claudine du Bruel and Charles-Édouard de La Palférine as narrated by Nathan and written up by Mme de La Baudraye, who then reads it aloud to Nathan, does not have a dénouement in Balzac's novella, but the *act of narration* recorded in Mme de La Baudraye's story, which stages Nathan narrating to the marquise Béatrix de Rochefide, a narrator whom we occasionally hear from in intrusions of the frame into the narration, has an ending that lies in the effect of the narrated story on Béatrix: she has fallen in love with La Palférine after listening to Nathan's skillful portrait of the cynical, capricious prince of bohemia. Then *this* story—the story that ends with Béatrix falling for La Palférine—has what can only be called a delayed and displaced dénouement: it will take place in the future and in another novel, *Béatrix,* which ends with Béatrix returning to her husband Rochefide. Inscribing Mme de La Baudraye in his own role as writer, exploiting narration and its effects, giving his parable a moral at second or third remove, Balzac gives form to the idea: love turns into money to redefine social position and identity.

Pierre Grassou gives greater consistency to this essential strategy of *La Comédie humaine.* Grassou, the mediocre painter of copies and pastiches, resembles La Palférine for the cheerful cynicism that characterizes him. He ekes out a paltry living until he sells copies of old masterworks to the unscrupulous dealer Elias Magus, who, unbeknownst to him, sells them as originals for vast sums after having artfully aged them. The copies, snapped up by the bourgeoisie, sell far better than originals, eventually turning Grassou into an affluent and respected member of the bourgeoisie: Grassou succeeds because he is recognized by the bourgeois citizens as one of them, as primarily a businessman rather than an impecunious artist. One of the chief buyers of Grassou's copies is M. Vervelle, a wealthy industrialist; when Grassou reveals that he is the author of the Rubens, Rembrandts, and so on in Vervelle's collection, Vervelle doubles his daughter Virginie's dowry; via marriage to Virginie, the painter obtains a title. The happy ending crowning his success, called a euphoric ending by Anne-Marie Meininger (6: 1089), ratifies his abilities, in stark contrast to other Balzacian mediocrities who end badly, such as Lucien de Rubempré. The moral of the story seems to be that the end justifies the means: why not succeed through mediocrity rather than superiority?

A brilliant opening page sets the underlying theme with lapidary precision. What used to be art has turned into commerce; no longer does the Salon maintain an aristocracy of art. "Depuis 1830, le Salon n'existe plus. Une seconde fois, le Louvre a été pris d'assaut par le peuple des artistes, qui s'y est maintenu" [Since 1830, the Salon no longer exists. For the second time, the Louvre has been besieged—by the artist populace who has maintained its position there] (6: 1091). Instead of a society of elites, instead of honors, a crown, and passionate discussions about art, the keywords of this opening are *foule, émeutes,* and *bazar*: popular insurrection and commercialism instead of art. "Au lieu d'un tournoi, vous avez une émeute; au lieu d'une Exposition glorieuse, vous avez un tumultueux bazar; au lieu du choix, vous avez la totalité" [Instead of a tournament, you have a riot; instead of a glorious Exhibition, you have a tumultuous bazaar; instead of choice, you have totality] (6: 1092). This theme opposing art and merchandise, elite and the crowd, selection and election, is maintained from the beginning to the end. By the ending, which arrives at the historical present in 1839, art as commerce has been ratified in lofty regions. The bourgeois circle in which Grassou evolves considers him "un des plus grands artistes de l'époque" [one of the greatest artists of the period] (6: 1111). In the list of his accomplishments and honors there is the commission for a battle scene for the museum of Versailles, another iconic location, like the Louvre, of *ancien régime* aristocracy and a true indicator of quality. But the ironic reason for his bourgeois success, "la grande raison des Bourgeois" [the great bourgeois rationale], is the money he makes: "il place vingt mille francs par an chez son notaire" [he invests twenty thousand francs a year with his financial advisor] (6: 1111). The ending fully realizes, in this fashion, the success of the bourgeoisie announced in the opening page; as Boris Lyon-Caen writes (170), the figure Grassou emblematizes the rise of the bourgeoisie after 1830.

If his success is crowned by monetary reward, Grassou is nevertheless not of the same stuff as the merchant class as illustrated elsewhere in *La Comédie humaine*, for instance by the Rogrons of *Pierrette*. He has qualities that deserve recognition, even if they are precisely the opposite of a great artist's qualities; he is modest, simple, good, gentle, hard-working, patient, honest, reliable, obliging, loyal, punctual, and dutiful; but the most important of these descriptions lasting a page and a half is that he has energy (6: 1101). Energy is a Balzacian virtue that, as Anne-Marie Meininger remarks, is never without reward (6: 1089).

So why not succeed via mediocrity? The answers that would give the resoundingly negative response to this rhetorical question reside in several significant places in *La Comédie humaine*. Grassou is commonly opposed to Frenhofer, who in *Le chef-d'œuvre inconnu* not only illustrates the concept of the artist driven by the passion of an idea but also teaches the artist's function to younger painters. "La mission de l'art n'est pas de copier la nature, mais de l'exprimer! Tu n'es pas un vil copiste, mais un poète!. . . . Nous avons à saisir l'esprit, l'âme, la physionomie des choses et des êtres" [The mission of art is not to copy nature but to express it! You are not a vile copier, you are a poet! . . . Our task is to grasp the spirit, the soul, the physiognomy of things and beings] (10: 418). But Grassou *is* a vile copier. Can he be a creator? In contrast, the satirical depiction of Grassou's success leads him to this ironic realization: "Inventer en toute chose, c'est vouloir mourir à petit feu; copier, c'est vivre" [To invent at every moment is to want to die a slow death; to copy is to live] (6: 1101)—again, quite the opposite of Frenhofer, who did die for inventing. Anne-Marie Meininger sounds the depth of this contrast between the two kinds of painting by musing that if a cataclysm were to destroy all but *Le chef-d'œuvre inconnu* and *Pierre Grassou*, readers would find it difficult to believe that the Balzac of the one was the Balzac of the other (6: 1079). Although the theme of the artist as man of passion is central in *La Comédie humaine*, giving automatic precedence to the Frenhofer model, this slight tale of the mediocre painter has a disproportionately important function. What *Pierre Grassou* institutes is a serious questioning of the very idea of the copy.

In the story itself, Joseph Bridau, another model for the artistic creator, admonishes Grassou: "Aborde donc la Nature comme elle est! . . . Veux-tu avoir plus d'esprit que la Nature?" [Approach Nature as she is! . . . Are you trying to be cleverer than Nature?] (6: 1107). Given Balzac's ambitions, this line invites us to place Balzac into the model of the copier. The painter and the writer both toil tirelessly to make imitations while thereby gaining fame and fortune, consideration and credit, a prosperous wife, and, in Grassou's case, a decoration and a title. To be sure, mediocrity was never a good descriptor for the grand creator of *La Comédie humaine,* and most of Balzac's many avatars, like Louis Lambert, fly high in the empyrean ether. Yet if we consider the idea of the copy (imitation) as *copy,* the product of writing, we are not far from a model for how Balzac did in fact succeed, producing so many lines of fiction a month.

For Balzac, love of his art turned of necessity into money. The Frenhofer model fails to communicate the beauty of the vision to the receiver; this is the theme that *Le chef-d'œuvre inconnu* illustrates. To communicate the vision, to "approach Nature as she is," the artist must *compromise* the very art it is his passion to illustrate; to convey the spirit, the soul, and the physiognomy of things and beings, Balzac does in fact create copy, and copies. Arlette Michel, in discussing the value of the real for Balzac, writes: "Le créateur ... doit inscrire l'Idée dans la Forme pour la rendre communicable, même si, évidemment, l'Idée est allusion à l'absolu donc rebelle à la Forme, toute forme étant réductrice" [The creator ... must inscribe the Idea into the Form so as to make it communicable, even when, as is likely, the Idea is an allusion to the absolute and therefore rebellious to the Form, all form being reductive] (*Le réel* 84–85). The form is the copy and money; the idea is the expression of nature, the soul, and love. In *Pierre Grassou* even the form of the painter's name is a copy of aristocratic naming conventions, where the land owned by the family has given its name to the family: Grassou is more often called Fougères or Grassou de Fougères than simply Grassou (Fougères occurs 60 times, Grassou 40 times). And Grassou de Fougères is a perfect imitation, or copy, or phony version of the aristocratic practice—a little reminiscent of the Balzac family's imitative mutation into de Balzac. In analyzing *Massimilla Doni,* Max Milner also pointed to the danger for an artist who is locked into the sphere of ideas and first principles—the way Cataneo and Capraja are in that novella. Milner writes that the creator runs the risk of not being able to return to earth and of losing "le contrôle de ce système raisonné de moyens en-dehors duquel il n'existe pas d'art communicable" [control of that rational system of methods without which there is no communicable art] (48)—with the accent on "communicable." *Pierre Grassou* goes far to illustrate Balzac's understanding of this risk to artistic creation, beginning with himself.

Marrying for money is of course the height of cynicism in the romantic context. Grassou marries the Vervelle daughter because her dowry has doubled, because he covets their beautiful country home, because he has discovered "un filon plein d'or" [a vein full of gold] (6: 1101) in the family's wealth, because "Le veau d'or jeta sur cette famille son reflet fantastique" [The golden calf cast its fantastic reflection upon this family] (6: 1104). The monetary value of painting is made equivalent to marriage: Vervelle's collection of paintings is worth one hundred thousand francs, which is also the amount of Virginie's dowry, according to Elias Magus, before Vervelle doubles it. If the Pierre Grassou model reveals a double bind for the creator, enveloping the artist in a necessary cynicism, in a Faustian struggle for the soul, the mediocre, bourgeois artist emerges unscathed and morally unblemished because the god of capitalism justifies turning love into money. Motivated by love, which is the Idea, the artist nevertheless must reduce it to a Form, which will always be a copy.

But not just the god of capitalism. It is also a matter of the activity of the artist. Where does the Idea lie, in relation to the Form? To transform the idea into a form, as Arlette Michel has pointed out, it takes the agency of the artist: the portrait is not a copy but a transformation of the real; the artist has to seize the real, analyzing the character, to turn it into the portrait. What Grassou achieves with his painting turns the business of copying into a transformation of nature. And that is the Balzacian act. As we can read in *Un prince de la bohème*, "En France le style vient des idées et non des mots" [In France, style comes from the ideas, not the words] (7: 823).

13

Voyages of Reflection, Reflections on Voyages

"La pensée," says Balzac in *Le curé de village,* "est constamment le point de départ et le point d'arrivée de toute société" [Ideas are invariably the departure point and the arrival point of any society] (9: 708). Expressing the concept of thinking by means of a metaphor of displacement, this Balzacian "axiom of social science" formulates how an initial thought wends its way toward an ultimate thought and suggests that, to result in an idea, to achieve *la pensée,* society journeys. Few and far between are the lines that Balzac dedicates to the description of his characters' actual displacements, because he is often content merely to mention the trip, and the journey is most often little more than a parenthesis or pause in the narration of actions. It would seem that Balzac agrees with Flaubert's complaint that the voyage genre "est par soi-même une chose presque impossible" [is in itself an almost impossible thing] (561).

But when he does take the time to recount a voyage, he is likely to associate it with reflection. For instance, Sabine du Guénic excuses herself for not being able to write to her mother during her honeymoon, because "notre esprit est alors comme les roues" [our mind goes like the wheels] (*Béatrix,* 2: 845); the mind moves as much as the body does. The hero of *Le message* describes the intimacy that arises during travel when two young men of similar fortune find themselves similarly in love with older women (like Balzac as a young man). Marked by the rhythm of the leagues covered and the cities through which the stagecoach passes, the journey metonymically expresses and explains such a delicate thing as love for a noble (and married) woman—until the vehicle overturns past Pouilly, about fifty-one leagues from Paris, and kills the narrator's companion in love. Gaston de Nueil follows Mme de Beauséant, in *La femme abandonnée,* all the way to Geneva, asking himself why she has left Paris: "Entre les mille réflexions qui l'assaillirent pendant ce voyage, celle-ci: 'Pourquoi s'en est-elle allée?' l'occupa plus spécialement" [Among the thousands of reflections that assailed him during this voyage, the one that preoccupied him especially was: "Why did she leave?"] (2: 491). Gaston has the entire length of this trip to think about it, but he finds what he considers to be the correct answer in so little time that Balzac allots it only a few lines: "Si la vicomtesse veut m'aimer, il n'y a pas de doute qu'en femme d'esprit, elle préfère la Suisse où personne ne nous connaît, à la France où elle rencontrerait des censeurs" [If the viscountess is willing to be my lover, there is no doubt that as a woman of intelligence she prefers Switzerland, where no one knows us, to France, where she would encounter disapproval] (2: 491).

In the examples studied here of journeys of reflection, thoughts change during the trip, prompting a reflection on journeys and an ultimate reflection on narration. Points of departure and arrival contribute to the definition of the Balzacian narrative of society, providing elements of the two branches that are its Prime Movers and key descriptors, Love and Money.

In *Les Chouans,* a highly geographical novel, several vehicles furrow the routes between Alençon and Fougères, passing through Mayenne and Ernée, with a round trip as well between Fougères and Saint-James and a loop into and out of la Vivetière. Marie de Verneuil will always be linked to these conveyances. At the moment we see Mlle de Verneuil for the first time, she has just arrived in Alençon by the mail coach. Already this first journey presents her full of emotion, excited and transformed by her trip. The paragraphs that initially introduce her suggest that Marie seems destined to undergo important changes during her travels. "J'aime ce renaissant péril qui nous environne," she says. "Toutes les fois que la route prend un aspect sombre, je suppose que nous allons entendre des détonations, alors mon cœur bat, une sensation inconnue m'agite . . . c'est le jeu de tout ce qui se meut en moi, c'est la vie" [I love this constantly renewed peril that surrounds us. Every time the road takes on a somber aspect, I imagine that we are going to hear detonations. Then my heart beats, an unknown sensation agitates me . . . it is the action of everything that stirs in me, it is life] (8: 968–69). Clearly her exalted excitement the moment she arrives in the land of the Chouans, where she confronts dangers and evils, is the fruit of a reflection about the mission she has been charged with, a reflection that will have tried to "étouffer [s]a conscience" [stifle her conscience]. She admits that "je me surprends à penser comme si j'avais cinquante ans, et à agir comme si j'en avais encore quinze" [I am surprised to realize that I am thinking as if I were fifty and acting as if I were still fifteen] (8: 969). In this narrated journey, thinking results in a consciousness of the harm she must do, but the goal of her trip will deviate from this toward the pole of love.

Going on from Alençon to Mayenne, Marie de Verneuil travels in the company of Montauran along with a republican escort. What Lucienne Frappier-Mazur in her introduction has so rightly termed their "escrime amoureuse" [love sparring] (8: 886) will last fifteen pages until the ambush just before the loop toward la Vivetière; it is, unless I am mistaken, the longest voyage of reflection in *La Comédie humaine*. Dispersing the clouds, the sun presides over the first moments of this *innamoramento* which is lengthened by the places through which they travel. The avid glance that Montauran casts on Marie in the intimacy of the carriage and the subtle actions that Marie directs toward Montauran have the function of putting them on their guard as their love grows but takes on a structure of combat. Seriously engaged, the struggle changes from jestful to grave; it adopts the weapons of conversation while the two strangers climb the hill on foot. Internal reflection goes on at the same time as the external struggle, each one trying to know the other. Marie wins one round by guessing the identity of her companion, but she has the grace and kindness to believe in the assumed name that Montauran has given himself, vicomte de Bauvan. After this interlude on the hillside, once again in the vehicle, each one keeps silent; "s'ils avaient l'un et l'autre trouvé matière à d'amples réflexions, leurs yeux ne craignirent plus désormais de se rencontrer" [although they had each found matter for ample reflection, their eyes no longer feared to meet each other] (8: 1012). Observing one another, they feel themselves pulled each toward the other, "car ils avaient réciproquement reconnu chez eux des qualités qui rehaussaient encore à leurs yeux les plaisirs qu'ils se promettaient de leur lutte ou de leur union" [for they had mutually recognized in themselves the qualities that heightened in their eyes the pleasure they were promising themselves from their struggle or from their union] (8: 1012). This sympathy of souls will take an immense step forward with the revelation of their common passion for knowing what their destiny is to be. It is not through serious reflection, but by the "chances du hasard" [chances of fortune] that they attempt to find a necessary dénouement to what has no obvious outlet. Marie's imagination helps her contemplate "toute sa vie en se complaisant à l'arranger belle, à la remplir de bonheur, de grands et de nobles sentiments" [her entire life, taking pleasure in arranging it into a beautiful one, filling it with happiness and grand and noble sentiments] (8: 1013). And it is love that comes to them, following the reflections that were nourished by the journey.

The ambush that puts an end to this reflection has the goal of bringing the conflict back into the center of the idyll. When the chevalier de Valois tells Montauran to be wary of the girl with whom he is traveling, everything changes; death glides into Marie's soul, while the marquis blushes and pales in turn: "Une compression violente détruisait la gracieuse courbure de ses lèvres, et son teint jaunissait sous les efforts d'une orageuse pensée. Mlle de Verneuil ne pouvait même plus deviner s'il y avait encore de l'amour dans sa fureur" [A violent compression destroyed the graceful curve of his lips, and his complexion was turning yellow under the actions of a stormy thought. Mlle de Verneuil could no longer even guess if love still existed within his fury] (8: 1019). She searches in vain for the cause of this change, but "les événements de cette journée appartenaient à un mirage de l'âme qui se dissipait alors" [the events of this day belonged to a mirage of the soul that was then dissipating] (8: 1019–20), and she concludes: no sooner loved, no sooner abandoned. From the depths of the carriage as from the depths of her reflections, she knows her destiny: "de toujours voir le bonheur et de toujours le perdre!" [always to see happiness and always to lose it] (8: 1020)—a fair statement of the end to which the novel is headed. But, before the fatal detour towards la Vivetière, she will have recognized the noble chief of the Chouans and, her love triumphing over all (according to Balzac), she happily continues to "marcher au hasard" [walk in fortune's path] (8: 1025), sealing their bourgeoning liaison with a smile.

Balzac sought to demonstrate, with *Les Chouans,* that "les sentiments suivent peu la route commune" [sentiments rarely take the common routes] (8: 1003) in these times of terror. In the same manner, we could say that this romantic novel scarcely follows the common pathways of romantic narrative; its route is traced in advance not by private politics (as in *Pierrette*) but by governmental and military politics. The love that asserts itself here, thanks to the movements between the Brittany and Normandy towns in 1799, the struggle for a happy union (see chapter 3), comes to an ending determined by the struggle between two ideas of the novel: as a scene of military life and as a novel of romance. It is almost as if Balzac says to himself: A little too much love? Thin it out with military action. Too much political intrigue? Time to return to love. And death justifies this mix in the end, the only arrival point of the two journeys and the final image of their unity.

In *Béatrix,* Sabine du Guénic falls head over heels in love with her husband while in a carriage between Paris and Brittany during her honeymoon. The honeymoon may well be considered a special case of the reflective journey. To present the intimate thoughts of the character in this crucial passage from girlhood to married woman, the novel briefly becomes epistolary. Comparing Sabine to Louise de Chaulieu, both young women perfected by their intelligence and wit, their grand airs, and their good taste, Balzac mentions the *Mémoires de deux jeunes mariées* to evoke the epistolary genre of narration, where the written word reveals the self. Writing and voyaging, this reflecting person is thus the only voice determining the content and orienting the reader. While the journey takes one from place to place, thoughts pass from one state to another.

Balzac takes care to situate this crucial moment in a context that will make the reader reflect on the trip. In one of those places in *La Comédie humaine* where Balzac gives his text over to explanation—where he writes the instruction manual for his writing—he introduces this epistolary episode and the narrative of the honeymoon by commenting on the role that honeymoon trips play in human evolution. Just as a marriage is a lottery whose terms and dangers are known by women, he says, a honeymoon, of uncertain length, announces the character of the marriage it inaugurates. Because Sabine is intelligent and already thinks of herself as a woman (2: 845), she is the same type of non-virginal virgin as Modeste Mignon, a young woman whose intelligence in matters of love is not dampened by her innocence. Writing about the journey to Brittany and its moral consequences, Sabine puts this intelligence to use and confirms her new status as a woman, showing a profound understanding of the situation in a way that owes all its pathos precisely to her innocence. By an effect of his rhetoric, Balzac employs a particular tone and manner to introduce Sabine's letters that prepares us for the style of elliptical and expressive subtlety that characterizes the letters: he makes his narrator innocently intelligent.

The newly married Mme du Guénic has so well disobeyed her mother's recommendations that in a few hours of travel she has fallen in love with her husband. According to the letters (2: 845–59), it is precisely by traveling that she has learned how to love: "J'aime Calyste comme s'il n'était pas mon mari. C'est-à-dire que si, mariée à un autre, je voyageais avec Calyste, je l'aimerais et haïrais mon mari" [I love Calyste as if he were not my husband. Which is to say that if, married to another, I were traveling with Calyste, I would love him and hate my husband]. The experience that she has acquired "en quelques jours, et pourquoi ne . . . dirai-je pas en quelques heures" [in a few days, and why not . . . say in a few hours] permits her to find the delicate words that one needs to speak of the things that make up the experience itself. Her mother had told her to "rester grande, noble, digne et fière" [remain grand, noble, dignified, and proud], to not do as those new brides who "commencent par la facilité, par la complaisance, la bonhomie, la familiarité, par un abandon" [begin with facility, with indulgence, good nature, familiarity, with an abandonment], who come perilously close to being like a courtesan. But Sabine is the one who will announce that she began with "cette catastrophe qui termine, selon vous, la lune de miel des jeunes femmes d'aujourd'hui" [this catastrophe that brings to an end, or so you claim, the honeymoons of young women today].

The "catastrophe" is inaugurated by a kiss, her first, given and received eight hours after the marriage ceremony, when the tale that Calyste tells of his love for Béatrix, meted out in small fragments, gives Sabine the right and the desire to take possession of her husband. This kiss will be followed by the "naufrage de cette demi-vertu" [shipwreck of this semi-virtue] that was her dignity, and which, according to Sabine's reflection in her mother's absence, will determine the possibility of happiness in her marriage (which happiness finally arrives, let it be said, only after several detours). "Si j'étais restée dans ma dignité," she says, "j'aurais eu les froides douleurs d'une sorte de fraternité qui certes serait tout simplement devenue de l'indifférence. Et quel avenir me serais-je préparé? Mon dévouement a eu pour résultat de me rendre l'esclave de Calyste" [If I had held on to my dignity, I would have had the frigid agonies of a sort of fraternal love that certainly would have simply become indifference. And what future would I have prepared for myself? My devotion has had the result of making me Calyste's slave], where the word "devotion" takes the place of an active engagement in the sexual relations, and the word "slave" hardly needs commentary. Balzac needed to possess this intelligence of the woman's heart during her honeymoon season, which comes here through Sabine's reflections on her honeymoon trip, to be able to ground this marriage on a bed of complete happiness. Sabine finishes her first letter by saying: "mais que pourrai-je vous dire, si déjà mon bonheur est au comble?" [but what can I tell you, if already my happiness is at its peak?].[1] The final effect of the honeymoon trip is to provoke reflection on the new condition of the bride and to give permanent form to the marriage.

---

1. At its first publication, this part of the novel was called *La lune de miel*.

In *La muse du département,* Dinah de La Baudraye makes a short trip in a carriage, but her organdy dress, quickly wrinkled by Lousteau, suffices to determine the remainder of the novel. The famous episode is announced by the chapter title (which Balzac later suppressed), "Le sentiment va vite en voiture" [Sentiments go quickly in a vehicle]. Everything is premeditated and well calculated so that Dinah comes back from Cosne to La Baudraye alone with Lousteau in the wrong carriage—one that is not in good repair. The setting is such that a familiar topos seems to be announced, the topos of the vehicle that breaks down, thus favoring the initiation of a liaison between its two occupants; it is a motif that Mérimée exploited brilliantly for his long novella, "La double méprise." But in *La muse du département* the decrepitude of the vehicle will play only a picturesque role, designed to provide supplementary effects of provincialism to characterize the provincial muse before her stay in Paris.[2]

Dinah seeks to make an impression and wears an extraordinary dress—one ill-suited for travel. But it is this very detail that provokes reflection about this journey. During the trip from the chateau d'Anzy to Cosne, passing through Sancerre, Mme de La Baudraye and Lousteau speak of "l'amour en théorie, ce qui permet aux amants *in petto* de prendre en quelque sorte mesure de leurs cœurs" [the theory of love, which allows the lovers *in petto* to take stock of each other's hearts after a fashion] (4: 723). It is a process of reflection by two people whose spoken words are only the tip of the iceberg. Lousteau's purpose is to seduce Mme de La Baudraye, and she allows herself to be seduced, since for three days "la conversation des deux Parisiens avait agi sur cette femme à la manière des livres les plus dangereux" [the conversation of the two Parisians had acted on this woman the way the most dangerous books would]. These thoughts show on her face as "la rêverie que donne l'irrésolution" [the reverie that indecision brings]. As for Lousteau, speed is the theme of his reflections. He fears he has wasted his time in this remote department, and so he recounts an example of rapid love, of the kind experienced by a woman who "pouvait succomber en quelques heures à une pensée, à un ouragan intérieur" [could succumb in a few hours to a thought, to a hurricane inside], hoping to inspire, during this quick trip, just this sort of thought in Dinah. At Cosne, while walking with Mme de La Baudraye, Lousteau pursues an interior reflection on organdy dresses, which the reader has also perhaps begun: "Il n'y a plus que les femmes de province qui portent

---

2. "A Cosne, il s'attroupa beaucoup de monde autour de la vieille calèche repeinte sur les panneaux de laquelle se voyaient les armes données par Louis XIV" [At Cosne, a mob of people gathered around the old repainted carriage, on whose panels one could see the coat of arms given by Louis XIV] (4: 724).

des robes d'organdi, la seule étoffe dont le chiffonnage ne peut pas s'effacer. . . . Cette femme, qui m'a choisi pour amant, va faire des façons à cause de sa robe. Si elle avait mis une robe de foulard je serais heureux" [Nobody but a provincial woman would wear an organdy dress, the only cloth whose wrinkles cannot be erased. . . . This woman, who has chosen me as a lover, will make a fuss because of her dress. If she had put on a silk dress, I would be more fortunate] (4: 725). Yet it is in opposition to this thought and directly because of it that Lousteau will think of behaving as he does in the carriage crossing the bridge: thinking that the game is lost, and fearing that the jealous Gatien is about to return to the carriage on horseback, Lousteau declares his love point-blank and takes the split-second decision to wrinkle the organdy dress in the instant that precedes Gatien's return. Consequently, Mme de La Baudraye finds herself "dans un état à ne pas se montrer" [in such a state that she could not show herself] (4: 726). These words apply to Lousteau's quick attack in a few seconds on the bridge at Cosne, but, devious in their suggestiveness, they are better suited to a shameful or embarrassing condition, such as an advanced pregnancy might be.

To find out what Balzac himself thought about Dinah's choice of an organdy dress for this trip, one can read an amusing paragraph from a letter of 9 April 1843 to Mme Hanska. Balzac claims the Chamber of Deputies was in an uproar and had attacked the Minister of the Interior on the subject of Dinah's dress:

> Étienne Lousteau qui reconduit avec elle Bianchon à une voiture, se trouve seul avec elle pendant le temps que la calèche traverse le pont de Cosne. Le journaliste déclare sa passion à Dinah, et comme Dinah fait des façons, le journaliste qui voit arriver un jeune homme à cheval venu pour les accompagner et les surveiller, a l'idée, pour faire croire que Dinah s'est rendue, de lui chiffonner sa robe. Vous lirez cela; c'est assez drôle. Les députés ont cru à la plus atroce saloperie et à *une action impossible*, vu le peu de temps! Quand, au *Messager*, on m'a dit cela, les bras me sont tombés. Il y a cependant là des fabricants qui doivent savoir que ce qu'ils pensaient aurait pu se faire sur toute espèce de robe, que l'organdi seul se prêtait à cette plaisanterie. (*Hanska* 1: 666–67)

[Étienne Lousteau, accompanying Bianchon to a coach with her, finds himself alone with her for the length of time the carriage is crossing the bridge at Cosne. The journalist declares his passion and, because she makes a fuss, the journalist, seeing a young man arriving on horseback to accompany them and keep an eye on them, has the idea of mussing her dress to make it seem that Dinah has succumbed. You'll read this; it's quite funny. The Deputies believed in the most atrocious filth and *an impossible action,* given the short time! When they told me that at the *Messager* office, my jaw fell open. And yet there are manufacturers in the Chamber who must know that what they were thinking could have been done to any sort of dress, and that only organdy lent itself to this joke.]

(The bridge at Cosne was 356 meters long.) For Balzac, only the organdy dress allowed the scene to be played as Lousteau played it: as a piece of theatrical farce. With any other dress, the situation would have been more ambiguous. Yet what is truly astonishing is that Balzac has his other characters assume that Dinah has lost her virtue to Lousteau, thereby behaving just like the Chambre des députés he finds so unbelievably filthy-minded. And that is the desired effect of this short journey, one that is absolutely necessary for the continuation of the narrative and for its eventual outcome.

After having changed her dress at La Baudraye, Dinah continues the journey as far as Anzy with her mother and Lousteau, but when people notice the change in dress, the two contradictory explanations given by Lousteau complete the condemnation of the muse in her department. The journey has made her, if not a fallen woman, at least a compromised one, and certainly a libeled one: "La chute de la Muse du Berry, du Nivernais et du Morvan fut accompagnée d'un vrai charivari de médisances, de calomnies et de conjectures diverses parmi lesquelles figurait en première ligne l'histoire de la robe d'organdi" [The fall of the Muse of Berry, of Nivernais, and of Morvan was accompanied by a true racket of slander, calumnies, and diverse conjectures among which was featured the story of the organdy dress] (4: 730). For everyone else, this has become a story of love-making in a carriage, but not for Dinah de La Baudraye—yet another case where the character is pronounced "happy" long before she actually is, for it is only during the weeks after the voyage to Cosne that she will truly become a woman in love.

The reader who wonders why Dinah de La Baudraye put on an organdy dress will perhaps come to the conclusion that an irresolute poetess needs someone else to take the decisive step. When Lousteau wrinkles her dress, she reacts in the most stereotypical fashion: "Ah! monsieur! . . . s'écria majestueusement Dinah" [Ah! Sir! . . . Dinah cried out majestically] (4: 727). "Vous m'avez défié" [You challenged me], answers the Parisian: the organdy dress was above all a challenge that he had to answer or else find himself removed from the list of suitors. The maneuver that Lousteau accomplishes after the change of dress, by letting people think that there was a crueler reason for which Dinah had to abandon her organdy dress, will confirm his position as winner of the contest of suitors—a glorifying trial after the central one—and the rest of the novel follows, a vast reflection of the smaller journey by carriage.

In *Illusions perdues,* Lucien de Rubempré journeys on foot between the Houmeau and Angoulême to reach Mme de Bargeton's mansion. His mind travels while the body does; like Sabine du Guénic, his physical movement favors the movement of ideas. After having read his poems for the first time at his muse's house, he takes the long way home,

> afin d'entretenir par la marche le mouvement d'idées où l'on se trouve, et au courant desquelles on veut se livrer. . . . Chemin faisant, il ôtait un à un les traits envenimés qu'il avait reçus, il se parlait tout haut à lui-même, il gourmandait les niais auxquels il avait eu affaire; il trouvait des réponses fines aux sottes demandes qu'on lui avait faites, et se désespérait d'avoir ainsi de l'esprit après coup. (5: 211–12)

> [to let walking encourage the movement of ideas in which one finds oneself and to savor the flow of the thoughts. . . . Along the way, he removed one by one the poisonous darts he had received, he spoke out loud to himself, he rebuked the simpletons he had had to deal with; he found shrewd responses for the foolish inquiries they had made, and he was in despair at having such wit after the fact.]

Here is an excellent illustration of Lucien's capacity to deceive himself (nicely explaining the novel's title) and of another of his character traits: his lack of a ready wit, foreshadowing the disappointments in Paris in the second part of the novel.

Along the return path he meets David Séchard and Ève Chardon, whose marriage will be decided during their stroll. Following a clearly marked structure, the two walks of opposite character meet physically and clash morally. David, resolved to speak about himself, "ne trouva plus rien à dire quand il donna le bras à la belle Ève pour traverser l'Houmeau" [found nothing else to say when he gave the beautiful Ève his arm to cross the Houmeau] (5: 212), and rather than speak of himself, he speaks of Lucien: "Chère Ève, épousez-moi par amour pour Lucien" [Dear Ève, marry me for the love of Lucien] (5: 215). Yet it is during this evening of promenades that David will expose his ambitions as inventor and as lover to Ève, in such a way that the contrast with Lucien is stressed when the poet tells the enraged and egotistical tale of his wounded ambitions. These two contradictory manners of thinking recall the two directions that alternatively pull at Rastignac in *Le père Goriot*—to work nobly and piously for an honest destiny, or to succeed by playing the world at its game.

While walking, Lucien has been constructing a whole future for himself starting with the imaginary death of M. de Bargeton, followed by his marriage with Mme de Bargeton and his certainty of dominating this arrogant world. David and Ève have meanwhile arrived at a perfect agreement which will make their marriage one of the four happy marriages of *La Comédie humaine,* according to Arlette Michel's pessimistic census: "Les seuls mariages heureux de la *Comédie humaine* sont ceux d'Ève Séchard, de Constance Birotteau, d'Ursule Mirouët et de Modeste Mignon" (*Le mariage et l'amour* 3: 1528). Lucien, who was dreaming of marrying his sister to some powerful family to support his own position, sees in this marriage nothing but an obstacle to his ambitions. "Il venait de se voir dominant la Société, le poète souffrait de tomber si vite dans la réalité" [He had just pictured himself dominating Society; the poet was pained to see himself falling so quickly into reality] (5: 224), while Ève and David believe that his silence signifies that he is overwhelmed by David's generous plans for him. It is a misunderstanding on both sides. In the same paragraph nevertheless, with the help of the walking, the three young people will reach unison, says Balzac: "Lucien, charmé par la voix de David et par les caresses d'Ève, oublia sous les ombrages de la route, le long de la Charente calme et brillante, sous la voûte étoilée et dans la tiède atmosphère de la nuit, la blessante couronne d'épines que la Société lui avait enfoncée sur la tête" [Lucien, charmed by David's voice and Ève's caresses, forgot in the shadings of the road, along the calm and shining Charente, under the starry arch and in the warm atmosphere of the night, the cutting crown of thorns that Society had thrust down upon his head] (5: 224). The entire scene, with the two walks that melt into one another, does much to emphasize Lucien's mobile character and clearly establishes the diagram of the movement of his state of mind in the second part of the novel and beyond.

The last journey in *Illusions perdues* shows Lucien walking towards Mesle with the intention of killing himself. It is another journey on foot; access to a carriage comes after he meets Carlos Herrera. While walking, "il tomba dans la résolution des moyens" [his thoughts fell to the resolving of the means] (5: 688), the methods of suicide; this reflection completes a short anthropological discussion on the varieties of suicides. Lucien remembers a deep basin in the river where his body will not be found, in the direction of

Marsac. "Il chemina donc vers Marsac, en proie à ses dernières et funèbres pensées, et dans la ferme intention de dérober ainsi le secret de sa mort, de ne pas être l'objet d'une enquête, de ne pas être enterré, de ne pas être vu dans l'horrible état où sont les noyés quand ils reviennent à fleur d'eau" [So he trudged towards Marsac, prey to his last and gloomy thoughts, and with the firm intention of thus concealing the secret of his death, of not being the object of an inquiry, of not being buried, of not being seen in the horrible state of drowned men returning to the surface of the water] (5: 689). It is this reflection prompted by vanity that makes him leave the main road when the stagecoach arrives, throwing himself onto a little sunken path, to return to the main road directly behind Carlos Herrera who is climbing the slope. It is a well-known scene and one that recalls a similar extra-vehicular moment in *Les Chouans*. The stories told by the Spanish priest quickly bring about an interesting change in Lucien's thoughts. How quickly is shown by a narrative device: having refused the first offer of a cigar under the pretext that his death is imminent, he accepts the second offer by telling himself: "Il a raison, j'ai toujours le temps de me tuer" [He is right, I have all the time in the world to kill myself] (5: 693). Some four hundred pages later, at the end of the third part of *Splendeurs et misères des courtisanes,* it will indeed finally be the right time. His destination point is inscribed in the departure point of this scene.

Walking creates not only a change in the state of mind but a philosophical change in *L'auberge rouge*. Trying to escape insistent thoughts about murdering the rich traveler in the inn, Prosper Magnan walks away; once back in his room, he will no longer be tempted by murder, thanks to his voyage of intense reflection. The goal of his walk is precisely to strengthen the return to goodness that comes to him by means of a miracle—a voice accompanied by a light. At the point of striking Walhenfer, he throws away the instrument of murder and places himself in front of the open window. "Là, il conçut la plus profonde horreur pour lui-même; et . . . craignant encore de succomber à la fascination à laquelle il était en proie, il sauta vivement sur le chemin et se promena le long du Rhin, en faisant pour ainsi dire sentinelle devant l'auberge" [There, he conceived the most profound horror of himself; and . . . still fearing to succumb to the fascination that held him in prey, he sprang briskly onto the path and walked along the Rhine, acting as if he were a sentinel in front of the inn] (11: 103). As he paces, he goes all the way to Andernach on one side and all the way to the direction he had come from on the other. He falls into a reverie, qui le ramena par degrés à de saines idées de morale. La raison finit par dissiper complètement sa frénésie momentanée. Les enseignements de son éducation, les préceptes religieux, et surtout . . . les images de la vie modeste qu'il avait jusqu'alors menée sous le toit paternel, triomphèrent de ses mauvaises pensées. Quand il revint, après une longue méditation au charme de laquelle il s'était abandonné sur le bord du Rhin, en restant accoudé sur une grosse pierre, (11: 103)

[which brought him back by degrees to the sane ideas of morality. In the end, reason completely dissipated his momentary frenzy. The teachings of his education, the religious precepts, and above all . . . the images of the modest life he had until now led under the paternal roof triumphed over the evil thoughts. When he returned, after a long meditation under whose charm he had abandoned himself on the banks of the Rhine, leaning on his elbows on a large rock,]

the temptation to steal has passed. In the room, Prosper falls asleep immediately, without noticing that his fellow traveler has departed, leaving Walhenfer's head on the ground and his body in the bed.

This voyage of reflection is not a displacement from one place to another, but a physical swinging movement in harmony with the mental swings and wavering of Prosper's thoughts. At the same time, it is this oscillating walk that permits the real assassin to go to work, since Prosper's steps draw far enough in each direction for him to lose sight of the window, allowing his companion to escape: "Souvent, il atteignait Andernach dans sa promenade précipitée; souvent aussi ses pas le conduisaient au versant par lequel il était descendu pour arriver à l'auberge; mais le silence de la nuit était si profond, il se fiait si bien sur les chiens de garde, que, parfois, il perdit de vue la fenêtre qu'il avait laissée ouverte" [Often his hurried walk took him as far as Andernach; often also his steps led him to the hillside he had come down to reach the inn; but the silence of the night was so deep, he trusted the guard dogs so well, that he sometimes lost sight of the window he had left open] (11: 103). Reflection or meditation turn out to be not very practical—completely the opposite of an alert behavior that could have potentially saved his life. The reflective pacing is thus the event that determines the dénouement for Prosper Magnan, the hinges on which his story turns, like the shutters of the window that he was unfortunate enough to leave open. Now and then, in front of the window or facing the Rhine, Prosper, as a good romantic hero, leans on his elbows in the classic pose of contemplation, the engine of virtue, but his reflection does not save his life.

A short journey of reflection happens in *Ursule Mirouët,* and its speed is part of its significance for this novel. The doctor Minoret is returning to Nemours after a quick trip to Paris to observe and judge a demonstration of magnetism (see chapter 11). Balzac devotes only a rather short paragraph to this moment, describing the material modalities of the rapid return to Nemours, in which the character does not meditate or reflect over a course of time and distance, but in which we can readily see the symbolic incarnation of his conversion to a new way of thinking. Speed of reflection contributes to the drama of the conversion: the fast trip symbolizes the lightning rapidity of this change. The paragraph (3: 834) serves as the hinge between the doctor's disbelief and his newfound belief.

Late at night, taking leave of his friend the doctor Bouvard with whom he has participated in the magnetism experiment, Minoret races to Nemours: after rushing to rent a bourgeois carriage for Fontainebleau, letting the horse rest at Essonne, finding a place in the stagecoach for Nemours, dismissing his driver, arriving home at 5 in the morning, Minoret is tired from the speedy travel, and "il se coucha dans les ruines de toutes ses idées antérieures sur la physiologie, sur la nature, sur la métaphysique" [he went to bed in the ruins of all his former ideas about physiology, nature, and metaphysics]. This race to Nemours is speedy because Minoret wants to verify what the somnambulistic subject saw in her last vision: Ursule getting ready for bed; "je voudrais avoir des ailes, aller à Nemours vérifier ses assertions" [I would like to have wings to go to Nemours and verify her assertions] (3: 832). While reflection normally takes advantage of the slowness of the journey to pass through stages, this is a case where the character's reflection, to which the demonstration of magnetism has given its first impulse and a giant step along the way, would like to gallop to catch up with the somnambulist's vision. The same speed of reflection makes the doctor young again: a new man will emerge from the rapid journey. Meditation on the facts and their confirmation, the realization of the truth of everything he saw, in short the completion of the change of thought will come after the return.

Love in a carriage, quite different from the ones in *Les Chouans* and *La muse du département,* takes place in *Splendeurs et misères des courtisanes.* The baron de Nucingen is returning to Paris after having dined with a colleague in the Brie, at eight leagues from the city. The drunken driver is asleep, the valet is snoring, and the baron wants to think, but "la douce somnolence de la digestion lui avait fermé les yeux" [the sweet somnolence of digestion had closed his eyes] (6: 492). In the bois de Vincennes, the unguided horses come to a stop at a roundabout inhabited by other carriages, and Nucingen, feeling that the vehicle is no longer moving, awakens. Comes a vision:

> il fut surpris par une vision céleste qui le trouva sans son arme habituelle, le calcul. Il faisait un clair de lune si magnifique qu'on aurait pu tout lire, même un journal du soir. Par le silence des bois, et à cette lueur pure, le baron vit une femme seule qui, tout en montant dans une voiture de louage, regarda le singulier spectacle de cette calèche endormie. A la vue de cet ange, le baron de Nucingen fut comme illuminé par une lumière intérieure. . . . Le vieux banquier ressentit une émotion terrible: le sang qui lui revenait des pieds charriait du feu à sa tête, sa tête renvoyait des flammes au cœur; la gorge se serra. (6: 493)

[he was overcome by a celestial vision that found him without his usual weapon, calculation. The moonlight was so magnificent that one could have read anything, even an evening newspaper. In the silence of the park, in this pure glow of light, the baron saw a woman entering a rented carriage alone while gazing at the singular spectacle of this sleeping carriage. At the sight of this angel, the baron de Nucingen was as if illuminated by an interior light. . . . The old banker felt a terrible emotion: blood flowing back from his feet trundled fire to his head, his head broadcast flames to his heart; his throat tightened.]

The angel flees, the baron's carriage cannot reach it, and the travel scene ends.

At age 60, the baron has already purchased all the forms of love; he has experienced everything and given up on everything except real love. "Cet amour venait de fondre sur lui comme un aigle sur sa proie" [This love had just descended upon him like an eagle on its prey] (6: 494). Driving through all the parks of the area for eight nights in a row fails to turn up "cette sublime figure de juive" [that sublime face of the Jewess] (6: 494) that he has before his eyes at every moment, Esther Gobseck. Not only Nucingen's but also Lucien de Rubempré's destiny is determined in this moment.

It is a short trip, and the character is asleep; once awake, his love comes like the proverbial thunderbolt, the result of no reflection. Is this a case that contradicts the others? While Nucingen needs no reflection, the reader is nevertheless invited to reflect—on the conduct of the narrative. Clearly this journey in a carriage plays the part of chance, which Balzac called a powerful novelist, and determines a continuation of the diegesis that could not have existed otherwise. But it is also evident that everything in the presentation of this scene is calculated to focus the moment in the reader's mind: the late hour, the effect of the light from the moon, the singular situation of the sleeping characters, the solitude of the courtesan and the baron in their carriages, the lightning glance, the fugitive gaze, a theatrical lexicon, even the roundabout that encircles the encounter as if to frame a unique, special moment and hold it up like a medallion. Completing the somewhat Stendhalian catalog of the types of love that Nucingen has possessed thanks to his money, the real love that comes now has not only the function of inflecting the direction of the plot but also, more importantly, of completing the character who until now had lacked this weakness common to mortals. Losing his stature as a "loup-cervier," a lynx of finance, he becomes incapable of carrying on his business affairs and for the first time in his life glimpses "quelque chose de plus saint et de plus sacré que l'or" [something more saintly and more sacred than gold] (6: 498). No doubt this can be considered a degraded version of the Balzacian idea of love as unique and predestined, uniting two beings fortunate enough to have met during their lifetimes; the portrait of the money man turned soupy with love is the fruit of an instant where love at first sight prohibits any reflection, just as sleep had replaced thought.

Journeys may represent a pause in the narration of the plot—a temporary halt in the action made necessary by the fact that the characters must find themselves elsewhere in order to continue their destiny. When travel is for a reason that is not contained in the trip itself, the narration does not show the characters' thoughts during the journey, which is most frequently the case in *La Comédie humaine*. In *La Rabouilleuse,* Agathe Bridau and her son Joseph make their way toward Issoudun to save an inheritance, and the necessity of thinking about the goal of the journey—to assemble the elements of a legal case against a fraudulent claim—makes them ignore the distractions of the landscape. The two characters are reflecting, but for the mother, troubled by the imprisonment of her favorite son and worried for the artist Joseph who is so unskillful in practical matters, their incapacity to play this role is revealed above all in the paucity of their thinking. At the end of their trip, they are no further along.

In the examples dealt with here, to which one could add others, journeys offer the time for a change in status that would not be possible without them.

But the goal of the voyage and the intent of the narration do not always work with the same effect. The characters go elsewhere for a precise reason—Lucien de Rubempré to kill himself, Marie de Verneuil to spy, Sabine du Guénic because she has to travel on her honeymoon and meet her Breton relatives, Dinah de La Baudraye to find herself alone with Lousteau, Prosper Magnan to escape from the power of his thoughts—but something else occurs that these people have not foreseen. Thus, Lucien, wrapped up in his illusory ambitions, changes course when he encounters David and Ève's sane ideas; later, instead of killing himself, he will begin a new life because of the chance encounter with Jacques Collin. Marie de Verneuil finds love, a true love that can be expressed only through death, which is an unforeseen result of the struggle she takes on in accepting her role as republican spy. Sabine undergoes radical changes under the direct effect of the trip; her case serves the author's momentarily anthropological designs, which present it as an illustration of the effect of honeymoons on young women. Dinah de La Baudraye finds herself compromised in her department and thus embarks on her Parisian adventure; the decision to leave and become Lousteau's mistress has been taken for her. Prosper Magnan sets out on a path of virtue, but finds himself instead headed for capital punishment; when he finishes his oscillating walk, he believes he has won the strength to be virtuous and feels liberated from the claws of evil, but he will be punished nevertheless and as a direct result of his walk. Nucingen was merely sleeping off the effects of a dinner with other bankers outside Paris when happenstance changed the focus of his life from money to love.

These examples where a change in status occurs because of a change in location show the intimate relationship of voyages to narration. When thoughts transform during these trips, their direction is not always foreseen or foreseeable. It turns out that the journeys in a carriage or on foot work to accomplish the purposes not of the traveler but of the novelist, and that these determine an unexpected diegetic consequence. Thus the reflection of the trip on the narrative consists in bending it toward the novel's goals. Voyages of reflection reflect the movement of the narrative according to the effects of fate; they are thus the reflections of narrative journeys, and in Balzac's narrative "journey," the direction changes upon reflection.

III

Mimetic Structures of Realism

Balzac and Poe
Realizing Magnetism

In September 1839, in the first version of "The Fall of the House of Usher" published in *Burton's Gentleman's Magazine,* Edgar Allan Poe wrote that Roderick Usher's excited and highly distempered ideality led him to perform "a certain singular perversion and amplification of the wild air of the last waltz of Von Weber" (*Selected Writings* 145). This sentence is found in subsequent versions as well (1840, 1842, 1845, 1847, and 1850). Almost two years later in June or July 1841, in *Ursule Mirouët,* Balzac wrote that his exquisitely sensitive heroine Ursule "jouait à son parrain des variations sur la *Dernière Pensée* de Weber" [played for her tutor variations on Weber's *Last Thought*] (3: 841).

Serendipity—the chance rereading of both texts at about the same time—brought to my attention this Close Encounter of the Musical Kind, and curiosity provoked me to seek its significance. My investigation took me through historical information about both the music and the literary works and beyond that to the authors' common purpose of making magnetism realistic.

As critical editions of both Poe and Balzac inform us, the "last waltz of Von Weber" or "Weber's *Last Thought*" is not by Carl Maria von Weber (1786–1826) at all but by his friend Karl Gottlieb Reissiger (1798–1859). It is the fifth piece of Reissiger's "Danses brillantes pour le pianoforte," opus 26, written in 1822; its title, "Webers letzte Gedanke," explains how both Poe and Balzac referred to it. According to Pollin in *Discoveries in Poe* (85), it was published in 1824. A New York publication by Firth & Hall (figure 14.1) gives the title "Von Weber's Last Waltz," under the presumed authorship of Weber, but with no mention of Reissiger's name and no date; a librarian's notation mentions 1831.[1]

Balzac probably did not know Weber's music well. The composer is mentioned only four times in the index to the Pléiade edition of *La Comédie humaine,* including once in *Pierrette* in June 1839 and once in *Illusions perdues,* about the same time, and no piece is named in those cases. Weber does not have the stature of other composers in Balzac's writing, such as Beethoven, Chopin, or Rossini. As for Reissiger, he is never mentioned in *La Comédie humaine.* Hector Berlioz in his memoirs gives some justification for Balzac's error, apparently a common one, by mentioning how little Reissiger is known in Paris: "La chapelle de Dresde, longtemps sous les ordres de l'Italien Morlacchi et de l'illustre auteur du *Freyschütz* [Weber], est maintenant dirigée par MM. Reissiger et Richard Wagner. Nous ne connaissons guère, à Paris, de Reissiger, que la douce et mélancolique valse publiée sous le titre de *Dernière pensée de Weber*" (Berlioz, *Mémoires*) ["The Dresden kapelle, for long under the command of the Italian Morlacchi and the illustrious composer of *Freischütz* [Weber], is now directed by Messrs. Reissiger and Richard Wagner. We know almost nothing of Reissiger's in Paris, apart from the mild and wistful waltz published under the title 'Weber's Last Thought'" (*The Memoirs of Hector Berlioz* 302)]. Berlioz's trip to Germany occurred in 1842–43, soon after Balzac's novel, 1841–42; this passage comes from a letter to the violinist Ernst written in 1843. Not only did Berlioz know the real composer of the waltz, but his comment also testifies to the familiarity of the piece to Parisians.

But Berlioz also described it as gentle and melancholic (rendered as "mild and wistful" in David Cairns's translation), and the description does not fit perfectly well with the two publications of the piece I have been able to find, particularly the older one (Firth & Hall). The waltz is in B-flat major, in the form of a minuet with two eight-measure phrases on different themes, each repeated, followed by an eight-measure trio in E-flat major, also repeated; there is a da capo and the first two sections are played again, without repeats, in typical minuet fashion. In the older edition, the piece is marked

---

1. My thanks are due to Bill McClellan, former librarian of the Music Library at the University of Illinois at Urbana-Champaign, who helped me identify the piece originally via a BBC music library cross-reference to Reissiger from Weber. There is a short biographical notice of Reissiger in the new *Grove Dictionary of Music*. Nicholas Temperley, professor of musicology emeritus at the University of Illinois, recorded the waltz on tape for me; my research turned up no available recording. A Peters edition from 1824 was republished in France several times in the nineteenth century.

Figure 14.1 Waltz by Reissiger

"Energico"; in the newer edition, "Andante." When performed, andante seems the appropriate tempo. Both editions give the dynamic "piano" (soft), but the older edition notes "il Basso ben marcato" (the bass well marked) for the first section, and both indicate "espressivo" for the trio. In fact, the trio alone might be considered melancholic, but the first two themes, whether played energico or andante, do not suggest sadness; wistfulness, perhaps. At an andante tempo or slower, and without a thumping bass, the opening phrase might be considered "gentle," especially in the sense of delicate or light. In all, as a short dance piece (about one minute, 20 seconds), "Webers letzte Gedanke" suits the style of early romantic salon music.

There may be some justification for melancholy in the odd history that led to the confusion of authorship. Introducing "The Fall of the House of Usher," Thomas O. Mabbott notes that "Roderick . . . plays a dirge based on a musical air supposed to have been written on the last day of its composer's life" (Poe, *Tales and Sketches* I: 395). His endnote on the sentence concerning the waltz repeats the comment that Usher is playing a dirge for himself and cites in support of this the Library of Congress copy of the waltz published about 1830 with the following mention: "Weber's Last Waltz/Composed by him a few hours before his death/for the Piano Forte" (Mabbott I: 418). Weber was in England and had copied out Reissiger's waltz to play it at concerts, when he died suddenly of tuberculosis. Found among his papers, the waltz was published under his name. This odd coincidence connecting the piece with Weber's death is perhaps the only reason Poe uses the word dirge and Berlioz connects it with melancholy. As for the adjective "wild" in "the wild air of the last waltz of Von Weber," little seems to explain it, unless the harmony of the piece's second phrase, with its chromatic coloring, can be made to suggest savage, uncontrolled emotion—an unlikely stretch.

Both Poe and Balzac have their characters playing variations—Roderick Usher in a deranged manner more decidedly in keeping with the gothic tone of the story: "a certain singular perversion and amplification." Variations on the waltz were not uncommon. I have found a "Fantasy on Weber's Last Waltz" written by Henri Cramer (1818–77) and arranged by Harold T. Brasch in the 1960s for euphonium with band. After an introductory flourish, this fantasy restates Reissiger's opening theme, and this is followed by two variations of a virtuoso stamp, including cadenzas. The Cramer piece was apparently part of the "Fantasies [read Fantaisies] élégantes" for piano, op. 74, and was called "Last Idea," as far as one can tell. There is no date of composition, but Cramer would have been only twenty-one in 1839. Pollin also mentions three other variations: the Fantaisie for piano and clarinet by Friedrich Berr; piano Variations Brillantes by Henri Herz; and a four-hand duet by Henry Karr (85). I have been unable to find editions or recordings of any of these three. Johann Peter Pixis wrote a "Fantasia" on the theme, thinking it was Weber's, and sent it to Reissiger (Pollin 85). Pixis was in Paris from 1825 to 1845, where he might well have played variations on Reissiger's air, calling it Weber's (*Johann Peter Pixis,* online). In addition I found the opening theme of Reissiger's waltz used by Karl Reinecke (1824-1910) in the second movement of his Toy Symphony together with several other little tunes, in the style of the popular ditty for simple instruments; the notes by Raymond Lewenthal on the LP jacket list the little waltz as a piece by Weber, his "Letzter Gedanke." As Pollin can conclude about Roderick Usher's performance on the guitar, his variations "induct him into the large company of musical enthusiasts who were varying Reissiger's air" (86)—and I can add the same about Ursule Mirouët.

Did Balzac, who wrote *Ursule Mirouët* almost two years after "The Fall of the House of Usher," read Poe's story? It is highly unlikely. To prove it, one would at least have to find a very early translation into French, since Balzac did not read English. One old source claims authoritatively that the earliest French translation of Poe was "Le Scarabée d'or" in the *Revue Britannique* in November 1845 (Cambiaire 30). On the other hand, it is clear, though not immediately relevant for this encounter, that Poe knew Balzac's work (Cambiaire 166). Messac, writing in 1929, also indicates that Poe had read Balzac, without saying what and when, but establishing several likely comparisons.[2] However, it is painfully obvious that Poe did not read *Ursule Mirouët* before writing his story, because *Ursule Mirouët* was written at the earliest two years after "The Fall." In the absence of a direct influence of one author on the other, I can only observe a commonality of interest highlighted by the use of the Reissiger waltz. The fact that both authors specify variations on the piece suggests that they may have actually heard performances in which variations were played.

A second conjecture about this conjuncture is that both authors had a common source. The likeliest are Walter Scott, E. T. A. Hoffmann, and possibly Mary Wollstonecraft Shelley.

    2. Messac compares "Monos et Una" to *Séraphîta* with a common source in Swedenborg; also "Ligeia" and "Morella" (35ff); *Louis Lambert* is linked with "William Wilson" and "The Tale of the Ragged Mountain" (42ff); and *La Grande Bretèche* with "The Cask of Amontillado." See also Eisenzweig, who compares *Maître Cornélius* with "The Murders in the Rue Morgue." Other encounters of Balzac with Poe include the theme of burial alive in *Le colonel Chabert* and in "The Premature Burial" and "The Cask of Amontillado," as well as "The Fall of the House of Usher." *L'Interdiction,* February 1836 (3: 428), has the house seen by an "Observateur," and it appears solid; compare to the observer at the beginning of "The Fall" and its lack of solidity due to its age.

Balzac was of course a fervent reader of Walter Scott and thought to improve on Scott's creation of the historical novel in his own vast historical sweep of society. In *Ursule Mirouët,* Balzac mentions "les récits de Walter Scott sur les effets de la *seconde vue*" [Walter Scott's narratives about the effects *of second sight*] among the proofs and manifestations of "la science des fluides impondérables" [the science of weightless fluids] (3: 824). Lucy Ashton, the heroine of Scott's *The Bride of Lammermoor,* written in 1819 (three years before Reissiger's waltz), is sensitive like Balzac's heroine, but not to the degree of somnambulism that Ursule attains. Neither mesmerism nor magnetism plays a part in her psychological makeup, but there is an episode of communication with the dead. In the woods, the ghost of old blind Alice, servant of Edgar's father, appears to the Master of Ravenswood at the Mermaiden's Well just at the moment of her death, to warn him again against marrying Lucy (Scott 235-37). She had strongly urged him not to contemplate this marriage earlier. Her extreme desire to see Edgar to warn him again makes it possible for her spirit to appear before him. Edgar wonders, in terms that Balzac must have approved: "can strong and earnest wishes, formed during the last agony of nature, survive its catastrophe, surmount the awful bounds of the spiritual world, and place before us its inhabitant in the hues and colouring of life?" (Scott 239). In *Ursule Mirouët* (see chapter 11), the dead doctor Minoret similarly surmounts the bounds of the spiritual world, his spirit surviving its last catastrophe, to convey an urgent message to Ursule; he appears in her dreams to tell her where he has hidden her inheritance and to show her just exactly how his relatives have stolen it. It is also in this novel that Balzac writes that Swedenborg had proved that communication with the dead is possible (3: 962).

If there are comparisons to be made between Scott's novel and Poe's story, they begin with the description of the castle of Ravenswood, gothic like the house of Usher, and its fall as a house in the sense of a family: "the final fall of the house of his fathers" occurs when Ravenswood's house burns down (Scott 265). Communication from the dead does not occur, strictly speaking, in Poe's story, but Madeline's desperate attempts to be heard from the tomb where she is buried alive can be considered an effort of her spirit to survive the last catastrophe. Unlike Balzac, Poe does not make us privy to the thoughts or visions of Roderick Usher until one frenzied outburst just before the nearly dead body of Madeline appears at the door; but if he does not see his sister materially present before him, the way Ursule sees Minoret, he has had a mental vision:

"Said I not that my senses were acute? I *now* tell you that I heard her first feeble movements in the hollow coffin. I heard them—many, many days ago—yet I dared not—I *dared not speak!* . . . Will she not be here anon? Is she not hurrying to upbraid me for my haste? Have I not heard her footsteps on the stair? Do I not distinguish that heavy and horrible beating of her heart? MADMAN!"—here he sprang furiously to his feet, and shrieked out his syllables, as if in the effort he were giving up his soul—"MADMAN! I TELL YOU THAT SHE NOW STANDS WITHOUT THE DOOR!" (*Selected Writings* 156)

In Balzac's novel and in the Poe story, playing variations (wild or not) on Reissiger's air demonstrates both characters' excessive sensibilities, so that the musical reference can be considered a semantic device that lends support to the strategic narrative device of the spirit passing an urgent message. Poe was not the great explicator that Balzac was, and to atmospheric effects alone, including the wild music, he confides the task of conveying Usher's unique hypersensitivity. But there is no chance that either Balzac or Poe found such a use of this music in *The Bride of Lammermoor,* because Scott's novel predates Reissiger's waltz by three years.

E. T. A. Hoffmann's tales were translated into French by Loève-Veimars in 1829–33, and he is mentioned often in the *La Comédie humaine,* for instance in *Le cousin Pons, La muse du département,* and a sketch of *Les martyrs ignorés.* He is particularly present in the context of magnetism, and the Hoffmann tales mentioned are "Casse-noisette," "Maître Floh," "L'homme au Sable," and "Petit Zack." Influences of Hoffmann on Balzac have been very well examined by Wanuffel, Guise ("Balzac, lecteur"), Jamin, and Wais. See also the excellent summary of Balzac's appreciation of Hoffmann in Pierre Brunel's preface and notes to the Folio edition of *Sarrasine, Gambara,* and *Massimilla Doni.* There is no mention of Reissiger's (or Weber's) waltz in these studies nor in Hoffmann's 1822 tales "Des Vetters Eckfenster," "Genesung," "Meister Floh," and "Der Feind" (Hoffmann died the year Reissiger's waltz was published, 1822), or in "Schnellpfeffer," date unsure. The story "L'archet du Baron de B . . .," published in 1828 in a review called *Le Gymnase* which Balzac printed, portrays a mad violin teacher whose wild playing on the violin recalls especially Roderick Usher's playing (see Wais 153). Like Frenhofer with his unknown masterpiece (*Le chef-d'œuvre inconnu*), the baron thinks his music shows genius, but only dreadful sounds are heard. This rapid review of the presence of Hoffmann in Balzac, in many other ways quite significant, nevertheless shows that Balzac almost certainly did not borrow the idea of variations on "la dernière pensée de Weber" from Hoffmann.

The influence of Hoffmann on Poe is also well documented, by Alterton, Stedman, and Cobb, among others. Alterton opposes "The Fall of the House of Usher" to the Hoffmann tale that she claims is its source, "Das Majorat" (1817), which was translated in 1826 into English as "The Entail" (17). Yet in none of these studies are there mentions of Weber or Reissiger. Walter Scott also wrote an article on Hoffmann, published in the *Foreign Quarterly Review* in 1827, which Poe read; Poe "got his Hoffmann" through Scott, according to Alterton (93). Other than themes of the occult, then, I found nothing in Hoffmann that might have functioned as a common source for the musical reference in Poe and Balzac.

In Mary Wollstonecraft Shelley's *The Last Man*, there is a mention of "the wild eastern air of Weber introduced in Abon [sic] Hassan" (173). This operetta by Weber was performed in England in 1825. According to Pollin (83–86), the Wollstonecraft novel is a source for Poe's "The Masque of the Red Death," and Pollin rather adventurously makes a connection between this allusion to the "wildness" of Abon Hassan and the "wild air of the last waltz of Von Weber" in "Usher," while going on to admit that Reissiger's salon piece would hardly strike a modern ear as wild (and we have already seen how unsuitable that adjective would have been to Berlioz's ear). From that admission stems what is possibly a creditable hypothesis, that Poe's reference to a piece by Weber as "wild" borrows its adjective, if not its identity, from the Wollstonecraft novel, rather than from a hearing of the piece itself. As for Balzac, there is no reason to believe that the reference to Weber in *The Last Man* had any influence on him.

I arrive then at my third set of conjectures, which measure the significance of the Close Encounter. If no tangible linkage between these Balzac and Poe narratives can be proved, as I believe, there is instead a major point to be made about this complex of intertextual and musical reference as a creative method in literature in general, and Balzac in particular. To begin with, it is well-known that both authors shared a preoccupation with mesmerism, magnetism, somnambulism, excessive sensibilities, and other such theories of the material manifestation of the immaterial. Magnetism will serve as a general term for those several phenomena. In both narratives, whatever the source or influence, the authors have created structures to make magnetism consonant with their realism, thus naturalizing the occult phenomena. And in both texts the music has the same function: it underscores and symbolizes the protagonists' mental disposition, both of whom similarly play variations on the Reissiger piece. Both characters have a similar ability to see beyond the visible; both are visionaries whose gifts are revealed in their music. The atmospheric function of the music helps to win the implicit wager both authors make to naturalize the spiritual phenomena and make them enter the world of realism and of their realistic writing.

The case of Poe has been well studied, and I intend to add little here. Its gothic characteristics are the subject of a recent study by Perry and Sederholm. Roderick Usher suffers from "a morbid acuteness of the senses" and "an excited and highly distempered ideality" (*Selected Writings* 143, 145). The morbid condition of his auditory nerve renders "all music intolerable to the sufferer with the exception of certain effects of stringed instruments"; Usher's confining himself to the guitar "gave birth, in great measure, to the fantastic character of his performances" (146). In the wildness of his notes and "the fervid *facility* of his *impromptus,*" Poe's narrator detects "that intense mental collectedness and concentration to which I have previously alluded as observable only in particular moments of the highest artificial excitement" (146). Except for their morbidity, these exalted states come the closest to those of Balzac's heroine in her moments of somnambulism, when her love makes visible to her not only the spirit of her dead tutor, Minoret, but also letters from Savinien de Portenduère the night before they arrive. Poe's text is of course overloaded with many other symbolic objects (such as Usher's paintings in a manner outdoing Fuseli), and scores of pages have been written on the heavy-handed atmospheric charge of the story.

The heroine Ursule Mirouët counts among her idealized qualities a special talent for playing the piano, and there are several scenes of music in the novel, some of which stress this idealization in contrast to the stupidity and cupidity of Minoret's blood relatives. If Ursule is to be described as playing the piano, suitable salon pieces must be named, and "la *Dernière pensée de Weber,*" a recent, fashionable piece, readily falls into that category. As such, Reissiger's familiar waltz might have served only to provoke a minor "effet de réel," alluding to what Barthes called a reality seen but not demonstrated (*Le plaisir du texte* 73–74)—only one of thousands of such products of contemporary reality found in *La Comédie humaine*. But this piece of music enters into a system of meanings far beyond this little touch of realism, meanings in which intangible realities become consonant with the famous Balzacian realism.

The piece is mentioned as if incidentally, in a subordinate clause: "Pendant que la filleule jouait à son parrain des variations sur la *Dernière Pensée de Weber*" [While the goddaughter played for her tutor variations on Weber's *Last Thought*] (3: 841). In spite of the attenuation of this incidental mention, the reader will notice this clause because it comes at the start of a paragraph just after one of the high points in the novel, Minoret's conversion under the effect of the powerful demonstration of animal magnetism. Already in this opportune mention there is a suggestion of a link between the piece and spirituality. Nevertheless, in case we do not pay much attention to this connection when it occurs at this relatively early point in the novel (about one-third), a later paragraph extensively develops this link between music and magnetism and does not allow us to be indifferent to it. I will quote from this paragraph at length (briefly discussed in chapter 11 as well):

> Il arrive souvent qu'un morceau pauvre en lui-même, mais exécuté par une jeune fille sous l'empire d'un sentiment profond, fasse plus d'impression qu'une grande ouverture pompeusement dite par un orchestre habile. Il existe en toute musique, outre la pensée du compositeur, l'âme de l'exécutant, qui, par un privilège acquis seulement à cet art, peut donner du sens et de la poésie à des phrases sans grande valeur. (3: 890)

> [It often happens that a piece of slender means on its own terms, when performed by a young woman under the sway of a deep emotion, makes more of an impression than a grand overture pompously pronounced by a skillful orchestra. One finds in all music, in addition to the composer's ideas, the soul of the performer, who, by a privilege pertaining only to this art, can give meaning and poetry to phrases lacking much value.]

Reissiger's little waltz could indeed be called "pauvre en lui-même"—it is nothing special; but inventing variations on it places the accent on Ursule's execution of the piece, in which her soul expresses itself. The ideal example of such execution on the piano is Chopin, mentioned here, and Ursule is like him:[3]

---

3. Compare to this description of Schmucke playing the piano in *Le cousin Pons*: "Il trouva des thèmes sublimes sur lesquels il broda, des caprices exécutés tantôt avec la douleur et la perfection raphaëlesque de Chopin, tantôt avec la fougue et le grandiose dantesque de Liszt, les deux organisations musicales qui se rapprochent le plus de celle de Paganini. L'exécution, arrivée à ce degré de perfection, met en apparence l'exécutant à la hauteur du poète, il est au compositeur ce que l'acteur est à l'auteur, un divin traducteur de choses divines" [He made up sublime themes which he ornamented, caprices performed sometimes with the sadness and Raphaelesque perfection of Chopin, sometimes with the verve and Dantesque grandiose of Liszt, the two musical organizations who come closest to Paganini's. Performance at this degree of perfection raises the performer to the apparent height of the poet; he is to the composer what the actor is to the author, a divine translator of divine things] (7: 705). Schmucke is the piano teacher who has brought Ursule's talent to perfection.

Chopin prouve aujourd'hui pour l'ingrat piano la vérité de ce fait déjà démontré par Paganini pour le violon. Ce beau génie est moins un musicien qu'une âme qui se rend sensible et qui se communiquerait par toute espèce de musique, même par de simples accords. Par sa sublime et périlleuse organisation, Ursule appartenait à cette école de génies si rares. (3: 890)

[Chopin today proves for the ungrateful piano the truth of this fact already demonstrated by Paganini for the violin. This admirable genius is less a musician than a soul that makes itself visible, that can be communicated by any kind of music, even by simple chords. By her sublime and perilous organization, Ursule belonged to this school of rarefied geniuses.]

As she plays now for both Minoret and Savinien, her soul goes out with the music:

Par un jeu à la fois suave et rêveur, son âme parlait à l'âme du jeune homme et l'enveloppait comme d'un nuage par des idées presque visibles. . . . Savinien admirait Ursule dont les yeux arrêtés sur la boiserie semblaient interroger un monde mystérieux. . . . Les sentiments vrais ont leur magnétisme, et Ursule voulait en quelque sorte montrer son âme. . . . Savinien pénétra donc dans ce délicieux royaume, entraîné par ce cœur qui . . . empruntait la puissance du seul art qui parle à la pensée par la pensée même, sans le secours de la parole, des couleurs ou de la forme. (3: 891)

[Through her at once suave and dreamy playing, her soul spoke to the soul of the young man and enveloped it, like a cloud, with nearly invisible thoughts. . . . Savinien admired Ursule whose eyes resting on the woodwork seemed to interrogate a mysterious world. . . . True feelings have their magnetism, and Ursule wished to reveal her soul, as it were. . . . Thus Savinien penetrated into this delicious domain, carried along by her heart which . . . borrowed its power from the only art that speaks to thought by means of thought itself, without the aid of words, colors, or shapes.]

Music is thought without words. It would have been singularly appropriate to mention "la *Dernière Pensée* de Weber" among the pieces she plays during this evening, given the emphasis on speaking to another's thought through thought. And that is exactly what we find in the manuscript version of this passage dating from June and July 1841, where Balzac had written: "Sur sa demande Ursule joua le mélancolique morceau appelé la dernière pensée de Weber" [On his request Ursule played the melancholy piece called

Weber's last thought] (3: 1611). But this sentence disappeared from the final version of the paragraph; instead of answering her tutor's request, it is she who chooses to play a caprice by Hérold, in the final version: "*Le Songe de Rousseau,* morceau choisi par Ursule, une des compositions de la jeunesse d'Hérold, ne manque pas d'ailleurs d'une certaine profondeur qui peut se développer à l'exécution; elle y jeta les sentiments qui l'agitaient" [*Rousseau's Dream,* the piece chosen by Ursule, one of Hérold's youthful compositions, is actually not lacking in a certain profundity, which can be demonstrated in the performance; she filled it with the emotions that were troubling her] (3: 891). Along with this change of music, Balzac engages in a significant reworking of the passage for the text published in *Le Messager* from August 25 to September 23, 1841. Most of Balzac's analysis of the soul making itself visible through the musical art—the paragraph quoted above—was written during this revision for the *Messager* version, with much new language, and this new language seems to entail the removal of the mention of Weber's last thought. It is almost as if the words "la dernière pensée de Weber" stood as a place-holder, in Balzac's manuscript, for the development of this musical theory he no doubt had in mind in June or July and would write out about two months later.

Balzac has given to music, unique among all the arts, the privilege of revealing the intangible, placing it even above the ability of words to express meaning.[4] For a writer driven by the passion to convey knowledge to his readers, for a man whose only expressiveness was in the power of his words, this priority given to music is remarkable. In *La recherche de l'Absolu,* written in 1834, an extended analogy with music illuminates the moment when two people predestined to fall in love first meet. Marguerite Claës and Emmanuel Solis each discovers the other as the one they have seen in their dreams, and the effect, as Balzac analyzes it, is like the astonishment a child feels on first hearing music: "Parmi les enfants, les uns rient et pensent, d'autres ne rient qu'après avoir pensé; mais ceux dont l'âme est appelée à vivre de poésie ou d'amour écoutent longtemps et redemandent la mélodie par un regard où s'allume déjà le plaisir, où poind la curiosité de l'infini" [Among children, some laugh and reflect, others laugh only after reflecting; but those whose soul is called upon to live on poetry or love listen for a long time and request

---

4. Berlioz concludes a chapter of his *Memoirs* with similar reflections on music's power: "No other art has music's power to affect one retroactively. Not even the art of Shakespeare can evoke the past with this degree of poetic intensity. Only music appeals at one and the same time to the imagination, the intellect, the feelings *and* the senses: and from the reaction of senses on intellect and feelings, and vice versa, come the phenomena which people with the right physiological mechanism are susceptible to, but which to those not so endowed (otherwise known as philistines) will always remain a sealed book" (438).

the melody again by a glance in which pleasure is already alight, in which the yearning for the infinite appears] (10: 741). The aspiration to the infinite found here characterizes the poetic soul from the start of Balzac's writing of *La Comédie humaine*. In *Massimilla Doni*, written in 1837 and 1838 and published in 1839, music conveys ideal love. *Gambara*, dating from the same period, portrays the maniacal composer through theories of doubling and unity in music, ideas that are also central to Balzac's preoccupations as "historian" of society. By 1841, when Balzac was writing *Ursule Mirouët*, the mysticism of music has deepened and strengthened to the point that it serves to motivate the spirituality without which the novel could not come to its happy and necessary conclusion, the restoration of the doctor's fortune to Ursule. This resoundingly realistic effect of Ursule's somnambulism forces the reader to accept spirituality as an element of materialistic reality and wins for Balzac the wager to naturalize magnetism.

15

Chemistry and Composition
La recherche de l'Absolu

Love and money are very much at play in *La recherche de l'Absolu,* a novel whose foundation in science carries forward the interplay of materiality and spirituality found in *Ursule Mirouët.* Like that novel, there are pairs of semiotic terms. The objectives and processes of chemical science can be said to group into two large classes: composition and analysis. Of these, composition cannot be more central to Balzac, while analysis necessarily involves anyone who would read him with understanding. It is fitting that in the last novel of *La Comédie humaine,* the last of the *Études philosophiques,* composition preoccupies its maniacal hero, Balthazar Claës. This man whose name contains Balzac's is as obsessed with finding a chemical composition that has not existed before as was his creator in search of the written composition, a connection Balzac does not fail to provide for us: "La puissance de vision qui fait le poète, et la puissance de déduction qui fait le savant, sont fondées sur des affinités invisibles, intangibles et impondérables que le vulgaire range dans la classe des phénomènes moraux, mais qui sont des effets physiques" [The power of vision that defines the poet and the power of deduction that defines the scientist are founded on invisible, intangible, and imponderable affinities, which the common people set in the category of moral phenomena, but which are physical effects] (10: 723).[1] Jacques Neefs also notes how

1. Compare this pairing of creation with composition in *La peau de chagrin,* where the special effect of the antiquarian shop on Raphaël de Valentin is described in these chemical

analysis serves composition: "cette prose narrative doit conquérir une incomparable puissance 'analytique,' pour que ce qui est rendu visible reçoive un nom, entre dans un ordre concevable, répertorié, pour que les lois de cette 'nature sociale' puissent être élaborées" [this narrative prose must master an incomparable 'analytical' power so that what is made visible can receive a name, can enter into a conceivable order and be inventoried, and so that the laws of this 'social nature' can be formulated] ("Figurez-vous . . ." 42). Balzac grounds his composition in science throughout this novel.

The defense of writers, composed "dans l'intérêt des écrivains" [in the interest of writers], takes scientific form immediately, in the first sentence. Barel-Moisan and Déruelle comment that this opening is often taken for a Balzacian manifesto (306), and Andrea Del Lungo connects it to Balzac's desire for "une prise de parole qui soit un véritable acte de genèse du monde représenté" [a speech-taking that constitutes a veritable genesis of the represented world] (32). Intending to describe the Claës house in Douai as a necessary, didactic preparation for the information that will follow, and anticipating impatient readers' possible objections, the narrator fustigates such "personnes ignorantes et voraces qui voudraient des émotions sans en subir les principes générateurs, la fleur sans la graine, l'enfant sans la gestation. L'Art serait-il donc tenu d'être plus fort que ne l'est la Nature?" [ignorant and voracious people who would like to feel emotions without subjecting themselves to their generating principles—the flower without the seed, the child without gestation. Should Art be expected to be stronger than Nature?] (10: 657). What was to begin like many a Balzac novel with the description of the house to explain its inhabitants turns instead to justifying art as a science, on a par with nature and capable of growing a story the way nature grows flowers and babies, from seeds.

And the novel contains several of those "personnes ignorantes et voraces" who do not allow art or nature to take their time—anti-scientific characters who see only smoke where there is composition. It seems that the scientist who composes will be misunderstood, as Balzac shows us first in Joséphine Claës's ignorance about what her husband is doing in the laboratory (10: 694) and later in the reaction by the Douai citizens to Claës's scientific work. One such is Pierquin, the notary, motivated by money. His first warning that the family fortune has dissipated comes in these anti-science terms: "Toute

---

terms: "Semblable en ses caprices à la chimie moderne qui résume la création par un gaz, l'âme ne compose-t-elle pas de terribles poisons par la rapide concentration de ses jouissances, de ses forces ou de ses idées?" [Doesn't the soul, comparable in its capriciousness to modern chemistry which understands creation as a gas, compose terrible poisons by the rapid concentration of its pleasures, its strengths, or its ideas?] (10: 74).

votre fortune, moins la maison et le mobilier, s'est dissipée en gaz et en charbon" [All your fortune, minus the house and the furniture, has vanished into gas and carbon] (10: 696). He also calls the scientific equipment and chemicals that Claës buys in Paris "brimborions" [baubles]. Everyone is muttering about Balthazar's actions: what can he be seeking to compose, if not gold or the philosopher's stone? Pierquin cites a judge who deplores "qu'un homme de votre sorte cherchât la pierre philosophale" [that a man of your kind would search for the philosopher's stone] (10: 707). Not one of the Douaisiens admires the perseverance of the scientific genius: "on le calomniait en le flétrissant du nom d'alchimiste, en lui jetant au nez ce mot:—Il veut faire de l'or!" [they slandered him, branding him with the name alchemist, flinging these words in his face: "He wants to make gold!"] (10: 830). And children gesture to their bottoms to imply that that is where Balthazar makes his gold. It is this very scene, which ends in the children's attacking him with stones and mud, that precipitates Claës's apoplexy and the consequent aphasia, making it impossible for him to communicate his discovery of the absolute.

One of the few comical moments in the novel opposes Lemulquinier, Balthazar's assistant, to the faithful servant Martha: when Lemulquinier complains there is no butter for lack of money, she spouts: "Comment, vieux monstre, si vous faites de l'or dans votre cuisine de démon, pourquoi ne vous faites-vous pas un peu de beurre?. . . . Si vous voulez des douceurs, vous avez vos fourneaux là-haut où vous fricassez des perles, qu'on ne parle que de ça au marché. Faites-vous-y des poulets rôtis" [What, you old monster, if you can make gold in your devil of a kitchen, why don't you make yourselves a little butter?. . . . If you're wanting goodies, you've got your furnaces up there where you fricassee pearls, like that's all they talk about at the market. Go ahead and make yourselves some roast chickens] (10: 782). Vulgar and ignorant people—the notary, servants, merchants, children, judges, and ordinary townspeople—constitute the underside of these "hautes régions de la Science" [high regions of Science] (10: 696), this high-minded composition. Raising up the specter of uncomprehending readers, Balzac's text erects its scientific system to ward off those who would prevent his search and his "research" for the ideal form.

The initial subject of the second paragraph, two pages long, is a kind of architectural archeology whose model, as an explanation of principles, is zoology. The tone is reminiscent of the paean to Cuvier in the famous paragraph of *La peau de chagrin* where the zoologist is admired for his ability to reconstruct whole organisms out of mere fossils. Similarly, "la plupart des observateurs peuvent reconstruire les nations ou les individus dans toute la vérité de leurs habitudes, d'après les restes de leurs monuments publics ou par l'examen de leurs reliques domestiques" [most observers can reconstruct nations or individuals in all the reality of their customs, based on the remains of their public monuments or by the examination of their domestic relics] (10: 657). The great observer that is Balzac's omniscient narrator will do exactly that, following the design of cause to effect that lies at the root of the entire structure:

> La cause fait deviner un effet, comme chaque effet permet de remonter à une cause. . . . De là vient sans doute le prodigieux intérêt qu'inspire une description architecturale quand la fantaisie de l'écrivain n'en dénature point les éléments; chacun ne peut-il pas la rattacher au passé par de sévères déductions; et . . . lui raconter ce qui fut, n'est-ce pas presque toujours lui dire ce qui sera? (10: 658)

> [From a cause one can guess at an effect, just as each effect allows one to go back to a cause. . . . No doubt the prodigious interest that an architectural description inspires, when the writer's fancy does not distort the elements, comes from this; isn't it true that anyone can connect it to the past by means of severe deductions; and . . . isn't telling what existed almost always to tell what will exist?]

The writer Balzac here justifies his overall realistic strategy as well as the structure of this novel: in particular, he is claiming that he does not denature the elements of the description, the simple bodies or elements (in the chemical sense) of his writing out of which he composes the entity that constructs the past and announces the future, the novel. Thus Joséphine Claës fearfully predicts future disaster based on the past (e.g., 10: 693–94), and the narrator stresses the ineluctable chain of events contained in supreme moments of crisis: "Ce moment terrible ne contenait-il pas virtuellement son avenir, et le passé ne s'y résumait-il pas tout entier?" [Didn't this terrible moment to all intents and purposes contain her future, and wasn't the past entirely summed up in it?] (10: 698). The reader who follows the writer's severe deductions will be guaranteed a faithful knowledge of past, present, and future.

Many pages expose chemistry, the unitary chemistry that regained fashion as of 1816 and continued to hold sway in the 1830s, and key names give this chemistry its letters patent, Lavoisier especially. (For useful explanations of nineteenth-century science, see Thiher's *Fiction Rivals Science*.) Balzac removed other names, like Berzélius, from proofs. There are early mentions of famous scientists, though not necessarily chemists, as if to inscribe science into the novelistic language: Gall (10: 671), Lavater, Swedenborg (10: 673), in addition to Lavoisier (10: 674). Pépita reads books by chemists and a few other scientists for good measure; the weighty list of names reads like a bibliography for Balzac's science (10: 700). Balthazar knows how to explain nature in chemical terms: the colors of tulips result from "Une combinaison d'hydrogène et d'oxygène [qui] fait surgir par ses dosages différents, dans un même milieu et d'un même principe, ces couleurs qui constituent chacune un résultat différent" [A combination of hydrogen and oxygen [which], through its different dosages, in the same environment and by the same principle, makes these colors appear, each constituting a different result] (10: 710). The most consequential scene, in chemical terms, shows Balthazar vaunting his scientific achievements to Joséphine:

> Mais tu ne sais donc pas ce que j'ai fait, depuis trois ans? des pas de géant! . . . J'ai combiné le chlore et l'azote [an explosive combination!], j'ai décomposé plusieurs corps jusqu'ici considérés comme simples, j'ai trouvé de nouveaux métaux . . . j'ai décomposé les larmes. Les larmes contiennent un peu de phosphate de chaux, de chlorure de sodium, du mucus et de l'eau. (10: 719)
>
> [Don't you have any idea what I've done in the last three years? I've taken giant steps! . . . I've combined chlorine and nitrogen [an explosive combination!], I've decomposed several compounds that were considered elements until now, I've found new metals . . . I've decomposed tears. Tears contain a little bit of calcium phosphate, some sodium chloride, mucus, and water.]

He has done real science and obtained new results. The key terms here are *décomposer* and *combiner.*

Like Raphaël de Valentin in *La peau de chagrin,* Balthazar Claës receives from an outside agent the gift that becomes the motor driving the story: the magic skin in the earlier novel, information about the absolute from a Polish man in this one. As others have justly noted, Adam Wierzchownia provides chemical explanations about the unity of composition that broadly inform about Balzac's writing. Thus the concept of a single unitary entity variously diversified underlies both the chemistry that Balzac knew about and his own composition. "[T]outes les productions de la nature devaient avoir un même principe. Les travaux de la chimie moderne ont prouvé la vérité de cette loi, pour la partie la plus considérable des effets naturels" [All of nature's products were to have the same principle. Work in modern chemistry has proved the truth of this law for the greater proportion of the effects in nature] (10:

715). While organic chemistry has shown that only four chemical elements—the three gases nitrogen, hydrogen, and oxygen and the non-metallic solid carbon—produce the immense diversity of animal and vegetable nature, fifty-three elements diversely combined form all the products of inorganic nature, "si peu variée, dénuée de mouvement, de sentiment, et à laquelle on peut refuser le don de croissance" [with such little variation, devoid of movement, of feeling, and to which the gift of growth can be refused] (10: 715). To the Polish chemist, and then to the Flemish one, this disparity seems illogical: "Est-il probable que les moyens soient plus nombreux là où il existe moins de résultats? . . . Aussi . . . ces cinquante-trois corps ont un principe commun, modifié jadis par l'action d'une puissance éteinte aujourd'hui, mais que le génie humain doit faire revivre" [Is it probable that the means should be more numerous where fewer results exist? . . . Thus . . . these fifty-three elements have one principle in common, modified in the past by the action of a power that is extinguished today, but that human genius must revive again] (10: 715). What could that "puissance éteinte aujourd'hui" be if not the absolute?

> Eh bien, supposez un moment que l'activité de cette puissance soit réveillée, nous aurions une chimie unitaire. Les natures organique et inorganique reposeraient vraisemblablement sur quatre principes, et si nous parvenions à décomposer l'azote, que nous devons considérer comme une négation, nous n'en aurions plus que trois. (10: 715–16)

> [Well then, suppose for a moment that the activity of this power were awakened, we would have a unitary system of chemistry. Organic and inorganic nature would likely rest on four principles, and if we managed to decompose nitrogen, which we must consider as a negation, we would have only three left.]

And three is the magical number of antiquity and medieval alchemy, but what exactly is its import?

Wierzchownia describes an experiment with watercress which results in the hypothesis of "un élément commun aux corps contenus dans le cresson, et à ceux qui lui ont servi de milieu" [a component common to the compounds contained in watercress and to those that served as environment to it] (10: 716); this unitary element is "un principe commun errant dans l'atmosphère telle que la fait le soleil" [a common principle wandering in the atmosphere as the sun has created it] (10: 717). By deductions, severe or otherwise, Wierzchownia identifies this principle as the absolute:

Une substance commune à toutes les créations, modifiée par une force unique, telle est la position nette et claire du problème offert par l'Absolu. . . . Là vous rencontrerez le mystérieux Ternaire, devant lequel s'est, de tout temps, agenouillée l'Humanité: la matière première, le moyen, le résultat. Vous trouverez ce terrible nombre Trois en toute chose humaine. . . . La MATIÈRE UNE doit être un principe commun aux trois gaz et au carbone. Le MOYEN doit être le principe commun à l'électricité négative et à l'électricité positive. Marchez à la découverte des preuves qui établiront ces deux vérités, vous aurez la raison suprême de tous les effets de la nature. (10: 717)

[A substance common to all creations, modified by a single force: such is the distinct and clear statement of the problem offered by the Absolute. . . . There you will find the mysterious Ternary, before which Humanity has forever knelt: the primary substance, the means, the result. You will find this terrible number Three in all human things. . . . The PRIMARY SUBSTANCE must be a principle common to the three gases and carbon. The MEANS must be the principle common to negative and positive electricity. Strive to discover the proofs that will establish these two truths, and you will have the supreme reason for all the effects of nature.]

Observable effects and principles need only the middle term, the means.

In the second half of the novel, after the interruption of Balthazar's research following Joséphine Claës's death, he is drawn once again into science because "La Science avait donc marché" [Science had advanced, then] (10: 770). Chemistry has indeed progressed. Here, in case the reader is inclined to side with the vulgar and to mistrust Balthazar's aims and claims, we are told about other scientists who have progressed toward the very goal he had sought: "Les gens adonnés à la haute science pensaient comme lui, que la lumière, la chaleur, l'électricité, le galvanisme et le magnétisme étaient les différents effets d'une même cause, que la différence qui existait entre les corps jusque-là réputés simples devait être produite par les divers dosages d'un principe inconnu" [People who were devoted to the high sciences thought as he did, that light, heat, electricity, galvanism, and magnetism were the different results of the same cause, that the difference which existed between the elements that were considered simple until then must be produced by the various dosages of an unknown principle] (10: 770). With Marguerite, Balthazar's daughter, we enter the laboratory for the first time and see precisely described machinery designed to focus the sun's rays, and we hear Balthazar vaunting his novel experiment: "J'ai les moyens de soumettre les métaux, dans un vide parfait, aux feux solaires concentrés et à des courants électriques" [I have the means of submitting metals in a perfect vacuum to concentrated solar heat and to electrical current] (10: 780). Earlier he was convinced that the absolute was a hair's breadth away: "Pour gazéifier les métaux, il ne me manque plus que de trouver un moyen de les soumettre à une immense chaleur . . . dans un vide absolu" [In order to volatilize metals, I only need to find a means to submit them to an immense heat . . . in an absolute vacuum] (10: 733).

Why these extensive explanations? Balzac "does science" not only for our sake—so we can follow the story, believe Balthazar a man of genius, credit the reality of the creation, and intimately comprehend the man of passion—but also for his own sake: Balzac's absolute would grasp the secret that underlies the unity of his own composition. Unity of composition is for Balzac the premise as well as the end point of his philosophy. Balthazar's famous cry "je répète la nature!" [I am repeating nature!] (10: 720) repeats Balzac's assertion that his art equals nature, like the good artist Pierre Grassou could not be; he makes diamonds out of basic elements. (Frenhofer, in Le chef-d'œuvre inconnu, similarly demands that art "express" nature, rather than copying it.) The mysterious ternary governs the global structure of La Comédie humaine; primal matter is found in the Études analytiques, the means are the laws of human life expounded in the Études philosophiques, and the results are the far more numerous products in the Études de mœurs. Beyond this rather obvious application of unitary chemistry to Balzac's composition, we can also think of a given novel as containing a primal matter, the drama or story which for Balzac clearly exists somewhere in reality (often in the form of stories he has heard from his family or friends), and a means, the created characters and the structures and language by which they come into existence, and the result: the fully developed novel we read in its myriad details. Since it is of enduring interest to understand how words written on a page create in the reader's mind characters and events that the reader accepts as if they were real, readers also follow the inverse route from result to primal matter, and that of course is the route of analysis or decomposition. Archeology, whether architectural or not, does not merely justify Balzac's descriptions, it is the model for the flow of knowledge from a primary substance to a result and back again.

For the reader of La recherche de l'Absolu, decomposition, crystallization, completion, fire, and other chemical processes become expressive metaphors for Balzac's writing. This rhetoric of composition determines our "chemical"

analysis, which takes apart the secret of Balzac's composition to reveal the ferocious irony that simultaneously undermines it.

Fire, flame, burning, ardor, and combustion are everywhere, in proper and figurative forms, a symbol forged in the furnaces of Balthazar's chemical laboratory. Besides the domesticated fire of the parlor, source of small comfort for Joséphine wringing her hands in the wing chair (e.g., 10: 687) and witness to her final illness (10: 747), there are several versions of fire and combustion in the laboratory experiments, including the one with watercress that Adam Wierzchownia describes (10: 716). Some of these are quickly compared to the fires of hell, especially by the pious Joséphine: "Ah! dit-elle, je me jetterais dans le feu de l'enfer qui attise tes fourneaux pour entendre ce mot" ["Ah!" said she, "I would throw myself into the hell fire that stokes your furnaces to hear that word"] (Balthazar has just promised "nous nous comprendrons en tout!" [there will be complete understanding between us] [10: 700–701]); also: "Le Tentateur peut seul avoir cet œil jaune d'où sortait le feu de Prométhée" [Only the Great Tempter could have that yellow eye from which Prometheus's fire escaped] (10: 718).

Figurative uses begin with the flashing Spanish eyes of Joséphine: "deux yeux noirs qui jetaient des flammes" [two black eyes that cast flames] (10: 668), sometimes in anger: "Je veux briser ton laboratoire et enchaîner ta Science, dit-elle en jetant du feu par les yeux" [I want to smash your laboratory and fetter your Science, she said, sparks flying from her eyes] (10: 723). Balthazar's eyes are equally sparkling: "Les sentiments profonds qui animent les grands hommes respiraient . . . dans ces yeux étincelants dont le feu semblait également accru par la chasteté que donne la tyrannie des idées, et par le foyer intérieur d'une vaste intelligence" [The deep sentiments that animate great men breathed . . . in these sparkling eyes whose fire seemed increased equally by the chastity inherent in the tyranny of ideas and by the internal fire of a vast intelligence] (10: 671). Passion and intelligence, grandeur in science, genius all take the form of figurative fire: Balthazar embraces Lavoisier's science with ardor—three mentions on one page (10: 674–75), interestingly put on a par with his love for Joséphine (e.g., 10: 679–80); he receives "dans mon âme le feu de ce raisonnement" [the flame of this reasoning in my soul] (10: 718) from Adam Wierzchownia; and when explaining his science, "son visage parut alors à sa femme plus étincelant sous le feu du génie qu'il ne l'avait été sous le feu de l'amour" [his face then appeared to his wife to gleam more from the fire of genius than it had from the fire of love] (10: 719). The gift of science came from a man with fire in his eyes too, Adam Wierzchownia ("ses deux yeux semblables à des langues de feu" [his two eyes similar to tongues of fire] [10: 714]). When Balthazar is forced to quit his research, the fire goes out: "les yeux de Balthazar perdirent leur feu vif, et prirent cette teinte glauque qui attriste ceux des vieillards" [Balthazar's eyes lost their lively fire, and took on that glaucous tinge that gives a gloomy appearance to those of old men] (10: 729), but fire returns to his eyes when aphasia prevents him from speaking of the discovery he has made entirely in thought, while paralyzed: "il désirait parler et remuait la langue sans pouvoir former de sons; ses yeux flamboyants projetaient des pensées" [he wanted to speak and moved his tongue without being able to form any sounds; his flaming eyes projected thoughts] (10: 834).

The fire in the furnaces of the laboratory, a fire that should forge new compositions, turns against the household to burn the family fortunes and collections. Smoke is the antithesis of composition here: "Prends, jette dans ton fourneau, fais-en de la fumée" [Take it, throw it in your furnace, make smoke out of it] (10: 721); "le notaire avait calculé que trois ans suffiraient pour mettre le feu aux affaires" [the notary had calculated that three years would suffice for the venture to go up in flames] (10: 772). On her return from Spain, "Marguerite entra dans le parloir pour y faire mettre ses bagages, et frissonna de terreur en en voyant les murailles nues comme si le feu y eût été mis" [Marguerite went into the parlor to have her luggage put there, and shuddered in terror upon seeing the walls as bare as if a fire had burned there] (10: 828); "L'idée de l'Absolu avait passé partout comme un incendie" [The idea of the Absolute had spread everywhere like wildfire] (10: 829). Thanks to Balzac's writing, the literal fire blends into the figurative fire.

Combustion is the principle of life itself: "quand la vie est bien active, quand les foyers en sont bien ardents, l'homme laisse aller la combustion sans y penser" [when life is very active, when the hearths are quite blazing, the human being lets combustion occur without even thinking about it] (10: 682). Balthazar's important explanation to Joséphine connects combustion to creation according to a triple ternary schema: "Toute vie implique une combustion" [All life implies a sort of combustion], but mineral is destroyed slowly because "la combustion y est virtuelle, latente ou insensible" [in it, combustion is virtual, latent, or undetectable], whereas vegetable matter refreshing itself continuously by means of combination producing humidity lasts indefinitely (10: 719). But the animal organisms into which nature has injected "le sentiment, l'instinct ou l'intelligence, trois degrés marqués dans le système organique, ces trois organismes veulent une combustion dont l'activité est en raison directe du résultat obtenu" [sentiment, instinct, or intelligence, three degrees marked in the organic system, these three organisms demand a combustion whose activity is directly proportional to the result obtained] (10: 719). This ternary system among animal organisms then splits into a ternary system unique to humanity: "L'homme, qui représente le plus haut point de l'intelligence et qui nous offre le seul appareil d'où résulte un pouvoir à demi créateur, *la pensée!* est, parmi les créations zoologiques, celle où la combustion se rencontre dans son degré le plus intense et dont les puissants effets sont en quelque sorte révélés par les phosphates, les sulfates et les carbonates" [The human being, who represents the highest level of intelligence and who offers us the only apparatus which results in a half-creative power—*thought!*—is, among the zoological creations, the one where combustion can be seen in its most intense degree and whose powerful effects are in some sort revealed by the phosphates, the sulfates, and the carbonates] (10: 719).

The next moment in the building of this ternary structure provides the link to electricity, humanity's means of creation: "Ces substances ne seraient-elles pas les traces que laisse en lui l'action du fluide électrique, principe de toute fécondation? L'électricité ne se manifesterait-elle pas en lui par des combinaisons plus variées qu'en tout autre animal" [Would not these substances be the traces left in him by the action of electrical fluid, the principle of all fecundation? Would not electricity manifest itself in him in combinations more varied than in any other animal], and humanity absorbs greater portions of the absolute which it assimilates into itself "pour en composer dans une plus parfaite machine, sa force et ses idées!" [to compose, in a more perfect machine, its power and its ideas!] (10: 719–20). Thus all these forms and manifestations of fire come down to electricity, the middle term of the ternary structure, the means, or the Force in another terminology: "la Matière, la Force et le Produit" [Matter, Force, and Product] (10: 718).

The action of fire on matter is of two opposing sorts: decomposition and combination (or completion), the two key terms I mentioned above.[2] "J'allais peut-être décomposer l'azote" [I might have decomposed nitrogen] (10: 691), Balthazar protests to Joséphine when, early on, she has the temerity to come to the laboratory and disrupt an experiment. For the modern reader, the moment is rife with irony: nitrogen is an element and cannot be decomposed (although scientists were not sure about this at the time). The irony intensifies to the crisis point when Mme Claës is dying and Claës has to be brought down from the laboratory by force; she gently protests: "*Tu allais sans doute décomposer l'azote*" [You were no doubt going to decompose nitrogen] (10: 753), provoking this joyous response: "C'est fait. . . . L'azote contient de l'oxygène et une substance de la nature des impondérables qui vraisembla-

---

2. On decomposition and its relation to creation, see Uhden.

blement est le principe de la . . ." [I've done it. . . . Nitrogen contains oxygen and an imponderable-like matter that likely is the principle of . . .] (10: 754), falling silent only because the family is horrified. Modern chemists too. Yet, as we learned during the chemical explanation by the Polish man, Balzac needed to decompose nitrogen to arrive at the mysterious ternary so central to his composition. Decomposition appears then as a necessary action preceding composition, and we can compare it to the *conception* Balzac so often opposed to the *execution* of an idea, as for instance in the preface to *Le Cabinet des Antiques*. Decomposition would be a kind of pre-analysis of the primal substance by the writer, of the sort occasionally visible in Balzac's letters and some prefaces, which guide the reader's later decomposition or analysis. It is left to Joséphine to say "Décomposer n'est pas créer" [To decompose is not to create] (10: 720) and to the man of knowledge to reassert his optimistic intent: "Si je trouve la force coercitive, je pourrai créer" [If I can find the coercive force, I will be able to create] (10: 720). Again, we hear Balzac speaking about his art.

The electric force will allow combination or its important result, completion. The first bit of science we hear about, before the *explication nécessaire* that takes us back to the previous life of Balthazar and the history of his involvement with chemistry, is this sentence that pops into his speech like a log surfacing out of some deep preoccupation: "Pourquoi ne se combineraient-ils pas dans un temps donné?" [Why wouldn't they combine after a given time?] (10: 674). Joséphine can only wonder if he has gone crazy. This is the first strand of a thread concerning combination of which the most striking culmination is the diamond produced during the absence of the scientists (10: 823–24). "Je fais les métaux, je fais les diamants, je répète la nature!" [I am making metals, I am making diamonds, I am repeating nature!] Balthazar exults (10: 720)—the last a cry that surely Balzac uttered more than once. Balthazar thinks he has come close to making a diamond: "cristalliser le carbone" [crystallizing carbon] (10: 700) is the process, and later he seeks only "un dissolvant du carbone" [a solvent for carbon] to manufacture diamonds aplenty (10: 781). Facts of science prepare the diamond that does actually get made, in a page-long explanation involving a capsule containing a combination of carbon and sulfur and wires from a Volta cell; carbon is the electropositive pole, crystallization will begin at the negative pole, "et, dans le cas de décomposition, le carbone s'y porterait cristallisé" [and, in the case of decomposition, the carbon will form there crystallized] (10: 805), and so on. But when the diamond is found after Balthazar's return from exile, the scientific term crystallization must give way to the most unscientific term "miracle" (10: 823) or to chance: "Oui, la puissance effrayante due au mouvement de la matière enflammée qui sans doute a fait les métaux, les diamants . . . s'est manifestée là pendant un moment, par hasard" [Yes, the frightful power proper to the movement of enflamed matter that doubtless made the metals, the diamonds . . . showed itself there for a moment, by chance] (10: 824). Balzac, contradicting his own pretentions, did admit that chance was the greatest of novelists.

Marriage is incidentally a means of achieving completion: "il sentit le besoin de se marier pour compléter l'existence heureuse dont toutes les religions l'avaient ressaisi" [he felt the need to marry to complete the happy existence which all religions had called on him to achieve] (10: 675). Men are essentially incomplete unless married, and before becoming an enraged chemist, Balthazar considers conjugal love "une œuvre magnifique" [a magnificent work] (10: 679), which suggests alchemical processes and from which he wishes to banish anything imperfect. That is the attitude of the seeker of the absolute as well, to be completed by attaining the object of the search. In the archeology or genealogy that governs the house of Claës, the necessary completeness of the collection of art works is not to be discounted among the images of combination and completion: "Une génération s'était mise à la piste de beaux tableaux; puis la nécessité de compléter la collection commencée avait rendu le goût de la peinture héréditaire" [One generation had set itself on the trail of fine paintings; then the necessity of completing the collection that had been started made the taste for paintings hereditary] (10: 683); it took three centuries to complete the collection. Marguerite astonishingly recreates the house—in the plural sense of the fortune, the collection, and the basis of the family—in a few years, made to seem even shorter by the small number of pages devoted to it. The completion of the house is thus parallel to the chemical process of completion.

In a strategy that I find characteristic of *La Comédie humaine,* Balzac gives us this panoply of chemical terms as figures of his mimesis. Balthazar incarnates the aspiration to the Promethean theme of acquiring for humanity the fires proper to the gods: no less does Balzac by writing.

The Capital of Money and the Science of Magnetism
Melmoth réconcilié

Melmoth réconcilié lies among Balzac's *Études philosophiques* and illustrates a visionary power in the pages describing the hero Castanier at the height of his fantastic abilities. But these moments of high-minded exposition of what Balzac considered a science degrade into satire and comic veniality as the novella comes to a close. High philosophical matter framed in a satirical manner also characterizes *L'elixir de longue vie* and *Massimilla Doni,* but it is in *Melmoth réconcilié* that a focus on money supplies the social satire. Balzac borrowed the character John Melmoth from the famous gothic narrative *Melmoth the Wanderer,* written by the Irish Huguenot clergyman Charles Robert Maturin in 1820. In that novel, Melmoth, as Victor Sage comments, appears to others and offers to exchange with them the pact he has made with the devil; in spite of the promise of an immediate end to their misery, none welcomes the exchange:

> The Wanderer appears at crises of suffering and despair in the lives of a range of men and women. In the main . . . he does not cause their predicament, but he predicts it, witnesses it, and makes his offer: if they will change places with him, their *fleshly* sufferings will cease. His peals of demonic laughter partly register his inexpressibly self-contradictory emotion at the suspicion that he is predestined to fail over and over again, and therefore to remain where he is, neither properly in nor outside human history. (*Melmoth the Wanderer* xvi)

221

In such Faustian narratives the hero typically seeks ultimate knowledge, a philosophical insight, but Balzac's recycling of the model distills such power into mere money, and he does this to begin with by putting Melmoth in Paris, the capital of money.

In Balzac's satire, Melmoth's victim is appropriately enough a cashier. The witty prologue to the tale describes the zoological species of the *caissier,* a hybrid and irreproducible species that Civilization obtains in the Social Realm as botanists do flowers in the garden: "Cet homme est un caissier, véritable produit anthropomorphe, arrosé par les idées religieuses, maintenu par la guillotine, ébranché par le vice, et qui pousse à un troisième étage entre une femme estimable et des enfants ennuyeux" [This man is a cashier, a veritable anthropomorphic product, watered with religious ideas, supported by the guillotine, pruned by vice, and growing on a fourth floor between an estimable wife and tedious children] (10: 345). Frequently calling him "le caissier" instead of by his name, Balzac brings anthropological irony to bear on the zoological specimen or the type—the mere handler of money. At the close of the prologue, Balzac's narrator warns that this preparatory observation should help sufficiently intelligent minds to fathom "les véritables plaies de notre civilisation qui, depuis 1815, a remplacé le principe Honneur par le principe Argent" [the true scourges of our civilization, which, since 1815, has replaced the principle of Honor with the principle of Money] (10: 347). This phrase closes the prologue on a note of sarcastic irony; Honor is a matter of principles, but there can be no principles where Money is concerned (see *La Maison Nucingen*), and while most of the prologue satirizes the species known as cashier, the government's treatment of people of talent is the deeper object of criticism. The date of 1815 points to a Restoration that was not the restoration of *ancien régime* power, based on birth, land, and honor, but rather an instauration of the new plague of capitalism, or Money, that fails to provide principles like those of Honor. Françoise Gaillard, who wrote a strong analysis of the story ("Aux limites du genre"), incidentally ennobles money by insisting on money as a principle, which determines realistic meaning, but I see Balzac primarily showing up money as the barest, lowest form of power—power sought for materialistic and egotistical reasons in opposition, for instance, to idealistic and altruistic purposes such as revolution, social benefit, or religious fervor.

Melmoth suddenly appears to Castanier, Nucingen's cashier, just as the cashier is forging the banker's signature on a quittance of five hundred thousand francs, the amount he has stolen from the cash drawer. The very fact that Melmoth penetrates the vault through its multiple barriers—human, stone, and metal—immediately symbolizes the superiority of a power based on total knowledge over one based on money. That evening, at the theater and at the apartment of Castanier's mistress, Melmoth convinces Castanier that he is going to be caught and hanged for his crime unless he takes his place. Castanier accepts the deal, thereby acquiring Melmoth's powers; he brushes off the unfaithful Aquilina and indulges in vast orgies of self-gratification, which are accurately pegged as petit-bourgeois by Françoise Gaillard: "L'ancien caissier reste 'rond de cuir' dans ses envies" [The former cashier remains a 'pencil pusher' in his desires] ("Aux limites" 130).

What high philosophical matter might one find among such tawdry characters and events? First, there is the portrait of the Balzacian visionary type. Melmoth describes the powers he possesses because of his pact with the devil in terms that are strikingly similar to words that describe Balzac's not supernatural visionary characters, Vautrin in particular. Melmoth's supernatural abilities materialize as "un regard de feu qui vomissait des courants électriques, espèces de pointes métalliques par lesquelles Castanier se sentait pénétré, traversé de part en part, et cloué" [a fiery look that belched forth electrical currents, like metallic spikes which Castanier felt penetrate him, go clean through him, and pin him down] (10: 366). When Melmoth speaks, we can imagine Vautrin subjugating Rastignac in *Le père Goriot:* "Qui donc est assez fort pour me résister? . . . Ne sais-tu pas que tout ici-bas doit m'obéir, que je puis tout? Je lis dans les cœurs. . . . Mon œil perce les murailles" [But who is strong enough to resist me? . . . Don't you know that everything here on earth must obey me, that I can do anything? I read in the hearts of men. . . . My eyes penetrate walls] (10: 364–65). He literally makes "la pluie et le beau temps" [rain and fair weather] (10: 368).

There is also the important philosophical conception of human desire, which echoes *La peau de chagrin.* Describing the condition of the visionary as represented in Castanier, after his exchange with Melmoth, Balzac shows us a man for whom every desire is satisfied except desire itself: "Ses lèvres devinrent ardentes de désir, comme l'étaient celles de Melmoth, et il haletait après l'INCONNU, car il connaissait tout" [His lips became ardent with desire, as were Melmoth's, and he gasped for the UNKNOWN—because he knew everything] (10: 375–76). Having satisfied every wish, "ce fut une dissipation de toutes les forces et de toutes les jouissances. . . . Cette énorme puissance, en un instant appréhendée, fut en un instant exercée, jugée, usée. Ce qui était tout, ne fut rien. Il arrive souvent que la possession tue les plus immenses poèmes du désir, aux rêves duquel l'objet possédé répond rarement" [there was a dissipation of all his strength and of all his pleasures. . . . This enormous power, seized in one moment, was in one moment exerted, judged, worn out. What had been all was nothing. It often happens that possession kills the most immense poems of desire, with whose dreams the object, once possessed, rarely complies] (10: 374). Possession of the entire earth means nothing to him (10: 376). At the moment when the cashier comes to realize the "mot terrible" (10: 380), that he will be as he is for all eternity, Balzac tells us how desire is yet born in him: if there is merely a point on the earth or in the heavens that is forbidden to him, he becomes preoccupied with it.

We are clearly in *Études philosophiques* territory, but it is philosophy reduced to money, which supplies the anthropological analysis when Balzac, with a studied caution, compares the cashier's obsession to a banker's:

> S'il était permis de comparer de si grandes choses aux niaiseries sociales, il ressemblait à ces banquiers riches de plusieurs millions à qui rien ne résiste dans la société; mais qui, n'étant pas admis aux cercles de la noblesse, ont pour idée fixe de s'y agréger, et ne comptent pour rien tous les privilèges sociaux acquis par eux, du moment où il leur en manque un. (10: 380)

> [If one may be permitted to compare such great things to the piddling nonsense of social life, he resembled those rich bankers who own several million and against whom nothing in society resists; but who, not being admitted into noble circles, have the *idée fixe* of joining them and consider all the social privileges they have acquired as nothing, as long as one of them is missing.]

The power of money to acquire social privilege is only a degraded power, in comparison to noble birth. The reader may well think of Nucingen in this image of a banker stupidly yearning for the one thing he cannot buy; how much more *niais* is Castanier, the mere cashier! The cashier is the banker without privilege.[1]

In spite of the inanity of this comparison, the notion of the *idée fixe* points us to the loftiest philosophical topic of the tale. The point forbidden to Castanier and the driving force of the scientific thought in *Melmoth réconcilié,* the "si grandes choses" that really undergird Balzac's appropriation of Maturin's conceit—these serious matters are the thought of religion and the comforts

---

[1]. Note that the hero is called "le caissier" as well as Castanier in the part of the narrative that recounts his stealing from Nucingen, the affair with Aquilina, and the eventual "sale" of the demonic power, but at the philosophical high points, the hero is called only Castanier for seven pages (10: 374–81).

provided by religious salvation. "En se voyant exclu de ce que les hommes ont nommé le ciel dans tous leurs langages, [Castanier] ne pouvait plus penser qu'au ciel" [Seeing himself excluded from what people, in all their languages, have named heaven, [Castanier] could think only about heaven] (10: 376–77). He becomes violently agitated with religious feeling: "il ne pensait plus qu'à l'avenir de ceux qui prient et qui croient" [he thought only about the future of those who pray and have faith] (10: 377). After observing Melmoth reconciled, calm in death and transfigured after his repentance, transformed by the hand of God (10: 378), Castanier becomes a mere man after having been a demon for several days, and he comes to know divine power. "Il eut bientôt dans la physionomie, comme Melmoth, quelque chose de grand" [Like Melmoth, his physiognomy soon held greatness] (10: 382).

But showing the power of religion is not Balzac's final purpose in *Melmoth réconcilié*, as both Gaillard and Émeline Dhommée argue more fully than I do here, the latter especially. Immediately after this "quelque chose de grand" shows that Castanier knows divine power, he stumbles on the idea of trading off his power, just as he had accepted it from Melmoth as his replacement in the pact with the devil, and he realizes that the current social climate of "fatale indifférence en matière de religion" [fatal indifference as concerns religion] (10: 382) will make it easy to find a buyer for the pact. This articulation between the high and the low moments of the story occurs with the realization that there is a place for trading, and it is that representation of capitalism, the Bourse: "Si je puis trouver une âme à négocier, n'est-ce pas là?" [If I am to find a soul to trade, wouldn't it be there?] (10: 382). From this point forward, no lofty philosophy remains—only satire: "Castanier alla joyeux à la Bourse, en pensant qu'il pourrait trafiquer d'une âme comme on y commerce des fonds publics" [Castanier went cheerfully to the Bourse, thinking he would be able to barter a soul in the same way one trades government bonds] (10: 382–83). The soul becomes an object to which a monetary value can be given, and this *Étude philosophique* reveals its grounding in an *Étude de mœurs*. Commerce, *le négoce*, takes the place of perceptions of the infinite, just as the cashier had taken the place of Melmoth; the romance of the fantastic falls to the banal realities. At the Bourse, transformations have nothing to do with the grandeur of the soul's aspirations; they are merely business affairs, according to the cashier hawking his diabolical wares: "N'est-ce pas une affaire comme une autre? Nous sommes tous actionnaires dans la grande entreprise de l'éternité" [Isn't it a transaction like any other? We are all shareholders in the great enterprise of eternity's firm] (10: 383–84).

And he is right. Just as the prologue announces, the cashier has no trouble making the sale: he quickly finds a buyer in the suitably venal Claparon (10:

384), who sells it to a notary after paying off his debts. In two sentences, the pact with the devil is bought and sold several times, losing in value at each sale and also tumbling down the social ladder. It starts at the level of banker-businessman with Claparon; it costs seven hundred thousand francs for the notary, five hundred thousand francs for a real estate developer, three hundred thousand francs for an ironmonger, and finally two hundred thousand francs to a carpenter, after which buyers for this "inscription sur le Grand-livre de l'enfer" [stock certificate on Hell's ledger] (10: 385) become scarce for lack of faith. By the end of the afternoon, barely an hour and a half after the first sale, the owner of the pact is a house painter, too low down on the social ladder even to recognize the power he holds: "Ce peintre en bâtiment, homme simple, ne savait pas ce qu'il avait en lui-même. *Il était tout chose,* dit-il à sa femme quand il fut de retour au logis" [This house painter, a simple man, did not know what he had in himself. "*He felt all funny,*" he said to his wife when he returned home] (10: 386).

This could have been the end of the story, but Balzac, never one to resist a joke when the opportunity arises, tacks on yet another replacement, this time a notary's clerk, favored object of Balzac's joyful satires and placed de facto at the very bottom of the ladder. Amossy and Rosen (163) point out that the notary's clerk is a double of Castanier. All this fellow needs is ten thousand francs to buy his Euphrasie a shawl so she will sleep with him. If ever the holders of Melmoth's immense power were brought to reflect on the even greater immensity of God's power, as Castanier does at the height of his, such philosophy is lost for good: the notary's clerk thinks only of sex with Euphrasie: "comme il avait le diable au corps, il y resta douze jours sans en sortir en y dépensant tout son paradis, en ne songeant qu'à l'amour et à ses orgies au milieu desquelles se noyait le souvenir de l'enfer et de ses privilèges" [as he was a lusty devil, he stayed there twelve days without leaving and spent all of his paradise, thinking only about love and orgies, in the midst of which the memory of hell and its privileges were drowned] (10: 387). Thanks to such thoughtless behavior, the power discovered by the Irishman is lost to humanity, and neither Orientalists, nor mystics, nor archeologists concerned with such matters are able to rediscover the means of evoking the demon. On the thirteenth day the clerk dies from an accidental overdose of a mercury-laced drug, taken, one gathers, to cure a venereal disease, and his soul presumably goes to the devil, thus ending the chain of replacements. The sheen of mercury is silvery but not silver—not "argent" but "vif argent"; Gaillard notes this pun ("Aux limites" 130). Melmoth's power has fallen down the money ladder to the level of raw sex, its value becoming finally too low to continue to be worth even a narrative.

Here the story really did end, until Balzac added, on proofs, a page of dialogue, capping the joke: he stages an encounter between the other clerks, with their particular sort of witticisms, and a German demonologist who solemnly believes it when the clerks tell him their comrade was "emporté dans la planète de Mercure" [carried off to the planet Mercury] (10: 387). In the dialogue constituting this final scene, the demonologist quotes Jakob Boehm, the German mystic, as translated by Saint-Martin, the French mystic, prompting mystifying remarks by the clerks, so that the story ends on Balzac's satire of the German demonologist: "Quoiqu'il fût un démonologue de première force, l'étranger ne savait pas quels mauvais diables sont les clercs; il s'en alla, ne comprenant rien à leurs plaisanteries, et convaincu que ces jeunes gens trouvaient Boehm un génie pyramidal.—Il y a de l'instruction en France, se dit-il" [Although he was a demonologist of the first order, the foreigner did not know what little devils clerks can be; he went away, understanding nothing of their jesting and convinced that these young men found Boehm to be a colossal genius. "People are educated in France," he said to himself] (10: 388). And these are the last words of the ending. We are now down at the level of the inane witticisms of the "esprit clerc," in which any silly remark is good because it is not serious. Both *Les employés* and *Le colonel Chabert* portray the low wit of clerks. One almost has the feeling that Balzac attached the whole ending so he could make the atrocious pun about clerks being such "mauvais diables"—and I suppose they are *poor* devils because in them the devil's power is lost. In an article entitled "*Melmoth réconcilié* ou un diable peut en cacher un autre," Émeline Dhommée has done the definitive study of the diabolism—the division, scission, and disunion—that defines money as "mauvais diables."

But what makes *Melmoth réconcilié* important for understanding Balzac? The story is neither a "sequel" to Maturin's *Melmoth the Wanderer* nor a "parody" of the last great gothic novel, as people writing outside the Balzacian context are wont to say: "*Melmoth réconcilié* is Balzac's sequel to Maturin's novel, and it becomes extremely interesting as it attempts to lead us out of the Gothic into the world of proper bourgeois writing" (Lanone 77). Victor Sage in his edition of Maturin's novel writes: "In 1835, Balzac wrote his famous parody, *Melmoth Reconcilié*" [sic] (xiii), and Sage accuses it of not being "even" (xiv). Michel Butor also writes: "*Melmoth réconcilié*, c'est l'achèvement et la correction du livre de Maturin" [*Melmoth réconcilié* is the completion and correction of Maturin's book] ("La pollution bancaire" 46).

In the 1970s, interpreters of literature might have said that the exchange of the gift of quasi-immortality is a figure for the exchange of knowledge with the reader—and it is worth a moment's reflection to recognize such hubris and the irony of its outcome.[2] Now, in the twenty-first century, I would suggest that the motif of the exchange of power figures the story's own definition, its ability to cohere. Does it in fact cohere? Dhommée thinks Melmoth's diabolical manipulations resemble Balzac's, "[qui] n'est pas dupe de sa prétention réaliste qui consiste sans cesse à occulter et dissimuler les origines discursives du récit" [[who] is not a dupe to his realist pretensions which consist in repeatedly hiding and dissimulating the discursive origins of the tale] (54). But the ending is such a tumble, a *dégringolade* from the high fantastic into buffoonery, that it raises the question of Balzac's real intent. (The intentional fallacy is intentional on my part.) Are we reading high comedy, as in *La Comédie humaine* or for that matter *divine,* or is it low farce?

Like the change of venue from Ireland to Paris, the exchanges of the power down the degrading ladder resolve the story on the satire of Paris, where Balzac's point is that Melmoth would have found millions of people ready to take his place, had Maturin only thought to put him in the capital of money, which is pointedly incarnated in the ironic hero, the cashier. Gaillard speaks of the relativity of all values in modernity: "Or avec *Melmoth réconcilié* nous quittons l'univers de la transcendance des valeurs pour entrer dans celui de leur relativité; nous quittons le monde de l'hétéronomie qui est celui des sociétés traditionnelles pour entrer dans le monde de l'autonomie qui est celui des sociétés modernes" [But with *Melmoth réconcilié* we leave behind the universe where values are transcendent to enter one where they are relative; we leave behind the world of heteronomy, the domain of traditional societies, and enter the world of autonomy, the domain of modern societies] ("Aux limites" 125). It is understood that "modern society," in Balzac, indexes nascent capitalism. The simple principle is that power comes with money and money with power: the holder of the power gets all the money he would need to buy love—but the irony about Paris, "cette succursale de l'Enfer" [that branch office of Hell] (10: 346), is that he does not get love. The story realizes this intention fully with the ending, where social satire re-orients the entire plot and undermines its serious message. And yet, paradoxically, and this is Anne-Marie Meininger's point in her introduction in the Folio edition (25), by turning Melmoth's power into a financial force that loses value and disappears, Balzac "saves" the visionary aspect of this

---

2. I have in mind a well-written article by Léo Mazet, "Récit[s] dans le récit: l'échange du récit chez Balzac."

power. Philosophy may be lost in the capital of money, but the *Études philosophiques* and Balzac himself, visionary of the real, seek to preserve all its value deep in the vaults of the human comedy.

Human comedy, governed by "le principe Honneur," perdures behind the low farce and relativizing force of "le principe Argent." Turning the exchange of a philosophical power into a monetary negotiation symbolizes the risks the narrative takes, as an item of value, if there are no buyers for lack of faith— faith in the ability of the narrator to tell a story worth knowing about. Balzac exposes himself to this loss of value every time he writes. And yet we continue to believe in the reality of his inventions, for that is the job his writing assigns to the reader: to bring unity in the face of relentless diabolical disunity. I see Balzac himself in the figure of Melmoth, empowered and yet tormented by his immense ability, but finally dying the death of a mere human, reconciled with the ordinary, having passed his power on to others less great. The sufficiently intelligent reader, imbued with the principles guiding Balzac's anthropology, knows what it takes to reconcile Balzac, so he may expect peaceful eternity. It is indeed a lucky thing that "Il y a de l'instruction en France" [People are educated in France], for if that were not the case, without readers, humanity would have to accept the loss of greatness: the only writers left at the end of *Melmoth réconcilié* are mere scribblers, copiers, and jokesters.

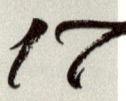

Love, Music, and Opium
Medical Semiotics *of* Massimilla Doni

> La phrase est griffes d'acier au cœur!
> [Sentences are steel clawing at the heart!]
> —*Hanska* 1: 509, May 1840

In May 1837, Balzac wrote to Mme Hanska in words now familiar to readers of the "artistic" stories of the *Études philosophiques,* explaining the principle behind *Massimilla Doni:*

> *Massimilla Doni* et *Gambara* sont, dans les *Études philosophiques,* l'apparition de la musique, sous la double forme d'*exécution* et de *composition,* soumise à la même épreuve que la pensée dans L[ouis] Lambert, c'est-à-dire l'œuvre et l'exécution tuées par la trop grande abondance du principe créateur, ce qui m'a dicté le *Chef-d'œuvre inconnu* pour la peinture. (*Hanska* 1: 382–83, 24 May 1837)

> [*Massimilla Doni* and *Gambara* are, in the *Études philosophiques,* the appearance of music, under the double form of *execution* and *composition,* put to the same trial as is thought in *Louis Lambert,* that is to say the work and its execution killed by too great an abundance of the creative principle, the subject that dictated the *Chef-d'œuvre inconnu* to me as concerns painting.]

This abundance of the creative principle, the root of the novella's philosophy, expresses itself in the three forms of content my title begins with, objects of men's desires and figures of the semiotics governing meaning in this story "rich in figures," in Jeannine Jallat's description (74). Music, love, and opium are the three passions expressed differentially by the duc de Cataneo, Emilio Memmi, and Marco Vendramini, Venetians to whom the officious French doctor seeks to bring nothing less than a cure. Although the chief focus of the plot is on Emilio and his love for the duchesse de Cataneo, Massimilla Doni, Balzac brings these three forms of desire together in key passages. Identified as three representations of the same human capacity, they together tie down what Balzac called the "psychological subject" of his novella, which he said was a "marvel" and a "mythical page" difficult to write (*Hanska* 1: 437–38, 22 January 1838). As Arlette Michel has put it, "Tous ont choisi le parti suicidaire de vivre de manière absolue et radicale la division en eux du corps et de l'âme" [They have all chosen the suicidal route of living absolutely and radically the division within themselves of body and soul] (*Le réel* 245).

The "trop grande abondance" of these lethal creative passions, the psychological subject of the novella, is expressed not only in the descriptions of these characters and their stories but also in Balzac's use throughout of highly figural language. As abundance is the topic of the story, so its execution, its forms of expression, represent abundance by excessive imagery. Forms of content and forms of expression are matched; the content is mirrored in the expression. It is as if Balzac sought to illustrate his principle, the underlying subject, not only by characters and events and situations, but also in the very language used to bring them to the reader. This figural language is poetic. In *Modeste Mignon,* the familiar opposition between "reality" and "poetry" aligns with that between Money and Love; in *Massimilla Doni,* poetry is opposed to "brutal nature," and that contrast is made visible in the writing, most strikingly in the last two paragraphs.

Love

The contrast between the psycho-philosophical subject matter and the narration of sexual union accompanies the first mention of love in the story, "l'amour d'une duchesse et d'un joli jeune homme, lequel est une œuvre de poésie fort éloignée des fins de la brutale nature" [the love between a duchess and a handsome young man, which is a work of poetry far removed from the purposes of brutal nature] (10: 545). Love has conflicting sexual and emotional expressions.[1] Thus the obscenity for which Balzac feared readers

---

1. For an excellent and concise explanation of this conflict, see Max Milner's introduction to his edition of the story.

would (again) reproach him is immediately connected with this philosophical subject. Brutal nature's ends are exactly what love comes to on the last page of the story, by which point the poetic and impotent Emilio has overcome his problem and the duchess is quite pregnant. But for most of the story, "ils s'aimaient trop" [they loved each other too much] (10: 546). Desire for Massimilla makes Emilio impotent with her, until his friends conspire to put her in his bed instead of the famous and adulated soprano he was to sleep with, Clarina Tinti. Already their love had strikingly illustrated the Platonic conception of reunited souls. When they first met, "une voix cria: *le voilà!* dans les oreilles de la duchesse. . . . ces deux ignorances se confondirent comme deux substances de la même nature qui n'en font qu'une seule en se rencontrant" [a voice cried out: *he is the one!* in the duchess's ears. . . . these two unknowing people blended like two substances of the same nature which become only one when they meet] (10: 547).

Emilio's soul has so taken up his body (10: 547), and he has placed Massimilla so high above him (10: 548), that he cannot consummate his love. The too-full heart makes the body empty, just as Emilio's brilliant palace in Venice is empty and his principality broke: "une âme sans action sur le corps . . . un corps vide et un cœur plein, mille antithèses désespérantes" [a soul that cannot act on the body . . . an empty body and a full heart, a thousand heart-breaking antitheses] (10: 552). Massimilla has only to ask him what he desires, and "life" leaves his body (made ignoble, at that point, because he has been deflowered by la Tinti) to take refuge in his heart (10: 564). In writing to Ève Hanska, Balzac calls la Tinti a "misérable fille" [wretched girl], perhaps because of her talent for sex. That the wretched girl sees Emilio as a child shows that he was a novice in sex until the opera singer's actions taught him to know this other kind of love.

A page-long allegory (10: 560–61) contrasting poetry and brutal nature in terms of landscapes opposes these two sides of love. Balzac's authorial presence is palpable in this passage addressed directly to the reader, as he pulls out all the romantic stops in a highly detailed description: "Si vous n'avez pas voyagé en Suisse, vous lirez peut-être avec plaisir cette description, et si vous avez grimpé par ces Alpes-là, vous ne vous en rappellerez pas les accidents sans émotion" [If you haven't traveled in Switzerland, you will perhaps read this description with pleasure, and if you have climbed on those Alps, you will not recall that rugged terrain without emotion]. Hidden in a valley between high peaks lies a vast and deep basin, of blue like sapphires or green like emeralds (depending on the light), nourished by waters flowing down from the St. Gothard or the Simplon. Nothing better represents "les idées de profondeur, de calme, d'immensité, de céleste affection, de bonheur éternel, comme ce diamant liquide" [ideas of depth, calm, immensity, heavenly affection, and eternal happiness than this liquid diamond]. So calm is this bed of water that its surface shows no ripple: "vous ne voyez aucun trouble à la surface où la voiture se mire en passant" [you see no disturbance on the surface where the carriage is reflected in passing]—and the word that Balzac chooses to speak of what is lacking on the water's surface is also the one that connotes sexual excitement, "trouble"—precisely what Emilio cannot feel for Massimilla. His love for Massimilla is a sleepy pond and a beautiful blue stream flowing calmly in the Alps—and we know that blue codifies purity in Balzac.

But whip the horses round a bend, and you are assailed with an opposite image: "tout à coup rugit un horrible concert de cascades se ruant les unes sur les autres; le torrent, échappé par une bonde furieuse, se brise en vingt chutes, se casse sur mille gros cailloux; il étincelle en cent gerbes contre un rocher tombé du haut de la chaîne qui domine la vallée" [all of a sudden, you hear the roar of a horrible concert of waterfalls rushing one atop the other; the torrent, escaping with a furious bound, divides into twenty cascades, and breaks on a thousand stones; it sparkles in a hundred sprays against a boulder that has fallen from the tops of the mountain chain that dominates the valley]. Sex with Tinti comes like an exploding cannon, and the numbers are suspiciously high.

But in case the allegorical nature of this brilliant passage has escaped the inattentive reader, Balzac will follow it with a summary that makes the interpretation explicit, according to a narrative design characteristic of his interpretations: "Si vous avez bien saisi ce paysage, vous aurez dans cette eau endormie une image de l'amour d'Emilio pour la duchesse, et dans les cascades bondissant comme un troupeau de moutons, une image de sa nuit amoureuse avec la Tinti. Au milieu de ces torrents d'amour, il s'élevait un rocher contre lequel se brisait l'onde" [If you have grasped this landscape well, you will have in this sleeping pond an image of Emilio's love for the duchess, and in the waterfalls bounding like a herd of sheep an image of his night of love with la Tinti. In the middle of these torrents of love arose a rock against which the wave broke]. Note that the broken wave is not without hints of the broken love instrument and the rock a suggestion of the immobility of this kind of love.

In writing to Mme Hanska that the work would be misunderstood, in spite of the "énormes travaux [qu'elle me donne] par ses difficultés" [immense labor [it is costing me] because of its difficulties], the language Balzac used glosses the idea of the psychological subject: "mais je n'ai rien tant caressé que cette page mythique, parce que le mythe est bien profondément enfoui sous la réalité" [but nothing have I caressed so much as this mythical page, because the myth is buried quite deep under the reality] (*Hanska* 1: 414, 20 October 1837). Reality, as often when Balzac uses this word, has to do with vulgar matters of everyday life—in this case, simplifying only a little, sex. The careless, uncomprehending reader will see that obscene story, but the deeply buried myth is what the author called the "sujet psychique," the wonderful story of art in the form of execution being slaughtered by an excess of the creative principle.

In 1838, when the story was almost finished, Balzac anticipated the usual "mauvaises et méchantes sottises" [mean, stupid criticisms] from readers, as he wrote to Mme Hanska:

> Vu d'un côté, le sujet donne prise à la critique, on dira que je suis un homme obscène, mais voyez le sujet psychique, c'est une merveille selon moi. Mais il y a longtemps que je suis fait à ces détractions. . . . Dans cinq ans, *Massimilla Doni* sera comprise comme une belle explication des plus intimes procédés de l'art. Aux yeux des lecteurs du 1er jour, ce sera ce que ça est en apparence, un amoureux qui ne peut posséder la femme qu'il adore parce qu'il la désire trop et qui possède une misérable fille. Faites-les donc conclure de là à l'enfantement des œuvres d'art! . . . (*Hanska* 1: 437–38, 22 January 1838)

> [Seen from one side, the subject lays itself open to criticism; they will say I am an obscene man, but look at the psychological subject; in my opinion it is a marvel. But I have been accustomed to this disparagement for a long time. . . . In five years, *Massimilla Doni* will be understood as a fine explanation of the most intimate processes of art. But in the eyes of the first readers, it will be what it appears to be, a lover who cannot possess the woman he adores because he desires her too much and who possesses a wretched girl. From that to the birthing of works of art, get them to draw any conclusions! . . .]

Admitting that most readers will not see beyond the apparent subject of impotence stemming from too much idealized love, Balzac explicitly links this subject to the real but occulted one, the birthing of a work of art. The link makes of love a semiotic figure of creation. Those happy readers who see that the story illustrates, in this form of content and again in the other two, the proposition that an excess of desire makes one impotent, will have captured the essence of the story even from its apparent subject, guided by this semiotic figure of its creation.

Music

If love furnishes the core of the moral plot, music constitutes its philosophy. Music possesses the ability to speak directly to the heart, while writing addresses the intelligence; the painter Balzac admired most, Raphael, gave music priority over poetry (10: 581–82), and Balzac devoted great care to the effort to place music on the supreme plane. It is through Massimilla Doni's sensitive illustration of Rossini's opera *Mosè* that Balzac expresses the position he ascribes to music in this novella: "Là où les autres arts cerclent nos pensées en les fixant sur une chose déterminée, la musique les déchaîne sur la nature entière qu'elle a le pouvoir de nous exprimer" [Whereas other arts encircle our thoughts by fixing them on a specific thing, music lets them loose on all of nature, which it has the power to express for us] (10: 588). The poetic Capraja is the "rêveur" [dreamer] and "théoricien fantasque" [whimsical theorist] (10: 580) of harmony and melody, but the passion of music has for its chief figure a grossly caricatured duc de Cataneo.

The duke is a premature old man who has sold his body to debauchery in search of excessive pleasures: "La Débauche avait détruit la créature humaine et s'en était fait une autre à son usage. . . . En héritier avide, chaque vice avait marqué sa part du cadavre encore vivant" [Debauchery had destroyed the human creature and had created another for its personal use. . . . Each vice, like an avid heir, had marked its share of the still living cadaver] (10: 555–56). Only music can bring him pleasure now, la Tinti explains. Soul, intelligence, heart, sinews, "tout ce qui produit chez l'homme un élan et le rattache au ciel par le désir ou par le feu du plaisir, tient non pas tant à la musique qu'à un effet pris dans les innombrables effets de la musique, à un accord parfait entre deux voix, ou entre une voix et la chanterelle de son violon" [everything that produces an impetus in a man and links him with the heavens through desire or through the fire of pleasure results not so much from music as from an effect found among the innumerable effects of music, a perfect accord between two voices, or between a voice and the highest string of his violin] (10: 561). When the perfect harmony occurs, the duke experiences what can only be described as a parody of an orgasm: "ce vieillard tombe alors en extase, ses yeux morts jettent leurs derniers feux, il est heureux, il se roule à terre comme un homme ivre. . . . Il mourra dans quelque attaque d'accord parfait" [this old man then falls into ecstasy, his deadened eyes emit their last sparks, he is content, he rolls on the ground like a drunken man. . . . He will die in an attack of some perfect chord] (10: 561–62). Death by music.

And it is not even music with a subject or theme, as defended poetically by Capraja, but the mere principle of harmony and the science of sounds, which have a magical power:

> L'accord de deux voix ou d'une voix et du violon, l'instrument dont l'effet se rapproche le plus de la voix humaine. . . . Cet accord parfait nous mène plus avant dans le centre de la vie sur le fleuve d'éléments qui ranime les voluptés et qui porte l'homme au milieu de la sphère lumineuse où sa pensée peut convoquer le monde entier. . . . je sais embrasser l'infini! (10: 582)

> [The harmony of two voices or of one voice and the violin, the instrument whose effect is the closest to a human voice. . . . This perfect harmony leads us forward into the center of life on the elemental river that reanimates sensual pleasures and lifts a man into the middle of the luminous sphere where his thoughts can summon up the entire world. . . . I can embrace infinity!]

The philosophy that illuminates this power of music is, like the moral action of love in the story, a semiotic figure of Balzac's creation. The achievement of the perfect harmony allows the creator to embrace infinity.

Opium

Opium is probably not as familiar as music and love, but comparisons make it comprehensible for this novella. While love is the moral symbol and music the philosophical one, opium is in fact the key symbol of creative power. To begin with, the state of mental excitation brought on by opium is compared to the effects of excessive coffee use: not unlike Balzac himself, Emilio Memmi uses coffee as a crutch for his idealized passion, "pour se soutenir jusqu'au soir dans une excitation nerveuse, sur l'abus de laquelle il comptait pour mourir" [to sustain himself until nighttime in a nervous excitation, the abuse of which he was counting on in order to die] (10: 551); in the same way, Vendramini uses opium: "Vendramin comptait, lui, sur l'opium" [As for Vendramin, he counted on opium] (10: 551). The comparison de-marginalizes opium and opium use, and it becomes the physiological expression of the passions of love and music. In the same manner, Cataneo faces death from a perfect chord, and idealization in love has an opium-like effect: "Or, sur un jeune homme assez puissant pour idéaliser une maîtresse au point de ne plus y voir de femme, l'arrivée trop subite de la fortune devait faire l'effet d'une dose d'opium" [Now, for a young man powerful enough to idealize a mistress to the point of no longer seeing a woman in her, the too sudden arrival of good fortune must have the same effect as a dose of opium] (10: 554).

Opium also leads the user to art. Thanks to the brilliant vapors of his intoxication, Vendramini sees Massimilla Doni as the highest expression of art, a Raphael portrait (10: 572), and opium makes his mind contain multitudes like an opera (10: 576). In Vendramini's lapidary formulation about those whose passion is music, love and music are as addicting as opium: "ils vont dans l'Art là où te conduit ton extrême amour, là où me mène l'opium" [they go into Art the way your extreme love directs you, the way opium leads me] (10: 584). This single sentence fragment identifies the three figures as three versions of the same principle. The de-marginalized opium lends powerful consistency to all three mind-expanding passions.

It is the *opium* addict who describes Cataneo's passion for *music,* the science of sounds, in a way that makes Emilio understand his *love,* in a passage where abundance of imagery dominates:

> Tu viens d'expliquer mon amour pour la Massimilla, dit Emilio. Cher, il est en moi-même une puissance qui se réveille au feu de ses regards, à son moindre contact, et me jette en un monde de lumière où se développent des effets dont je n'osais te parler. . . . Le désir soulève mon crâne en y remuant ce monde invisible au lieu de soulever mon corps inerte; et l'air devient alors rouge et pétille, des parfums inconnus et d'une force inexprimable détendent mes nerfs, des roses me tapissent les parois de la tête, et il me semble que mon sang s'écoule par toutes mes artères ouvertes, tant ma langueur est complète. (10: 585)

> [You have just explained my love for la Massimilla, said Emilio. Dear friend, there is within me a force that reawakens with the fire of her glances, at the slightest contact with her, and projects me into a world of light where effects that I dared not tell you about develop. . . . Desire raises up my skull and agitates the invisible world in it instead of lifting up my inert body; and the air then becomes red and sparkles, unknown fragrances calm my nerves with an inexpressible force, roses carpet the inner walls of my head, and my languor is so complete, it seems like my blood flows out of all my open arteries.]

"Ainsi fait mon opium fumé" [That is what my smoking opium does] (10: 585), Vendramini replies, and I am almost ready to say that writing does the same to Balzac.

All three men are taken over by their passions and suffer a loss of self. The drama is the greater for it being a man who loses the self to a passion. For this impotence redefined broadly, opium serves as the most telling model, because it is a physiological, psycho-pharmaceutical one. Love and music would be more metaphorical expressions of the same inherently psychological principle. Yet precisely the point of the comparison or blending of the three passions is that love and music are as powerful, physically, as the known mind-altering substance that opium is. In Vendramini's description of the passion that Capraja submits to, it is a question of the belief that sounds encounter within us a substance analogous to that which engenders the phenomena of light, a substance that produces ideas in man: "l'homme a des touches intérieures que les sons affectent, et qui correspondent à nos centres nerveux d'où s'élancent nos sensations et nos idées" [the human being has internal keys that are affected by sounds and that correspond to the nerve centers from which our sensations and our ideas are launched] (10: 584). Having lost the self, the man of passion is freed, poetically, to embrace the infinite; his narrow mind expands to contain the universe, and he can create:

> Imagine une création sublime où les merveilles de la création visible sont reproduites avec un grandiose, une légèreté, une rapidité, une étendue incommensurables, où les sensations sont infinies, et où peuvent pénétrer certaines organisations privilégiées qui possèdent une divine puissance, tu auras alors une idée des jouissances extatiques dont parlaient Cataneo et Capraja, poètes pour eux seuls. (10: 585)

> [Imagine a sublime creation where the marvels of visible creation are reproduced with incommensurable grandiosity, lightness, rapidity, and breadth, where the sensations are infinite, and where certain privileged organizations that possess a divine power can penetrate, and you will have an idea of the ecstatic raptures of which Cataneo and Capraja spoke, poets for themselves alone.]

Such men surpass "la sphère où s'enfantent les œuvres plastiques par les procédés de l'imitation, pour entrer dans le royaume tout spirituel des abstractions où tout se contemple dans son principe et s'aperçoit dans l'omnipotence des résultats" [the sphere where the plastic arts are given birth through procedures of imitation, in order to enter the entirely spiritual kingdom of abstractions, where everything can be observed in its principles and is seen in the omnipotence of the results] (10: 585). These words, spoken by the opium addict, describe music; Emilio understands music in terms of his love, which he then describes with poetic expressions; Vendramini then applies those terms to his feelings with opium. In short, opium gives us a physiological, analytical model for a philosophical formulation, music, which expresses itself in a moral action, love. The tripartite structure mirrors that of *La Comédie humaine* in its entirety. In this passage, the three passions unite in this entirely spiritual realm of abstractions where the creator sees the beginnings of everything and the omnipotence of his results, the incorporeal essence of a thought captured by poetry and brought forth in powerful illustration.

What could be more Balzacian? It is a Frenchman, and a doctor at that, in whom we can easily recognize a partial double of Balzac, who undertakes to cure the opium addict, the manic musician, and the impotent lover. Vendramini's opium passion connects to death, a voluptuous and not vulgar death; to political empire, saving Venice from its slavery; to music, captured by every pore; to love, enhanced beyond the limits of the flesh (10: 574–75); but primarily, it expresses itself in the desire for Venice's political freedom during his opium dreams: "Oui, pour trois livres d'opium il meuble notre arsenal vide" [Yes, for three pounds of opium, he furnishes our empty arsenals] (10: 575). Though the French doctor aspires to cure the opium user, it is the only one of the three passions that he will fail to cure, and that is because the political realities oppose poetic aspirations: "L'amour d'une patrie qui n'existe plus est une passion sans remède" [Love of a fatherland that no longer exists is a passion without remedy] (10: 619). Massimilla explains the genius of music to the Frenchman, "car il faut être à la fois poète et musicien pour comprendre la portée d'une pareille musique. Vous appartenez à une nation dont la langue et le génie sont trop positifs pour qu'elle puisse entrer de plain-pied dans la musique" [for one must be at once a poet and a musician to comprehend the full significance of such music. You belong to a nation whose language and genius are too positive for it to be able to enter music on an equal footing] (10: 587). Nevertheless, she reassures him that the French can succeed in loving this new music because France is "compréhensive." Having erected an artistic system, the novella, in which he captures the poetic principle of music, Balzac slyly places himself among those comprehending elite.

The fact that the duchess becomes pregnant signals that the doctor has cured Emilio of his passion. Martine Léonard opposes the "mode vulgaire" by which this pregnancy is signified on the last page, the four words set off in their own paragraph, "La duchesse était grosse" [The duchess was pregnant], to the "mode poétique" constituting the fifteen-line, single sentence final paragraph, in which "la phrase se gonfle à l'infini des figures de l'art" [the sentence swells infinitely with the figures of art], as Léonard aptly puts it (67). The opposition echoes that between "la brutale nature" and "la poésie" (10: 545). In spite of the necessary vulgarity of a "grossesse" (and that is not even the most euphonic word Balzac could have used), poetry tries to reassert its prerogatives in the long last sentence—and what is held decisively at bay by this long accumulation of poetic figures is the sex act of which the pregnancy is irrefutable evidence. As in many of Balzac's endings, the authorial narrator takes his leave with a flourish, a final bow that restores his presence on the stage as the one in charge and indicates the direction interpretation should take. In this poetic inflation—poetic partly because it simulates the puffing up of Massimilla Doni's figure while it also allows us to think how her pregnancy brings *Massimilla Doni,* the novella, to fulfillment—artistic feminine angelic figures from the civilized world hasten to her bedside and weep. They signal the duchess's capitulation to her lover, the highest moment of sublime parody, as Max Andréoli has shown ("Sublime et parodie" 28 and passim):

> Les péris, les ondines, les fées, les sylphides du vieux temps, les muses de la Grèce, les vierges de marbre de la Certosa da Pavia, le Jour et la Nuit de Michel-Ange, les petits anges que Bellini le premier mit au bas des tableaux d'église, et que Raphaël a si divinement peints au bas de la Vierge au donataire, et de la madone qui gèle à Dresde, les délicieuses filles d'Orcagna dans l'église de San-Michele à Florence, les chœurs célestes du tombeau de saint Sébald à Nuremberg, quelques vierges du Duomo de Milan, les peuplades de cent cathédrales gothiques, toute la nation des figures qui brisent leur forme pour venir à vous, artistes compréhensifs, toutes ces angéliques filles incorporelles accoururent autour du lit de Massimilla, et y pleurèrent! (10: 619)

> [The peris, the undines, the fairies, the sylphs of olden times, the muses of Greece, the marble virgins of the Certosa da Pavia, the Day and the Night by Michelangelo, the little angels that Bellini was the first to put on the bottom of his church paintings and that Raphael so divinely painted on the bottom of the Virgin of the Donee and of the Madonna freezing in Dresden, the delicious girls by Orcagna in the San-Michele church in Florence, the celestial choruses of the tomb of Saint Sebald in Nuremberg, a few virgins from the Duomo in Milan, the peoples of a hundred gothic cathedrals, the entire nation of figures who break their material forms to come to you, comprehensive and comprehending artists, all these incorporeal angelic women hurried to Massimilla's bedside, and wept!]

One little phrase in this swollen sentence, a phrase summarizing the host of angelic figures, alludes to how artists created them: "toute la nation des figures qui brisent leur forme pour venir à vous, artistes compréhensifs." Balzac thus places himself among these comprehending and comprehensive artists (it is the French who are "compréhensifs," as Massimilla had assured the doctor) capable of receiving the incorporeal, formless essences of these artistic incarnations and making of them the figures we can see in "cent cathédrales gothiques" and in the works of Bellini, Raphael, Orcagna, and many others.

That is not all. Charles Nodier had given a particular meaning to the adjective "compréhensif" in an article published in the *Revue de Paris* in 1832 which prompted Balzac's "Lettre à M. Ch. Nodier" in October of that year in the same review. Nodier's "De la palingénésie humaine et de la résurrection" imagines a future form of humanity that will surpass even the most evolved human being; he called this future being "l'être compréhensif." It is perfectly plausible that, in choosing to reuse the word "comprehensive" in this final paragraph, recalling its only other use in *Massimilla Doni* to describe the French, in particular the understanding French doctor, Balzac wished to allude to Nodier's notion of the superior being to come, as a way to reassert the unique nature of the artist among present humanity. I have suggested, in translating the quotation, that the adjective is already polyvalent, meaning both all-inclusive and understanding and even providing a connection between these two meanings. To this polyvalence, in his final paragraph, Balzac adds the hint of Nodier's utopian reverie, crowning the idea of the artist as the *only* person who can clothe ideas in words.

Balzac believes he possesses the mind-expanding passion he has triply illustrated. He can place himself among the one or two men of genius per century that Massimilla talks about, who have the power to "devancer les temps, et qui formulent ces mélodies pleines de faits accomplis, grosses de poèmes immenses" [be ahead of their time, and who formulate these melodies full of accomplished facts, pregnant with immense poems] (10: 609). How can we but think of these adjectives "pleines" and "grosses" in the context of the ending to which Balzac brought his novella? Thanks to the passion but also thanks to its cure, a narrative will be born out of the difficult conception, executed according to a sublime ideal that loses nothing for being vulgarly real: "Car il ne suffit pas que l'artiste, pour mériter ce nom, aperçoive l'idéal: il doit encore le confronter au réel en en donnant une image dans l'ordre du sensible, faute de quoi l'œuvre disparaît" [For it is not enough that the artist, to merit that name, perceives the ideal: he must also confront it with reality by providing an image within the order of the senses, without which the work will disappear] (Andréoli, "Sublime et parodie" 16).

18

The Language of Sex

> Oh! monsieur, cela se dit et ne se raconte pas . . .
> [Oh! sir, people speak of it but never recount it . . .]
> —*Splendeurs et misères des courtisanes*

Love as Prime Mover in the Balzacian world would not be Balzacian if it did not include physical love. The word *amour* is ambiguous; *le plaisir* also. But among the different meanings of these *words,* there is one *action* that can be defined fairly unambiguously: sexual intercourse. The set of actions that we call sexual love, whatever its many and diverse forms, can be designated by technical terms (those, for example, that the vicomte de Valmont boasts of having taught Cécile Volanges in *Les liaisons dangereuses*). Yet, in spite of the clarity and distinctness of sex, or perhaps because of these qualities, writers who are not primarily writers of sex speak of sex without recounting it. In a fine article, "Tabou or not Tabou," on Maupassant's "self-censure," Floriane Place-Verghnes cites the many ways that the language of sex engages the reader. As she notes, "Le corpus regorge de *personnages* qui font mais ne disent pas" [The corpus is packed full of *characters* who do but don't say] (372). She inventories the "diverses figures de style allant de la périphrase à la métaphore, de l'euphémisme au jeu de mots, avec une typographie qui se fait à l'occasion l'alliée de la dérision" [various figures of speech ranging from periphrasis to metaphor, from euphemism to play on words, with a typography that occasionally becomes the ally of derision] by which Maupassant accomplishes this self-censure (375). As she notes, "l'euphémisme, la métaphore, le blanc typographique permettent d'écrire le tabou tout en ne l'écrivant pas. Au récepteur de comprendre le non-dit" [the euphemism, the metaphor, and the unprinted blank allow the taboo to be written while not writing it. It's up to the receiver to understand what's unsaid] (382). In similar fashion, Balzac goes to considerable lengths to create particular expressions that one would nevertheless hesitate to call "clean" or "proper." Avoiding the most technical language for the most technical definition of *l'amour*, Balzac invents a language of sex.

"Comment dire le sexe?" asked Éric Bordas ("Ne touchez pas le H" 23). "Quelle pratique énonciative pour quelle pratique désirante?" [How can one speak about sex? What enunciative practice for what desiring practice?]. The analysis that follows does not record the various "desiring practices" in Balzac but shows rather how the complete sexual event translates into words; it is the writing of sex, so to speak: the way to write what people do not narrate. Bordas's purpose instead is to show how metaphors and euphemisms work in the semiotic system and in the narrative programs configuring meaning, as in his article, "Ne touchez pas le H de Natalie." Others are concerned to develop the range of desires and sexual activities in *La Comédie humaine*. But my purpose is simpler. I am not seeking to enumerate the diversity of forms of pleasure or physical love among Balzacian characters, nor to inventory the social types within sexual relations—these are forms of content—but rather to examine the forms of expression that take the place of the act.

Many critical studies have addressed the question of Balzacian eroticism, elucidating Balzac's vision of the diversity of sexual relations and following the traces of the more or less hidden forms of physical love, in their practice and in their social insertion. These studies, constituting a veritable industry around Balzacian eroticism, are indispensable for both our sociological and narratological knowledge of the world of *La Comédie humaine*. Nicole Mozet's analysis of *La fille aux yeux d'or*, a story in which sex is a prime mover, has the merit of precision in its examination of details, illuminating the eroticism of the novella especially by reestablishing the lines of feminine power that were previously unappreciated. To this type of approach I am adding a more strictly linguistic view, focusing on the language that takes the place of the act. As Mozet incidentally observes in her analysis of *La fille aux yeux d'or*, "il était évidemment impossible à Balzac de parler de l'homosexualité autrement que par sous-entendu" [it was naturally impossible for Balzac to speak of homosexuality other than by innuendo] (*Balzac au pluriel* 128). It is precisely this impossibility that provokes the reader's interest, and this innuendo that calls for analysis. Mozet elsewhere comments that the novel has constantly "adopté un discours détourné sur la chair, le plaisir, et la luxure" [adopted a roundabout discourse on matters of the flesh, pleasure, and erotic love] ("Par le biais" 203). My purpose is to examine the precise nature of this diverted discourse.

Moïse Le Yaouanc's indispensable study on "Le plaisir" will serve as a background for this examination. Le Yaouanc writes:

> l'entrée des personnages dans les draps marque la fin des hardiesses de langage chez l'auteur. Soucieux de respecter les bienséances quand il s'agit d'un genre sérieux qui s'adresse à la communauté des lecteurs, l'auteur de *La Comédie humaine* devient alors discret, tout au moins dans ses mots, et aussi prudent que s'il parlait dans un salon d'autrefois . . . : sans choquer, il adresse des signes aux gens avertis. ("Le plaisir" [1973] 211)

> [the moment when the characters slip between the sheets marks the end of the author's boldness of language. Anxious to respect decency in a serious genre addressed to the community of all readers, the author of *La Comédie humaine* becomes discreet at that moment, at least in his words, and as prudent as if he were speaking in an old-time drawing room . . . : he avoids shocking anyone while sending signals in the direction of well informed people.]

The "salon d'autrefois" represents a place of well-chosen metaphorical expressions, spoken most likely in the rhetorical forms of preterition as practiced by *ancien régime* nobility, where good form allowed one to "parler de choses basses avec élégance et de distractions grossières avec distinction" [speak of base things with elegance and of coarse distractions with distinction], according to Robert Ellrich (218). By sending "des signes aux gens avertis," Balzac sets up a language of sex that is both coded and clear.

But, says Le Yaouanc, "Il serait illusoire de prétendre découvrir toujours des sous-entendus. Balzac se place assez souvent sur le plan de l'affirmation générale sans avoir en vue aucune pratique particulière. . . . Mais souvent aussi il donne à entendre, et la meilleure lecture est celle qui se montre la plus attentive à ses signes, même les plus discrets" [It would be illusory to claim to always discover hidden meanings. Balzac places himself rather frequently on the level of general affirmations without having any particular procedure in mind. . . . But also he often gives things to be understood, and the best reading is one that pays the most attention to these signals, including the most discreet ones] ("Le plaisir" [1973] 211). Balzacian eroticism works by innuendos, to be sure. Yet the discreet signals on which Le Yaouanc insists are sometimes the clearest ones. *Clarity* refers to a very specific quality of this language, which employs neither the proper or technical term nor an insignificant, vague, or general one, but something specific and agreed upon whose meaning the alert reader immediately understands and which serves to hide the referent.

If Adrian, Genestas's son in *Le médecin de campagne,* suffers from the "disease" of onanism, according to Le Yaouanc's diagnosis in *Nosographie de l'humanité balzacienne* (208–10), it is only through coded words that the reader penetrates the mystery of his behavior, which is explained by his "mauvaises habitudes de collège" [bad habits of high school boys] (9: 585). The expression is a coded sign immediately understood, but coded all the same. Comprehension and knowledge come from the relationship of the words with each other, rather than the relation of the words with the actions (which are characterized rather by understatement ["Le plaisir" [1972] 284]). Similarly, it is one thing to say that a man is "aimé, très aimé" [loved, much loved] by Valérie Marneffe, but it is another thing to say "souvent aimé" [often loved] (*La cousine Bette* 7: 395). Like the word *amour, amant* or lover can be plurisemantic, ambiguous as to sexual relations, but the context can give it the clear meaning of sexual partner. For Mme de Beauséant in *La femme abandonnée,* where all society knows that Ajuda-Pinto is her lover, this word will always have a sexual meaning, to the extent that when Gaston de Nueil visits her, as an enamored lover, it is enough to make people believe that there are sexual relations going on. In *La Rabouilleuse,* Balzac does not tell us in technical terms how Flore Brazier "cessa d'être une honnête fille" [ceased being an honest girl] (4: 400); it is by metonymy that he designates the sexual act thus given to be understood, by giving the date on which the servant Fanchette leaves the household, offended in the name of morality. Finally, one of the correspondents in *Mémoires de deux jeunes mariées* employs the laconic "quand on a été heureuse" [when a woman has known joy] (1: 274) to discreetly mean: after we have slept with a man. All these expressions yield their significance instantaneously.

This clear if not proper language is widespread and not unusual. Yet Balzac also knows how to vary his tone to multiply and "thicken" meanings. The language of sex involves witty inventions such as "la femme comme il faut" vs. "la femme comme il en faut" [the well behaved woman of the world vs. the type of woman men need] (*Autre étude de femme* 3: 694; *La vieille fille* 4: 936); conventional language such as a woman's very neutral "fautes" [erring ways]; the delicate "vœux de la nature trompée" [yearnings of cheated nature] (*La vieille fille* 4: 860) and the brutal "viol" [rape] feared by the duchesse de Langeais; the mostly "horrible" "scènes conjugales" [conjugal disputes] (*L'enfant maudit* 10: 877; *La femme de trente ans*); and the romantic "poèmes de leur double vie secrète" [poems of their secret life together] also of *La femme de trente ans* (2: 1115). In this last novel, a poetic language translates the woman's orgasm in terms of "notre nature, dont la mélodieuse harmonie ne s'émeut jamais que sous la pression des sentiments" [our nature, whose melodious harmony is roused only by the urgings of our emotions] (2: 1118–19). The language of sex is often composed of figures of speech that eliminate or remove proper terms, obtaining clarity on the topic as a result: ordinary ellipses, even extremely ordinary (in *Béatrix*, after having dined with the seductive Béatrix, the unfaithful Calyste "rentra vers deux heures du matin" [went home around two in the morning] [2: 871] without anything mentioned that could have filled up his time since dinner); ellipses as suspension points: Foedora the hard-hearted woman spied upon in her boudoir by Raphaël de Valentin says: "Quel est l'homme auquel je pourrais me . . ." [Where is the man to whom I could bring myself . . .] (*La peau de chagrin* 10: 183), or else this comment by the very innocent mother of *L'enfant maudit*: "La sainte Vierge n'a-t-elle pas conçu sans . . ." [Didn't the holy Virgin conceive without . . .] (10: 877); narrative compression that allows one to skip over the "coquetteries charmantes" [charming coyness] (*La femme abandonnée* 2: 491] or those "petits protocoles du boudoir" [little protocols of the boudoir] (2: 492); and finally total silence, as in *La muse du département*, where Dinah de La Baudraye becomes pregnant without the slightest word about sexual intercourse.

Not all proper terms are absent, however. Thus, Mme de Beauséant in *La femme abandonnée* exclaims: "il m'a possédée ne m'aimant plus" [he took me even when he no longer loved me] (2: 499). "Posséder," whose meaning is unambiguous in context, is as direct and targeted as the angry viscountess's thoughts—she is about to send Gaston de Nueil to his death. More interesting is the mundane euphemism, as when Mme de Beauséant laments: "parce que j'ai été faible, le monde veut donc que je le sois toujours?" [because I was weak once, does the world expect me therefore to always be that way?] (*La femme abandonnée* 2: 479). The worldly metaphor can be elegant; the pious metaphor is perhaps less so, like the example in *La Maison du Chat-qui-pelote* (1: 73): "l'amour saint et permis du mariage" [the saintly and permitted love of marriage], in which the adjective "permitted" also permits the expression. But the pretense of decency of the Balzacian text produces twists in the language that are often more enticing than they are modest. Thus M. Marneffe has become hideous, destroyed "par ces débauches particulières aux grandes capitales, décrites par les poètes romains, et pour lesquelles notre pudeur moderne n'a point de nom" [by debaucheries of the kind that happen in the great capital cities, as described by the Roman poets, and for which our modern-day modesty has no name] (*La cousine Bette* 7: 194). This feigned inability to give a name to the debaucheries creates an enigma and obliges one to search among poets: does Balzac mean to suggest something like the sadistic practices of a scene from *Venise sauvée,* mentioned in *La Rabouilleuse?* In that novel, Flore Brazier makes her master play "ces scènes ensevelies dans les mystères de la vie privée" [scenes buried in the mysteries of private life], that "réalise[nt] le magnifique de l'horrible!" [make what is magnificently horrifying real!] (4: 403). To understand that this language of sex refers to sadism, one has to be familiar with the work by Otway; the language is indirect and comes to us through an embedded intertextual allusion.

To speak of the prince de Cadignan's impotence, the language of sex alludes to the king Charles X, "puni . . . pour avoir . . . trop plu dans sa jeunesse" [punished . . . for having . . . been too admired in his youth] (*Les secrets de la princesse de Cadignan* 6: 982). The completion of the sexual act in spite of this impotence is expressed by periphrasis: "le bonheur inespéré de se donner un héritier" [the unexpected good fortune of giving oneself an heir] (6: 983). Rouget in *La Rabouilleuse* has become "caduque" [decrepit] (4: 519); after his marriage with the young Flore, the danger of sexuality in old age is expressed by an allusion to the death of Louis XII.

It is clear that the most attractive expressions are distorted, indirect, or detoured. Neither the proper term nor the general term, the language of sex is something else that is more suggestive, a third term that reveals while it plays at hiding. The examples that follow are grouped according to several categories.

Outside of Marriage

A negotiation about sex occupies the entire second chapter of *La duchesse de Langeais.* Beyond the banalities about the "senses," "possession," "voluptuousness," and the "pleasures" that perpetuate love, Balzac skillfully varies the language. This language is moreover deeply appropriate, in that the ambiguity that characterizes the boundaries of the act is reproduced in the ambiguity of the words. Thus, the line between permitted caresses and shameful acts is described as the "*nec plus ultra* de passion; et quand [Montriveau] en arrivait là, elle se fâchait toujours [s'il] faisait mine d'en franchir les barrières" [*ne plus ultra* of passion; and when [Montriveau] got to that point, she always became angry if he made as if to cross those barriers] (5: 966). When he naively lets out the expression "conserver les apparences" [keeping up appearances], Mme de Langeais cries out with the shocked morality she knows how to feign: "Vous ai-je donné le moindre droit de penser que je puisse être à vous?" [Have I in the least given you the right to think that I could be yours?] (5: 962). Later the marquis makes "la demande farouche de ses droits illégalement légitimes" [the brutal request of his illegally legitimate rights] (5: 974)—rights that are made legitimate in his mind by the compromising actions already performed by the duchess, but illegal because they are outside of marriage. But upon the duchess's refusal, he indulges in amusing phraseology: "Madame la duchesse, je suis au désespoir que Dieu n'ait pas inventé pour la femme une autre façon de confirmer le don de son cœur que d'y ajouter celui de sa personne" [my dear madame duchess, I am in despair that God has not invented another way for women to confirm the gift of their heart than by adding to it the gift of their person] (5: 977)—which by contention the duchess calls "désirs prodigieusement vulgaires" [prodigiously vulgar desires]. For a rather long time, she limits Montriveau to the preliminaries, the "péchés véniels" [venial sins] (5: 981), a feminine jurisprudence that Balzac veils with the following sentence: "pour l'honneur du faubourg Saint-Germain, il est nécessaire de ne pas révéler les mystères de ses boudoirs, où l'on voulait tout de l'amour, moins ce qui pouvait attester l'amour" [for the honor of the faubourg Saint-Germain, we cannot reveal the mysteries of its boudoirs, where everything was expected of love except what could bear witness to love] (5: 978)—let us say, for example, a pregnancy, possible result of the "péché positif" [positive sin], of the "grand péché mortel" [great mortal sin] (5: 981). Montriveau's attempt to "donne[r] le *mat* en trois coups, à volonté" [checkmate in three moves, at will] (5: 983), will fail, and, as everyone knows, in spite of so many words spent on the subject, there is no sex in this novel. Is it because Antoinette had touched Montriveau's castrating axe (see the analysis by Bordas, "Ne touchez pas le H" 30–31)?

In *La muse du département* Dinah de La Baudraye, who is considering a very sexual transgression, commits one against originality when she speaks of the "dénouement" of "ce beau roman" [this fine novel] (4: 671) to indicate the act of love. Normally Balzac does not fall into such platitudes except to make fun of them. In this novel there is an unrealized *fiacre* scene (love in a carriage) (4: 726). But only Mme de La Baudraye's organdy dress is mussed, for Étienne Lousteau returns from Sancerre and from the provincial muse "sans y plus toucher" [without having touched her any more] (4: 735) than one touches a fancy dessert before someone cuts it. By a curious displacement effect, nevertheless, this nonhappening is made to take the place of the act that puts an end to Dinah's virtue, for we will find her pregnant nine pages later without the slightest elucidation on the event. Here is a case where no words let the act that produces a pregnancy find a place in our reading. At the most, we have the word *fiacre,* about which *La physiologie du mariage* merely comments that taxicabs are a place where a husband can be made into a cuckold (11: 989).

From the trivial to the sublime: in *Le père Goriot,* the language of sex becomes lyrical and noble when Eugène de Rastignac and Delphine de Nucingen sleep together after a long, chaste love affair:

> Rastignac et Delphine s'étaient rencontrés dans les conditions voulues pour éprouver l'un par l'autre les plus vives jouissances. Leur passion bien préparée avait grandi par ce qui tue les passions, par la jouissance. En possédant cette femme, Eugène s'aperçut que jusqu'alors il ne l'avait que désirée, il ne l'aima qu'au lendemain du bonheur: l'amour n'est peut-être que la reconnaissance du plaisir. (3: 262–63)

> [Rastignac and Delphine had met under the conditions needed for them to feel the liveliest enjoyment of one another. Their well-prepared passion had grown by what kills most passions—by its satisfaction. In possessing this woman, Eugène realized that until then he had only desired her; he loved her only after the fulfillment of his happiness. Perhaps love is nothing but the recognition of pleasure.]

Véronique Bui, in commenting on Mme de Mortsauf's death in *Le lys dans la vallée,* mentions this passage to support her interpretation of the sexual nature of Henriette's behavior during her agony, and adds: "La synonymie entre bonheur et jouissance est ici explicite" [There is an explicit synonymy between "happiness" and "orgasm" here] (79). She also cites Pierre Barbéris, who affirms with no uncertainty that this meaning is "normal depuis le classicisme. Bonheur égale satisfaction sexuelle" [normal from classicism on. Happiness equals sexual satisfaction] (Bui 80).[1] Raphaël and Pauline achieve a similar bliss in *La peau de chagrin* through their sexuality: "Leur mariage, retardé . . . et le bonheur leur ayant révélé toute la puissance de leur affection . . . de part et d'autre même délicatesse, même pudeur, même volupté . . ." [their marriage having been delayed . . . and their sexual happiness having revealed to them all the power of their affection . . . on both sides the same delicacy, the same modesty, the same voluptuousness . . .] (10: 234). Delicacy and modesty are terms that, in Balzac, augment voluptuous pleasure without repressing it.

   1. As part of his argument, Barbéris cites the language that tells us that Lucien de Rubempré sleeps with Coralie every day: "heureux tous les jours avec Coralie" [made happy every day with Coralie] (notes to *La femme de trente ans* 357).

Le curé de village is interesting because it involves an illicit love affair that is not recounted, contrary to the explanatory manner that widely characterizes *La Comédie humaine*. The mystery and secret are kept until the end. Véronique Graslin's "nature" balks in the face of marriage, "ce dur métier" [this difficult job] (9: 667), and she is happy when her husband sleeps elsewhere in the house (9: 681). But when she becomes pregnant, ambiguity resurfaces, because her husband has only just returned to the conjugal bedroom (9: 681). No more is told us; the sexual act is simply absent.

It is literally veiled in *Les Marana*. Here, once again, a bastard child will be created, after a two-week seduction. Montefiore knows how to "contenir ses désirs pour en mieux assurer le contentement" [contain his desires the better to assure their contentment] (10: 1058); for, "sûr du succès, l'Italien se donna les plaisirs ineffables d'une séduction allant à petits pas" [sure of his success, the Italian allowed himself the pleasure of a slow-paced seduction] (10: 1059). During these approaches, Juana remains, if not chaste, at least virgin.[2] Montefiore chooses the eve of his departure to consume his prey entirely, like a tiger, but this sexual act takes place behind the following words: "La porte en tapisserie retomba sur eux, sur leurs folies, sur leur bonheur, comme un voile, qu'il est inutile de soulever" [The tapestry door fell shut on them, on their folly, on their happiness, like a veil we do not need to lift] (10: 1060). And that is all.

Specialties and Specialists

The "specialties" are first and foremost those of the specialists, particularly in *La cousine Bette*: "Valérie possédait des spécialités de tendresse qui la rendaient indispensable à Crevel aussi bien qu'au baron" [Valérie possessed specialties of tenderness that made her indispensable to Crevel as well as to the baron] (7: 192). Balzac does not further elucidate these practices that perpetuate desire; the language of sex remains perfectly euphemistic. Sleeping with Valérie is expressed by this metaphor of the sexual act: "Crevel . . . avait payé le droit de prendre, aussi souvent qu'il le pourrait, sa revanche de l'enlèvement de Josépha" [Crevel . . . had paid for the right to take his revenge as often as he could for the abduction of Josépha] (7: 191). As for Baron Hulot, never in the last twenty-five years, he protests to Valérie, has his wife "gêné [s]es plaisirs" [gotten in the way of his pleasures] (7: 303)—and this is once

---

2. This opposition between chasteness and virginity is often found in Balzac's works, especially in *La fille aux yeux d'or* (5: 1092); *La physiologie du mariage* (11: 1156): "tout à la fois vierge et savante!" [virgin and knowing at the same time!]); and *Modeste Mignon*.

again an expression of the language of sex, signifying that the Hulot couple have not been sleeping together for twenty-five years.

In *La vieille fille*, the smart milliner Suzanne needs to have a language that expresses the sexual act so she can pretend to be pregnant, as she does. But while she speaks only of a "bonheur" [good fortune] for which du Bousquier should be glad to pay dearly (4: 833), he wonders if he ever has "chiffonné autre chose que sa collerette! . . ." [wrinkled anything more than her ruff! . . .] (4: 836). The difference between these two expressions highlights what could be called female innocence and male competence (quite ironically, as it will turn out): Suzanne borrows a conventional term of the least precise sort, while du Bousquier's rhetoric describes an act of foreplay, however limited.

Les secrets de la princesse de Cadignan supplies an entire vocabulary of the language of sex. The banal "adventures," the flat "liaisons," the worn-out "frivolities," and the perfectly insignificant "inconsequences" (6: 966) compose the fabric on which the Parisian princess will embroider the secrets that make her worthy of her own novella. No well-informed reader has any trouble translating these terms, in the same way that society interprets the beautiful Diane's actions, but it is difficult to imagine how she could have conceived a child, when we hear her say to d'Arthez, on the subject of her son: "Eh bien, sa naissance est un hasard ou le fait d'une convention de ma mère et de mon mari. Je suis restée longtemps jeune fille après mon mariage" [Well, his birth is a stroke of luck or the result of an agreement between my mother and my husband. I remained a virgin long after my wedding] (6: 991). The object of her secrets being her innocence, she must make others believe in her virginity—but there is no possible "agreement" that makes one pregnant, nor a stroke of luck that lets a mother remain a maid. It is true that five pages later she admits to "une mauvaise nuit de mariage" [one wretched wedding night] (6: 995). When the princess wants d'Arthez to understand that he may sleep with her—that in fact he will definitely sleep with her—she simply tells him: "vous ferez croire au monde que nous sommes purement et simplement frère et sœur" [you will make everyone believe that we are purely and simply brother and sister] (6: 1000), in which the idea of sex is transmitted by language that would proclaim the opposite of sex. In fact, d'Arthez has had a liaison with a lower-class woman, but he has not yet known love with a noble woman, and this contrast between the sexual act and the sentiment of love is expressed thus: "peut-être aimait-il mieux faire la part à la Nature et garder ses illusions en cultivant son Idéal?" [perhaps he preferred to satisfy the needs of Nature and preserve his illusions by cultivating his Idéal?] (6: 964).

In *Splendeurs et misères des courtisanes,* Esther has hidden her past as a courtesan from Lucien de Rubempré, but has she or hasn't she slept with him? Here is how we learn that she has: when Esther wants to kill herself because "le voile d'innocence qu'[elle avait] est tombé" [the veil of innocence that she had has fallen aside], Carlos Herrera speaks with her thus: "Votre voile d'innocence? . . . dit le prêtre, vous avez donc traité Lucien avec la dernière rigueur?—Oh! mon père, comment vous, qui le connaissez, me faites-vous une semblable question! . . . On ne résiste pas à un Dieu" [Your veil of innocence? . . . said the priest, have you then refused Lucien your most intimate favors?—Oh father, you who know him, how can you ask me such a question? . . . One does not resist a God] (6: 453). Notable is the language that makes a religion out of this love, while the relationship between Esther and Nucingen, later on, is expressed through an entirely financial language, when Esther says for example: "Vous avez payé, je me dois. . . . Je veux payer dans une seule nuit toutes les sommes qui sont hypothéquées sur ce fatal moment et j'ai la certitude qu'une heure de moi vaut des millions" [You have paid, I owe myself to you. . . . I want to pay up in a single night all the sums that are mortgaged on this fatal moment, and I am certain that an hour with me is worth millions] (6: 603). Her specialty is rich with interest.

What Love Brings to Girls

In *Béatrix,* Sabine du Génic describes her honeymoon in her letters to her mother (see chapter 13). A girl becomes a woman (a word full of meaning in Balzac's works) as a result of the act of love in marriage, or outside of it. In spite of the desire to reconcile passion with marriage, the women suffer in the gulf that separates them—as does *Honorine,* for whom the sexual act with a husband is diametrically opposed to the love of a lover. To speak of the pleasure Honorine knew with her unworthy lover, the language of sex resorts to oxymorons: "cruelles délices" [cruel delights], "délire mortel" [mortal delirium] (2: 581), and "des voluptés gravées en traits de feu" [sensual pleasures etched with strokes of fire] (2: 581). For the sexual love that she finally agrees to grant her husband Octave, the language of sex says only: "quand vous le voudrez, je serai votre femme" [when you wish it, I will be your wife] (2: 592). To be a wife says everything without recounting much.

Mémoires de deux jeunes mariées proposes a particularly developed case of the language of sex in the context of a young woman's love and marriage. The serious Renée will have the fruits of the sexual act (children) without knowing its flowers, while the passionate Louise will have the flowers without the fruit (1: 316). Renée in her marriage of reason negotiates her sexual initiation and speaks of "consentement entier" [complete consent] (1: 252), in contrast to passive obedience "comme ma très honorée mère vient de me le recommander" [as my most honored mother has just recommended] and to duty (1: 253). Keeping her "libre arbitre" [free will], Renée does not have sex as long as she does not want to (1: 255). When the initiation takes place, she calls it a "fête" and, to keep it secret, even from her intimate friend, this is how she writes of it to Louise:

> Sache cependant que rien n'a manqué de ce que veut l'amour le plus délicat, ni de cet imprévu qui est, en quelque sorte, l'honneur de ce moment-là: les grâces mystérieuses que nos imaginations lui demandent, l'entraînement qui excuse, le consentement arraché, les voluptés idéales longtemps entrevues et qui nous subjuguent l'âme avant que nous nous laissions aller à la réalité, toutes les séductions y étaient avec leurs formes enchanteresses. (1: 255)

> [Know, however, that nothing was lacking of what the most delicate love seeks, nor of that unexpectedness that is in some ways the honor of that moment: the mysterious graces that our imagination demands of it, the allurement that excuses it, the consent that is won, the ideal sensual pleasures long foreseen that subjugate our souls before we let ourselves suffer the reality, all the seductions were there in their enchanting forms.]

These words, although not particularly metaphorical, weave a veil through which one must discern Renée's sexual happiness, in particular by means of the connotations of the word "réalité"—the positive, concrete reality of the sex act. Nevertheless, she feels unhappy because she is experiencing a conflict between conjugal duty and passion (1: 278). Renée thus has the role of symbolizing the failure of marriages that require the wife to give herself to her husband as a duty, and that, because of this, exclude sexual passion.

With more elaborate flowers of rhetoric, Louise de Macumer later describes the "terrible passage" (1: 303) from maidenhood to womanhood and from love to happiness:

> Comment! on a nommé un devoir les gracieuses folies du cœur et l'irrésistible entraînement du désir. Et pourquoi? Quelle horrible puissance a donc imaginé de nous obliger à fouler les délicatesses du goût, les mille pudeurs de la femme, en convertissant ces voluptés en devoirs? Comment peut-on devoir ces fleurs de l'âme, ces roses de la vie, ces poèmes de la sensibilité exaltée, à un être qu'on n'aimerait pas? Des droits dans de telles sensations! (1: 306)

[What! People have called the graceful follies of the heart and the irresistible surrender to desire a duty! But why? What horrible force has thought to oblige us to trample upon delicate tastes, the thousand modesties of women, by converting these sensual pleasures into duties? How can one owe these flowers of the soul, these roses of life, these poems of exalted sensibility, to a being whom we may not like? Rights, among such sensations!]

Here, reunited once again, are scruples and modesty with sensual pleasure. On the bed called an altar there takes place "le terrible fait qui change la fille en femme et l'amant en mari" [the terrible act that changes the girl into a woman and the lover into a husband] (1: 299). Through this language, we can see that a husband is not a lover, as the following remark also states: "Faire de son mari son amant est une œuvre aussi délicate que celle de faire de son amant son mari" [To make a lover out of one's husband is as delicate a task as is making a husband out of one's lover] (1: 302).

Julie d'Aiglemont, in *La femme de trente ans,* suffers in her new sexuality as a married woman because her "lansquenet" [warrior] (2: 1066) of a husband "[la] cherche trop souvent" [seeks her out too often] (2: 1065); the euphemism "chercher" returns several times to designate "ce qui [la] tue" [what is killing her] (2: 1066), the act that renders her Victor happy. "Toujours jeune fille en dépit du mariage" [still a virgin in spite of marriage], says the narrator (2: 1075)—we have to interpret this to mean that she does not know the blossoming that love brings to a woman—she will nonetheless have a daughter, which will allow her a cessation in her sexual relations, and that is called a "bonheur négatif" [negative happiness] (2: 1075). What is going badly in this conjugal love is expressed by the verb "succomber encore une fois" [to succumb once again] (2: 1084) and by the terrible logic of the sentence: "elle se donnait, contre son cœur et contre le vœu de la nature, à un mari qu'elle n'aimait plus" [she gave herself, against her heart and against the wishes of nature, to a husband she no longer loved] (2: 1085). The refusal of sex will be translated by the qualifier "widow" (2: 1091), and when the narrator says that "elle ne pouvait plus être une créature complète" [she could no longer be a complete being] (2: 1108), this means that she no longer has a sex life.

Driftings

Paquita Valdès, in *La fille aux yeux d'or,* is introduced as an enigma, a mystery, and a charade because she knows physical love even though she has never slept with a man: "si la *Fille aux yeux d'or* était vierge, elle n'était certes pas innocente" [if the *Girl with the Golden Eyes* was a virgin, she was certainly not innocent] (5: 1091). She knows the refinements of sensual pleasure, "tout ce que pouvait connaître Henri de cette poésie des sens que l'on nomme amour" [all that Henri could know about that poetry of the senses that one calls love] (5: 1091). In this paragraph, which recounts the first act of love between Henri de Marsay and Paquita, there is no direct expression of sex. The language of sex is borrowed here from the domain of oriental poetry, of which, however, no rhyme could translate "l'extase pleine de confusion et la stupeur dont cette délicieuse fille fut saisie quand cessa l'erreur dans laquelle une main de fer la faisait vivre" [the ecstasy full of confusion and the stupor that seized this delicious girl when the error in which an iron hand was forcing her to live came to an end] (5: 1092). The expression is distorted and twisted, especially because the reader does not yet know that a woman was responsible for Paquita's loss of innocence, and that the error is homosexuality (of which, according to Mozet, it is impossible to speak [*Balzac au pluriel* 128]). But the ecstasy, the confusion, the stupor are words that indicate her first sexual pleasure with a man.

When the marquise de San-Réal finds Paquita again, she examines her and discovers that she is no longer a virgin; Paquita herself says: "il est bien facile de voir que je ne suis plus la même" [it is very easy to see that I am no longer the same] (5: 1099). This quasi-medical examination is expressed by the following language: "Tous les flambeaux allumés, un parfum délicat qui se faisait sentir, certain désordre où l'œil d'un homme à bonnes fortunes devait reconnaître des folies communes à toutes les passions, annonçaient que la marquise avait savamment questionnée la coupable" [All the lit torches, a delicate scent that one could smell, a certain disorder in which a man of experience would readily recognize the follies that all passions have in common, told that the marquise had skillfully questioned the guilty girl] (5: 1106). In this "parfum" that no doubt exudes from a human body, and especially in these "folies" that two impassioned beings can commit together, men or women, and even in the irony of the adverb "savamment," we should be able to read, if we exercise mental gymnastics, a sexual act.[3] Mozet attracts our attention to the fact that "Margarita n'intervient donc qu'au dénouement, pour l'acte décisif" [Margarita thus does not intervene until the dénouement, to accomplish the decisive act] (*Balzac au pluriel* 128).[4]

---

3. I am not at all convinced by the examination of this passage by Drevon and Guichardet, nor by their conclusion: "ce n'est pas Gomorrhe" [it is not Gomorrah] (273).

4. Mozet in her astute analysis concludes that Balzac "a choisi de parler *à la fois et en même temps* des lesbiennes et des ouvriers" [chose to speak *at the same time and simultane-*

Everything that has needed to be said about *Une passion dans le désert* is said by Janet Beizer in her book *Family Plots*—while Balzac says almost nothing about sex between the soldier and the panther. In this case of a bestial sexual partnership, where the subject matter is the least proper, the language is the most chastised, the most inhibited. Such is not the case for at least one reader of the story, Philippe Berthier, who has certainly dotted the i's and crossed the t's: "C'est en faisant l'amour avec sa geôlière, *en plein orgasme,* qu'un faux mouvement, un geste mal interprété amène la tragédie. Elle se croit menacée, il la poignarde" [It is while making love with his jailor, *at the moment of orgasm,* that a false movement, a misinterpreted gesture brings about the tragedy. She thinks she is threatened, he stabs her] ("Le désir" 83; emphasis added). For an opposite tendency, there is the intelligent reading by Anne-Marie Baron arguing that the real occulted passion is the mystical, disincarnated one of Christ:

> Cette nouvelle fascinante cache bien son jeu. Car ce n'est pas une perversion sexuelle que Balzac a voulu dissimuler, c'est un sens mystique qu'il a cherché à occulter par une apparente perversion, jetée comme leurre au lecteur. Texte plus édifiant que provocant, moins érotique qu'arétologique, *Une passion dans le désert,* comme toutes les vies d'ermites, répète symboliquement la vie du Christ, jusque dans sa crucifixion. (*Les hiéroglyphes* 147)

> [This fascinating story plays its cards close to the chest. For it is not a sexual perversion that Balzac wanted to hide, it is a mystical meaning that he sought to occult by an apparent perversion, flung to the reader like a decoy. More an edifying than a provocative text, less erotic than aretological, *Une passion dans le désert,* like all the hermits' lives, symbolically repeats the life of Christ, right up to his crucifixion.]

As Beizer recognizes, the story about sex is the one of our second reading—the one that is not naive and that sees the erotic relation between man and panther (52); and it is a reading that Balzac has arranged for us to uncover, "a rather simplistic secret core of this text" (57) while pretending not to.

In the famous passage of sexual pleasure in *Sarrasine,* this "histoire du contresens sexuel du sculpteur Sarrasine" [story of sexual misinterpretation by the sculptor Sarrasine] (Bordas, Introduction to *Sarrasine* 12), I will only

---

ously of lesbians and workers], since it was impossible for him to develop a complete discussion on each of them (*Balzac au pluriel* 142).

note that the ecstasy of the sculptor that takes place while Zambinella is singing is not solely "toute nerveuse" [completely nervous], as Le Yaouanc would have it ("Le plaisir" [1973] 230). One would have to be as naive as Suzanne Simonin, Diderot's nun, not to accept seeing sexual pleasure written here, or more clinically speaking, an orgasm, to be exact. In my opinion, this is how it is written. Balzac is no less crafty at inventing a language for homosexual sex than he is for sex between a man and a woman.

Why a Language of Sex?

Balzac "s'intéresse extrêmement à la vie charnelle de ses personnages" [is extremely interested in the carnal life of his characters], says Le Yaouanc ("Le plaisir" [1973] 211–12)—and also in the language he uses to speak it, I would add. This is why we should try to "percevoir, à travers ce que Balzac a dit, ce qu'il a tu" [perceive, through what Balzac has said, what he has not said] (Drevon and Guichardet 257). Mental gymnastics, a suspicious reader's attitude, bold intellection, sincerity or insincerity—this is what we need as we read the language of sex in Balzac's works. Often a child must be conceived before we are able to say with certainty that the couple has had sexual relations. And yet this language is not "flat": neither proper nor dull, as I have said, but evocative, provocative, ultimately clear. For it is understood that one cannot recount sex, in proper terms. Not only is this simply not done (a question of social norms), but also, is it not true that indirect language speaks more than direct language? The mental effort that translates this language not into acts but into another language is rewarded by the price that is attached to it: the greater pleasure of the text. The language of Balzacian sex takes place in the domain of the *obvious hidden meanings* (I am reformulating one of Michel Butor's notions about the second pavilion scene in *La princesse de Clèves* [*Répertoire* 1: 76]).

But Balzac is perfectly conscious of the stakes involved in such a language with respect to his global project. What he called the obscenity of *Massimilla Doni* elucidates his personal and particular reasons for the choice of such language, a language that represents an image of literary creation. *Massimilla Doni* represents for Balzac creation as *execution,* the execution being the realization, at the price of arduous work on language, of the *conception* that is born in the spirit, fertile in inventing subjects for novels. Sexual love represents literary creation and gives "une belle explication des plus intimes procédés de l'art" [a fine explanation of the most intimate processes of art]; but to arrive at "l'enfantement des œuvres d'art" [the birthing of works of art], one must go past the barriers that separate the bodies. Love, of the kind that may conceive a child, brings to fruition an imagined creation. Balzac thus tells us about sexual unions, and to do this, he conceives a language of sex.

19

Composed Past and Historical Present

"Le passé composé," in addition to being a verb tense (past or perfect), can be taken to refer to the past as Balzac composed it in any given text. By analogy with chemistry, the complement of composition is analysis. Together, these two processes constitute Balzac's method: everything is either composition or analysis in *La Comédie humaine*. My analysis of *La recherche de l'Absolu* was based on this premise.

An interesting approach to this relation between composition and analysis lies in the way the past links to the present in the figurative form of the historical present. Nineteen of Balzac's novels and novellas finish in a present tense diegesis, sometimes at a considerable distance from the time of the rest of the plot. Closing the composed past, the instances of historical present ideally situate the reader in the moment of analysis that follows immediately. In the preface to *Une fille d'Ève* (1839), one of those Balzac wrote and then later suppressed for the Furne edition, he put these two processes in relation to each other, as follows: "Aussi l'affaire de l'auteur est-elle principalement d'arriver à la synthèse par l'analyse" [Therefore the author's task is principally to reach synthesis through analysis] (2: 267–68). Portraying the characters and their histories, he composes their past and at the same time the immense physiognomy of his century; the reader's task is to take up the analysis and produce the synthesis. The following sketches show how the text prompts the reader to do the synthesis.

In *La Maison du Chat-qui-pelote,* the jump to the present tense is as abrupt as possible. In chapter 2, I analyzed the elliptical semiosis of this story, which leaves a gaping hole between the composed past and the historical present. The last scene between Augustine de Sommervieux and her husband, in which Théodore violently destroys his portrait of her, ending the composed past, suddenly results in the scene depicting her gravestone at the Montmartre cemetery. The use of the historical present, like the immediately symbolic memorial marker, eternalizes the drama. Each November 2nd the unnamed friend of this timid soul, an image of Balzac himself, sees in the tomb the last act of a drama—the actual death of Augustine. In other words, the grave takes the place of a scene that was not actually "composed"—her suffering and death; that scene occurs only in the vision of the first-person witness. The friend makes the narrative endure like her memory: "Chaque année, . . . il ne passe jamais devant ce jeune marbre sans se demander s'il ne faut pas des femmes plus fortes que ne l'était Augustine pour les puissantes étreintes du génie. 'Les humbles et modestes fleurs, écloses dans les vallées, meurent peut-être, se dit-il, quand elles sont transplantées trop près des cieux, aux régions où se forment les orages, où le soleil est brûlant'" [Each year, . . . he can never pass in front of this new marble without wondering if the powerful embraces of geniuses did not require stronger women than Augustine had been. "Humble and modest flowers, blooming in the valleys, may die," he told himself, "when they are transplanted too close to the heavens, in the regions where storms are formed, where the sun burns strong"] (1: 93–94). The analysis formulates and finalizes the story's fundamental theme, a theme that endures in an always renewed present.

In *Modeste Mignon,* after having written and rejected two or three detailed descriptions of Modeste's marriage with Ernest de La Brière, her children, and her life, descriptions written mostly in the past tense, Balzac finally substituted an eight-line paragraph using the present tense. According to this paragraph, the marriage, which the novel has composed in its writing, is not a harsh reality and does not exclude the romantic ideal, as will be seen, writes Balzac, elsewhere in *La Comédie humaine:* "les connaisseurs remarqueront alors combien le mariage est doux et facile à porter avec une femme instruite et spirituelle; car Modeste, qui sut éviter selon sa promesse les ridicules du pédantisme, est encore l'orgueil et le bonheur de son mari comme de sa famille et de tous ceux qui composent sa société" [people in the know will then note how marriage can be sweet and easy to bear with an educated and intelligent woman; for Modeste, who knew to avoid the ridicule of pedantry as she had promised, is still her husband's pride and joy, and also that of her family and of all those who make up her society] (1: 714).

Certainly a masculine prejudice prevails in this "précieuse ridicule" analysis, but the "feminine" reading I prefer obtains in the composition, because of the wily device of the anonymous correspondence between Modeste and La Brière. The historical present identifies a direction for the reader's analysis to take: showing that Modeste has corrected any and all errors and is perpetually smart and sweet, it begins to solve the key problem of interpretation of *Modeste Mignon:* Is this a happy marriage, as Arlette Michel characterizes it (*Le mariage et l'amour* 3: 1528), or one of the most depressing endings in *La Comédie humaine,* as Anne-Marie Meininger forcefully writes ("Préface" 29)? My view is entirely on the side of the happy marriage, to which the historical present lends an aura of permanence typical of fairy-tale endings.[1]

Oscar Husson had much to learn in *Un début dans la vie,* and one paragraph before the end Balzac enumerates how everything turned out well after all. In sum: "Devenu sage et capable, il fut heureux" [Having become wise and capable, he was happy] (1: 887). His happiness is guaranteed by the protection of well-placed individuals. Such is his recovery from error that he now becomes a model, and this is what constitutes the historical present (as I have redefined it): "Oscar est un homme ordinaire, doux, sans prétention, modeste et se tenant toujours, comme son gouvernement, dans un juste milieu. Il n'excite ni l'envie ni le dédain. C'est enfin le bourgeois moderne" [Oscar is an ordinary, gentle, unpretentious, modest man, who always keeps himself, like his government, within the happy medium. He excites neither envy nor disdain. In all he is the modern bourgeois] (1: 887). Irony aside, present tenses like this one establish a type. This is Balzac the anthropologist, doing a service to the human sciences by composing the past that explains the model, for our better comprehension of his society and especially of the disdain in which he held the politics of 1830. To the ending pertains the analytical mode of knowledge and the wider scope that takes in the physiognomy of a century.

The case of *Albert Savarus,* analyzed in chapter 5 as an important example of self-narration, presents interesting peculiarities in its ending. First we learn that Rosalie de Watteville, having wreaked her vicious harm on Albert and Francesca, now lives the life of the eccentric, in the present tense: "[elle] passe pour une personne extrêmement originale. Elle est une des célébrités de l'Est. . . . On dit d'elle: '*Elle a des lubies!*'" [she passes for an extremely eccentric person. She is one of the celebrities of the East. . . . They say about her: "*She's full of whims!*"] (1: 1019). The first version ended essentially in

---

1. See Mortimer, *Writing Realism* (103–24), for an extended analysis of the romantic realism of *Modeste Mignon.*

this historical present, in which Rosalie receives no comeuppance for her dastardly behavior. Not content to let this undistinguished ending endure, however, Balzac then returned briefly to composing in the past tense by recounting the horrible, freakish accident that took Rosalie's arm and leg and scarred her face, in 1841, three years after the first historical present. This is the punishment that then endures in the permanent present, according to the last words: "sa santé soumise à des troubles horribles lui laisse peu de jours sans souffrance. Enfin, elle ne sort plus aujourd'hui de la Chartreuse des Rouxey où elle mène une vie entièrement vouée à des pratiques religieuses" [her health, troubled by horrible disturbances, allows her few days without suffering. In short, today, she no longer goes out of the Chartreuse des Rouxey, where she leads a life entirely dedicated to religious practice] (1: 1020). To a horrible cruelty pertains a terrible punishment, and it was this stodgy maxim that turned Balzac's text backward (in verb tenses) to finish the composition with Rosalie's accident—or finish it off, with a more definitive equilibrium, balancing a life lost to love with another life lost to love. Ebguy, pointing to this ending as an instance of the author's achieving silence, comments: "L'interruption de la démarche herméneutique—dire le sens d'une conduite—est caractéristique de la distance entre le narrateur et le personnage" [The interruption of the hermeneutic process—which gives the meaning of a particular behavior—is characteristic of the distance between the narrator and the character] ("Description d'une (dé)composition" 37). The hermeneutic process is what I am calling the composed past; the arrival at the historical present marks this taking of distance.

The very short *Étude de femme* typifies the simplest case of the present-tense ending: "Depuis seize jours, elle ne va plus dans le monde" [It has been sixteen days and she no longer goes out in society] (2: 179). What can the virtuous marquise de Listomère make of the fact that Eugène de Rastignac wrote her address on a love letter intended for another woman? When she obtains proof that Rastignac's letter was not for her but for Delphine de Nucingen, the "petite crise nerveuse" [little attack of nerves] that she suffers arises from the interpretive crisis that occurred in the story, which is now left in the hands of those who know—starting with Bianchon, her doctor and our narrator, and including the Balzacian reader skilled in Restoration manners and style, on which our analysis bears. Her secret is that she not only envies Delphine for Eugène's fidelity but also suffers from the seductive attack on her sensitivity that Eugène's letter produces ("*O cher ange d'amour, trésor de vie et de bonheur!*" [Oh sweet angel of love, treasure of life, of happiness!] [2: 175]). The high-minded marquise, who has never taken a lover, is nevertheless defenseless against the crystallization of these words in her mind—

and yet Rastignac did not address them to her; what caused him to think of her, if not a desire to seduce? To arrive at this analysis, the reader must deploy an intelligence on a par with Bianchon's. Not only that perspicacious doctor, but also Stendhal and Freud help us to analyze Mme de Listomère's enduring, present-tense attack of nerves.

Like *Albert Savarus, La fausse maîtresse* comes to two moments of historical present. The first ended the manuscript with a quite typical phrase indicating the arrival in the present: "Voici trois ans que Thaddée est parti. . . . La comtesse Laginska s'intéresse énormément aux expéditions de l'empereur Nicolas, elle est russe de cœur" [It has been three years since Thaddée left. . . . Countess Laginska is enormously interested in Emperor Nicolas's expeditions, she is Russian in her heart] (2: 243). The comtesse Laginska has just learned that comte Thaddée Paz loved her in secret—and kept a fake mistress to dispel suspicion; for three years now, she has wondered what has become of him in the Russian army: "elle lit avec une espèce d'avidité toutes les nouvelles qui viennent de ce pays" [she reads with a kind of avid eagerness all the news that comes from that country]. And the manuscript ended with her falsely indifferent question asking what has become of comte Paz. But Balzac, not satisfied to leave his heroine in this suspended state of doubt, added five paragraphs containing a "moral of the story" and a new dramatic event. The paragraph containing the moral turns Clémentine Laginska into a type and a warning, by which Balzac laments the fact that many a devoted lover, like Paz, will go ignored and unrecognized; that this is an indirect message to Mme Hanska has been noted. Three-quarters of a page later, the second historical present consists of only one line; it comes at the end of a final episode Balzac added to the composed past on proofs, as he so often did (for example, in *La Maison du Chat-qui-pelote* and *Albert Savarus*); this additional episode has concision, melodrama, and impact, all the best qualities to conclude a novel, as Balzac points out, and directly responds to the countess's wondering what has become of Paz. Just as she is about to be tricked into being seduced by the callous La Palférine (the prince de la bohème), late one night after a ball, a vigorous pair of arms seizes her and puts her safely into her own carriage; the countess recognizes her secret lover and realizes he has not left Paris, and the story ends finally on this single line: "À toute heure, Clémentine espère revoir Paz" [At every moment, Clementine hopes to see Paz again]. A purgatory of hope: let all women take heed, Balzac seems to be saying, and not neglect a true lover until it is too late. The historical present gives the tale all the virtues of a lesson for all time.

Une fille d'Ève closes off Marie de Vandenesse's story of adulterous temptation as something well over with, like a return to health after a disease:

"Mme de Vandenesse eut un mouvement de honte en songeant qu'elle s'était intéressée à Raoul" [Mme de Vandenesse, remembering that she had been interested in Raoul, felt a pang of shame] (2: 382). The historical present focuses instead on Raoul Nathan, who becomes thus an emblem of the enduring, continuing change in principles, government, and people since 1830, the turning point of *La Comédie humaine*. Today Nathan lives in shameful peace in the shadow of a ministerial paper, a hypocritical capitulation. "Cette conduite illogique a son origine et son autorité dans le changement de front de quelques gens qui, durant nos dernières évolutions politiques, ont agi comme Raoul" [This illogical conduct finds its origins and authority in the change of face of a few people who, during the recent political evolutions, acted like Raoul] (2: 383). Analysis thus points the reader in the direction of political explanation, the root of the depiction of Paris after 1830. In the face of the rising powers of finance and capitalism, the insufficiency of great political men in the July Monarchy reflects the weakness that threatened the marriage of Marie-Angélique and Félix de Vandenesse.

After the past of *Ursule Mirouët* brings the heroine to a well-deserved happy ending—"Trois mois après ces événements . . . Ursule épousa Savinien du consentement de Mme de Portenduère" [Three months after these events . . . Ursule married Savinien with Mme de Portenduère's consent] (3: 986)—two more pages tour the horizon of all the destinies remaining and also provide a final, enduring image of the marriage of Ursule and her husband, of which we are told "Il n'y a pas deux ménages semblables dans Paris" [There are not two households like this one in Paris] (3: 987). While the composed past dramatized the conflict between the bourgeoisie of Nemours and Ursule's select society, all the elements of the historical present show the malicious folk turned to good under her influence, or at least to benign neutrality. Minoret-Levrault's reversal is the most dramatic, just as he was the most harmful to Ursule—he has become a model of charity; Goupil serves one and all, and Dionis is one of the "ornaments" of the chamber of deputies; Bongrand and his son flourish in the magistrature; and Mme Crémière continues to regale all hearers with her malapropisms. This is not just tying up loose ends, however. Analysis proves that the good emanating from Ursule must inevitably flow into all the nasty crevices until the conflict resolves into unity. The historical present then gives permanence to what the past composed.

Eugénie Grandet's historical present arrives mid-paragraph in a turn of the hand: "[Eugénie] fut veuve à trente-trois ans, riche de huit cent mille livres de rente, encore belle, mais comme une femme est belle à près de quarante ans. Son visage est blanc, reposé, calme" [[Eugénie] was widowed at the age of thirty-three, with eight hundred thousand pounds of income, still beautiful, but in the way that a woman is beautiful when she is close to forty years old. Her face is white, rested, calm] (3: 1198). Two detailed paragraphs continue in this vein, including the famous sentence, "Eugénie marche au ciel accompagnée d'un cortège de bienfaits" [Eugénie strides toward heaven accompanied by a retinue of good actions]. Balzac's analysis is concise but complete and he summarizes it and the entire composition with the most direct of phrasings: "Telle est l'histoire de cette femme qui n'est pas du monde au milieu du monde, qui faite pour être magnifiquement épouse et mère n'a ni mari, ni enfants, ni famille" [Such is the story of this woman who is not from society but lives among society, who, born to be a magnificent wife and mother, has neither husband, nor children, nor family]. This was the ending in the manuscript, followed by an epilogue. In the text as it was originally published and retained in the Furne edition, nine more lines now follow the summary sentence, beginning: "Depuis quelques jours, il est question d'un nouveau mariage pour elle" [In the last few days, there is talk of a new marriage for her] (3: 1199). This sentence constitutes the bud of a new composed past, but—quickly nipped in the bud: those said to be aiding this marriage plot are not capable of understanding the corruption in the world. No, the composition will not make a new start. Instead, the epilogue, which Balzac removed for the Furne edition, reaffirmed and extended the analysis made in the present-tense passage, calling woman an intermediate creation between man and angel, while, among women, Eugénie "sera peut-être un type, celui des dévouements jetés à travers les orages du monde" [would perhaps be a type, one of self-sacrifice cast among worldly storms] (3: 1202). Arising in the composition, this quasi-anthropological analysis serves society, making a lesson of the unique story.

Joseph Bridau's finally happy fate is the object of the brief historical present that arrives on the last page of *La Rabouilleuse:* "Joseph, à qui son beau-père . . . amasse tous les jours des écus, possède déjà soixante mille francs de rente. . . . Par suite d'une clause de l'érection du majorat, il se trouve comte de Brambourg, ce qui le fait souvent pouffer de rire au milieu de ses amis, dans son atelier" [Joseph, whose father-in-law . . . amasses money for him daily, already possesses sixty thousand francs of income. . . . As a result of a clause raising his property to a *majorat,* he has become comte de Brambourg, which often makes him burst out laughing among his friends, in his studio] (4: 540). Just about everyone else has died, and he has inherited his cruel brother Philippe's property and his title, which means nothing to him. Extensive revisions brought the story well beyond the period of its melodramatic events, the complex intrigues of noxious characters—Jean-Jacques Rouget, Maxence Gilet, and Philippe Bridau. To achieve this happy present tense, Balzac lengthened the ending, bringing it to 1839 and the Algerian war, during which Philippe is attacked by Arabs in a bloody combat, abandoned by his own troops, and savagely hacked to pieces. The year 1839 happens to be the year when Balzac started to write the novel, suggesting that one of the elements of its historical present would be to safely consign the story to writing. In contrast to *Pierrette,* in which the historical present eternalizes the gains made entirely at Pierrette's expense by the political factions around her, this novel brings the composed past to the point where the only meritorious character still living is at last rewarded for his patience and virtue. Analysis here suggests that the writing had to continue Philippe's story until it could achieve his death and Joseph's happy destiny after 1839.

A famous arrival in the present closes *Les secrets de la princesse de Cadignan* (to be discussed in detail in chapter 20): "Depuis ce jour, il n'a plus été question de la princesse de Cadignan, ni de d'Arthez" [From this day on, there was no further mention of the princesse de Cadignan or of d'Arthez] (6: 1004). Like the ending of *La Maison du Chat-qui-pelote,* the historical present comes after an abrupt lapse of time, jumping from their first kiss to the months spent in that villa in Geneva which, for Balzac, seems to indicate total sexual happiness. However, the understated and inadequate phrase "il n'a plus été question de la princesse," when it had, precisely, "been a question" of the princess for all her scandalous life, marks the refusal to continue supplying the details—the facts, the intimate stories about both characters, the very matter that had made the composed past worth telling—a juicy telling, indeed. This refusal to tell is a real turnabout. There follow the well-known lines: "Est-ce un dénouement? Oui, pour les gens d'esprit; non, pour ceux qui veulent tout savoir" [Is this a dénouement? Yes, for intelligent people; no, for those who want to know everything] (6: 1005), urging the reader to proceed with the analysis that is now needed to figure out what is going on in the villa. The "gens d'esprit" will analyze the present-tense moments—d'Arthez's absences, the excessive rarity of his publications "depuis ce jour"—and produce the meaning to which all the composition led: it really was true love at last.

Pierre Grassou, the mediocre painter, arrives at good fortune even though he is not a genius. His success "aujourd'hui" also indicates the passage to the bourgeois commercial mentality and its robust progress after 1830, as analyzed in chapter 12. By 1839, middle class successes could have a destiny: "Pierre Grassou ne sort pas d'un cercle bourgeois où il est considéré comme un des plus grands artistes de l'époque" [Pierre Grassou remains within a bourgeois circle where he is considered one of the greatest artists of the period] (6: 1111). Reason governs this valuation, in bourgeois Paris, for

Grassou is making money. A good copy is as good as an original—or better; originality has no value or a negative value (think of Augustine's family's assessment of Théodore de Sommervieux). In the context of *La Comédie humaine, Pierre Grassou,* for all its minor status, carries a disproportionately major meaning; it gives reality to that impossible contradiction made possible by 1830, the "artiste bourgeois." The historical present to which the story arrives initiates the analysis of this new way of being a "genius" in the new forms the world is taking. When Balzac praises Grassou in the final words, the reader is led to produce the analysis of mediocrity that constitutes the composition, which concludes with a wonderful sort of "punch line" when Grassou discovers that the Vervelles' Rembrandts and Titians are actually his own copies, artistically aged by the dishonest art dealer Elie Magus. It is the bourgeois artist Grassou who now buys paintings from famous artists "quand ils sont gênés" [when they are short on funds] (6: 1111), so that an ingredient of this analysis must be that even "les peintres célèbres" [famous painters] are not guaranteed material happiness or success. While *Le chef-d'œuvre inconnu* has often been taken as an icon of Balzac's creation, the brilliant success of the humble copier Pierre Grassou must also stand as a consolation for the "artiste bourgeois" that Balzac could not help being.

Another copier brings an end to *Le cousin Pons.* When the historical present arrives, Pons is dead and his collection already appropriated by his cousins, the Camusot de Marville. Like *Pierrette,* the historical present concerns those who endure after having immolated their victim. The example would be unremarkable were it not for its most enigmatic final line: "Excusez les fautes du copiste!" [Excuse the clerical errors!] (7: 765). While I suspect there is an intertextual allusion here that has not yet been identified, a comic line possibly from a popular play, I also think Balzac himself poses as the mere *copiste* in contrast to Providence, to whom the novelist is indebted for bringing about the death of the greedy Rémonencq, an event that is narrated in the historical present: "Cette fin, digne de ce scélérat, prouve en faveur de la Providence que les peintres de mœurs sont accusés d'oublier, peut-être à cause des dénouements de drames qui en abusent" [This end, worthy of this villain, proves in favor of Providence, which depicters of mores are accused of forgetting about, perhaps because of overuse by the dénouements of dramas] (7: 765).

Finally, when the marquis de Léganès is forced to execute his own family in literature's most horrendous instance of plea-bargaining, he becomes El Verdugo, the executioner, and this identification is given in the historical present. As the paragraph that explains why the story is called *El Verdugo,* it is this permanent condition that endures, that dramatically eternalizes the horror Juanito has suffered: the name sticks. In spite of his noble titles, "il est dévoré par le chagrin, il vit solitaire et se montre rarement. Accablé sous le fardeau de son admirable forfait, il semble attendre avec impatience que la naissance d'un second fils lui donne le droit de rejoindre les ombres qui l'accompagnent incessamment" [he is devoured by grief, he lives a solitary life and rarely shows himself. Weighed down under the burden of his admirable offense, he seems to be waiting impatiently for the birth of a second son to give him the right to join the shadows that accompany him ceaselessly] (10: 1143). A past tense could not have conveyed the impatience of this suspended suicide, nor especially its lack of resolution. It was a smart move on Balzac's part to remove El Verdugo the executioner from the composed past, in which he too would have died the noble death of his parents and siblings, and to leave him with the reader in the moment of analysis, where he incarnates a superlative of heroism, surpassing his family's and guiding our interpretation.

What observations to draw from this discussion? First, one cannot say that the procedure is common. It is not overwhelmingly characteristic for Balzac to bring the past into the present after the closure of the story's event, although in several other novels besides these he reaches into a future diegesis.[2] Perhaps for that very reason the procedure is remarkable—if not for its quantity, then for the kind of reflection it can provoke. The present, unlike the past, has only one definition: it is now. So when events are occurring now—when people *still* aren't talking about la princesse de Cadignan, when Eugénie is *still* striding toward heaven—we as readers find ourselves included in this frame of time. We are engaged in the process to which the past Balzac composed has led us, when all that is left after the composition concludes is the analysis by which we can explain it. The historical present gives a role to the reader complementary to the heavy task the composer assumed, to analyze and explain now. It situates the reader in that always ideal moment of analysis.

That a composed past had to exist in relation to some kind of present of analysis was felt by Balzac as a kind of anxiety: he feared to be misunderstood. Balzac was haunted by wholeness. Because of the system of recurring characters, the composed past stretches over many different titles in *La*

---

2. An interesting graphic rendition of the time covered in novels, along with extensions to the past and the future, can be seen on a website, http://hbalzac.free.fr/temps.php, showing twenty-six works with extensions to future dates.

Comédie humaine; only after the different parts of their stories have been told, in whatever order, can a reader reassemble them into a whole. Failing that synthesis, the work will be tainted by a "capital vice" which, with surprising optimism, Balzac hopes will be viewed one day as a virtue: "Il s'applaudit de la grandeur, de la variété, de la beauté, de la fécondité de son sujet, quelque déplorable que le fassent, socialement parlant, la confusion des faits les plus opposés, l'abondance des matériaux, l'impétuosité des mouvements. Ce désordre est une source de beautés" [He congratulates himself on the grandeur, variety, beauty, and fruitfulness of his subject, however deplorable, socially speaking, the confusion of the most opposing facts, the abundance of source materials, and the impetuosity of movements may make it. Such disorder is a source of beauty] (2: 264). This persuasive argument marks the 1839 preface to *Une fille d'Ève* as one of the most important documents about Balzac's ambitions. It is also in this preface that one finds the image of the mosaic, so readily applicable to *La Comédie humaine* as a whole. The nineteenth century gave Balzac the gift of its "disorder"; from it, Balzac forged beauty by composing its past: "Vous ne pouvez raconter chronologiquement que l'histoire du temps passé, système inapplicable à un présent qui marche" [Chronological narration applies only to the history of times past, a system that is not applicable to the ongoing present] (2: 265). The reader working in the historical present arrives at the composed past through its analysis.

Eventually, closer study may show how Balzac's magnificent project resulted in a *passé surcomposé*—which would not only be a verb tense but also an *overcomposed* past.

20

Problems of Closure

Realistic closure goes without saying. It normally lacks nothing and requires no complex elaboration, for when we think of narrative closure in a realistic work we usually have in mind the resolution of problems posed by the narration, producing the feeling of satisfaction that accompanies the completion of finished models. We associate such a strong sense of closure with the "grand roman réaliste ou naturaliste" [great realistic or naturalist novel], as Lucien Dällenbach correctly generalized ("Du fragment au cosmos" 420), and many are the readers who include Balzac's novels in that definition. As Bersani wrote in *Balzac to Beckett,* describing the fatality of the childhoods of Félix and Henriette in *Le lys dans la vallée,* "[all that follows] has the superfluity characteristic of a Balzacian novel, where the *dénouement* often strikes us as an almost unnecessary proof of the predictive, containing powers of the exposition" (85). Sentiments such as this encourage the belief that the realistic work achieves what we may well call a norm of narrative closure.

The taxonomic achievements of studies on closure make an inventory of typical endings easy: final morals, concluding frames, death of main characters, a fate meted out to each, final tag lines, and so on; there is a plethora of such structural and rhetorical moves in *La Comédie humaine.* Yet the phenomena that best illustrate the norm may well be those that diverge from it. A subtle proof of this rests on the premise that any attempt to problematize closure depends on the prior recognition that we habitually submit to the necessity of a strong and artistic ending, corresponding to the expectation raised by the text. *Autre étude de femme* illustrates such a strong and artistic ending with a complete mimetics and semiotics of closure, while the analyses of *Les secrets de la princesse de Cadignan, La Maison Nucingen,* and *Honorine* concern endings made ambiguous by changes in the final pages.

Enclosure
Autre étude de femme

There is no better way to apprehend the nature of narrative closure in Balzac than to follow the trace of its signs in this novella, which presents the richest possible thematic and formal material for analysis. Composed of fragments from as early as 1831, the novella was still incomplete in the 1842 volume of *La Comédie humaine,* but modern editions have long obeyed Balzac's manuscript note in the Furne corrigé and appended to *Autre étude de femme* the best known, longest, and most important section, the narrative known as *La Grande Bretèche. Autre étude de femme* appeared in volume II of the Furne edition without *La Grande Bretèche,* which was published in volume IV (1845), subtitled at that time "Fin de Autre étude de femme." On his personal copy of the Furne edition, Balzac crossed out this subtitle and wrote "Ceci doit être reporté à la suite de '*Autre étude de femme*'" [This should be transferred to the end of "*Autre étude de femme*"] (3: 1510). *La Grande Bretèche* had first appeared in 1832 as the second of the two parts of *Le conseil* in the *Scènes de la vie privée,* with *Le message;* it reappeared in 1837 and finally took its definitive place in *Autre étude de femme* after five other stories narrated within the frame of an intimate after-dinner conversation among several familiar recurring characters.

This tardy reassignment of *La Grande Bretèche* has its own importance for the story as a whole, but what strikes the reader at an initial reading is the wealth of clotural signs this added narrative possesses. The ending of *La Grande Bretèche* has itself a strongly marked closure in addition to bringing about the closure of *Autre étude de femme,* while reiterating allusively all the other anecdotes which it surpasses and outdoes. The subject of the tale is such that one could hardly find a more powerful way of closing off the novella: inside the Grande Bretèche manor, absolutely and mysteriously closed since the death of its proprietors, a lover caught by a suspicious husband has been entombed alive in a walled-up closet. This literal enclosure immediately resonates with the multiple signs of figurative closures throughout the narrative.

It is certain that the fatal cloistering of Mme de Merret's lover, Bagos de Férédia, a noble Spanish prisoner of Napoleon, is so horrifying that it admits of no reopening of the story, as Balzac makes particularly evident. The house is literally a tomb. To this thematic closure is added the formal closure created by the carefully articulated structure of *La Grande Bretèche,* which begins with the logical ending and saves for a total dénouement the account of the walling-in. The enigmatic manor house, closed and untouchable, the concrete and durable outcome of the drama that Bianchon will uncover, is the subject of the first of the four secondary narrations that structure *La Grande Bretèche*. Wandering within its forbidden enclosure, Bianchon dreams of "de délicieux romans" [delicious romances] and "un drame assez noir" [a rather dark drama] (3: 712), in what is actually a prologue to the three further parts, narrated by the notary Regnault, the innkeeper Mme Lepas, and Rosalie, formerly Mme de Merret's maid. Table 20.1 shows that the four parts are not in chronological order.

Table 20.1

Part	Narrator	Subject	Logical Order
1st (prologue)	Bianchon	description of the house	4th (epilogue)
2nd	Regnault	death of Mme de Merret, her will	3rd
3rd	Mme Lepas	introduction of characters, disappearance of Férédia	1st
4th	Rosalie and Bianchon	Férédia buried alive	2nd

Proposing successive enigmas, this structure figures the pursuit of the secret, a pervasive effect in Balzac's hermeneutics. Thus, in the second part Regnault explains the mystery of the manor by revealing Mme de Merret's unusual will, which requires that the Grande Bretèche remain sealed and untouched for fifty years after her death. Of course, that partial explanation only deepens the initial enigma and whets Bianchon's curiosity, which Mme Lepas's account detailing the mysterious and total disappearance of Napoleon's prisoner does nothing to dissipate (although the knowing reader might have a pretty good inkling). The accumulation of these unexplained facts and partial revelations underscores the situation of the last part, which will necessarily supply the answers. According to Rosalie's account, Mme de Merret hides her lover in a closet built into the wall when her husband comes unannounced to her room; M. de Merret makes her swear on her crucifix that there is no one there, and then cruelly orders a mason to wall up the closet.

He then remains in her room for two weeks and, at each muffled sound that passes through the wall, he reminds her (and this is the last sentence of *La Grande Bretèche*) that she has sworn on her cross "qu'il n'y avait là personne" [that there was no one there] (3: 729). To the extent, then, that the narrative principle is that of the pursuit of a secret, the last segment furnishes a formal closure in that it finally reveals the most hidden part of the story. The last part is both solution and resolution; in supplying the answer to all riddles, it has the last word.

Clearly, the story too is "buried alive," walled up in silence and secret. The semiotic process takes down this wall, stone by stone, to uncover and resuscitate the story for the benefit of dramatic interest, just as Mme de Merret hoped to save Férédia by offering a bribe to Rosalie for trying to persuade the mason to leave a hole. Where Mme de Merret fails, Bianchon succeeds, but not without brandishing the weaponry of love—a feigned courtship—for Rosalie is described, significantly, as "un mur" [a wall] (3: 722). The action of the narration, then, consists in breaking down the walls that surround the story, particularly its ending, so that an audience that demands powerful emotions can relive it, for narrative profit depends on the possibility of making openings. The irony of this strategy is that the impossibility of breaking down a wall was just the point of the story worth discovering.

But a contrary metaphor also governs Rosalie's account as reported by Bianchon: it fills in the holes of an incomplete narration; it supplies "le dernier chapitre du roman" [the last chapter of the novel] (3: 723), which is placed between those of the notary and of the innkeeper "aussi exactement," says Bianchon, "que les moyens termes d'une proportion arithmétique le sont entre leurs deux extrêmes" [as exactly as the middle terms of an arithmetical proportion are between the two extremes] (3: 724); it is "au centre même de l'intérêt et de la vérité" [at the very center of interest and of truth] (3: 723); it is "noué dans le nœud" [knotted into the knot]; it is like "la case qui se trouve au milieu d'un damier" [the square in the center of a checkerboard], a very inexact simile, as there are four squares in the center of a checkerboard, not one. It is striking that these descriptions of the last part, all stressing its centrality, are not in the least terminal and that it is the "last chapter" only in the temporality of the narration, not of the story. Imitating a possible method of laying bricks, the structure of the narration saves for last a piece out of the middle; the work of the narration will be completed only when the secret, finally revealed, fulfills the expectations of the audience, thus completing the story—and necessitating the death of the lover.

The thematics of the secret suffer from an equally paradoxical contradiction between dis-covering and closing up, to which Bianchon initially falls prey after illegally entering the courtyard of the Grande Bretèche. His instinct to fantasize must yield to the curiosity, even the necessity, of finding out the truth, since the notary takes it as a sacred duty to uphold Mme de Merret's testament. Trapped between illusion and truth, Bianchon both wants to know and does not, for knowledge can be both seductive and perilous (this is also true of the audience represented in the frame story, especially the women). The process of the narration may well break down walls and liberate truth, but the one who knows this truth loses a certain innocence in abandoning illusions and must submit to its effects, whatever they may be. Thus, the two series of figurative representations of this closure—making holes or filling them in, building or undoing walls, images that coexist and that supply the pattern of the tale—betray a preoccupation with the double attraction of the enigma and with its effect on the audience.

Unable to find the happy medium between saying too much and saying too little, between knowing and not knowing, Bianchon and the narrative reproduce the limits between which Mme de Merret also moves. Saying too little, she refuses to admit that a man is hidden in her closet, and her silence is fatal to Férédia; swearing on her crucifix, she says too much, and that too is fatal for Férédia. In the last paragraph, she tries to speak ("Joséphine voulait l'implorer pour l'inconnu mourant" [Josephine wanted to implore him for the sake of the dying stranger]), and her husband will not allow her "un seul mot" [a single word] (3: 729). After having been reduced to silence, Mme de Merret, like Férédia, dies in silence, of a self-imposed starvation, a kind of penance suitable to her sin. Her will imposes a further fifty years of silence on her property.

Along with this double treatment of silence and secret, the conversation of the frame recounts "des secrets bien trahis" [well revealed secrets] (3: 675) that puncture the verbal form of the wall—silence—symbolized by the cracks that have appeared in the walls of the manor. Just as the desire to know the story has a negative side, so the desire to know the truth about women in general gives rise to an irony that pervades the entire novella, the vehicle of a negative judgment on female conduct. It is this relation between the themes of the anecdotes and the thematics of the frame that lends heightened importance to the end of the frame, quoted here in full in its final 1845 version, when Balzac decided to conclude *Autre étude de femme* by appending *La Grande Bretèche*: "Après ce récit, toutes les femmes se levèrent de table, et le charme sous lequel Bianchon les avait tenues fut dissipé par ce mouvement. Néanmoins quelques-unes d'entre elles avaient eu quasi froid en entendant le dernier mot" [After this narrative, all the women rose from the table, and the charm under which Bianchon had held them was dissipated by this movement. Nevertheless, some of them had felt almost chilled upon hearing the final word] (3: 729). The closures of *La Grande Bretèche* are fatal to the evening's gathering; the story goes too far, and all the women recognize as if with a common accord that no possible sequel can follow the closure definitively encoded in that account. The claustrophobic charm had held them transfixed. Frappier-Mazur has written that the story closes on a "point d'orgue" [fermata], but I believe that can only be understood as sustaining silence rather than a phrase ("Lecture d'un texte illisible" 725). The final sentence is heavy with implications of silent accusation against the women who had lovers.

As the last instance of punished adultery, *La Grande Bretèche* depletes the central thematics of infidelity and revenge in *Autre étude de femme*. It strikes the final blow to a certain form of worldliness, as well as to facile women. Just as Rosalie's part of the story concludes the other parts of *La Grande Bretèche* and completes its construction with an emphatic, accentuated, and central ending, *La Grande Bretèche* concludes the entire novella by concentrating in a single focal point the motifs and themes bundled together by its de facto construction. *La Grande Bretèche* brings out this unity of vision of *Autre étude de femme* in spite of the disparate origins of its constituent parts. But this ultimate unity is achieved only after a significant revision made in 1845: the reduction of the final portion of the frame to the few lines quoted above, about which there is a great deal to say before recognizing that in fact after this closure there is nothing more to say. In 1832, in *Le conseil* (whose two anecdotes were told to Mme d'Esther by M. de Villaines to advise her to remain faithful to her husband), the text of *La Grande Bretèche* was essentially the same and finished on exactly the same words as in the final version ("Vous avez juré sur la croix qu'il n'y avait là personne" [You swore on the cross that there was no one there]). However, the end of the frame in *Le conseil*, a page and a half long, did much to minimize the glacial effect of the tale by showing Mme d'Esther's confused gratitude, by portraying the characters of the frame continuing their moralizing commentary, and by showing M. de Villaines "passionnément épris de Mme d'Esther" [passionately enamored of Mme d'Esther] (2: 1373).[1] Balzac's decision not to neutralize the acidity of the story's ending when adding it to *Autre étude de femme* did much to increase its powerful clotural effect.

Refusing to assimilate the events of the story, the new frame measures the distance between two forms of audience. In the fragmentary composition of the story, Frappier-Mazur has identified a kind of sliding of the dividing line

---

1. The Pléiade edition of *Le message*, which remained in *La Comédie humaine* as a separate publication, gives the text of the frame of *Le conseil* from the 1832 original publication.

between what she calls the old and the new, the former identified with the oral and aristocracy, the latter with the written and the bourgeoisie ("Lecture"). Léo Mazet also places this rupture between two narrative poles, on the one hand "la littérature du XIXe siècle et son public bourgeois réel dont elle récuse l'unification" [nineteenth century literature and its actual bourgeois audience, whose unification it challenges] and on the other "un public virtuel de coteries d'initiés tel que le connut le XVIIIe siècle" [a virtual audience of coteries of the initiated like those that existed in the eighteenth century], nostalgically evoked (132). *Le conseil* of 1832 more than *Autre étude de femme* is a story in which an elite society of former times flourishes, portrayed in the frame. In one of the three or four salons that still exist in Paris, in which literature, criticism, and art—the "conversation française d'autrefois" [the French style of conversation from the past]—are still admired, there are ironic allusions to the "ruines de la France" [ruins of France] after July 1830 (2: 1369, 1370). When in the closing segment of the frame "chacun . . . cherchait des critiques à faire" [everyone . . . looked for criticisms to make] and M. de Villaines stresses the horror of the lesson in "cette affreuse tragédie . . . moins horrible . . . que le spectacle d'une jeune et jolie femme, encore pure, prête à devenir la proie d'un homme sans principes" [this ghastly tragedy . . . less horrible . . . than the spectacle of a pretty young woman, still pure, about to become prey to a man with no principles] (2: 1372), the result is that the moral point of the stories dominates, obliterating any effect of horror. The tale of the Grande Bretèche was thus appropriated and assimilated into the aristocratic conversation of times past, a conversation that, imperturbably, "prit un autre cours" [took a different direction] (2: 1372). Lacking the other anecdotes of *Autre étude de femme*, *La Grande Bretèche* did not yet enjoy its full dramatic power.

For not only does the theme of infidelity and revenge unify the capricious ensemble of the novella, in spite of its far too obvious seams, but many of the motifs of *La Grande Bretèche* also exist in the first five parts of *Autre étude de femme*. In "La maîtresse de notre colonel" the faithless wife is barricaded in a house that is then burned to the ground, introducing the motif of the sealed house in which a terrible revenge takes place, and the husband, an Italian captain, resembles M. de Merret in that both have jealous personalities hidden behind a cool façade. Merret also resembles the colonel of that anecdote, who harbors a choleric temperament that comes to the fore in critical situations. The sketch of "la femme comme il faut," the second part of the story, could well serve as an introduction to the character of Mme de Merret, who incarnates a certain morality in spite of being a countess and an adulteress. Just like the first mistress of de Marsay, according to the first section of the novella, Mme de Merret is able to keep her composure while lying to her husband. Her excessive emaciation and the saintly quality of her death reproduce very closely the death of the duchess recounted by Bianchon in the fifth part. Likewise, Rosina, in the fourth part, was in "un déplorable état de maigreur" [a deplorable state of emaciation] (3: 706). Even the praise of Napoleon by Canalis, in the third section (3: 700–701), throws a certain light on the emperor's honorable treatment of Férédia, and indeed what Frappier-Mazur calls a Napoleon cycle ("Lecture" 715) links three of the episodes in a common social-historical frame. Lastly, somewhat like a parody, the three secondary narrators of *La Grande Bretèche*—Regnault, Mme Lepas, and Rosalie—provide a kind of narrative frame for this tale, like *Autre étude de femme*. These examples should suffice to demonstrate that *La Grande Bretèche* unites in its enclosure elements from all the rest of the novella. Balzac was right to add it to his disjointed masonry, for it fills in the holes and carries the illustration of the theme to its highest and most somber point, the maximum degree of proof.

With this new dignity, the novella can express its modern lesson alone, without the calming and reassuring closing segment of the 1832 frame; there is no flattening of the point. The new text requires the critical work of the reader to reestablish the deeper meaning revealed by the capital fact that *La Grande Bretèche* brings the after-dinner conversation to a close: that kind of congenial, elite, and old-fashioned society in which *La Grande Bretèche* had found its first illustration in 1832 (where its moral was perfectly neutralized) is drawing to a close. The anecdotes that "pétillèrent et se pressèrent sans apprêt" [sparkled and crowded upon each other without affectation] (3: 675) and that characterize a type of outmoded audience whose "literature" is not yet worthy of the name give way at the end of the story to the far too crude realities of a new genre of literature whose carefully devised structure will be the death of the old eighteenth-century–style anecdote. This opposition is explicit in the text: "Là [dans ce salon dernier asile de l'esprit français d'autrefois], nul ne pense à garder sa pensée pour un drame; et, dans un récit, personne ne voit un livre à faire. Enfin, le hideux squelette d'une littérature aux abois ne se dresse point" [There [in this salon, last refuge of the French wit of the past], no one thinks to keep his thoughts for a drama; and in a tale none sees a book to be constructed. Lastly, the hideous skeleton of literature at bay does not rise up] (3: 674). Rejecting *un drame, un livre, une littérature* [a drama, a book, a literature] in favor of the *récit,* which implies an oral narration, is a way of reclaiming the *"ancien,"* or the eighteenth-century audience. (The rejection of literature is a theme addressed with a different approach in *La Maison Nucingen;* see chapter 7.) But the definitive version of

Autre étude de femme, with the radical change of the closing segment of the frame, stresses the cloturing power of the artistic, dramatic, and architectonic structure of *La Grande Bretèche,* marking the end of this "eighteenth century" and the start of a new realism.

A part of this power remains to be demonstrated: it is the rich semiotics of closure, a virtual thesaurus whose terms uphold the closure fatal to witty anecdotes and futile conversations. On one side are these signs: *cacher, emmurer, haie, mur, passer sous silence, imposer silence, dissimuler, ensevelir, enterrer, clôture, cloître, enclos, fermer, tirer le rideau, disparaître, barricader, secret, mystère, énigme, enceinte* [to hide, to wall in, hedge, wall, to pass over in silence, to impose silence, to dissemble, to entomb, to bury, fenced-in enclosure, cloister, enclosed, to close, to draw the curtain, to disappear, to barricade, secret, mystery, enigma, walled-in enclosure], all in the story; on the other, also taken from the text, are *brèche, bretèche, grille, trous, parole, récit, vérité, connaissance, révéler, mettre au jour, faire sauter des briques, briser le charme, casser la vitre, crevasse* [breach, a kind of balcony with open work, iron gate, holes, utterance, narration, truth, knowledge, to reveal, to bring to light, to tear away the bricks, to break the charm, to break the window, crevice]. With the death of Férédia in the sealed-up closet, the tale results in the depletion of the signs of closure, in the totalizing sense that, following Greimas, I attribute to his term *épuisement* (261–62). This fatal closure depletes the possibilities of narration; it is material and metaphysical; it causes the cloture of the session giving rise to narration, after which there is nothing further to say. The stories have attained a maximum degree of finitude. Actualizing closure on the thematic, lexical, spatial, and narrative planes, *La Grande Bretèche* is a kind of paradigm of the whole story, and beyond that of realistic representation in general.

Forcefully at play in *Autre étude de femme* is a kind of closure that literally goes without saying, a vast international manner of writing in which Balzac's participation, usually taken for granted, is actually highly problematic. For Balzac did not always strike so mortal a blow to his stories. Coexisting with a long list of closing devices and many examples of powerful realistic closures, there is a strange reluctance to complete, to untie, or to satisfy in the last sentences of many of his stories. Such closures leave a trace of a reaction against the realistic norm. Although it is sometimes difficult to unearth this hesitation to finish in the final published versions, additions and suppressions in the last pages best reveal how Balzac came to deny the text the last word. This rewriting often resulted in willful ambiguity. Is it not possible that in rereading himself—especially in the proofs to which he brought extensive changes—Balzac sometimes deplored a too strong sense of an ending, that such ambiguous endings are the signs of a contrary movement toward opening up the text, and that their coexistence with strong definitive closures runs parallel to those tensions between fragment and whole that Dällenbach so persuasively identified in two articles in *Poétique*? It is always interesting to consider how an author has changed his plots, but never more intriguing than when these changes occur in the conclusions. Among several such cases in *La Comédie humaine,* three are discussed here, a selection that is neither arbitrary nor exhaustive, but illustrative of different strategies for subverting closure. There are others with endings made interesting by revision, but these cases are striking for reasons inherent to them. In what must be described as a negative way, they too illustrate the power of realistic closure.

Disclosure
Les secrets de la princesse de Cadignan

In her preface to this story for the Club Français du Livre edition of *La Comédie humaine,* Claude-Edmonde Magny is moved to claim that most of Balzac's short stories end with a kind of "rature" [erasure], leaving us rather uncertain as to what we should think about them, in contrast to the long novels that dispose unambiguously of their principal characters (235). What Magny calls "erasure"—"dire vraiment ce qu'il avait à dire en ne le disant pas" [to say what he actually had to say by not saying it] (260)—is very much like the definition of the perverse secret that Guy Rosolato has given in *Essais sur le symbolique* (278): "cacher pour montrer sans dire" [to hide to show without saying]. This is an apt description of the princess's strategy. Without presenting in detail the kinds of techniques used to render endings ambiguous, Magny cites at least four examples in a highly interesting reflection prompted by Balzac's refusal to "mettre un point final" [put a full stop] to *Les secrets de la princesse de Cadignan.* This authentic reaction of one excellent reader of the story is certainly a fair indication of its problematic closure, which is not necessarily the obvious one.

The conquest of the virtuous author and genius Daniel d'Arthez by the very notorious and very impoverished princess, premeditated at length and executed as only this Balzacian *grande dame* can do it, finishes in the joint fall of the text and of the nobly chaste d'Arthez. Marking both the end of the plot and the start of the closure, this fall leads to the critical final scene and situates the last paragraph:

> Depuis ce jour, il n'a plus été question de la princesse de Cadignan, ni de

d'Arthez. La princesse a hérité de sa mère quelque fortune, elle passe tous les étés à Genève dans une villa avec le grand écrivain, et revient pour quelques mois d'hiver à Paris. D'Arthez ne se montre qu'à la Chambre. Enfin, ses publications sont devenues excessivement rares. Est-ce un dénouement? Oui, pour les gens d'esprit; non, pour ceux qui veulent tout savoir. (6: 1004-5)

[From this day on, there was no further mention of the princesse de Cadignan or of d'Arthez. The princess has inherited some fortune from her mother; she spends every summer in a villa with the great writer in Geneva, and comes back to Paris for a few months in winter. D'Arthez shows himself only in the Chamber. Lastly, his publications have become excessively rare. Is this a dénouement? Yes, for intelligent people; no, for those who want to know everything.]

Invalidating all other signs of finality, the final question and answer undermine the reader's certainty about the ultimate sense of the story and the concept of dénouement itself. But Balzac added those two sentences only in 1844 for the Furne edition—a striking example of a too strong ending made ambiguous for the final version. Until 1844 the final paragraph faithfully followed terminal conventions: the accounting of the characters' fates, the affective distance, and the switch to the present tense and even the perfect were all consonant with realistic closures. The inheritance compensating for the princess's penury is especially clotural. But with the last sentences Balzac redirects these closing summaries and subtly orients the story's meaning in a particular way.

In a simpler strategy for denying closure, *Un prince de la bohème* also puts the notion of a dénouement explicitly into question, in terms that may clarify what Balzac did here. The narrated story itself lacks any ending, and this failing is excused by the narrator in the closing frame: "Je ne crois pas aux dénouements . . . il faut en faire quelques-uns de beaux pour montrer que l'art est aussi fort que le hasard; mais, mon cher, on ne relit une œuvre que pour ses détails" [I don't believe in endings . . . you have to write some nice ones to show that art is as strong as chance; but, my dear fellow, one rereads a work only for its details] (7: 838). The two-part opposition between art and chance, on the one hand, and between dénouements and details, on the other, puts the parallel terms into obvious relation. Chance, the great novelist, produces details more fascinating than any artist's imagination; but it is to art that dénouements belong. Dénouements finish or close the unfinishable, although a great creator of closed worlds pretends not to believe in them. In the domain of "le hasard" Balzac elsewhere maintains the absence of dénouements, for, as he wrote in the postface to *La fille aux yeux d'or* in 1835, though the story is true "dans ses détails" [in its details], "rien ne se dénoue poétiquement dans la nature" [nothing winds up poetically in nature] (5: 1111), and the end to which Paquita came was an effect of art. To the details pertains the duty to be true: "Mais le roman ne serait rien si, dans cet auguste mensonge, il n'était pas vrai dans les détails" [But the novel, this august lie, would be nothing if it were not true in its details] (*Avant-propos* 1: 15).

In *Les secrets de la princesse de Cadignan,* the dénouement reserved for the "gens d'esprit" is also artistic. Rather than a banal clotural formula, the vague expression "être question de," to which only intelligent people will be able to restore meaning, signals a refusal to furnish the details. An artistic reading will see that only the text's silence protects this story from the risk of becoming another subject of dinner-table conversations, or another portrait to add to the princess's already bulging album of possible and probable lovers. Nor is there any reference to another volume of *La Comédie humaine* in which the curious reader would find the details of this new story (so frequent a practice elsewhere). In fact, in every other case where Diane and Daniel are mentioned, up to seven years after this story, there are no details. The final paragraph of the story offers only the symptoms of happiness; let the skillful readers conclude. Just what they must conclude concerns not only the princess, but the disclosure of d'Arthez's secrets as well, and this is why the closing summary is not a dénouement for those who want to know everything.

The silence of the ending, not unlike the women's refusal to discuss the lesson of *La Grande Bretèche* in *Autre étude de femme,* duplicates the program the princess opposes to Parisian society, refusing to answer its insistent questions: will she devour his fortune as she has her own (and that of her previous lovers)? Can he afford to abandon the literary and political scene he has only just conquered? Refusing to satisfy the curious reader, the text in its closure is the princess's accomplice. The fact that the ending is brought about by this (relative) silence allows the skillful reader to read into it the perfect love dreamed of by the princesse de Cadignan, thus making of such readers her accomplices as well. For the "gens d'esprit" are the good readers Balzac admires, and for whom there is a biological type for each sex: the "homme de génie" [man of genius] and the "femme supérieure" [superior woman]. (Among such good readers are the editors, who do not fail to cite a letter to Mme Hanska: "Des amants en Suisse, pour moi, c'est l'image du bonheur" [Lovers in Switzerland, for me, this is the image of happiness] [6: 1535].) But for those who want to know everything—the chroniclers of the *faubourgs,* the rumor-mongers and salon narrators—this story does not have a dénouement; it lacks closure.

Clearly, the most likely question such a society might ask is whether d'Arthez is happy at the price of being Diane's dupe. The typical reader will certainly assume so, like society, and the evident success of the princess's mendacious strategy, so finalistically summarized in the original closing paragraph, would seem to imply Daniel's total capitulation. Herein lies certainly the most troublesome paradox of the story, for the model of the good reader, in the story itself, is obviously the man frequently described as an "homme d'esprit," d'Arthez himself. Yet this penetrating hero of art, who has made a study of women in particular, "reads" so badly that he seems fooled by the princess's lies, throughout their lengthy exposition. To open his eyes Mme d'Espard invites him to dine with some of the most perspicacious of Balzac's men—Rastignac, Nathan, Maxime de Trailles, and Blondet among a host of other Balzacian personages—who gaily assassinate the character of Diane de Cadignan in fine detail. Can d'Arthez continue to be led by the nose by the arranged account the princess had given?

This account is an obvious referent of the secrets of the title, which are perverse (as in Rosolato's definition). By manipulating certain secrets, the princess obtains the secret of happiness, an art that pertains properly to her. A good Balzacian reader will do likewise and progress from the desire to know these secrets, like those who want to know everything, to the superior skill of those who have the secret of reading, like the "gens d'esprit." Shortly before the final paragraph, the dinner-party scene draws to a significantly ambiguous close in which the secret of the text lies hidden the better to reveal, and it is the express function of the two sentences added in 1844 to draw our attention to it and thus to d'Arthez's apparent lack of penetration, so as to require our active decoding.

What then are d'Arthez's secrets? His replies to Mme de Cadignan's moral assassins provoke unrestrained admiration from those members of the new society so prodigal of killing repartee. Nathan, for example, says "Il est aussi habile que difficile de venger une femme sans la défendre" [It is just as clever as it is difficult to avenge a woman without defending her] (6: 1003), a fine distinction replete with meaning, coming as it does from the wit, the social finesse, and expertise of a Nathan. It is in these terms that d'Arthez avenged the princess: "La princesse est une des héroïnes du parti légitimiste, n'est-ce pas un devoir pour tout homme de cœur de la protéger *quand même*? . . . Ce qu'elle a fait pour la cause de ses maîtres excuserait la plus folle vie" [The princess is one of the heroines of the legitimist party, is it not the duty of all courageous men to protect her *all the same*? . . . What she has done for the cause of her rulers would excuse the most extravagant life] (6: 1003). But to defend her, by denying false or true slander, would reveal that she has indeed fooled him, a social blunder so patent that none present would ignore such a delicious occasion for scorn. As Blondet says, "ne pas avoir pris la défense d'une femme aimée, faute qu'on attendait de vous, et qui eût fait triompher ce monde dévoré de jalousie contre les illustrations littéraires . . . Ah! permettez-moi de le dire, c'est le sublime de la politique privée" [not to have taken up the defense of a mistress, a fault that we expected from you, and which would have meant victory for this society consumed by jealousy against literary illustrations . . . Ah! Permit me to say it, that is the veritable sublime of private politics] (6: 1003). D'Arthez succeeds in taking the bait without falling into the trap. The distinction between "avenge" and "defend" is therefore of crucial connotation: it reveals Daniel's secrets in both senses. He wins his social medals by proving that he has penetrated the princess's secrets—namely, that she has adroitly altered the true facts—and that he will nevertheless keep his secret to himself: "Il joue serré" [He plays his cards close to his chest], says Nathan (6: 1004).

In short, after Mme d'Espard's dinner party, Daniel cannot hold to Diane's innocence, nor can he reveal his knowledge, and this is *his* secret, kept from the undiligent reader as it most certainly is from Diane de Cadignan. To all this Balzac supplied the clue in the last two sentences, enigmatic for those who do not know how to read them, but vital in preventing our possible misreading. Those who want to know everything will never arrive at this dénouement, for details are missing, and the text will remain an impenetrable secret. For the others, this closure depends on having the secret in the second sense. And it is such readers that Balzac hopes to find.

It is regrettable that not all of Balzac's readers of this story have been "gens d'esprit" as much as d'Arthez is. Anthony Pugh, for instance, in *Balzac's Recurring Characters,* summed up what is commonly said about this story, that the princess has successfully fooled the genial author and that Balzac's mocking irony extends to d'Arthez: "a character recently idolized for his noble qualities is here gently mocked for his lack of worldly wisdom" (240). This is the anticipated final meaning, the closure that, lacking the last two sentences, the reader would come to. For the actual meaning of the story to surface, the reader must make accommodation for those added sentences; we cannot just ignore them, no more than d'Arthez can ignore the attacks on his beautiful Diane. Pasco's fine analysis (*Balzacian Montage* 35–45) shows him to be a reader of wit, sensitivity, ingenuity, and cleverness (the four words by which Pasco translates *esprit*), as he proves that Balzac's unshakable belief in the "paradise of completely absorbing love" overturns every other consideration in the ending (44). In rereading himself, Balzac perhaps came to the realization that the noble character he modeled on himself would not emerge unscathed from what I have called the anticipated reading, and the final two sentences require that like Bianchon in *La Grande Bretèche* we ferret out the true story behind the façade. This means that the closure must include the complete knowledge of *his* secrets, not hers. In a word, I have claimed that the text is lying to those who want to know everything ("les curieux forcenés" [frenzied inquiring minds], in Magny's delightful phrase [234]), and that it will remain a cipher, perversely hiding the facts that it reveals without saying them, for any inattentive reader. By the simple addition of two sentences, Balzac addresses the final meaning of his story to the select few capable of appreciating it and leaves it unfinished for the others, who will be unable to decide if the Geneva idyll is to be taken as a reward or a punishment. Magny, no dupe herself, puts it finely: as d'Arthez is based on Balzac himself, "il ne saurait être question d'en faire une dupe" [it was out of the question to paint him as a dupe] (238).

Foreclosure
La Maison Nucingen

Published in 1838, *La Maison Nucingen* was revised more than most of the short texts of *La Comédie humaine*. Exceptionally, suppressions nearly equal additions throughout at least eight sets of proofs, in which, as Citron writes, money devours everything, beginning with love, as the "processus de modelage qui devait amener l'œuvre à sa perfection" [process of modeling that was to bring the work to its perfection] (6: 327) progresses. Essentially, the ending of the embedded story is lengthened while the frame shrinks after having been expanded. These terminal suppressions and additions are indeed capital for the interpretation of the story, but to say that they result in perfection is misleading at best.

The somewhat technical account of the intricate operations that enrich Nucingen and a few others, including Rastignac (see chapter 7), concluded in the first set of proofs with this "vérité pécuniaire" [pecuniary truth] delivered by Bixou, the primary narrator of the banker's "puff financier": "Le débiteur est plus fort que le créancier" [The debtor is stronger than the creditor] (6: 391). Starting with this maxim still quite close to the narrated events, at least three further statements added to the first set of proofs broaden the moral bearing of the new capitalism illustrated by the tale:

[1]—Les lois sont des toiles d'araignées à travers lesquelles passent les

grosses mouches et où restent les petites.—Où veux-tu donc en venir? dit Finot à Blondet.

[2]—Au gouvernement absolu, le seul où les entreprises de l'Esprit contre la Loi puissent être réprimées! Oui, l'Arbitraire sauve les peuples. . . . La Légalité tue la Société moderne. . . .

[3] [L]a royauté est éternelle: toute nation saine d'esprit y reviendra sous une forme ou sous une autre. (6: 391–92)

[1] ["Laws are the spider webs through which large flies pass and in which the little ones remain." "What are you getting at?" said Finot to Blondet.

[2] "Absolute government, the only one where the ventures of the Mind against the Law can be repressed! Yes, Arbitrariness saves the people. . . . Legality is killing modern Society." . . .

[3] "Royalty is eternal: every nation of a sane mind will return to it under one form or another."]

The first of these may still apply to Nucingen, the "banqueroutier frauduleux" [fraudulent bankrupt] who thumbs his nose at the laws, but the apology of an absolute government crosses the technical borders of the financial subject matter to enter the territory of political opinions, of which the last word seems to lie in the third formula. Reflections on capitalism may well have a necessary ending in the choice of a morally sound system of government. But this royalist conclusion is at the very least surprising; it confuses the issues, leaving the reader somewhat perplexed: Balzac the absolutist contests therein Balzac the advocate of the "société moderne" and the apologist of genius (*l'Esprit*).

Nor does the frame solve the contradiction. At the end of the original version Balzac did not even recall the presence of the narrator, the "secretary" next door, until he was correcting the first proofs, to which he added a sentence that has been retained in the final version: "Tiens, il y avait du monde à côté, dit Finot en nous entendant sortir" [Well well, there were people next door, said Finot, hearing us go out] (6: 392). In the following proofs, the closing portion of the frame continued to grow longer. On the third proof, Balzac appended to the sentence just quoted a direct criticism of journalism, which became the fourth additional closing formula: [4] "Le journalisme est l'opération d'un chimiste [l'alchimie de l'intelligence—fourth proof] dis-je à ma voisine étonnée, vous venez d'en voir les plus beaux *précipités!*" ["Journalism is the operation of a chemist [the alchemy of intelligence—fourth proof]," I said to my astonished companion, "you have just seen its most amazing *precipitates!*"] (6: 1307–8). Obviously, this moral concerning the four narrators is even farther from the events of the story itself than the first three. The operations of the "intimate conversations" (as this narrative is ironically called) between intelligent people are thus the subject of this last formula, rather than those of finance, and this attack against journalism is then developed at length on the fourth set of proofs, the narrator opposing it to the sentimentality of "le beau idéal" [the ideal of beauty], which produces both virtue and art.

Thus the closure of the longest version of the frame contrasted journalism (linked to *esprit*) and art (here tied to sentiment), so that anyone possessed of *esprit* could not be an artist. Denouncing intelligence and wit, Balzac clearly supported an art based on sentiment. This closure could be described as one that conveys a final meaning about the narrative style in this story but does nothing to clarify the ending of the narrated account. Closure was diverted from the muddy moralities of the narrated financial or political events to a value-laden pronouncement closer to Balzac's preoccupation with art. But on the fifth set of proofs, a major revision suppressed everything that followed the discreet departure of the characters of the frame, hence the entire attack against journalism as "l'alchimie de l'intelligence" and all the analysis of art as the "beau idéal." Instead, Balzac excused himself in a marginal note: "j'ai supprimé la copie de la précédente épreuve, il n'y avait pas à conclure, il faut laisser penser ce que j'y disais" [I deleted the text of the previous proof, it was not necessary to conclude, let the reader think what I was saying in it] (6: 1308). Opting thus for a silence heavy with significance, Balzac leaves the closure in the hands of the reader, refuses his own clotural power, and makes an esthetic choice for thinking, a necessity ("il faut") on which the ultimate meaning of the story rests. The closing section of a frame always establishes a critical distance from the inserted story, often proposes a sketch of an interpretation that orients our reading. In suppressing that frame, Balzac indicated that he no longer wanted unambiguously to dedicate his text to that particular interpretation and chose instead to rest on the contradictory ethics pronounced mostly by Blondet, a journalist. As a result, the end remains suspended, with competing results. The utter silence of the erstwhile speechifying "secretary" leaves only a trace: "Il y a toujours du monde à côté, répondit Bixiou, qui devait être aviné" ["There are always people next door," replied Bixiou, who must have been drunk] (6: 392, last sentence in the final version), an indirect allusion to the critic.

And the critic does indeed run the risk of always being "à côté" or beside the point, for it is impossible to arrive at a final truth for this novella as it stands. Is it an apology of modern society or of royalty? of legality or of "l'Arbitraire"? of the "Esprit" or of law? of the fat "flies" or the little ones? All efforts to come down on one side or the other fail. Magny finds that the end is lost among the inebriated remarks of the narrators; *La Maison Nucingen* "ne conclut pas du tout" [does not conclude at all] (235). Or, as Barbéris writes, though it is true that "dès 1831, Balzac s'affirme *royaliste*" [as early as 1831, Balzac asserts he is a *royalist*], there is also in this story "quelque chose qu'il est impossible de mobiliser ou de récupérer pour un finalisme" [something that is impossible to call up or retrieve for a finality] (*Une mythologie réaliste* 203, 231). What is more, it is highly doubtful that the critic would think exactly what Balzac said in the development he suppressed, since nothing in the morals of the story predicts the new direction of his thoughts. Though debate on politics may well grow out of considerations of finance, by what pathways do politics lead to art and intelligence? The artistic critic capable of following Balzac in this itinerary to the suppressed ending would have to superpose the laws of finance and those of narrative to recover that final thought, but would fall inevitably into the category of the *esprit* rather than the *sentiment*. The cynical intelligence that pervades the tale does indeed merit the moral on journalism (and one can find Balzac's opinion on it in other places, for instance in prefaces to first editions such as the one to *Illusions perdues*), so that the suppressed moral was an appropriate closure, at least at some time. Why then did Balzac go without saying it? No doubt to prolong the reader's reflection on the story, to make us reread the last paragraphs and seek their ultimate development, to interrogate the text.

In sum, there is no settled sense here, in part because the unusual suppressions brought foreclosure rather than closure, in part because the morals themselves are a reflection of the sliding axiology of regimes in Balzac in general, for a major threat to closure here is the difficulty of assigning a sure Balzacian value to the various modes of government between 1789 and 1838, when the story was written. The several added morals are the semiotic index of the competing ideologies that can claim to have value in a created world, but so much is thrown into the pot that no unique flavor survives. The task of closure, explicitly assigned to the "gens d'esprit" in *Les secrets de la princesse de Cadignan,* is here given to the "monde à côté," the critic who will eventually and necessarily conclude. Though these strategies are similar, and remarkably so, the subversion of the realistic closure in *La Maison Nucingen* has a different effect. Closure is simply made unrecognizable. I claimed that realistic closure goes without saying; here is a case where the author literally went without saying, and as a result the story lacks the usual closure.

A Pensive Text
Honorine

Maurice de l'Hostal, the French consul at Genoa, recounts the story of comte Octave, whose wife Honorine ran away with a lover, was abandoned, and lived for nine years as a simple worker under the secret and efficacious protection of her husband. Maurice intercedes to reunite her with Octave, but in spite of the good will of both spouses, her memories of irresistible "voluptés" [sensual pleasures] (2: 581) and her cult of the ideal love (2: 592) make the marriage impossible. Honorine languishes and dies. For his part, a very different Octave confesses to Maurice that he has her death on his conscience and that he will himself die of remorse. The characters of the frame interpret Octave's remorse and conclude: "il pouvait rester des vertus à une femme après sa faute" [a woman who has fallen can still be virtuous] (2: 531).

The entire frame, opening and closing portions, was hastily added in February 1843 and required a major revision of the ending of the inserted story, which Balzac had written in three days at the end of December 1842. Where the definitive version is pessimistic, fatalistic, and tragic, the manuscript simply had a happy ending: the reunited couple lived in eternal happiness, and Octave had only to wish for Maurice a similar wife and an equal happiness. All disturbances laid to rest, the thoroughly wrapped-up closure returned the marriage to normality.

So dramatic a reversal in the dénouement would be interesting in itself, but it is all the more so because one can pinpoint the spot where the text bifurcates toward the new direction. The last paragraph in the manuscript consisted of this brief letter from Octave: "Maurice, je suis heureux, ce mot vous est dû, sans quoi vous pourriez croire que je ne sais pas apprécier votre générosité. J'espère que Dieu, dans sa clémence, aura fait deux femmes semblables et que vous saurez trouver la seconde. Ai-je besoin de vous dire que je suis tout à vous" [Maurice, I am happy. I owe you this note, without which you might think that I do not know how to appreciate your generosity. I hope that God, in his clemency, will have made two identical women and that you will know how to find the second one. Do I need to tell you that I am yours faithfully] (2: 1439). The letter is short, for there is never very much to say when a couple has found happiness, which does not suffer narration. But in the definitive version it is precisely at the start of this letter from Octave that the dénouement bifurcates toward the tragic ending, confirming that happiness cannot be recounted nor accounted for: "Mon cher Maurice, si j'étais heureux je ne vous écrirais point; mais j'ai recommencé une autre vie de douleur" [My dear Maurice, if I were happy I would not be writing to you; but I have begun another life of suffering] (2: 590). And this new ending goes on for nearly three pages. In the different lengths of the two letters, in the change from "je suis heureux, ce mot vous est dû" to "si j'étais heureux je ne vous écrirais point," I find the most striking formal proof that a well wrapped-up ending supports no commentary, just as *La Grande Bretèche* brought closure to the intimate after-dinner conversation. Quite to the contrary, the addition of the frame entailed the reformulation of this letter as well as a last letter from Honorine to Maurice and a visit by Octave to Maurice. While the letter from Octave recounts the enduring incompatibility between husband and wife, the letter from Honorine describes the courage she deploys in order to make her husband think she is happy: "Déchirée, je souris!" [Torn to pieces, I smile!] (2: 593); "Je suis comédienne avec mon âme, et voilà peut-être pourquoi je meurs! J'enferme le chagrin avec tant de soin qu'il n'en paraît rien au dehors, il faut bien qu'il ronge quelque chose, il s'attaque à ma vie" [I am playing a part with my soul, and perhaps that is why I am dying! I shut up the grief with such care that it cannot be seen from outside; it has to gnaw at something; it is attacking my life] (2: 594). The discreet allusions to the cause of this death are to be completed by comparing it to Mme de Mortsauf's in *Le lys dans la vallée*. These letters stand in counterpoise. As for Octave's ambiguous explanation to Maurice after Honorine's death, it largely proves that there are still things to be said, and that one must interpret the meanings hidden in his words, or veiled by his silences, which are marked in the text by ellipses:

> Dans l'intérêt de la nature humaine, ne faudrait-il pas rechercher quelle est cette irrésistible puissance qui nous fait sacrifier au plus fugitif de tous les plaisirs, et malgré notre raison, une divine créature? . . . J'ai, dans ma conscience, entendu des cris. Honorine n'a pas crié seule. Et j'ai voulu! . . . Je suis dévoré de remords! Je mourais rue Payenne [his home] des plaisirs que je n'avais pas; je mourrai en Italie [having gone there to seek distractions] des plaisirs que j'ai goûtés! . . . D'où vient le désaccord entre deux natures également nobles, j'ose le dire? (2: 595; ellipses in the text)

> [In the interest of human nature, shouldn't we seek to know what this irresistible power is that makes us sacrifice a divine creature to the most fugitive of all pleasures, in spite of our reason? . . . I heard cries in my conscience. Honorine did not cry out alone. And I wanted to! . . . I am devoured by remorse! I was dying on the rue Payenne [his home] of the pleasures that I did not have; I will die in Italy [having gone there to seek distractions] of

the pleasures that I have tasted! . . . Whence comes this misunderstanding between two equally noble natures, if I may say so?]

By completing the text at each lacuna, the operation of reading will make it clear that the misunderstanding is of a sexual nature and that the count has forced his wife. And yet Octave too is a man of honor, a noble soul, an "être exceptionnel" [exceptional being]. The ending of the text maintains at the same time the grandeur of these equally noble souls and Honorine's inability to live with Octave—the impossible contradiction that turns this novella into an exceptional story. The dramatic change of outcome has the effect of freezing the text in that impossible contradiction. And the new frame extends the tragic dénouement to Maurice.

The consul Maurice had sent his wife away before recounting Honorine's story, for he had chastely played in it the role of the lover-friend and did not want his wife to know. Unfortunately, his wife has listened, and her name is . . . Onorina! But the frame recuperates this tragedy to prove that virtue can be found in a fallen woman, that one should honor Honorine and the "belles âmes" [beautiful souls] like her, and that "le mariage, avec un amour de cœur chez les deux époux, ce serait le Paradis" [a marriage with heartfelt love in both the spouses would be Paradise] (2: 596). In the face of these powerful values the possibility of a happy marriage must fall, as even the narrator loses his usual impunity.

The last sentence leaves the text in suspension: "Il se trouve donc encore de grandes âmes dans ce siècle! dit Camille Maupin qui demeura pensive, appuyée au quai, pendant quelques instants" ["So there are still great souls in this world!" said Camille Maupin, who remained pensive for a few moments, leaning on the pier] (2: 597). As Barthes said of *Sarrasine,* pensiveness has the structural function of infinite opening (*S/Z* 222–23). Lacunary but proof of recovered fullness, Camille Maupin's pensiveness equals that of the creator before his creation at the moment when it is necessary to bring it to an end. It is the moment when the author wonders in fact what he had meant to say, to what ending he had meant to come. (One might also explain the note on the fifth proof of *La Maison Nucingen* in such a way.) The silence that follows the end of a text is that of reading, in which that thinking will take place.

But what is one to think? If it is true, as the editor thinks, that the original version with the happy ending was intended as an indirect message to Mme Hanska, gently reminding her that true love can survive in a marriage, and even after "la faute de la femme" [the woman's misconduct], the pessimistic definitive ending is appropriated to serve the final truth pronounced by the author Camille Maupin ("Il se trouve donc encore de grandes âmes dans ce siècle!"), in which it is permitted to see Balzac preferring greatness of soul to the fugitive pleasures he has already enjoyed. Sacrificing the pleasure of a happy ending to the superior finality of sustaining greatness in exceptional souls, and artists in particular, the work of the text reproduces a movement of withdrawal from too neatly wrapped-up conclusions; a happy ending was truly unthinkable, given these values. (And a third possible outcome, perhaps more common yet, has been avoided by the same recourse to pensiveness: the edifying moral lesson of the repentant adulteress divinely punished.) A well-closed and cloturé ending leaves few traces; likewise, pleasures that one has enjoyed kill off the narrative, whereas pensiveness prolongs the reader's interest. There would be little critics could write about this story if Balzac had not added the frame. Pensiveness then is yet another strategy for leaving behind an ambiguous meaning, one that maintains the impossible contradiction of noble souls and marriage. A pensive reader will reflect on the refusal of a romantic norm in favor of an artistic closure that exists only for the "gens d'esprit" capable of reflection, and that denies pleasures even to—especially to—those who narrate.

Composition builds to a closed effect, but closure can be undermined to good effect as well. Like Camille Maupin in the final words of *Honorine,* the reader disassembles the composition in the act of analysis, only to put it together again, but differently. Inherent in the project to write the history of French society in its entirety is the recognition of a powerful sense of closure in the world, for in the belief that one day the edifice will be finished, repeated in several prefaces, in correspondences, and in the *Avant-propos,* there lies the certainty that there are conclusions, if not dénouements, to which one can aspire, and in which all the constituent parts will participate, even those with problematic closures. The illusory project, for it is of necessity unrealizable, is as lacking in dénouement as are these stories for "those who want to know everything."

21

Conclusion
Balzac's Invention of Realism

> Souvent la tête d'un drame est très éloignée de sa queue.
> [The head of a drama is often quite distant from its tail.]
> (4: 962)

Balzac was writing in what Dominique Rabaté has called the "age of happy metonymy" (48). It was a time when discourse was confident of its power to call forth, develop, and expand narrative to the extent of imagining that it might recreate a whole from a mere fragment.[1] For Balzac this notion validates the claim that *La Comédie humaine* contains the whole of French society of the time in its scope; "happy metonymy" grounds Balzacian realism. And if metonymy has the good hand, it is because Balzac conceives of causality as justified by bringing ends out of origins, notes Rabaté. Balzac's zoological and archeological models lay scientific foundations for the signifying chain of narrative matter that will conclude in a "triumphant metonymy" (Rabaté 49): "L'écrivain, comme l'archéologue ou le naturaliste, sait lire, à partir d'une trace, le processus entier; il fait se déplier, devant son lecteur ébahi, l'intégralité du caché, de l'enfoui. . . . Il n'empêche [contra Dällenbach] que c'est bien cette idéologie qui permet au romancier de bâtir l'édifice totalisant de *La Comédie humaine*" [The writer, like the archeologist or the naturalist, knows how to read the entire process from a single trace;

---

1. Dällenbach proposes to reread Balzac "en tant qu'ensemble bricolé et pluriel visant à la totalité sur le mode du fragment" [as a pluralistic ensemble cobbled together, aiming for totality by way of the fragment] (*La canne* 60).

for his astounded reader he unfolds an integral vision of what is hidden or buried.... Yet it is indeed [contra Dällenbach] this ideology that allows the novelist to build the totalizing edifice of *La Comédie humaine*] (49). Happy metonymy, Rabaté adds, rests on the writer's belief in the totality of his transmission: "Chez Balzac, l'opacité première du réel oblige justement l'écrivain à percer les apparences, à se faire déchiffreur. Si l'artiste est visionnaire, c'est par ce talent, et pourrait-on dire cet héroïsme herméneutique" [For Balzac, it is precisely the primary opacity of the real that obliges the writer to see beyond appearances, to turn himself into a decipherer. This talent—one could almost say this hermeneutic heroism—is what makes the artist a visionary] (51–52).

All this well describes the standard assessment of Balzacian realism, including perhaps the author's own, but the interpretive reader, while acknowledging this age of happy metonymy, seeks nuances to avoid a naive apprehension of the idea of realism. Naive realism holds that there is a reality "out there" that Balzac's text does a good job of reflecting in the mirrors of his novels. The reading I constantly prefer takes realism to be the creation of reality, where the prose is not the translation of a pre-existing reality but the experience of that reality itself. As Starobinski wrote in 1967: "l'écriture n'est pas le truchement douteux de l'expérience intérieure, elle est l'expérience même" [writing is not the dubious translation of intimate experience, it is this experience itself], in a formulation that applies equally well to the creativity of the novelist and the activity of the critic (18). At the end of the trajectory I have taken among Balzacian conceptions, I would like to connect these important questions of realism to the rhetoric of the Prime Movers.

The Rhetoric of Realism

> The nineteenth century, as we know it, is largely an invention of Balzac.
> —Oscar Wilde

I have asked in this study why people say that Balzac is a realistic author, that he represents the standard of realism. What actually constitutes the realism we call Balzacian?

A good place to begin to answer is the well-known passage about Cuvier in *La peau de chagrin,* about the famous bleached bones: "notre immortel naturaliste a reconstruit des mondes avec des os blanchis, a rebâti comme Cadmus des cités avec des dents, a repeuplé mille forêts de tous les mystères de la zoologie avec quelques fragments de houille, a retrouvé des populations de géants dans le pied d'un mammouth" [our immortal naturalist reconstructed worlds out of bleached bones, rebuilt cities out of teeth as Cadmus did, repopulated a thousand forests with all the mysteries of zoology from a few fragments of coal, found populations of giants in the foot of a mammoth] (10: 75). The hymn to creation that this famous passage intones prepares the mysterious Sabbath that Raphaël de Valentin is prey to an instant later, but it applies just as immediately to the creative force of Balzac's realism. Cuvier is invoked to give scientific validity to the concept; like him, Balzac reconstructed worlds out of the mere bones, teeth, or fragments of coal that are his words. Those elements were ready to hand; the "mœurs françaises" gave Balzac the gift of an enormous variety of types, dramas, thought, and movement. In France, "tout s'y dit, tout s'y pense, tout s'y fait" [everything can be said, everything can be thought, everything can be done] (preface to *Une fille d'Ève* 2: 264). It took a genius to create the signifying structure that would give life to those elements. A voice cries "Voyez!" and "Soudain les marbres s'animalisent, la mort se vivifie, le monde se déroule!" [Look! Suddenly the marble turns animal, death comes to life, the world unfolds!] (10: 75). Balzacian realism builds an entire population by describing single representatives.

A similar voice in the preface to *La peau de chagrin* asks, rhetorically, in a sentence that remains without answer but that Balzac's opus resoundingly assents to, "Les hommes ont-ils le pouvoir de faire venir l'univers dans leur cerveau, ou leur cerveau est-il un talisman avec lequel ils abolissent les lois du temps et de l'espace?" [Do men have the power to bring the universe into being in their minds, or are their minds the talisman with which they abolish the laws of time and space?] (10: 53). In spite of the balanced syntax, this is not an either-or alternative, for Balzac. If Balzac creates realism it is because he is fully invested in both principles. "Faire venir l'univers dans leur cerveau" points to the vast accumulation of real and real-like facts, people, cities, houses, furniture, events, and all the myriad data that constitute the raw material on which the brain as talisman works its creative energies by placing them into a system and a structure that abolish "les lois du temps et de l'espace." The talisman enables the writing of realism; the power to conceive of the materials of this realism provides the matter of the writing. On the one hand the *expression*, on the other the *observation* (10: 52); both the ability to do and to make—the verb *faire* from Latin *faber*—and the ability to conceive and to give life to what is made and done. The duality of the structure is ineluctable in *La Comédie humaine,* from the moment Balzac imagined the possibility of creating a society that informs in every particular about real society. "La réunion des deux puissances fait l'homme complet" [the union of the two powers makes man complete], the preface also says—and the key word *complete* is never insignificant in Balzac (10: 52)—but "l'homme de génie" [the man of genius] (10: 53) alone possesses as well the visionary possibility of *inventing* the real instead of or in addition to *observing* the real, the voice of the preface says.

Cuvier was a baron. Closer to the other end of the production of *La Comédie humaine,* in 1845, Balzac published a satirical article, "Entre Savants," in which a character called baron Total represents the analytical view. Baron Total is a believer in absolute divisions, which means he is an analyst whose total intellectual effort is dedicated to explaining the "phénomènes de l'animalité, et conséquemment de la terre" [phenomena of animality and consequently of the planet] (12: 525). In spite of the satire and the tone of persiflage of this article, quite the opposite of the tone in both the preface and the text of *La peau de chagrin,* what has remained the same since 1831 is the admiration for the analytical genius whose vision embraced the entire planet. Writing in 1833, in *Théorie de la démarche,* Balzac had again raised the analytical to the highest rank: "L'observateur est incontestablement homme de génie au premier chef. Toutes les inventions humaines procèdent d'une observation analytique dans laquelle l'esprit procède avec une incroyable rapidité d'aperçus" [The observer is incontestably a man of genius of the highest order. All human inventions come from an analytical observation in which the mind proceeds with an incredible rapidity of perceptions] (12: 276). Geniuses like Cuvier, mentioned in this paragraph, are the ones who see both cause and effect and who have induced the cause from the effect.

Such is, for Balzac, the ability of the writer. It was in the novel of 1831 that Balzac developed the concept of the visionary creator of reality who possesses the phenomenon of second sight that devolves only to the poet and writer and allows them to find truth: "C'est une sorte de seconde vue qui leur permet de deviner la vérité dans toutes les situations possibles; ou, mieux encore, je ne sais quelle puissance qui les transporte là où ils doivent, où ils veulent être. Ils inventent le vrai, par analogie, ou voient l'objet à décrire, soit que l'objet vienne à eux, soit qu'ils aillent eux-mêmes vers l'objet" [It is a sort of second sight that allows them to guess the truth in all possible situations; or, better yet, some unknown power that transports them to the place where they must be, where they want to be. They invent the true by analogy, or see the object to be described, whether the object comes to them or they go themselves toward the object] (10: 52).[2]

2. Balzac's "second sight" has been very well studied in the critical literature; see Arlette Michel's *Le réel et la beauté,* chapter 2.

A man of genius such as these texts proclaim was Etienne Geoffroy Saint-Hilaire, whose revision of the Cuvier position in the field of zoology coupled with Balzac's Cuvierism took Balzac's realism to new richness and uniqueness by adding the fertile concept of the *unity of composition*. Balzac praises the "immense progress" to which Geoffroy Saint-Hilaire brought natural science (3: 823). The debate between the two naturalists was a dramatic conflict in the zoological world, but in Balzac's it is more appropriate to speak of a complementary pairing: what I am calling the Cuvier tendency in *La Comédie humaine* takes up the analytical observation of the facts into the unity of composition posited by Geoffroy Saint-Hilaire. The myriad details of real life function together with the operators that put them into action to produce the Balzacian concept of realism. These ideas are exposed in the *Avant-propos*. Françoise Gaillard's analysis of the text in her article "La science: Modèle ou vérité," as published in *Balzac: L'invention du roman,* remains the best and most lucid exposition of this essential Balzacian duality, which opposes *matière* and *esprit* and the synthetic and the analytic and creates the necessary *liaison* and *système* to organize the vast real matter of existence, according to the method of observation and expression that makes the raw material into what we recognize as realism in the novel.

Geoffroy Saint-Hilaire's concept of the unity of composition holds that "L'organisme des animaux est soumis à un plan général, modifié dans quelques points seulement pour différencier les espèces" [The animal organism is subject to a general model, modified only in a few points to differentiate species] which he called the "principe d'unité typéale" [principle of the unity of type] (quoted by Allem 302). The principle possesses operative functionality: by explaining, interpreting, and putting into operation a set of facts, materials, or data, the man of genius realizes the creation of a composition of reality. No genius is complete without that ability to put into a system the facts it observes. Balzac put it this way in his preface to *Le Cabinet des Antiques:* "Cette manière de procéder doit être celle d'un historien des mœurs: sa tâche consiste à fondre les faits analogues dans un seul tableau, n'est-il pas tenu de donner plutôt l'esprit que la lettre des événements, il les synthétise" [This way of proceeding should be the one the moral historian uses. His task consists in blending analogous facts into a single picture. Isn't it his job to provide the spirit rather than the letter of events? He synthesizes them] (4: 962). And in the preface to *Une fille d'Ève,* the same double task is expressed in quasi-chemical terms: "Aussi l'affaire de l'auteur est-elle principalement d'arriver à la synthèse par l'analyse, de dépeindre et de rassembler les éléments de notre vie, de poser des thèmes et de les prouver tout ensemble, de tracer enfin l'immense physionomie d'un siècle en en peignant les principaux personnages" [The author's business is therefore principally to arrive at synthesis through analysis, to depict and to assemble the elements of our lives, to propose themes and prove them at the same time, finally to trace the immense physiognomy of a century by portraying its principal characters] (2: 267–68).

The two tendencies we can call "Cuvier" and "Geoffroy Saint-Hilaire," in shorthand fashion, explain the tension inherent in the Balzacian notion of *types,* one of the most important rhetorical devices in *La Comédie humaine.* It is the variety of types that allows Balzac to be so inventive in comparison to the paltry realisms that existed before him, as he claims in the preface to *Une fille d'Ève.* In the past, novels were constructed from simple elements—conflicts of class, kings, queens, and peasants, fixed characters like the merchant. Peasants were slaves, nobles were entirely free. Balzac credits *l'Égalité* with producing infinite nuances: "Jadis, la caste donnait à chacun une physionomie qui dominait l'individu; aujourd'hui, l'individu ne tient sa physionomie que de lui-même" [In the past, a caste gave each person a physiognomy that had dominance over the individual; today the individual takes his physiognomy entirely from himself] (2: 263). Such a notion of types creates a personal or psychological realism; the character types serve as the skeletons on which the body of *La Comédie humaine* is molded. Familiar examples are Gobseck the usurer; Grandet the miser; Rastignac the young malleable hero, who is also "adroit, hardi" [adroit, bold] (4: 960); Lucien de Rubempré the even younger and more malleable hero; the female heart in *Une fille d'Ève* or *Les secrets de la princesse de Cadignan;* male desire with Vautrin, among many others. Juliette Grange provides a different list of examples: "Dans la mesure où il définit des figures exemplaires, ce que Balzac appelle des types, le roman fabrique une réalité sociale à partir de la fiction. Parmi bien d'autres, la Femme de Trente ans, l'Artiste, l'Épicier, le Concierge, Paris, la Ville de Province, l'Ambition, l'Amour, l'Avarice" [To the extent that it defines exemplary figures, what Balzac calls types, the novel fabricates a social reality on the basis of fiction. Among many others, the Woman of Thirty, the Artist, the Grocer, the Concierge, Paris, the Provincial City, Ambition, Love, Avarice] (37). More abstractly, Arlette Michel makes the connection of the type to the imaginary: the type is "l'équivalent poétique et beau parce qu'il porte en lui à la fois la grandeur attachée à la généralité et la singularité propre à l'imaginaire" [the poetic, beautiful equivalent because it contains within itself both the grandeur of generalities and the singularity of the imaginary] (*Le réel* 39).

From the type to the imaginary creation of reality, the mechanism serves the realistic narrative.

Not just the readily identifiable and denominated social types, but scores of other characters serve Balzac's demonstration of the real world. César Birotteau's story is particular to him and he serves not just as the type of the *banqueroutier,* but more importantly as the entry into the Balzacian chronotope of the real story of bankruptcy. In *Splendeurs et misères des courtisanes,* "Corentin, Peyrade et Contenson représentent l'espionnage sous ses trois faces, comme Vautrin est à lui seul toute la corruption et toute la criminalité" [Corentin, Peyrade, and Contenson represent espionage in its three forms, just as Vautrin all by himself represents all corruption and all criminality], Balzac writes in his preface (6: 426). The ability of the type to represent gives it operative functionality and drives the writing toward its ultimate goal of completion; the type approaches totality by giving a single form to a diverse accumulation; it locates the uniqueness of the diversity and the mass. Types, moreover, are not limited to people, as there are cities, streets, dwellings, furnishings, and clothing that function as types as well. In *Le curé de village,* for example, Véronique Sauviat's home has archeological significance: it is the type of the dwelling that produced a character like Véronique.

But characters evolve, and so do cities, streets, and other things, so that the very definition of the type in Balzac is determined by the tension between a fixist view and an evolutionary one. The erstwhile wife of the colonel Chabert, Rose, now comtesse de Ferraud, is both a fixed type, from her origins as a *fille* working the alleys at the Palais Royal, and an evolved one, a countess after the return of the Bourbons, representing not only both positions in society, for women, but also the entire process by which such a change could occur: by virtue of her marriage to Chabert, she rose to the *noblesse d'Empire,* thence to marriage to a *ci-devant* count, Ferraud, thus encapsulating in her personal history an entire history of regime changes and all that stemmed from them, between the Revolution and the Restoration, not forgetting Napoleon. Yet Chabert's return threatens to expose her "real self," her origins as a lower-class woman, and that threat is a powerful motor of the plot. Balzac's types resemble the real all the more for displaying this inherent tension and instability. As Silvestre de Sacy wrote, "Les variations du type humain, matière romanesque inépuisable, soulignent l'unité et la constance du plan sur lequel est construit l'homme" [The variations of the human type, an inexhaustible material for the novel, underscore the unity and the constancy of the model on which the human being is constructed] (No. 1018, 304). That pairing of variation and unity, of evolution and fixism, characterizes Balzacian realism.

La Comédie humaine gives special importance to genealogies, which can be called the creation of types on the level of families. Their complexity is legendary; they represent the messy realities of real life; and, like types, they have operative functionality. Genealogies stack the deck against the individual; I studied three such examples in *Ursule Mirouët, La Rabouilleuse,* and *Pierrette*. Jean-Hervé Donnard speaks of "envahissement familial" [invasion by families] (345) with *Les paysans* in mind (and Thierry Bodin produced one of the best studies of genealogies in an article about that late novel). Balzac does not mince his words, in this as in much else: the genealogy in *Les paysans* is a "despotique cousinage bourgeois" [despotic bourgeois cousinage] (9: 186) or a "népotisme bourgeois" (9: 187), and in *Ursule Mirouët* he compares the heirs of Dr. Minoret to "des chiens à la curée" [dogs going for quarry] (3: 925).

To create an entire family structure is for Balzac to invent the basis for a story to be told. In addition to representing the multiple relations within families, genealogies play a structural role in the plots and in character development, exhibiting instabilities such as conflict, defects, excess, and deceit. In all cases, they function as schematic representations of the movemented relation of love to money—even if they often point to the failures of love or family to overcome the power of attraction that money possesses. The complexities of the money relations mirror the complexities of the genealogies; in *La Rabouilleuse,* the failed family ties correspond to the harmful actions occurring in the name of money; in *Ursule Mirouët,* love arises where there is no genealogical relation, in the coterie embracing Ursule, her tutor, and the mini society of chosen friends surrounding them. As for *Pierrette,* the branches of the genealogy stemming from the heroine's grandmother represent love, while anything to do with the Rogron brother and sister stands for money. Among the possible semiotic structures, these family structures based on Love and Money are powerful forces in the rhetoric of realism.

No conception of Balzac's reinvention of realism is possible without taking into account the basic strategy that characterizes the Balzacian narrator. Balzac is the great explicator. In the 1960s, Gérard Genette had spoken of "le démon explicatif, chez Balzac" [Balzac's explicating demon] ("Vraisemblance" 79). Jacques Neefs remarks that the analytical, in *La Comédie humaine,* is not limited to the *Études analytiques* but is also "une qualité de visée, de 'coup d'œil,' répandue dans l'ensemble du narratif balzacien" [a quality of purpose, of a "gaze," widespread throughout the Balzacian narrative world], operating wherever a description or an identification is needed ("Les trois étages" 154). Isabelle Tournier's article about the use of the expression "voici pourquoi" [here's why], which she inventoried using Frantext, identified nine functions: for instance, to start a narrative, show the narrator's control, stimulate interest, simulate orality, regulate the speed or eliminate the unnecessary, and most important for this discussion, operate verisimilitude by justifying the narration. I much prefer to speak of *explications nécessaires* to designate this tic of Balzacian narrative style which seeks to reveal, display, and explain what he knows and serves to justify the very existence of the narrative at all. For the narrative tells us: not only will you understand this story better, after following Balzac through his necessary explication, but you will not understand it if you do not—hence the strength of the necessity to inform.

Not just an operator of verisimilitude by inscribing causality, the *explication nécessaire* is an operator of a more acute form of realism than had been known before. (I am well aware that one finds authorial interventions before Balzac—*Jacques le fataliste,* for instance, is rife with the author's interruptions—but it is the coupling of this device with the scientific grounding of *La Comédie humaine* that distinguishes Balzac's practice.) Before final corrections, *Splendeurs et misères des courtisanes* included a chapter titled "Explications nécessaires" (6: 595). A fine article by Claire Barel-Moisan and Aude Déruelle, "Balzac et la pragmatique: Narration et lois du discours," shows that the Grician "maxim of manner," the injunction to be clear, occupies an excessive part: "[La maxime de modalité] apparaît comme un véritable impératif, au service duquel les autres maximes vont être sacrifiées, sans que ce soit réciproque. Le narrateur transigera sur la pertinence et la quantité pour garantir une plus grande clarté, mais pas l'inverse" [The maxim of manner appears as a veritable imperative in the service of which the other maxims are sacrificed without there being any reciprocity: the narrator will compromise on relevance and quantity to guarantee greater clarity, but not the reverse] (308). The same Aude Déruelle in her book on digressions considers the *explications nécessaires* as an instrument of "vraisemblabilisation" (91), certainly a word that deserves mentioning for the sheer pleasure of its poetic resonances. She writes that Balzac's explications construct a thread that explains the linkages among events while also maintaining the thread visible to the reader. Everywhere, *M. de Balzac s'explique*—or his narrator does; our only task is to follow him as he takes us through the flashbacks, the family histories, the political exegeses, the anthropological sociologies, the hidden truths and passions of all sorts that ground the stories—and primarily the passions of love and of money.

On the habitual understanding of "the Balzacian novel" as a standard of realism, consider also Fredric Jameson's view. The premise is that Balzac stands for everything that is traditional about representation: "so that Balzac may stand for unenlightened representationality when you are concerned to bring out everything that is 'textual' and modern in Flaubert, but turns into something else when, with Roland Barthes in S/Z, you have decided to rewrite Balzac as Philippe Sollers, as sheer text and *écriture*" (18).[3] This stance is similar to Lucien Dällenbach's more nuanced and complete appreciation of the status of Balzacian realism in his two parallel articles published in *Poétique* in 1979 and 1980, "Du fragment au cosmos" and "Le tout en morceaux." Dällenbach compares the Balzac novel to the type of the Claude Simon novel in which there is no "commentaire explicatif," according to "Le tout en morceaux" (161). The Balzacian novel is one that explains.

Love and Money and the Rhetoric of Realism

It is my contention that all the necessary explanations, all the genealogies, all the types, ultimately lead us, in our analytical and synthetic reading, to the two Prime Movers of *La Comédie humaine,* the root causes of everything, which are Love and Money. As Michel Nathan writes about *Ursule Mirouët,* "L'argent et l'amour circulent selon les désirs du romancier catholique" [Money and love circulate according to the desires of the Catholic novelist] (95).

Jacques-David Ebguy, in a Deleuzian reading of the effect of prose, speaks of the neutrality of the Balzacian prose, the famous "objectivity" by which it is often classically categorized in opposition to the disruptions of the modern. (Barthes in *Le plaisir du texte* and reading Balzac in *S/Z* opposed in such a way the classic and the modern.) Neutral because it mixes all types of language and all registers, Balzacian prose, Ebguy writes, seems to philosophers transparent or "white," in the sense of combining all colors, which in the French term *blanc* also has resonances of blankness. It is this blankness that justifies the assimilation of money and prose (specifically, Balzacian prose): "L'argent circule, dépourvu de propriétés intrinsèques, et, pareil aux phrases balzaciennes envisagées isolément, ne prend de valeur que dans l'échange ou la composition" [Money circulates, stripped of intrinsic properties, and like Balzacian sentences taken in isolation, it gains value only in exchange or in

---

3. Jameson also names Balzac as a marker of the emergence of realism (104).

composition] ("Balzac" 133). Like money when it is used, the signs signify when placed in composition.

But circulating paper money, according to Prendergast's reading, indicates the emptiness of money as sign. Prendergast quotes Bonald who connected this danger to the potential harm of taking language as a system of conventional signs:

> La parole est donc, dans le commerce des pensées, ce que l'argent est dans le commerce des marchandises, expression réelle des valeurs parce qu'elle est valeur elle-même. Et nos sophistes veulent en faire un signe de convention, à peu près comme le papier-monnaie, signe sans valeur, qui désigne tout ce qu'on veut, et qui n'exprime rien, qu'autant qu'il peut être échangé contre l'argent, expression réelle de toutes les valeurs. (Bonald 1: 71)

> [Language, in the commerce of ideas, is therefore what real money is in the commerce of merchandise: the real expression of value because it is itself value. And yet our sophists want to make of language a conventional sign, somewhat like paper money, a sign without value, which designates whatever one wants and expresses nothing except to the extent to which it can be exchanged for real money, the real expression of all values.]

Bonald, who wished to maintain that language was given to humanity as a primitive law from which all others naturally flow, including everything that defines value, castigates the human being who would claim to have made language:

> Mais si l'homme, au contraire, a fait lui-même sa parole, il a fait sa pensée, il a fait sa loi, il a fait la société, il a tout fait; il peut tout détruire: et c'est avec raison que dans le même parti qui soutient que la parole est d'institution humaine, on regarde la société comme une convention arbitraire, et qu'on a dit: "Un peuple a toujours le droit de changer ses lois, même les meilleures." (1: 53)

> [But if, on the contrary, man made his own language, then he has also made his way of thinking, he has made the law, he has made society, he has made everything; he can destroy everything. And it is true that the same opinion that holds that language was instituted by humans sees society as an arbitrary convention and says: "A society always has the right to change its laws, even the best ones."]

But language *is* a system of conventional signs. As Hélène Gomart observes: "Il faut également mentionner au préalable une analogie qui, de fait encadre conceptuellement la réflexion sur les rapports de la littérature et de l'argent: de Foucault jusqu'à J.J. Goux, la circulation du sens serait analogue à la circulation de l'argent, les mots et la monnaie vivant sous le même régime du signe" [At the outset, one should also mention an analogy that conceptually frames reflection about the relationship between literature and money: from Foucault to J. J. Goux, the circulation of meaning has been described as analogous to the circulation of money; words and money live under the same regime of signs] (18). Money and speech are exposed to the risk of being empty, like the "fictive capital" Balzac speaks of in *Illusions perdues* (5: 595). Just as the edifices of money Balzac erects grow via verbal excretions, building capital by expanding the numbers, so his amassed signs—his semiosis, his execution—build the realistic world through verbal excess. The underlying danger for Balzac lies in this obsession for excess. "Balzac est devenu, parmi les romanciers, celui dont le réalisme est le plus complet peut-être parce qu'il ne cesse de réunir, dans la critique et dans l'amour, dans le comique et la tragédie, le dépassement extatique du réel, son exaltation et sa cruelle dérision" [Balzac among novelists is the one whose realism is the most complete, perhaps because he continually unites, in criticism and in love, in comedy and in tragedy, the ecstatic surpassing of the real with its exaltation and its cruel derision] (Michel, *Le réel* 12).

Balzac acts in spite of the emptiness of his fictive signs. And his action fills the signs.

Writing in 1839, a year of intense creative activity, and with the perception of the vastness he will give to his work brewing in his mind, Balzac proclaims what makes his invention of realism distinct from other writers: it is easy for any person to *conceive,* but few can *execute.* The relation between conception and execution is of the greatest significance in Balzac. This is how he puts it in the preface to *Le Cabinet des Antiques:*

> Si tous les auteurs ont des oreilles, il paraît que tous ne savant pas entendre, ou pour être plus exact, tous n'ont pas les mêmes facultés. Presque tous savent concevoir. Qui ne promène pas sept ou huit drames sur les boulevards en fumant son cigare? qui n'invente pas les plus belles comédies? qui, dans le sérail de son imagination, ne possède les plus beaux sujets? Mais entre ces

faciles conceptions et la production il est un abîme de travail, un monde de difficultés que peu d'esprits savent franchir. (4: 963)

[While all authors have ears, it seems that not all know how to hear, or to be more exact, they don't all have the same faculties. Almost all know how to conceive. Doesn't everyone parade seven or eight dramas along the boulevards while smoking his cigar? Doesn't everyone invent the most attractive comedies? Who doesn't possess the most beautiful subjects in the harem of his imagination? But between these facile conceptions and actual production, there is an abyss of work, a world of difficulties that few minds know how to traverse.]

When one is Balzac, plunged into the abyss of work, one's conceptions grow: "toutes les proportions ont été dépassées à l'exécution" [all the proportions have been surpassed in the execution] (4: 961). *Massimilla Doni*, the topic of which is art as execution, illustrates this excess, this abundance in its execution. The "trop grande abondance" of the three lethal creative passions of Love, Music, and Opium is expressed not only in the descriptions of the characters and their stories but also in Balzac's use throughout of highly figural language. As excessive abundance is the conceptual topic of the story, so its execution, which constitutes its forms of expression, represents abundance by imagery of excess. Capraja is speaking in *Massimilla Doni*:

Quand un artiste a le malheur d'être plein de la passion qu'il veut exprimer, il ne saurait la peindre, car il est la chose même au lieu d'en être l'image. L'art procède du cerveau et non du cœur. Quand votre sujet vous domine, vous en êtes l'esclave et non le maître.... Sentir trop vivement au moment où il s'agit d'exécuter, c'est l'insurrection des sens contre la faculté! (10: 613)

[When an artist has the misfortune of being full of the passion he wants to express, there is no way he is able to portray it, because he is the very thing itself rather than its image. Art arises in the brain, not in the heart. When your subject overpowers you, you are its slave, not its master.... To feel too excessively at the moment when execution is needed is the revolt of the senses against the faculties!]

In another novel where art is the topic, one finds a similar formulation of the conception–execution pair. A two-page passage in *La cousine Bette* gives us an extended metaphor of maternity (developing the literal meaning of conception) and child rearing to describe the sculptor Wenceslas's effort (or lack thereof), in which capitalized words abound:

> Wenceslas, né poète et rêveur, avait passé de la Conception à l'Exécution, en franchissant sans les mesurer les abîmes qui séparent ces deux hémisphères de l'Art. Penser, rêver, concevoir de belles œuvres, est une occupation délicieuse. ... L'œuvre apparaît alors dans la grâce de l'enfance, dans la joie folle de la génération. ... Telle est la Conception et ses plaisirs. ... Mais produire! mais accoucher! mais élever laborieusement l'enfant ... c'est l'Exécution et ses travaux. (7: 241–42)

> [Wenceslas, born a poet and a dreamer, had passed from Conception to Execution by traversing the abyss that separates these two hemispheres of Art, without measuring its extent. To reflect, to dream, to conceive beautiful works of art is a delicious occupation. ... The work appears then in its childlike grace, in the wild joy of generation. ... Such is Conception and its pleasures. ... But to produce, to give birth, to laboriously raise the child ... that is Execution and its travails.]

That this pair lies deep in the heart of Balzacian realism is evident in the fact that the whole system I am describing was present from the start, in 1831 in the preface to *La peau de chagrin*.

The relation of conception to execution is analogous to the relation of *semiosis* to *mimesis* underlying this study. In Balzac's novels, characteristically, the semiotic forms an alliance with the mimetic; language in and of itself symbolizes what the story will tell. *La Maison Nucingen* remains for me the shining example of this essential strategy, and I have given several other examples as well. My readings are often based on a simultaneous interpretation of narrated events and an attention to the language in which they are told, even when this relationship is not foregrounded.

The Balzacian text operates its realism by establishing this relationship. The work shows its semiotic hand, lets the reader know how its signs work; what makes the work come to us, what "operates" it, is the symbolic expression of its content in its forms; it works because there is a congruence of the semiosis with the mimesis. Stéphane Vachon observes that Balzac founded his project on "la révélation que la littérature porte en elle son pli le plus intime, sa capacité à se représenter elle-même" [the revelation that literature carries within it its most intimate fold, its capacity to represent itself] ("Balzac théoricien" 30). Jean Starobinski put this fundamental principle of narration in these terms: "Il n'est point d'œuvre moderne qui ne porte en elle l'indice ou la justification de sa propre venue au monde" [There is not a single modern work that does not carry within itself the indication or the justification of its own birth] (24), a principle which I detour slightly to assert that the *signs* create a semiotic structure that matches the mimetic content of *story*, which bears within its forms the *signs* of its coming to us, its birth.

To the pairs of conjoined terms and patterns I have been considering in this conclusion, I would add another duplet to close. This pair of terms also comes from the preface to *Le Cabinet des Antiques:* "Aucune tête humaine ne serait assez puissante pour inventer une aussi grande quantité de récits, n'est-ce donc pas déjà beaucoup que de pouvoir les amasser" [No human head would be powerful enough to invent so large a quantity of narratives; is it not therefore already a great deal to be able to amass them?] (4: 963). *Inventer* and *amasser* appear here as if they are mutually exclusive terms, and yet both are needed—and they must function together—to achieve the objectives of *La Comédie humaine.* Balzac claimed to write true stories and put those claims repeatedly into his prefaces; the assertion of "truth" or "reality" is a powerful ingredient in his invention of realism. The very vastness of the project, what Balzac amassed, provides evidence for the demonstration of the claim, realizing the assertion of reality. Yet Balzac seems to say that it is impossible for a human mind to invent so many stories: no inventor he. But who would take Balzac at his word? We are compelled to consider Balzac's head powerful enough to have invented, and not just amassed, such a great number of stories; and it is the vastness and the mass that so compel us, in spite of what he claims.

Bibliography

Balzac, Honoré de. *La Comédie humaine*, ed. Pierre-Georges Castex et al. Paris: Gallimard, 1976–81. All references to Balzac's *Comédie humaine*, except where noted, are to this edition and appear in the text as volume and page number in parentheses.

Allem, Maurice. Notes in *Ursule Mirouët* by Honoré de Balzac, 289–321. Paris: Garnier, 1952.
Alterton, Margaret. *Origins of Poe's Critical Theory*. Iowa City: University of Iowa Press, 1925.
Amar, Muriel. "Autour de 'La maison du Chat-qui-pelote': Essai de déchiffrage d'une enseigne." *L'Année Balzacienne* (1993): 141–55.
Ambrière-Fargeaud, Madeleine. Notes in *Ursule Mirouët* by Honoré de Balzac, 358–407. Paris: Gallimard [Folio], 1981.
Amossy, Ruth, and Elisheva Rosen. "'Melmoth réconcilié' ou la parodie du conte fantastique." *L'Année Balzacienne* (1978): 149–67.
Andréoli, Max. "Sublime et parodie dans les 'Contes artistes' de Balzac." *L'Année Balzacienne* (1994): 7–38.
———. "Sur le début d'un roman de Balzac, 'Une ténébreuse affaire.'" *L'Année Balzacienne* (1975): 89–123.
Balzac, Honoré de. *Lettres à Madame Hanska. 1832–1844*, ed. Roger Pierrot. 2 vols. Paris: Robert Laffont, Bouquins, 1990.
———. "Lettre à M. Ch. Nodier sur son article intitulé 'De la palingénésie humaine et de la résurrection.'" *Œuvres diverses*, ed. Pierre-Georges Castex et al., 2: 1203–16. Paris: Gallimard, 1996.
Bara, Olivier. Introduction to *Le père Goriot* by Honoré de Balzac, 5–23. Paris: La Bibliothèque Gallimard, 2000.

Barbéris, Pierre. *Balzac: une mythologie réaliste*. Paris: Larousse, 1971.

———. *Mythes balzaciens*. Paris: A. Colin, 1972.

———. Notes to *La femme de trente ans* by Honoré de Balzac, 347–71. Paris: Folio, 1977.

———. *Le père Goriot de Balzac: écriture, structures, significations*. Paris: Larousse, 1972.

Barel-Moisan, Claire, and Aude Déruelle. "Balzac et la pragmatique: Narration et lois du discours." In *Penser avec Balzac*, ed. José-Luis Diaz and Isabelle Tournier, 293–310. Saint-Cyr-sur-Loire: Christian Pirot, 2003.

Barnett, Louise K. "American Novelists and the 'Portrait of Beatrice Cenci.'" *The New England Quarterly* 53 (1980): 168–83.

Baron, Anne-Marie. *Balzac ou l'auguste mensonge*. Paris: Nathan, 1998.

———. *Balzac, ou les hiéroglyphes de l'imaginaire*. Paris: Champion, 2002.

———. *Le fils prodige. L'inconscient de La Comédie humaine*. Paris: Nathan, 1993.

Barthes, Roland. *Le plaisir du texte*. Paris: Seuil, 1973.

———. *S/Z*. Paris: Seuil, 1970.

Beaver, Harold, ed. *The Science Fiction of Edgar Allan Poe*. Harmondsworth: Penguin, 1976.

Behrendt, Stephen C. "Beatrice Cenci and the Tragic Myth of History." In *History and Myth: Essays on English Romantic Literature*, ed. Stephen C. Behrendt, 214–34. Detroit: Wayne State University Press, 1990.

Beizer, Janet. *Family Plots*. New Haven: Yale University Press, 1986.

Berlioz, Hector. *Mémoires*. http://hector.ucdavis.edu/Berlioz2003/Memoires/Mem51A1VL05.htm. 2 February 2002.

———. *The Memoirs of Hector Berlioz, member of the French Institute, including his travels in Italy, Germany, Russia, and England, 1803–1865*. Trans. and ed. David Cairns. New York: Norton, 1975.

Bersani, Leo. *Balzac to Beckett: Center and Circumference in French Fiction*. New York: Oxford University Press, 1970.

———. "Le réalisme et la peur du désir." *Poétique* 22 (1975): 177–95.

Berthier, Philippe. "Accoucher au masculin (Balzac: *Mémoires de deux jeunes mariées*)." In *Corps, littérature, société (1789–1900)*, ed. Jean-Marie Roulin, 293–305. Saint-Étienne: Presses de l'Université de Saint-Étienne, 2005.

———. "Le désir, le désert." In *Figures du fantasme, un parcours dix-neuviémiste*, 75–85. Toulouse: Presses Universitaires du Mirail, 1992.

———. "Frauenlieben und Leben (*Mémoires de deux jeunes mariées*)." In *L'érotique balzacienne*, ed. Lucienne Frappier-Mazur and Jean-Marie Roulin, 157–70. Paris: Société d'édition d'enseignement supérieur, 2001.

———. Notes to *La vieille fille. Le Cabinet des Antiques* by Honoré de Balzac, 355–80. Paris: Garnier-Flammarion, 1987.

Bodin, Thierry. "Généalogie de la médiocratie dans 'Les Paysans.'" *L'Année Balzacienne* (1978): 91–101.

Bonald, Louis-Gabriel-Ambroise, vicomte de. *Législation primitive, considérée dans le dernier temps par les seules lumières de la raison, suivie de divers traités et discours politiques; par L. G. A. de Bonald*. 3 vols. Paris: Chez Le Clere, 1802. [An XI]

Bordas, Éric. Introduction to *Sarrasine* by Honoré de Balzac, 7–18. Paris: Livre de Poche, 2001.

———. "Ne touchez pas le H de Natalie. Écritures du détournement suggestif chez Balzac: pratiques et effets d'une contre représentation." In *L'érotique balzacienne*, ed. Lucienne Frappier-Mazur and Jean-Marie Roulin, 23–34. Paris: Société d'édition d'enseignement supérieur, 2001.

Bouvier, René. *Balzac homme d'affaires*. Paris, 1930.

Brunel, Pierre. "Mythanalyse et mythocritique." In *Lectures, systèmes de lecture*, ed. Jean Bessière, 37–51. Paris: Presses Universitaires de France, 1984.

———. Preface to *Sarrasine. Gambara. Massimilla Doni* by Honoré de Balzac, 7–32. Paris: Gallimard [Folio], 1995.

Brunet, Etienne. Concordance de Balzac. http://ancilla.unice.fr/~brunet/BALZAC/balzac.htm. 5 June 2009.

Bui, Véronique. *La femme, la faute et l'écrivain. La mort féminine dans l'œuvre de Balzac*. Paris: Champion, 2003.

Butor, Michel. "Balzac et la réalité." In *Répertoire I*, 79–93. Paris: Minuit, 1960.

———. *Paris à Vol d'Archange: Improvisations sur Balzac II*. Paris: Éditions de la Différence, 1998.

———. "La pollution bancaire: 'Melmoth réconcilié.'" In *Le Marchand et le Génie. Improvisations sur Balzac I*, 45–57. Paris: Éditions de la Différence, 1998.

———. "Sur la princesse de Clèves." In *Répertoire I*, 74–78. Paris: Minuit, 1960.

Cambiaire, Célestin Pierre. *The Influence of Edgar Allan Poe in France*. New York: Haskill House, 1970; first published 1927.

Cave, Terence. "Modeste and Mignon: Balzac Rewrites Goethe." *French Studies* 59 (2005): 311–25.

Chambers, Ross. "Reading and the Voice of Death: Balzac's 'Le message.'" *Nineteenth-Century French Studies* 18 (1990): 408–23.

Citron, Pierre. *Dans Balzac*. Paris: Seuil, 1986.

———. Preface to *Pierrette* by Honoré de Balzac, 21–47. Paris: Garnier-Flammarion, 1967.

Cobb, Palmer. *The Influence of E.T.A. Hoffmann on the Tales of Edgar Allan Poe*. Chapel Hill: University of North Carolina Press, 1908.

Conner, Wayne. "Story and Frame in Balzac." *L'Esprit Créateur* 7.1 (1967): 45–54.

Cramer, Henri. *Fantasies élégantes*, piano, op. 74. Last Idea; arr. s.l.:s.n., 196–.

Cropper, Corry. *Playing at Monarchy: Sport as Metaphor in Nineteenth-Century France*. Lincoln: University of Nebraska Press, 2008.

Curran, Stuart. *Shelley's* Cenci: *Scorpions Ringed with Fire*. Princeton: Princeton University Press, 1970.

Dällenbach, Lucien. *La canne de Balzac*. Paris: Corti, 1996.

———. "Du fragment au cosmos (*La Comédie humaine* et l'opération de lecture I)." *Poétique* 40 (1979): 420–31.

———. "D'une métaphore totalisante: la mosaïque balzacienne." *Lettere Italiane* 33 (1981): 493–508.

———. "Le tout en morceaux (*La Comédie humaine* et l'opération de lecture II)." *Poétique* 42 (1980): 156–69.

Danger, Pierre. *L'éros balzacien: Structures du désir dans* la Comédie humaine. Paris: Corti, 1989.

David, Gérard. "L'idée de bonheur dans *La Comédie humaine*." *L'Année Balzacienne* (1966): 309–56.

Del Litto, Victor. "Alexandre Dumas, Stendhal et 'les Cenci.'" *Stendhal Club* 29, No. 115 (1987): 230–32.
Del Lungo, Andrea. "Poétique, évolution et mouvement des *incipit* balzaciens." In *Balzac. Une poétique du roman*, ed. Stéphane Vachon, 29–41. Montréal: XYZ Éditeur, 1996.
Delattre, Geneviève. *Les opinions littéraires de Balzac*. Paris: Presses Universitaires de France, 1961.
Derrida, Jacques. "Le théâtre de la cruauté et la clôture de la représentation." In *L'écriture et la différence*, 341–68. Paris: Seuil, 1967.
Déruelle, Aude. *Balzac et la digression*. Saint-Cyr-sur-Loire: Christian Pirot, 2004.
Dhommée, Émeline. "*Melmoth réconcilié* ou un diable peut en cacher un autre." In *Réflexions sur l'autoréflexivité balzacienne*, ed. Andrew Oliver and Stéphane Vachon, 41–54. Toronto: Centre d'études du XIXe siècle Joseph Sablé, 2002.
di Maio, Mariella. "Avatars des Cenci: Stendhal, Artaud, Moravia." *Stendhal Club* 35, No. 138 (1993): 155–69.
Donnard, Jean-Hervé. *Balzac. Les réalités économiques et sociales dans La Comédie humaine*. Paris: Armand Colin, 1961.
Drevon, Marguerite, and Jeannine Guichardet. "Fameux Sexorama." *L'Année Balzacienne* (1972): 257–74.
Dumas, Alexandre. "Les Cenci." In *Crimes célèbres*, 3–57. Paris: Administration de Librairie, 1839.
Ebguy, Jacques-David. "Balzac ou 'L'autre modernité': Le Balzac des philosophes." In *Penser avec Balzac*, ed. José-Luis Diaz and Isabelle Tournier, 129–41. Saint-Cyr-sur-Loire: Christian Pirot, 2003.
———. "'Ce que racontent les romans': 'mise en scène' des situations et des langages dans *La Fausse Maîtresse*." In *Envers Balzaciens*, ed. Andrea Del Lungo and Alexandre Péraud, 181–98. Poitiers: La Licorne, 2001.
———. "Description d'une (dé)composition de quelques modalités de la construction balzacienne des personnages." In *Balzac et la crise des identités*, ed. Emmanuelle Cullmann, José-Luis Diaz, and Boris Lyon-Caen, 25–40. Saint-Cyr-sur-Loire: Christian Pirot, 2005.
Eco, Umberto. *Role of the Reader. Explorations in the Semiotics of Texts*. Bloomington: Indiana University Press, 1979.
Eisenzweig, Uri. "L'instance du policier dans le romanesque: Balzac, Poe et le mystère de la chambre close." *Poétique* 51 (1982): 279–302.
Ellrich, Robert J. "Modes of Discourse and the Language of Sexual Reference in Eighteenth-Century French Fiction." *Eighteenth-Century Life* 9.3 (May 1985): 217–28.
Falconer, Graham. "Balzac historien des mentalités? Lecture de *César Birotteau*." In *Réflexions sur l'autoréflexivité balzacienne*, ed. Andrew Oliver and Stéphane Vachon, 55–65. Toronto: Centre d'études du XIXe siècle Joseph Sablé, 2002.
Flaubert, Gustave. *Correspondance*. Vol. III. Paris: Gallimard (Pléiade), 1991.
Forclaz, Roger. *Le monde d'Edgar Poe*. Francfort: Peter Lang, 1974.
Frappier-Mazur, Lucienne. "Lecture d'un texte illisible: *Autre étude de femme* et le modèle de la conversation." *MLN* 98 (1983): 712–27.
———. "Max et les Chevaliers: famille, filiation, et confrérie dans *La Rabouilleuse*." In *Balzac, Pater familias*, ed. Claudie Bernard and Franc Schuerewegen, 51–61. Amsterdam & New York: Rodopi, 2001.

Gadenne, Paul. Preface to *Un prince de la bohème* by Honoré de Balzac. In *La Comédie humaine*, 9: 633–42. Paris: Club Français du Livre, 1966.
Gaillard, Françoise. "Aux limites du genre: Melmoth réconcilié." In *Balzac ou la tentation de l'impossible*, ed. Raymond Mahieu and Franc Schuerewegen, 121–32. Paris: Société d'édition d'enseignement supérieur, 1998.
———. "La science: Modèle ou vérité. Réflexions sur l'*avant-propos* à La Comédie humaine." In *Balzac: L'invention du roman*, ed. Claude Duchet and Jacques Neefs, 57–83. Paris: Belfond, 1982.
Gauthier, Henri. *L'image de l'homme intérieur chez Balzac*. Genève: Droz, 1984.
Genette, Gérard. *Seuils*. Paris: Seuil, 1987.
———. "Vraisemblance et Motivation." In *Figures II*, 71–99. Paris: Seuil, 1969.
Gille, Bertrand. *La banque et le crédit en France, de 1818 à 1848*. Paris: Presses Universitaires de France, 1959.
Gomart, Hélène. *Les opérations financières dans le roman réaliste. Lecture de Balzac et de Zola*. Paris: Champion, 2004.
Goux, Jean-Joseph. *Frivolité de la valeur. Essai sur l'imaginaire du capitalisme*. Paris: Blusson, n. d. [2000].
Grange, Juliette. "La prose comme institution du monde moderne." In *Balzac et le style*, ed. Anne Herschberg Pierrot, 35–40. Paris: Société d'édition d'enseignement supérieur, 1998.
Greimas, A. J. *Maupassant. La sémiotique du texte*. Paris: Seuil, 1976.
Guenther, Beatrice Martina. *The Poetics of Death: The Short Prose of Kleist and Balzac*. Albany: State University of New York Press, 1996.
Guise, René. "Balzac, lecteur des 'Elixirs du diable.'" *L'Année Balzacienne* (1970): 57–67.
———. Introduction to *La Rabouilleuse* by Honoré de Balzac, 7–19. Paris: Gallimard [Folio], 1972.
———. Introduction to *Une ténébreuse affaire* by Honoré de Balzac, 7–19. Paris: Gallimard [Folio], 1973.
Hjelmslev, Louis. *Prolégomènes à une théorie du langage*. Paris: Minuit, 1966, 1968–1971.
Hoffman, Léon-François. "Éros en filigrane: 'Le curé de Tours.'" *L'Année Balzacienne* (1967): 89–105.
Hunt, H. J. *Balzac's Comédie Humaine*. London: The Athlone Press, Univ. of London, 1959.
Jallat, Jeannine. "Petite poétique du corps empêché." *Littérature* (December 1985): 73–88.
Jameson, Fredric. *The Political Unconscious. Narrative as a Socially Symbolic Act*. Ithaca: Cornell University Press, 1981.
Jamin, Marie-France. "Quelques emprunts possibles de Balzac à Hoffmann." *L'Année Balzacienne* (1970): 69–75.
Jouve, Nicole Ward. "Balzac's *A Daughter of Eve* and the Apple of Knowledge." In *Sexuality and Subordination. Interdisciplinary Studies of Gender in the Nineteenth Century*, ed. Susan Mendus and Jane Rendall, 25–59. London: Routledge, 1989.
Jussien, Narendra. "Les périodes décrites par Honoré de Balzac." http://hbalzac.free.fr/temps.php. 16 December 2009.
Kanes, Martin. *Balzac's Comedy of Words*. Princeton: Princeton University Press, 1975.
Kinder, Patricia. "Un directeur de journal, ses auteurs et ses lecteurs en 1836: autour de 'La vieille fille.'" *L'Année Balzacienne* (1972): 173–200.

Kiriu, Kazuo. Vocabulaire de Balzac. http://www.paris-france.org/Musees/Balzac/kiriu/concordance.htm.

Kopp, Robert. Preface to *La vieille fille* by Honoré de Balzac, 7–19. Paris: Gallimard [Folio], 1978.

Lanone, Catherine. "Verging on the Gothic: Melmoth's Journey to France." In *European Gothic: A Spirited Exchange 1760–1960*, ed. Avril Horner, 71–83. Manchester: Manchester University Press, 2002.

Laubriet, Pierre. Introduction and notes to *César Birotteau* by Honoré de Balzac, xiii–clxxv. Paris: Garnier, 1964.

Le Yaouanc, Moïse. *Nosographie de l'humanité balzacienne*. Paris: Maloine, 1959.

———. "Le plaisir dans les récits balzaciens." *L'Année Balzacienne* (1972): 275–308; (1973): 201–33.

Léonard, Martine. "Le dernier mot." In *Balzac. Une poétique du roman*, ed. Stéphane Vachon, 55–68. Montréal: XYZ Éditeur, 1996.

Levine, Stuart, and Susan Levine. *The Short Fiction of Edgar Allan Poe. An Annotated Edition*. Indianapolis: Bobbs-Merrill, 1976.

Lewenthal, Raymond. Liner Notes, *Toy Symphonies and Other Fun*. Sound Recording. Angel S36080, p1975.

Lockridge, Laurence S. "Justice in the Cenci." *The Wordsworth Circle* 19.2 (1988): 95–98.

Lukacher, Ned. *Primal Scenes: Literature, Philosophy, Psychoanalysis*. Ithaca: Cornell University Press, 1986.

Lyon-Caen, Boris. *Balzac et la comédie des signes. Essai sur une expérience de pensée*. Saint-Denis: Presses Universitaires de Vincennes, 2006.

Madden, James C. *Weaving Balzac's Web. Spinning Tales and Creating the Whole of* La Comédie humaine. Birmingham: Summa, 2003.

Magny, Claude-Edmonde. Preface to *Les secrets de la princesse de Cadignan* by Honoré de Balzac. In *La Comédie humaine*, 8: 233–61. Paris: Club Français du Livre. Paris, 1966.

Mahieu, Raymond. "Le 'pli' du texte balzacien." In *Balzac. Une poétique du roman*, ed. Stéphane Vachon, 43–53. Montréal: XYZ Éditeur, 1996.

Marceau, Félicien. Preface to *César Birotteau suivi de la Maison Nucingen* by Honoré de Balzac, 5–14. Paris: Livre de Poche, 1966.

Massol, Chantal. *Une poétique de l'énigme. Le récit herméneutique balzacien*. Genève: Droz, 2006.

Maturin, Charles Robert. *Melmoth the Wanderer*, ed. and intr. Victor Sage. Harmondsworth: Penguin Classics, 2000.

Mazet, Léo. "Récit[s] dans le récit: l'échange du récit chez Balzac." *L'Année Balzacienne* (1976): 129–61.

Meininger, Anne-Marie. Preface to *La Maison Nucingen précédé de Melmoth réconcilié* by Honoré de Balzac, 7–64. Paris: Gallimard [Folio], 1989.

———. Preface to *Modeste Mignon* by Honoré de Balzac, 7–35. Paris: Gallimard [Folio], 1982.

Messac, Régis. *Influences françaises dans l'œuvre d'Edgar Poe*. Paris: Librairie Picart, 1929.

Michel, Arlette. "Balzac et la rhétorique: modernité et tradition." *L'Année Balzacienne* (1988): 245–69.

———. "Balzac juge du féminisme. Des *Mémoires de deux jeunes mariées* à *Honorine*." *L'Année Balzacienne* (1973): 183–200.

———. "Balzac ou l'idée contre l'idée reçue." In *Voix de l'écrivain: Mélanges offerts à Guy Sagnes*, ed. Jean-Louis Cabanès, 31–42. Toulouse: Presses Universitaires du Mirail, 1996.

———. Introduction and editorial material to *Mémoires de deux jeunes mariées* by Honoré de Balzac, 19–47, 297–311. Paris: Garnier-Flammarion, 1979.

———. *Le mariage chez Honoré de Balzac. Amour et féminisme*. Paris: Société d'édition 'Les belles lettres,' 1978.

———. *Le mariage et l'amour dans l'œuvre romanesque d'Honoré de Balzac*. 4 vols. Paris: Champion, 1976.

———. *Le réel et la beauté dans le roman balzacien*. Paris: Champion, 2001.

Miller, D. A. *Narrative and its Discontents: Problems of Closure in the Traditional Novel*. Princeton: Princeton University Press, 1981.

Milner, Max. Introduction to *Massimilla Doni* by Honoré de Balzac, 7–82. Paris: Corti, 1964.

Mortimer, Armine Kotin. "Balzac's *Ursule Mirouët*: Genealogy and Inheritance." *The Modern Language Review* 92 (1997): 851–63.

———. *Writing Realism: Representations in French Fiction*. Baltimore: Johns Hopkins University Press, 2000.

Mozet, Nicole. *Balzac au pluriel*. Paris: Presses Universitaires de France, 1990.

———. "Par le biais de l'anachronisme (Balzac, *La vieille fille*)." In *Limites du langage: Indicible ou silence*, ed. Aline Mura-Brunel and Karl Cogard, 203–11. Paris: L'Harmattan, 2002.

———. "Temps historique et écriture romanesque: '1830 a consommé l'œuvre de 1793.'" *L'Année Balzacienne* (1990): 233–41.

———. "*Ursule Mirouët* ou le test du bâtard." In *Balzac, Œuvres complètes: Le moment de* La Comédie humaine, ed. Claude Duchet and Isabelle Tournier, 217–28. Saint-Denis: Presses Universitaires de Vincennes, 1993.

———. *La ville de province dans l'œuvre de Balzac: L'espace romanesque: fantasmes et idéologie*. Paris: Société d'édition d'enseignement supérieur, 1982.

Naginski, Isabelle Hoog. "De la faute d'Ève au crime invisible et à la sublimation. Structures du désir dans la Comédie féminine de Balzac." In *L'érotique balzacienne*, ed. Lucienne Frappier-Mazur and Jean-Marie Roulin, 147–56. Paris: Société d'édition d'enseignement supérieur, 2001.

Napoléon. *Pensées politiques et sociales*, ed. Adrien Dansette. Paris: Flammarion, 1969.

"Narrative Endings." *Nineteenth Century Fiction* 33 (1978).

Nathan, Michel. "Religion et Roman: À propos de *Ursule Mirouët*." In *Balzac: L'invention du roman*, ed. Claude Duchet and Jacques Neefs, 85–98. Paris: Belfond, 1982.

Neefs, Jacques. "'Figurez-vous . . .'" In *Balzac et le style*, ed. Anne Herschberg Pierrot, 41–45. Paris: Société d'édition d'enseignement supérieur, 1998.

———. "Les trois étages du mimétique dans *La Comédie humaine*." In *Balzac, Œuvres complètes: Le moment de* La Comédie humaine, ed. Claude Duchet and Isabelle Tournier, 149–56. Saint-Denis: Presses Universitaires de Vincennes, 1993.

Oliver, Andrew. "Penser le roman: *Albert Savarus* ou le roman comme transgression." In

Penser avec Balzac, ed. José-Luis Diaz and Isabelle Tournier, 95–106. Saint-Cyr-sur-Loire: Christian Pirot, 2003.

Pasco, Allan. *Balzacian Montage. Configuring La Comédie humaine*. Toronto: University of Toronto Press, 1991.

———. "Process Structure in Balzac's *La Rabouilleuse*." *Nineteenth-Century French Studies* 34 (2005–6): 21–31.

———. "Ursule Through the Glass Lightly." *French Review* 65 (1991): 36–45.

Péraud, Alexandre. "La construction de l'identité du débiteur (des Physiologies au récit balzacien)." In *Balzac et la crise des identités*, ed. Emmanuelle Cullmann, José-Luis Diaz, and Boris Lyon-Caen, 151–64. Saint-Cyr-sur-Loire: Christian Pirot, 2005.

Perrot, Philippe. *Les dessus et les dessous de la bourgeoisie: Une histoire du vêtement au XIXe siècle*. Paris: Fayard, 1981.

Perry, Dennis R., and Carl H. Sederholm. *Poe, "The House of Usher," and the American Gothic*. New York: Palgrave Macmillan, 2009.

Pich, Edgard. *Mémoires de deux jeunes mariées d'Honoré de Balzac: Un roman de l'identité*. Lyon: JC2/ALDRUI Editions, 2004.

Pixis, Johann Peter. http://www.operone.de/komponist/pixis.html. 25 April 2002.

Place-Verghnes, Floriane. "Tabou or Not Tabou, Dire ou ne pas dire: Maupassant et l'autocensure." *Neophilologus* 88 (2004): 367–84.

Poe, Edgar Allan. *Collected Works*, ed. Thomas O. Mabbott. Cambridge, MA: Harvard University Press, 1978. Reprinted as *Tales and Sketches*. 2 vols. Urbana: University of Illinois Press, 2000.

———. *The Complete Works of Edgar Allan Poe*, ed. James A. Harrison. New York: Thomas Y. Crowell, 1902. Reprint AMS Press 1965.

———. *Selected Writings. Poems, Tales, Essays and Reviews*, ed. David Galloway. Harmondsworth: Penguin, 1970.

Poe Studies 5:1, June 1972.

Pollin, Burton Ralph. *Discoveries in Poe*. South Bend, IN: Notre Dame University Press, 1970.

Poulet, Georges. "Balzac." In *Les métamorphoses du cercle*, 203–30. Paris: Plon, 1961.

Prendergast, Christopher. *The Order of Mimesis: Balzac, Stendhal, Nerval, Flaubert*. Cambridge: Cambridge University Press, 1986.

Proust, Marcel. *Contre Sainte-Beuve*, ed. Pierre Clarac and Yves Sandré. Paris: Gallimard, 1971.

Pugh, Anthony. *Balzac's Recurring Characters*. Toronto: University of Toronto Press, 1974.

Queffélec, Lise. "*La vieille fille* ou la science des mythes en roman-feuilleton." *L'Année Balzacienne* (1988): 163–77.

Rabaté, Dominique. *Le chaudron fêlé: Écarts de la littérature*. Paris: Corti, 2006.

Rashkin, Esther. *Family Secrets and the Psychoanalysis of Narrative*. Princeton: Princeton University Press, 1992.

[Reissiger, Karl Gottlieb.] "Weber's Last Thought (Dernière Pensée Musicale)." By C. M. von Weber. In *Masterpieces of Piano Music: The Largest and Most Comprehensive Collection of Standard Piano Compositions Ever Published, Covering Completely all Fields of Classic, Modern, Light and Operatic Piano Music*. Selected and ed. Albert E. Wier, 47. New York: C. Fischer, c1918.

———. *Von Weber's Last Waltz*. New York: Firth & Hall, n.d.

Robert, Marthe. *Roman des origines et origines du roman*. Paris: Gallimard [Tel], 1972.
Rosolato, Guy. *Essais sur le symbolique*. Paris: Gallimard, 1969.
Sacy, Sylvestre de. "Balzac, Geoffroy Saint-Hilaire et l'unité de composition." *Mercure de France*, vol. 303 [May–Aug. 1948], No. 1018, June 1, 1948: 292–305; No. 1019, July 1, 1948: 469–80.
Schuerewegen, Franc. *Balzac suite et fin*. Lyon: ENS Éditions, 2004.
Scott, Walter. *The Bride of Lammermoor*. New York: E. P. Dutton (Everyman's Library), 1906; reprint 1909.
Shelley, Percy Bysshe. *The Cenci*, a Tragedy in Five Acts. Introduction by Alfred Forman and H. Buxton Forman. Prologue by John Todhunter. New York: Phaeton Press, 1970. Reprint of an 1886 edition by the Shelley Society.
Starobinski, Jean. *La relation critique*. Paris: Gallimard, 1970.
Stedman, Edmund Clarence. "Edgar Allan Poe." *Scribner's Monthly* 20 (May 1880): 107–24; also published separately as *Edgar Allan Poe*.
Stendhal. "Les Cenci." *Chroniques italiennes*. In *Œuvres complètes*, ed. Victor Del Litto, 1: 41–86; Appendix, 2: 135–58. Geneva: Cercle du Bibliophile, 1968.
Taylor, Françoise M. "Mythe des origines et société dans *Une ténébreuse affaire* de Balzac." *Nineteenth-Century French Studies* 14 (1985–86): 1–18.
Thiher, Allen. *Fiction Rivals Science: The French Novel from Balzac to Proust*. Columbia: University of Missouri Press, 2001.
Torgovnick, Marianna. *Closure in the Novel*. Princeton: Princeton University Press, 1981.
Tournier, Isabelle. "Un fait de style: Le 'voici pourquoi' balzacien." In *(En)jeux de la communication romanesque: Hommage à Françoise van Rossum-Guyon*, ed. Suzan van Dijk and Christa Stevens, 73–84. Amsterdam: Rodopi, 1994.
Tritter, Jean-Louis. "A propos des épreuves de *Pierrette*." *L'Année Balzacienne* (1973): 19–29.
Uhden, Raina F. "'Le charbon ardent' in Balzac's *La recherche de l'Absolu* and 'Des artistes.'" *Nineteenth-Century French Studies* 36 (2008): 241–54.
Vachon, Stéphane. "Balzac théoricien du roman." In *Écrits sur le roman*, 9–36. Paris: Librairie Générale Française, 2000.
———. "Chabert sur les chemins de l'ethnocritique. Le point de vue du balzacien." In *Horizons ethnocritiques*, ed. Jean-Marie Privat and Marie Scarpa, 217–50. Nancy: Presses Universitaires de Nancy, 2010.
———. *1850. Tombeau d'Honoré de Balzac*. Montréal: XYZ Éditeur; Paris: Presses Universitaires de Vincennes, 2007.
———. *Les travaux et les jours d'Honoré de Balzac. Chronologie de la création balzacienne*. Paris: Presses du CNRS, 1992; Presses Universitaires de Vincennes, Université de Paris VIII; Montréal: Les Presses de l'Université de Montréal, 1992.
Van den Doel, Ernst M. H. "Balzac's 'Pierrette': An Early Description of Chronic Subdural Hematoma." *Archives of Neurology* 43 (1986): 1291–92.
Vanoncini, André. "*Pierrette* et la rénovation du code mélodramatique." In *Balzac, Œuvres complètes: Le moment de La Comédie humaine*, ed. Claude Duchet and Isabelle Tournier, 257–67. Saint-Denis: Presses Universitaires de Vincennes, 1993.
Wais, Kurt. "Le roman d'artiste: E. T. A. Hoffmann et Balzac." In *La littérature narrative d'imagination des genres littéraires aux techniques d'expression*, 137–55. Paris: Presses Universitaires de France, 1961.

Wanuffel, Lucie. "Présence d'Hoffmann dans les œuvres de Balzac (1829–1835)." *L'Année Balzacienne* (1970): 45–56.
Wilde, Oscar. "The Decay of Lying." In *Critical Theory Since Plato*, ed. Hazard Adams, 673–86. New York: Harcourt Brace Jovanovich, 1971.
Wollstonecraft, Mary. *The Last Man*, ed. and intr. Hugh J. Luke, Jr. Lincoln: University of Nebraska Press, 1965.
Wooden, Thomas, ed. *Twentieth Century Interpretations of "The Fall of the House of Usher": A Collection of Critical Essays*. Englewood Cliffs, NJ: Prentice-Hall, 1969.
Wurmser, André. *La comédie inhumaine*. Paris: Gallimard, 1964.
———. Preface to *César Birotteau* by Honoré de Balzac, 7–31. Paris: Gallimard [Folio], 1975.

Index

Pages references in *italics* refer to illustrations.

Abraham, Pierre, 64
Abrantès, Laure Junot, duchesse d', 21, 22; *Mémoires*, 49
the absolute: Balzac's belief in, 285; in "Entre Savants," 295; in government, 104–5, 285; in love, 168; in *La recherche de l'Absolu*, 210, 212–15
Adieu (Balzac), 75–77; cinematic aspects of, 75, 76, 78; identity in, 75; misrepresentation in, 75–76, 78
adultery: in *Autre étude de femme*, 275; Balzac's mother's, 60; in *Le Cabinet des Antiques*, 151n1; in *La Grande Bretèche*, 276–77; in *La muse du département*, 10–11
Albert Savarus (Balzac): autobiography in, 69; composed past in, 262, 263; historical present of, 261–62; identity in, 68–70; narration of, 68, 79; self-narration in, 70–71, 261; versions of, 261–62
Algerian War, in *La Rabouilleuse*, 266

Alterton, Margaret, 202
Amar, Muriel, 26n2
Ambrière-Fargeaud, Madeleine, 155
Amossy, Ruth, 226
analogy, Balzac on, 296
analysis: anthropological, 265; in Balzacian narrative, 209, 299–300; Balzac on, 259, 296–97; in *Eugénie Grandet*, 265; in *La Comédie humaine*, 259, 296; composition and, 259, 290; of historical present, 269; as mode of knowledge, 261; in *La recherche de l'Absolu*, 216, 219, 259; synthesis through, 296–97
Andréoli, Max: on *Massimilla Doni*, 240; on *Une ténébreuse affaire*, 58
antagonisms, in Balzac's works, 4–5
anthropology, Balzacian, 261, 300; analysis in, 265; in *Un début dans la vie*, 261; in *Eugénie Grandet*, 265; in *Illusions perdues*, 185; in *La Maison du Chat-qui-pelote*, 25; in *Melmoth réconcilié*, 222, 224, 229; myth and,

109, 137; in *Pierrette,* 110; in *La vieille fille,* 109, 137
anthropology, French ignorance concerning, 109–10, 137–38
archeology, Balzacian, 292; architectural, 210; in *Le curé de village,* 298; in decor descriptions, 25; in *La Maison du Chat-qui-pelote,* 25; in *Pierrette,* 127; in *La recherche de l'Absolu,* 220; in *Une ténébreuse affaire,* 52, 54, 60, 61
Archimedes, fulcrum of, 3
Aristotle, Prime Mover of, 3
art: and chance, 280; commercialization of, 171–72, 266; communicable, 173; compromise in, 173; as execution, 304; and nature, 209, 215; role in politics, 287; transformation of the real, 174
Artaud, Antonin: *Les Cenci,* 120, 122
artists: bourgeois, 267; in *Le chef-d'œuvre inconnu,* 172–74, 230, 267; in *Massimilla Doni,* 173; nature of, 241; as visionaries, 293
L'auberge rouge (Balzac), voyage motif of, 186–87
autobiography, in Balzac's works, 64, 69, 283–84
Autre étude de femme (Balzac): closure of, 271, 275, 278; enclosure in, 276; frame of, 271; *La Grande Bretèche* in, 271; infidelity in, 275; narrative of, 277; revenge in, 275, 276; sexual language of, 245; unity of, 275. See also *La Grande Bretèche*

Le bal de Sceaux (Balzac): identity in, 73–74; self-narration in, 73, 74
Balzac, Anne-Charlotte-Laure de: adultery of, 60
Balzac, Henri de, 60, 151
Balzac, Honoré de: absolutism of, 285; admiration for Raphael, 235; on analogy, 296; on analysis, 259, 296–97; belief in will, 163; as businessman, 9n3; on celibacy, 129, 139; and Cenci portrait, 123, 124, 127; on chance, 190, 220, 280–81; conception of subjects, 257; and copy, 173; correspondence with Hanska, 88n3, 92, 182–83, 230, 232, 233–34, 281; double characters of, 18, 63; dualities of, 4, 19, 294, 296, 298; and duchesse d'Abrantès, 21, 22; family dynamics of, 63; family name of, 173; family secrets of, 60; fictional avatars of, 64, 69, 283–84; financial maneuvers of, 87, 88; fulcrum imagery of, 3; Hoffmann's influence on, 201; incompletion in, 19; interest in mesmerism, 202; knowledge of Clément kidnapping, 49–50, 56; and Poe, 195, 199–200; political writings of, 60; Proust on, 57, 60; reading of Scott, 200; rewriting by, 278–79; royalism of, 287; "second sight" of, 259n1; theory of unique love, 168; use of coffee, 236; use of hypothesis, 2; view of celibacy, 129; view of family, 16, 140; view of July Monarchy, 59–60, 110; view of law, 95, 127; view of Napoleon, 60; as visionary, 293, 295. *See also* narrative, Balzacian; rhetorical realism, Balzacian; *titles of works by Balzac*
Bara, Olivier, 4n2
Barbéris, Pierre, 104; on Balzac's royalism, 287; on Balzac's sexual language, 249
Barel-Moisan, Claire, 209; "Balzac et la pragmatique," 94, 300
Barnett, Louise, 123, 126
Baron, Anne-Marie: on *Le Cabinet des Antiques,* 151n1; on *Les Chouans,* 40; on *Mémoires de deux jeunes mariées,* 20–21; on *Une passion dans le désert,* 256. Works: *Balzac ou l'auguste mensonge,* 63; *Le fils prodige,* 63n1
Barthes, Roland: on *Sarrasine,* 290; on seen reality, 203; on symbolic code,

27. Works: *Le plaisir du texte,* 301; S/Z, 301
Béatrix (Balzac), 170; misrepresentation in, 77; sexual language in, 246, 252; voyage motifs of, 179–80; women's desire in, 133
Behrendt, Stephen C., 121
Beizer, Janet: *Family Plots,* 256
Bérard, Suzanne-J., 49, 50
Berlioz, Hector, 198, 202; on power of music, 206n4; on Reissiger, 196; on Weber, 196
Bernardin de Saint-Pierre, J.-H.: *Paul et Virginie,* 112, 122
Bersani, Leo: *Balzac to Beckett,* 270
Berthier, Philippe, 16; on *Mémoires de deux jeunes mariées,* 18; on *Une passion dans le désert,* 256; on unity, 20; on *La vieille fille,* 135
Berzélius, Jöns Jacob, 211
Bodin, Thierry, 154
Boehm, Jakob, 227
Bonald, Louis-Gabriel-Ambroise, vicomte de, 302
Bonaldism, 17
Bonapartism, hierarchy in, 60
Bordas, Éric, 130, 243
bourgeoisie: artists among, 267; as audience, 275–76; in *César Birotteau,* 83–84, 90–91, 92; conception of clothing, 132; evolution of, 91n4; in *La Maison du Chat-qui-pelote,* 25–26; mediocrity of, 151; in *Pierre Grassou,* 167, 171–72, 266; in *Pierrette,* 113, 118–19, 126; in *Un prince de la bohème,* 167; in *La Rabouilleuse,* 150, 151; in *Ursule Mirouët,* 152, 153, 154, 155, 158, 264
La bourse (Balzac): identity in, 67–68; self-narration in, 78
Bouvier, René, 87
Brasch, Harold T., 198
Brooks, Peter, 8
Brunel, Pierre, 201
Bui, Véronique, 73; on *Le lys dans la vallée,* 249; on *Pierrette,* 110

Butor, Michel, 31; on bourgeoisie, 91n4; on *Melmoth réconcilié,* 227; on *La princesse de Clèves,* 257

Le Cabinet des Antiques (Balzac), 30, 296; adultery in, 151n1; dualities in, 306; preface to, 303
capitalism: in *La Maison Nucingen,* 284–85; in *Melmoth réconcilié,* 222, 225; in modern society, 228; in *Le père Goriot,* 4; progress through, 104; in realistic novels, 4. *See also* credit; money; speculation, financial
Carnot, Lazare: in *Une ténébreuse affaire,* 49
Castex, Pierre-Georges, 49
causality, Aristotelian: in *La Comédie humaine,* 8
cause and effect, in *La recherche de l'Absolu,* 211, 214
celibacy: in Balzac's works, 129, 139; in *Pierrette,* 109, 112, 113, 115, 117, 120, 139; in *La Rabouilleuse,* 139–41, 144–51
Cenci, Beatrice: martyrdom of, 122–23; myth of, 110, 120, 121–24; in *Pierrette,* 118, 119–21, 122–24, 126–27; Reni portrait of, 123–24, *125,* 126, 127
César Birotteau (Balzac): bourgeoisie in, 83–84, 90–91, 92; composition of, 92–93; decadence in, 81, 89–90; double representation in, 80–93; as financial narrative, 85; grandeur in, 81, 83, 88–90, 92; identity in, 84–85; illusions in, 80–84, 87; money in, 80, 85–88; narrative structure of, 85; publicity for, 88; reality in, 81–84, 87; semiosis of, 87; title of, 81, 89; types in, 298
Chambers, Ross, 61
chance: art and, 280; Balzac on, 190, 220, 280–81
characters: double, 18, 63; interpretation of signs, 68; misrepresentation of, 64,

66–67, 69–70, 71–73, 77–78. *See also* types, Balzacian
Le chef-d'œuvre inconnu (Balzac), 201; the artist in, 172–74, 230, 267; model of composition in, 172
chemistry: in Balzac's works, 12; in *La recherche de l'Absolu*, 208, 210, 211–20; unitary system of, 212–14
Chopin, Frédéric, 204–5
Les Chouans (Balzac), 32–46, 186; and Balzac's family dynamics, 63; castle imagery in, 38–39; clothing in, 33–38; decor in, 44; disparity in, 32–36, 38–39, 43, 45–46; geography of, 32, 40, 45, 176; heterogeneity in, 32–35, 40, 41–42; heteronomy in, 33, 44–45; identity in, 177; landscape of, 40–41; marriage in, 43–44, 46; military life in, 32; mimesis in, 32; the nebulous in, 44–45; peasant characters of, 33–34, 36; point of view, 45; politics in, 178; realism of, 32, 42; self-representation in, 66–67; semiosis of, 32; uniformity in, 33, 36, 42, 43, 45; unity in, 33, 35–37, 39, 40, 43–46, 89; voyage motif of, 176–78
Citron, Pierre, 110; *Dans Balzac*, 63, 64; on *La Maison Nucingen*, 284; on *Pierrette*, 112
Clément de Ris, Dominique, 48; Balzac's knowledge of, 49–50, 56
closure, Balzacian, 12; of *Autre étude de femme*, 271, 275, 278; composition of, 291; of *La Grande Bretèche*, 271, 275, 277, 289; of *Honorine*, 288–91; of *Le lys dans la vallée*, 270; of *La Maison Nucingen*, 286, 287; problematic, 270–91; of *Les secrets de la princesse de Cadignan*, 279–84, 287; semiosis of, 278; subversion of, 279
clothing: bourgeois conception of, 132; in *Les Chouans*, 33–38; in *La muse du département*, 181–83
Cobb, Palmer, 202
coffee, Balzac's use of, 236
Le colonel Chabert (Balzac): clerks in, 227; identity in, 74–75, 78; and Poe's works, 199n2; self-narration in, 74–75; types in, 298
La Comédie humaine (Balzac): analysis in, 259, 296, 299–300; antagonisms in, 4–5; artists in, 172; Balzac's family dynamics in, 63; capitalists in, 4; causality in, 8; *Les célibataires*, 112; chaosmos of, 45; characters of, 64; closure in, 270; composed past in, 259, 268–69; composition in, 259; Cuvier tendency in, 296, 297; determinism in, 127; disorganization of, 92, 269; doctors in, 116; energy in, 2; *Études analytiques*, 91; *Études de mœurs*, 32, 91; *Études philosophiques*, 91–92, 208, 221, 224, 229, 230; explanation in, 179, 250; expression in, 294; family in, 63, 140; fathers in, 144; games in, 26n2; genealogies of, 12, 299; history in, 91, 92; Hoffmann in, 201; idea and form in, 173, 174; the infinite in, 207; July Monarchy in, 264; love in, 6, 140, 190; love/money connection in, 8–10, 66, 176, 301–3; marriage in, 185, 260; mediocrity in, 151, 172; merchant class in, 172; money in, 98–99, 104; mosaic imagery of, 269; observation in, 294; openings of, 65; points of view in, 15; politics in, 52, 109, 150; Prime Movers of, 8, 11, 176, 242, 301; realism in, 12, 203; recurring characters of, 268; role of *La Maison Nucingen* in, 103; role of *Le père Goriot* in, 3; role of political instability in, 52; *Scènes de la vie de Province*, 152; *Scènes de la vie militaire*, 32; *Scènes de la vie politique*, 114; *Scènes de la vie privée*, 229, 271; scientific grounding of, 300; sexual love in, 243–44; signifying structures of, 91; social climbing in, 169–70; as social document, 59; suitors in, 133; totalizing edifice of, 293; types in, 297–98; unities of, 5; voyages in,

12, 177, 190. *See also* narrative, Balzacian; rhetorical realism, Balzacian; titles of works by Balzac
completion: chemical process of, 220; in *La recherche de l'Absolu*, 215, 218, 220; through marriage, 220
composition: and analysis, 259, 290; of closure, 291; of reality, 296; in *La recherche de l'Absolu*, 208, 219, 259; unity of, 212, 214, 296
Le conseil (Balzac): elite society of, 276; frame of, 275–76; *La Grande Bretèche* in, 271, 275–76
content, form and, 11, 305
conversation, French style of, 276, 277
corsets, nineteenth-century, 130; in *La vieille fille*, 12, 128–38
Le cousin Pons (Balzac): historical present in, 267; Hoffmann in, 201; piano playing in, 204n3
La cousine Bette (Balzac): conception in, 304–5; execution in, 304–5; sexual language of, 246, 250–51
Cramer, Henri: "Fantasy on Weber's Last Waltz," 198
creation: abundance of, 230; chemical and written, 208–9; as execution, 257; in *Massimilla Doni*, 230–31, 238–39; in *La peau de chagrin*, 208n1, 293–94; of reality, 294–95; role of opium in, 236; use of signs in, 31, 294
credit (finance), 10, 28; in nineteenth-century France, 87n2. *See also* capitalism; money; speculation, financial
Cropper, Corry, 26n2
crystallization: of love, 40, 262
crystallization, chemical: in *La recherche de l'Absolu*, 215, 219–20
Le curé de village (Balzac): archeology in, 298; sexual language of, 250; types in, 298; voyage motif of, 175
Curran, Stuart, 122
Cuvier, Georges: in *La Comédie humaine*, 296, 297; in *La peau de chagrin*, 293; and Geoffroy Saint-Hilaire, 296, 297

Dällenbach, Lucien, 45–46; on closure, 270; on fragment and whole, 279, 292n1; on readers, 62
David, Gérard, 9
the dead, communication with, 200
Un début dans la vie (Balzac): anthropology of, 261; historical present in, 261
decomposition, in *La recherche de l'Absolu*, 212, 215, 218, 219
deduction, scientific, 208
Delattre, Geneviève, 121
Del Lungo, Andrea, 209
Derrida, Jacques, 120
Déruelle, Aude, 209; "Balzac et la pragmatique," 94, 300
desire, human: in *Massimilla Doni*, 231; in *Melmoth réconcilié*, 223–24; in *La peau de chagrin*, 223; philosophical conception of, 223; sexual, 130, 133–37; women's, 133. *See also* love, sexual; sexual language, Balzac's
Dhommée, Émeline, 225
Dickens, Charles: on Cenci portrait, 123
Diderot, Denis: *Jacques le fataliste*, 67, 68, 300; *Le Neveu de Rameau*, 99
Donnard, Jean-Hervé: on Balzacian families, 299; on *César Birotteau*, 87; on *Pierrette*, 110; *Les réalités économiques et sociales dans* La Comédie humaine, 9
doubleness: in Balzacian realism, 12, 18, 30, 63; in *César Birotteau*, 80–93. *See also* dualities, Balzacian
dreams: in *César Birotteau*, 80; erasure of, 92
Drevon, Marguerite, 255n3
dualities, Balzacian, 4, 294, 296, 298; in *Le Cabinet des Antiques*, 306; of conception and execution, 304–5; in *Mémoires de deux jeunes mariées*, 15–21; unity made from, 18–20. *See also* doubleness
La duchesse de Langeais (Balzac), sexual language of, 247–49
Dumas, Alexandre: "Les Cenci," 121

Ebguy, Jacques-David, 64; on *Albert Savarus,* 262; on Balzacian prose, 301; on *La fausse maîtresse,* 71
Eco, Umberto, 26–27
Eisenzweig, Uri, 199n2
electricity, in *La recherche de l'Absolu,* 214–15, 218, 219
L'elixir de longue vie (Balzac), social satire in, 221
ellipsis: in *Honorine,* 289–90; in *La Maison du Chat-qui-pelote,* 21–27, 260; meaning through, 27
Ellrich, Robert, 244
Les employés (Balzac), clerks in, 227
"Entre Savants" (Balzac), the absolute in, 295
Erasure: in Balzac's short stories, 279; of dreams, 92
Ernst, Heinrich Wilhelm, 196
Essai sur les forces humaines (projected work, Balzac), 93
Étude de femme (Balzac), historical present in, 262–63
Eugénie Grandet (Balzac): anthropological analysis in, 265; historical present of, 264–65; love and money in, 4; types in, 265; versions of, 265
explication: Balzac's, 47, 299; in *La Comédie humaine,* 179; in *Jacques le fataliste,* 300; of love/money connection, 301; *nécessaire,* 31, 81, 159–60, 163, 164, 300–301; in realistic novels, 47; in *Splendeurs et misères des courtisanes,* 300; in *Une ténébreuse affaire,* 47–62
expression: in *La Comédie humaine,* 294; forms of, 11; of sexual love, 243

Falconer, Graham, 84
family: Balzac on, 16; in *La Comédie humaine,* 140; in *La Rabouilleuse,* 140, 141, 143–45; types within, 299
La fausse maîtresse (Balzac), 69; historical present in, 263; love in, 168; misrepresentation in, 71–73; self-narration in, 72, 78; versions of, 263
La femme abandonnée (Balzac): sexual language of, 245, 246, 254; voyage motif of, 176
La femme de trente ans (Balzac): Cenci portrait in, 124, 126; narrator of, 254; sexual language of, 245–46, 254
Le Figaro, César Birotteau in, 88
La fille aux yeux d'or (Balzac): erotic love in, 243–44; love in, 10; love/money connection in, 8–9; postface to, 281; preface to, 296–97; sexual language of, 254–55; virginity in, 250n2
Une fille d'Ève (Balzac): fortune in, 30; historical present in, 263–64; initiating plot of, 29; interest in, 27–30; *lettres de change* in, 28–30; narrative of, 27, 28, 29; semiosis in, 29; preface of, 259; types in, 297
fire: action on matter, 218; in *La recherche de l'Absolu,* 215, 216, 218
Flaubert, Gustave: *Madame Bovary,* 84; the textual in, 301; on voyage genre, 175
form: and content, 11, 305; ideas and, 173, 174
Fortassier, Rose, 3
fortune, in *Une fille d'Ève,* 30
Fouché, Joseph: in *Une ténébreuse affaire,* 49–50, 56–57, 58–59, 62
fragment, and whole, 279, 292–93
France, disunity of, 44–45
Frappier-Mazur, Lucienne, 39, 46; on *Les Chouans,* 177; on *La Grande Bretèche,* 275–76, 277
fulcrum, Balzac's imagery of, 3

Gaillard, Françoise: on Balzacian duality, 296; on *Melmoth réconcilié,* 222, 223, 225, 226, 228; on science, 165
Gambara (Balzac), composition in, 207, 230
games, in Balzac, 26n2
Gauthier, Henri, 19–20

genealogies, Balzacian, 12; of *La Comédie humaine*, 299; evil in, 154; function of, 299; of *Les héritiers Boirouge*, 154; of *Les Paysans*, 154, 299; in *Pierrette*, 110, *111*, 154, 299; in *La Rabouilleuse*, 139, 140–41, *142*, *143*, 144–51, 154, 299; of *Ursule Mirouët*, 152–55, *156*, 157–66, 299
Genette, Gérard, 31, 48; on explication, 61, 299
Geoffroy Saint-Hilaire, 163, 165; and Cuvier, 296, 297; on unity of composition, 296
Gille, Bertrand: *La banque et le crédit en France*, 9
Girardin, Émile, 129
Gomart, Hélène: on *César Birotteau*, 81, 87; on language, 303; *Les opérations financières dans le roman réaliste*, 10
Goux, Jean-Joseph, 4
La Grande Bretèche (Balzac): centrality in, 273; closures of, 271, 275, 277, 289; in *Le conseil*, 275–76; dramatic power of, 276; enclosure motifs of, 271–79; infidelity in, 276–77; narrations of, 272–74, 277; and Poe's work, 199n2; revenge in, 276; secrets in, 273–74; semiotic process of, 273; silence in, 274; wall imagery of, 273–74. See also *Autre étude de femme*; *Le conseil*
greensickness, 116
Greimas, A. J., 278
Guenther, Beatrice Martina, 126
Guichardet, Jeannine, 255n3
Guise, René, 9, 47n1

Hanska, Ève, 69, 72; Balzac's correspondence with, 88n3, 92, 182–83, 230, 232, 233–34, 281
Hawthorne, Nathaniel: on Cenci portrait, 124
Heine, Heinrich, 167–68
Les héritiers Boirouge (Balzac), genealogy of, 154

hermeneutics, Balzac's, 262, 272
Hérold, Ferdinand: *Rousseau's Dream*, 205
history, reversals in, 89, 90, 91. See also present, historical
Hjelmslev, Louis, 11
Hoffmann, E. T. A., 199; influence on Balzac, 201; influence on Poe, 202
Honorine (Balzac): closure in, 288–91; ellipses in, 289–90; frame of, 288–89, 290; marriage in, 288; misrepresentation in, 77–78; pensiveness in, 290, 291; revisions to, 288, 290; sexual language of, 252; sexual love in, 288; silence in, 290
hypothesis (rhetoric), 2
hysteron proteron, in *Une ténébreuse affaire*, 48, 51, 57

the ideal, reality and, 241. See also love, idealized
ideas: conception of, 219; execution of, 219; and form, 173, 174
identity: in *Adieu*, 75; in *Albert Savarus*, 68–70; in *Le bal de Sceaux*, 73–74; in Balzac's works, 63, 64; in *La bourse*, 67–68; in *César Birotteau*, 84–85; in *Les Chouans*, 177; in *Le colonel Chabert*, 74–75, 78; in *Jacques le fataliste*, 67; in *Madame Firmiani*, 64–66; in *Un prince de la bohème*, 170; rhetorical figure of, 12. See also self-narration, Balzacian
illusions: in Balzac's works, 80; in *César Birotteau*, 80–84, 87; in financial speculation, 87
Illusions perdues (Balzac): anthropology in, 185; journalism in, 287; marriage in, 184–85; money in, 303; narrative of, 186; voyage motif of, 184–86
imagination, French, 99, 100
incompletion, in Balzac's works, 19
the infinite, in *La Comédie humaine*, 207
innocence, female, 250n2, 251
interest: in *Une fille d'Ève*, 27–30; rhetorical figure of, 12

Jallat, Jeannine, 231
Jameson, Fredric, 129n1, 301
journalism: in *Illusions perdues*, 287; in *La Maison Nucingen*, 285–86, 287
Jouve, Nicole Ward, 29n3
July Monarchy, 58; Balzac's view of, 59–60, 110; in *Pierrette*, 126; politicians of, 264; undermining of, 59–60

Kanes, Martin, 30n4
Karr, Henry, 199
Kinder, Patricia, 129
knowledge, analytical mode of, 261

Laclos, Pierre Choderlos de: *Les liaisons dangereuses*, 15, 16, 242
La Fontaine, fables of, 50
language: function in Balzac's realism, 305; human construction of, 302; as sign system, 11, 302–3. *See also* sexual language, Balzac's
Laubriet, Pierre, 87
Lavater, Johann Kaspar, 212
Lavoisier, Antoine, 211, 212, 216
law: Balzac on, 95, 127; in *La Maison Nucingen*, 104–5; in *Ursule Mirouët*, 159–61
Léonard, Martine, 239–40
"Lettre à M. Ch. Nodier" (Balzac), 241
lettres de change, in *Une fille d'Ève*, 28–30
Le Yaouanc, Moïse: *Nosographie de l'humanité balzacienne*, 245; "Le plaisir," 244; on *Sarrasine*, 257
literature: bourgeois audience of, 276; creative method in, 202; and money, 104, 105, 303; rejection of, 277; self-representation of, 305–6; truth in, 30–31
Loève-Veimars, François-Adolphe, 201
Louis Lambert (Balzac), 63; and Poe's work, 199n2; thought in, 230
love: absolute, 168; in *La Comédie humaine*, 6, 140, 190; crystallization of, 40, 262; idealized, 231–34, 236–37, 252, 288; in marriage, 179–80; in *Massimilla Doni*, 231–34, 238, 239, 304; misrepresentation of, 72; opium imagery of, 237; in Paris, 7, 9; as Prime Mover, 8, 242; in *La Rabouilleuse*, 10, 168; role in women's lives, 15
love, sexual: in *La Comédie humaine*, 243–44; expression of, 243; happiness in, 249, 253; hidden forms of, 243; in *Honorine*, 288; and idealized love, 231–34, 252; innuendo in, 244; as literary creation, 257–58; within marriage, 252–54; and money, 6–7; outside of marriage, 247–50; in *Le père Goriot*, 7; types within, 243. *See also* desire, human; sexual language, Balzac's
love/money connection, 4; in *La Comédie humaine*, 8–10, 66, 176, 301–3; explication of, 301; in *La fille aux yeux d'or*, 8–9; in *La Maison Nucingen*, 4, 284; in marriage, 5; in *Modeste Mignon*, 231; in *Le père Goriot*, 5–7; in *Pierrette*, 110, 299; power in, 7; in *Un prince de la bohème*, 168–69, 170; in *La Rabouilleuse*, 140, 147, 148–50, 169; semiotic structures of, 299; in *Splendeurs et misères des courtisanes*, 190; in *Ursule Mirouët*, 301
Lukacher, Ned, 60
Lyon-Caen, Boris, 172
Le lys dans la vallée (Balzac), 24, 289; closure of, 270; flower symbolism of, 25; sexual language of, 249; women's desire in, 133

Mabbott, Thomas O., 198
Madame Firmiani (Balzac): identity in, 64–66; narrator of, 65; self-narration in, 66, 78; social types in, 65
magnetism, animal: in Balzac's works, 12; in "The Fall of the House of Usher," 195, 202; in *Ursule Mirouët*, 153–54,

163, 165–66, 188, 195, 202–6, 207. See also mesmerism; somnambulism
Magny, Claude-Edmonde, 279, 284; on *La Maison Nucingen*, 287
Mahieu, Raymond, 4
La Maison du Chat-qui-pelote (Balzac): anthropological description in, 25; archeological description in, 25; bourgeoisie in, 25–26; composed past in, 260, 263; ellipsis in, 21–27, 260; historical present in, 260, 266; merchant class in, 26; portrait symbolism in, 22–26, 27; rhetorical realism of, 24; role in *La Comédie humaine*, 21; semiosis of, 260; sexual language of, 246; shop sign of, 26; title of, 26; versions of, 23–24, 25
La Maison Nucingen (Balzac): adventure novel in, 102–3; arbitrariness in, 105; capitalism in, 284–85; chiasmus structure of, 95, 97, 103; closure in, 286, 287; digressions in, 95, 97; embedded story of, 284, 285; external narrator of, 94–95, 99, 100; as financial narrative, 85, 94–105; foreclosure in, 284–87; French imagination in, 99, 100; government in, 104–5, 285, 287; interior framework of, 96, 98; journalism in, 285–86, 287; law in, 104–5; love/money connection in, 4, 284; mimesis in, 305; modern society in, 287; money imagery in, 101–2; narratives of, 85, 94–105, 286, 287; readers of, 97; revisions to, 284, 285, 286; role in *La Comédie humaine*, 103; royalty in, 285, 287; semiosis of, 287, 305; silence in, 286; storytelling ensemble of, 101–2; theatrical vocabulary of, 99
Maître Cornélius (Balzac), 66, 199n2
Les Marana (Balzac), sexual language of, 250
Marengo, battle of, 49–50
Margonne, Jean de, 60
Marivaux, 100
marriage: in Balzac's works, 10; in *Béatrix*, 179; in *Les Chouans*, 43–44, 46; in *La Comédie humaine*, 185, 260; completion through, 220; happiness in, 185; in *Honorine*, 288; in *Illusions perdues*, 184–85; in *Jacques le fataliste*, 68; love in, 179–80; love/money connection in, 5; in *Modeste Mignon*, 10, 260–61; for money, 173–74; passion in, 17; in *Pierre Grassou*, 173–74; in *Pierrette*, 115–16; for power, 115–16; provincial, 157; of reason, 17, 253; sex outside of, 247–50; sexual love in, 252–54; in *La vieille fille*, 128–29, 132, 134, 135, 137
Les martyrs ignorés (Balzac), Hoffmann in, 201
Masséna, André, 59
Massimilla Doni (Balzac), 10; art in, 173, 304; the comprehensive in, 239, 240, 241; creativity in, 230–31, 238–39; figural language of, 231; human desire in, 231; imagery of excess in, 304; loss of self in, 238; love in, 231–34, 238, 239, 304; medical semiotics of, 230–41; music in, 207, 230–31, 235–36, 238, 239, 304; narrative of, 233; obscenity of, 257; opium in, 236–39, 304; poetry in, 231, 232, 240; pregnancy in, 232, 239–40, 241; readers of, 233–34; sexual union in, 231–32, 233; social satire in, 221
Massol, Chantal, 47; on *Albert Savarus*, 71n4; on *La vieille fille*, 137
Maturin, Charles Robert: *Melmoth the Wanderer*, 221, 227
Maupassant, Guy de: self-censure by, 242
Mazet, Léo, 228n2, 276
meaning: circulation of, 303; creation of, 12; mimetic, 11; rhetorical, 11; semiotic, 11; through ellipsis, 27
Le médecin de campagne (Balzac), sexual language of, 245
Meininger, Anne-Marie, 21; on *Melmoth réconcilié*, 228–29; on *Modeste Mignon*, 261; on *Pierre Grassou*, 171, 172

Melmoth réconcilié (Balzac): anthropology of, 222, 224, 229; clerks in, 226, 227; commerce in, 225; demonic power in, 223–27; human desire in, 223–24; *idée fixe* in, 224–25; modern society in, 228; money in, 221–26, 228–29; narrative of, 222; proofs of, 227; religion in, 224–25; scientific thought in, 224; social satire in, 221–22, 225–26; the unknown in, 223; visionaries in, 223; zoological motifs of, 222

Melville, Herman: *Pierre*, 124

Mémoires de deux jeunes mariées (Balzac), 81; and Balzac's family dynamics, 63; Balzac's philosophy in, 17–18; dualities of, 15–21; letter reading in, 20–21; mimesis in, 19, 20; narrative of, 15–18, 21, 179; opposed values in, 16; point of view, 16; semiosis of, 18, 20; sexual language of, 252–54

merchant class: in *La Maison du Chat-qui-pelote*, 26; in *Pierrette*, 113, 114, 172

Mérimée, Prosper: "La double méprise," 181

mesmerism: Balzac's interest in, 202; in *Ursule Mirouët*, 163, 165–66

Messac, Régis, 199

Le message (Balzac), 271, 275n1; voyages in, 175–76

metonymy: Balzac's use of, 292–93; structural, 54; in *La vieille fille*, 129, 130, 133, 134

Michel, Arlette: on Balzacian realism, 303; on Balzacian types, 297–98; on Balzac's antagonisms, 4–5; on *Les Chouans*, 33, 36–37; on idea and form, 173, 174; on marriage, 185; on *Mémoires de deux jeunes mariées*, 17, 21; on *Modeste Mignon*, 261; on *Le père Goriot*, 3–4; *Le réel et la beauté*, 10

Milner, Max, 173

mimesis, Balzacian, 11, 30; chemical terms in, 220; in *Les Chouans*, 32; in *La Maison Nucingen*, 305; in *Mémoires de deux jeunes mariées*, 19, 20; moral purpose of, 31; in narrative, 64; relation to semiosis, 15–31, 155, 305–6; structures of, 12; in *Une ténébreuse affaire* (Balzac), 61; in *Ursule Mirouët*, 153, 166

Modeste Mignon (Balzac): feminine reading of, 261; historical present in, 260–61; love/money connection in, 231; marriage in, 10, 260–61; romantic realism of, 261n1; virginity in, 250n2

Molière, 100

money: agency of, 2; in Balzac's sexual language, 252; Balzac's writings about, 87, 88; in *César Birotteau*, 80, 85–88; circulation of, 158, 301; in *La Comédie humaine*, 98–99, 104; as demon, 227; in *Illusions perdues*, 303; in industrial society, 104–5; literature and, 104, 105, 303; in *La Maison Nucingen*, 101–2; marriage for, 173–74; in *Melmoth réconcilié*, 221–26, 228–29; as merchandise, 10; in Paris, 228; in *Le père Goriot*, 1–3, 11; in *Pierre Grassou*, 171–72, 173–74, 267; in *Pierrette*, 112; as Prime Mover, 8; principles concerning, 222; in provincial towns, 152; reduction of philosophy to, 224; rhetorical imagery of, 2; role in social privilege, 224; and sexual love, 6–7; as sign, 10, 104, 169, 302, 303; in *Ursule Mirouët*, 166; words and, 98, 103. *See also* capitalism; credit; love/money connection; speculation, financial

Montzaigle, Laurence de: death of, 24; marriage of, 21

Mozet, Nicole: on *La fille aux yeux d'or*, 243–44, 255; on *Pierrette*, 112; on *La Rabouilleuse*, 144; on *Ursule Mirouët*, 159–60, 161

La muse du département (Balzac): adultery in, 10–11; clothing in, 181–83; sexual language of, 246, 248–49; voyage motif of, 181–84

music: composition of, 230; execution of, 230; in "The Fall of the House of Usher," 38, 198, 199, 202–3; in *Gambara*, 207, 230; in *Massimilla Doni*, 207, 230–31, 235–36, 238, 239, 304; opium imagery of, 237; power of, 206n4, 234–36; in *La recherche de l'Absolu*, 206–7; role in Balzac's works, 206–7; salon, 198; in *Ursule Mirouët*, 38, 158, 159, 163–64, 195, 198, 201. *See also* Reissiger, Karl Gottlieb: "Webers letzte Gedanke"
myth: and anthropology, 109, 137; in *Pierrette*, 12, 109–20, 116, 119–21; in *La vieille fille*, 109, 137–38

Naginski, Isabelle Hoog, 27
Napoleon I (emperor of France), 92; Balzac's assessment of, 60; conspiracy against, 49–50; *Pensées politiques et sociales*, 58; in *La Rabouilleuse*, 151; in *Une ténébreuse affaire*, 54, 57–59, 60–61
narrative, Balzacian: of *Albert Savarus*, 68, 70–71, 79; analysis in, 209, 299–300; of *Autre étude de femme*, 277; of *César Birotteau*, 85; closure in, 270–91; of *La Comédie humaine*, 59, 63, 78, 127; composition of, 78; devices of, 12; epistolary, 21, 179; explication in, 299–301; external, 94–95, 99, 100; of *La femme de trente ans*, 254; of *Une fille d'Ève*, 27, 28, 29; first-person, 63; of *La Grande Bretèche*, 272–74, 277; of *Illusions perdues*, 186; justification of, 300; loss of value in, 229; in *Madame Firmiani*, 65; of *La Maison Nucingen*, 85, 94–105, 286, 287; of *Massimilla Doni*, 233; of *Melmoth réconcilié*, 222; of *Mémoires de deux jeunes mariées*, 15–18, 21, 179; mimesis in, 64; omniscient, 211; the oppositional in, 19; of *Pierrette*, 113; of *Un prince de la bohème*, 170; of *La recherche de l'Absolu*, 209, 211; scientific foundation of, 292; of *Les secrets de la princesse de Cadignan*, 280; semiosis of, 94; strategies of, 49, 64; of *Une ténébreuse affaire*, 49, 51, 53, 61; of *La vieille fille*, 129; of voyages, 190–91. *See also* self-narration, Balzacian
Nathan, Michel, 301
nature: art and, 209, 215; brutal, 231–32
Neefs, Jacques, 208–9; on Balzac's analysis, 299–300
Nodier, Charles: "De la palingénésie humaine et de la résurrection," 241
novels, epistolary, 21, 179; editorial mediation in, 16
novels, realistic: capitalism in, 4; explication in, 47. *See also* realism; rhetorical realism, Balzacian

Oliver, Andrew, 70
opium, in *Massimilla Doni*, 236–39, 304
Otway, Thomas: *Venise sauvée*, 247

Paris: love in, 7, 9; money in, 228; relationship to provinces, 152, 181
parricide, theatrical, 120
Pasco, Allan H.: on *La Rabouilleuse*, 140; on *Les secrets de la princesse de Cadignan*, 283; on *Ursule Mirouët*, 164. Works: *Balzacian Montage*, 65; "Process Structure in Balzac's *La Rabouilleuse*," 10
passion: in marriage, 17; religious, 256
Une passion dans le désert (Balzac), 10; sexual language of, 256
past, composed: in *Albert Savarus*, 262, 263; in Balzac's proofs, 263; in *La Comédie humaine*, 259, 268–69; function for readers, 268–69; hermeneutic process of, 262; in *La Maison du Chat-qui-pelote*, 260, 263; relation to historical present, 259; in *Ursule Mirouët*, 264; in *El Verdugo*, 268. *See also* composition

Les Paysans (Balzac), genealogy of, 154, 299

La peau de chagrin (Balzac), 212; conception in, 305; creation in, 208n1, 293–94; Cuvier in, 293; execution in, 305; human desire in, 223; power in, 2; preface of, 294; sexual language of, 246, 249; will and power in, 2; zoology in, 210

Peirce, Charles Sanders, 11

Péraud, Alexandre, 87n2

Le père Goriot (Balzac), 103, 185, 223; capitalists in, 4; love/money connection in, 5–7; misrepresentation in, 66; money in, 1–3, 11; role in *La Comédie humaine*, 3; sexual language of, 249; sexual love in, 7; truth in, 79n5

Perry, Dennis R., 203

La physiologie du mariage (Balzac), 249; virginity in, 250n2

Pich, Edgard: on dualities, 20; on *Mémoires de deux jeunes mariées*, 17n1, 18–19

Pierre Grassou (Balzac), 79, 215; bourgeoisie in, 167, 171–72, 266; commercialism in, 171; historical present in, 266–67; imitation in, 170–74; marriage in, 173–74; mediocrity in, 170–74, 267; money in, 171–72, 173–74, 267

Pierrette (Balzac): anthropology in, 261; archeology in, 127; bourgeoisie in, 113, 118–19, 126; Brittany in, 112; celibacy in, 109, 112, 113, 115, 117, 120, 139; Cenci myth in, 118, 119–21, 122–24, 126–27; chronology of, 113; genealogy of, 110, *111*, 154, 299; historical present in, 266; July Monarchy in, 126; liberals in, 113–15; love/money connection in, 110, 299; marriage in, 115–16; mendacity in, 116–19; merchant class in, 113, 114, 172; money in, 112; myth in, 12, 109–21; narrative of, 113; and *Paul et Virginie*, 112; politics in, 112, 113–16, 127, 266; Provins in, 112, 113, 114, 117, 118, 126; semiotic system of, 117; society in, 112–13; Stendhal's influence on, 121, 122; Weber in, 196

Pixis, Johann Peter: "Fantasia," 199

Place-Verghnes, Floriane: "Tabou or not Tabou," 242–43

Poe, Edgar Allan: and Balzac, 195, 199–200; Hoffmann's influence on, 202; interest in mesmerism, 202. Works: "The Gold Bug," 53; "The Masque of the Red Death," 202; "The Premature Burial," 199n2

Poe, Edgar Allan: "The Fall of the House of Usher," 38, 200–201; and *The Bride of Lammermoor*, 200; magnetism in, 195, 202; music in, 38, 198, 199, 202–3; narrator of, 203

poetry: and brutal nature, 231–32; in *Massimilla Doni*, 231, 232, 240; oriental, 254

politics: Balzac's writings on, 60; in *Les Chouans*, 178; in *La Comédie humaine*, 52, 109, 150; liberal, 113–15; in *Pierrette*, 112, 113–16, 127, 266; in *La Rabouilleuse*, 150–51; in reading, 62; role in art, 287

Pollin, Burton Ralph: *Discoveries in Poe*, 195–96, 198

Poulet, Georges, 154

Prendergast, Christopher, 54; on bills of exchange, 28; on mimesis, 30; on money, 10, 302

present, historical: in *Albert Savarus*, 261–62; analysis of, 269; in Balzac's works, 12, 259–60; in *Le cousin Pons*, 267; in *Un début dans la vie*, 261; in *Étude de femme*, 262–63; in *Eugénie Grandet*, 264–65; in *La fausse maîtresse*, 263; figurative form of, 259; in *Une fille d'Ève*, 263–64; function for readers, 268; in *La Maison du Chat-qui-pelote*, 260, 266; in *Modeste Mignon*, 260–61; in *Pierre Grassou*, 266–67; in *Pierrette*, 266; in *La Rabouilleuse*, 265–66; relation

Index 329

to composed past, 259; in *Les secrets de la princesse de Cadignan*, 266; in *Ursule Mirouët*, 264; in *El Verdugo*, 267–68
preterition, rhetorical forms of, 244
Prime Movers, 3; of *La Comédie humaine*, 8, 11, 176, 301; love as, 8, 242; rhetoric of, 293
Un prince de la bohème (Balzac), 71; bourgeoisie in, 167; dedication of, 167; diegetic story of, 170; discursive structures of, 170; identity in, 170; love/money connection in, 168–69, 170; mediocrity in, 167; misrepresentation in, 77; narrative of, 170; readers of, 167; style in, 174; title of, 169
La princesse de Clèves (Lafayette), 257
Proust, Marcel, 51; on Balzac's secrets, 60; on Balzac's style, 57
provinces, French: intermarriage in, 157; money in, 152; relationship to Paris, 152, 181
Pugh, Anthony: *Balzac's Recurring Characters*, 283
purity, color symbolism of, 233

Queffélec, Lise, 109, 138

Rabaté, Dominique: on Balzac's metonymy, 292–93
La Rabouilleuse (Balzac): Algerian War in, 266; bourgeoisie in, 150, 151; celibacy in, 139–41, 144–51; family in, 140, 141, 143–45; genealogies in, 139, 140–41, *142, 143*, 144–51, 154, 299; historical present in, 265–66; love in, 10, 168; love/money connection in, 140, 147, 148–50, 169; maternity in, 146–48; mediocrity in, 151; Napoleon in, 151; politics in, 150–51; readers of, 140; sexual language of, 247; versions of, 140–41, 265–66; voyage motif of, 190
Raphael, Balzac's admiration for, 235, 237

readers: acceptance of semiosis, 31; assumptions concerning, 30n4; bourgeois, 276; comprehension of, 79; eighteenth-century, 276, 277; function of composed past for, 268–69; interest of, 61–62; mistaken, 78; naive, 293
reading, as political process, 62
realism: Balzac's invention of, 292–306; beginnings of, 278. *See also* novels, realistic; rhetorical realism, Balzacian
La recherche de l'Absolu (Balzac): the absolute in, 210, 212–15; alchemy in, 210, 213; analysis in, 216, 219, 259; archeology in, 220; cause and effect in, 211, 214; chemistry in, 208, 210, 211–20; combustion in, 216–18; completion in, 215, 218, 220; composition in, 208, 219, 259; crystallization in, 215, 219–20; decomposition in, 212, 215, 218, 219; defense of writers, 209; diamond imagery in, 215, 219, 220; electricity in, 214–15, 218, 219; fire in, 215, 216, 218; music in, 206–7; narrative of, 209, 211; science in, 208–20; ternary structures in, 213–15, 217–19; zoology in, 210–11
reflection: displacement metaphors for, 175; voyages of, 175–91
Reinecke, Karl: Toy symphony, 199
Reissiger, Karl Gottlieb: "Webers letzte Gedanke," 195–96, *197*, 198–99, 201, 202, 203–5
religion: in *Melmoth réconcilié*, 224–25; in *Une passion dans le désert*, 256; in *Ursule Mirouët*, 153, 164–65
Reni, Guido: Cenci portrait, 123–24, *125*, 126, 127
representation, 12; double, 80–93
revenge: in *Autre étude de femme*, 275, 276; in *La Grande Bretèche*, 276
rhetorical realism, Balzacian, 293–97; blankness in, 301; of *Les Chouans*, 32, 42; closure in, 270–91; in *La Comédie humaine*, 12, 203; conception of, 303–5; content in, 11, 21, 305; creation through signs, 31, 294;

creative force of, 294; credibility of, 79; the disparate in, 45; displacement in, 175; doubleness in, 12, 18, 30, 63, 80–93; epistolary form in, 21, 179; evolution of, 46; execution of, 303–5; experience of reality through, 293; *explications nécessaires* in, 300–301; expression in, 294; figures of, 11–12; form in, 305; fragment and whole in, 279; function of language in, 305; invention of, 295; love/money connection in, 5, 299; in *La Maison du Chat-qui-pelote*, 24; metonymy in, 292; mimesis in, 11; misrepresentation in, 78; naive readers of, 293; observation in, 294, 295; openings in, 65; plot in, 11; Prime Movers of, 8, 11, 136, 301; self-narration in, 78; semiosis of, 11, 15–31, 305; strategies of, 211; structures creating, 11–12; types in, 297–98; verbal excess in, 303; of *La vieille fille*, 128

Riffaterre, Michael, 8
Robert, Marthe, 49
Rosen, Elisheva, 226
Rosolato, Guy: *Essais sur le symbolique*, 279
Rossini, Giacomo: *The Barber of Seville*, 101; *Mosè*, 235
Rougemont, Denis de, 122
royalty, in *La Maison Nucingen*, 285, 287

Sacy, Silvestre de, 298
Sage, Victor, 221, 227
Sagnes, Guy, 66
Saint-Martin, Louis Claude de, 227
salons, French, 276, 277
Sand, George: on *Mémoires de deux jeunes mariées*, 17, 18
Sarrasine (Balzac): misrepresented characters of, 66; pensiveness in, 290; sexual language of, 256–57
Schumann, Robert, 167
science: in Balzac's realism, 292; in *Melmoth réconcilié*, 224; in *La recherche de l'Absolu*, 208–20; role in *La Comédie humaine*, 300; of sounds, 236; in *Ursule Mirouët*, 163, 164, 165. See also chemistry; zoology

Scott, Walter, 199; Balzac's reading of, 200; *The Bride of Lammermoor*, 200–201; on Hoffmann, 202

secrets: Balzac family's, 60; in *La Grande Bretèche*, 273–74; in realistic fiction, 47; in *Une ténébreuse affaire*, 54, 56, 59, 60, 61

Les secrets de la princesse de Cadignan (Balzac): closure in, 279–84, 287; disclosure in, 279–84; historical present in, 266; narrator of, 280; readers of, 266, 281–82, 283; revisions to, 280; secrets in, 281, 282–83, 284; sexual language of, 247, 251; silence in, 281; types in, 297; women's desire in, 133

Sederholm, Carl H., 203
self-narration, Balzacian, 63–79; in *Albert Savarus*, 70–71, 261; in *Le bal de Sceaux*, 73, 74; in *La bourse*, 78; in *Le colonel Chabert*, 74–75; in *La fausse maîtresse*, 72, 78; in *Madame Firmiani*, 66, 78; in third-person narratives, 74. See also identity

semiosis, Balzacian: of *César Birotteau*, 87; of *Les Chouans*, 32; of closure, 278; concept of circulation, 87; conveying of information, 11; euphemisms in, 243; of *Une fille d Ève*, 29; of *La Grande Bretèche*, 273; in love/money connection, 299; of *La Maison du Chat-qui-pelote*, 260; of *La Maison Nucingen*, 287, 305; of *Massimilla Doni*, 230–41; of *Mémoires de deux jeunes mariées*, 18, 20; metaphors in, 243; mimetic figures of, 15–31, 155, 305–6; moral purpose of, 31; of narration, 94; of *Pierrette*, 117; readers' acceptance of, 31; in structures of realism, 11, 15–31, 305; of *Une ténébreuse affaire*, 61; uniform patterns of, 32; of *Ursule Mirouët*, 152, 154, 157, 162, 165, 166, 208;

of *La vieille fille*, 134, 137, 138. See also signs
Séraphîta (Balzac), 199n2
sexual language, Balzac's, 6, 130n2, 242–58; in *Béatrix*, 246, 252; of bestiality, 256; clarity in, 244–45, 246, 257; coded, 244, 245; of *La cousine Bette*, 246, 250–51; of *Le curé de village*, 250; of *La duchesse de Langeais*, 247–49; of *La femme abandonnée*, 245, 246, 254; of *La femme de trente ans*, 245–46, 254; figures of speech in, 246; of *La fille aux yeux d'or*, 254–55; hidden meanings in, 244; homosexual, 254; of *Honorine*, 252; of *Le lys dans la vallée*, 249; of *La Maison du Chat-qui-pelote*, 246; of *Les Marana*, 250; in *Le médecin de campagne*, 245; of *Mémoires de deux jeunes mariées*, 252–54; money in, 252; in *La muse du département*, 246, 248–49; from oriental poetry, 254; of *Une passion dans le désert*, 256; of *La peau de chagrin*, 246, 249; of *Le père Goriot*, 249; of *La Rabouilleuse*, 247; reading of, 257; religious, 256; of *Sarrasine*, 256–57; of *Les secrets de la princesse de Cadignan*, 247, 251; shadings of, 245–46; specialties in, 250–52; of *Splendeurs et misères des courtisanes*, 252; of *La vieille fille*, 245, 251; virginity in, 250n2, 251. See also love, sexual
Shelley, Mary Wollstonecraft, 199; *The Last Man*, 202
Shelley, Percy Bysshe: *The Cenci*, 120, 121, 122, 123, 124
Sieyés, Abbé: in *Une ténébreuse affaire*, 49
signs: characters' interpretation of, 68; constitution of, 11; creation of realism, 31, 294; double use of, 30; in-dwelling, 12; language as, 302–3; money as, 10, 104, 169, 302, 303; of natural language, 104. See also semiosis, Balzacian
silence: in *La Grande Bretèche*, 274; in *Honorine*, 290; in *La Maison Nucingen*, 286; in *Les secrets de la princesse de Cadignan*, 281
sixteenth century, as medieval, 121
social satire: in *L'elixir de longue vie*, 221; in *Massimilla Doni*, 221; in *Melmoth réconcilié*, 221–22, 225–26
Sollers, Philippe, 301
somnambulism, in *Ursule Mirouët*, 154, 162–63, 165, 188, 200, 203, 207
souls, reunited, 232
sounds, science of, 236
speculation, financial: in *César Birotteau*, 85; illusion in, 87; in *La Maison Nucingen*, 105. See also capitalism; credit; money
spirituality, in *Ursule Mirouët*, 153–54, 162, 164, 165, 166, 200, 203, 204, 207, 208
Splendeurs et misères des courtisanes (Balzac), 10, 186; explication in, 300; love/money connection in, 190; sexual language of, 252; types in, 298; voyage motif of, 188–90
Starobinski, Jean, 306
Stedman, Edmund Clarence, 202
Stendhal, 190, 263; "Les Cenci," 120–21, 123; crystallization imagery of, 40; influence on *Pierrette*, 121, 122
Swedenborg, Emanuel, 200, 212

Taine, Hippolyte: on Cenci portrait, 123
Talleyrand, in *Une ténébreuse affaire*, 49, 51, 59
Taylor, Françoise M., 52
Une ténébreuse affaire (Balzac): archeological description in, 52, 54, 60, 61; *cachot* of, 52–53, 54, 62; canine imagery of, 62; chronology of, 51; completion of, 60; complication in, 51–52; drafts of, 50; explication in, 47–62; Fouché in, 49–50, 56–57, 58–59, 62; historical truth and, 52, 54–57, 61, 62; hysteron proteron in, 48, 51, 57; the inaccessible in,

52; mimesis in, 61; Napoleon in, 54, 57–59, 60–61; narratives of, 49, 51, 53, 61; readers of, 62; relationship to history, 48; secrets in, 54, 56, 59, 60, 61; semiosis of, 61; sun imagery in, 58; tenebrosity in, 48–49, 50–53; title of, 48, 50

ténébreux (adjective), 48

Théorie de la démarche (Balzac), 295

Tournier, Isabelle, 300

Tritter, Jean-Louis, 110, 114

Trollope, Anthony: on Cenci portrait, 123

truth: historical, 52, 54–57, 61, 62; literary, 30–31

types, Balzacian, 34, 281; in *César Birotteau*, 298; in *Le colonel Chabert*, 298; in *La Comédie humaine*, 297–98; in *Le curé de village*, 298; in *Eugénie Grandet*, 265; evolution of, 298; in families, 299; in *Une fille d'Ève*, 297; function of, 298; in *Madame Firmiani*, 65; in *Les secrets de la princesse de Cadignan*, 297; within sexual relations, 243; in *Splendeurs et misères des courtisanes*, 298; tensions within, 297, 298; unity of, 296; in *La vieille fille*, 129–30; visionary, 223

unity: of *Autre étude de femme*, 275; in *Les Chouans*, 33, 35–37, 39, 40, 43–46, 89; of composition, 212, 214, 296; made from duality, 18–20; rhetorical figure of, 12; of types, 296; of *Ursule Mirouët*, 157, 162, 163, 165, 166; variation and, 298

Ursule Mirouët (Balzac): bourgeoisie in, 152, 153, 154, 155, 158, 264; chimera metaphor of, 165; Christian religion in, 153, 164–65; cognomonism in, 157; composed past in, 264; genealogy of, 152–55, 156, 157–66, 299; historical present in, 264; illegitimacy in, 159, 165; inheritance in, 152–55, 157–66; kaleidoscope imagery of, 155; law in, 159–61; love/money connection in, 301; magnetism in, 153–54, 163, 165–66, 188, 195, 202–6, 207; materiality in, 153–54, 162; maternity in, 144; mesmerism in, 163, 165–66; mimetic structures of, 153, 166; money in, 166; music in, 38, 158, 159, 163–64, 195, 198, 201; Nemours in, 152, 153, 155, 158, 188, 264; readers of, 157, 165; semantic structures of, 164; semiosis of, 152, 154, 157, 162, 165, 166, 208; somnambulism in, 154, 162–63, 165, 188, 200, 203, 207; sources of, 199, 201; spirituality in, 153–54, 162, 164, 165, 166, 200, 203, 204, 207, 208; unity of, 157, 162, 163, 165, 166; voyage motif of, 188; Walter Scott in, 200

Vachon, Stéphane, 305–6; on identity, 74; *Tombeau de Balzac*, 63

Vanoncini, André, 114, 126

El Verdugo (Balzac): composed past in, 268; historical present in, 267–68

La vieille fille (Balzac): anthropological conclusion of, 137; corset metaphor of, 12, 128–38; critical reception of, 129; inundation imagery of, 132, 137; marriage in, 128–29, 132, 134, 135, 137; modern myth in, 137–38; mythic dimension of, 109; narrative of, 129; readers of, 129; semiosis of, 134, 137, 138; sexual desire in, 130, 133–37; sexual language of, 245, 251; title of, 128–29; types in, 129–30; use of metonymy, 129, 130, 133, 134

virginity, in Balzac's sexual language, 250n2, 251

vision, poetic, 208

visionaries: artists, 293; in *Melmoth réconcilié*, 223

Voltaire, *Candide*, 99

voyages: in *L'auberge rouge*, 186–87; in Balzac's works, 12; in *Béatrix*,

179–80; in *Les Chouans,* 176–78; in *La Comédie humaine,* 12, 177, 190; in *Le curé de village,* 175; diegetic consequences of, 191; effects of, 191; Flaubert on, 175; goal of, 191; in *Illusions perdues,* 184–86; in *Le message,* 175–76; in *La muse du département,* 181–84; narration of, 190–91; in *La Rabouilleuse,* 190; in reflection, 175–91; of *Splendeurs et misères des courtisanes,* 188–90; in *Ursule Mirouët,* 188

Weber, Carl Maria von, 195; *Abu Hassan,* 202; Berlioz on, 196; death of, 198. *See also* Reissiger, Karl Gottlieb: "Webers letzte Gedanke"
Wharton, Edith, 124
will, Balzac's belief in, 163
women: desire of, 133; double, 18; innocent, 250n2, 251; miseducation of, 22, 24; role of love for, 15
Wurmser, André: on *César Birotteau,* 81, 82, 85; on *Une ténébreuse affaire,* 48

zoology: in *Melmoth réconcilié,* 222; in *La peau de chagrin,* 210; in *La recherche de l'Absolu,* 210–11

www.ingramcontent.com/pod-product-compliance
Lightning Source LLC
Chambersburg PA
CBHW030105010526
44116CB00005B/112